COLD WAR
SECRET
NUCLEAR BUNKERS

By the same author
Secret Underground Cities
(Leo Cooper, 1998)

COLD WAR SECRET NUCLEAR BUNKERS

The Passive Defence of the Western World during the Cold War

N.J. McCamley

LEO COOPER

First published in Great Britain in 2002 by
LEO COOPER
an imprint of
Pen & Sword Books Ltd
47 Church Street
Barnsley
South Yorkshire
S70 2AS

Copyright © N.J. McCamley 2002

ISBN 0 85052 746 5

A CIP catalogue record for this book is
available from the British Library

Typeset in 10.5/12.5 Plantin by
Pen & Sword Books, Barnsley, South Yorkshire

Printed and bound in England by
CPI UK

CONTENTS

Foreword vii

Glossary x

Introduction 1

Chapter 1   The American 'Big Bunkers' 5

Chapter 2   North American Radar 24

Chapter 3   NORAD and the Cheyenne Mountain Complex . . . 49

Chapter 4   The Ballistic Missile Early Warning System 58

Chapter 5   Cold War Bunkers in Canada 63

Chapter 6   The ROTOR Radar System 71

Chapter 7   The Royal Observer Corps and UKWMO 123

Chapter 8   Civil Defence and the Nuclear Bunker Programmes
in the United Kingdom 147

Chapter 9   Emergency Regional Government of the United
Kingdom under Nuclear Attack 152

Chapter 10 Local Authority Bunkers 193

Chapter 11 The GPO Secret Underground Exchanges and the
Essential Services Bunkers 230

Chapter 12 The Central Government Emergency War
Headquarters 248

Conclusion 279

Index 282

DIAGRAMS

1.   Raven Rock Mountain 7
2.   North American Radar - 1962. 41
3.   ROTOR Radar Stations 77
4a. Typical ROTOR Guardhouse Bungalow 79
4b. ROTOR Type R1 Bunker 79
4c. ROTOR Type R3 Bunker 80
4d. ROTOR Type R4 SOC - Lower Floor 80
4e. ROTOR Type R4 SOC - Upper and Middle Floors 82
4f. ROTOR Type R9 - Converted Happidrome 82
5.   Lansdown Anti-Aircraft Operations Room 119
6.   R.O.C. Underground Observation Post 129
7.   UKWMO HQ, Longley Lane, Preston. 135
8.   R.O.C. Group Control Room 135
9.   Regional War Room - Typical Layout 154
10. London Group Control 161
11. Cambridge Regional Seat of Government - RSG4 164
12. Warren Row - RSG6. 165
13. Drakelow - RSG6. 172
14. RGHQ 9.1 Swynnerton 181
15. RGHQ 8.2 Brackla, Bridgend 182
16a. Chilmark RGHQ - Section 190
16b. Chilmark RGHQ - Plan 191
17. Somerset County Council Emergency Centre 213
18. Kingsway Deep Level Telephone Exchange 231
19a. GPO Type PR2 Repeater Station - Section. 240
19b. GPO Type PR2 Repeater Station - Plan 241
20. Severn-Trent Water Emergency Control Bunker 244
21. Corsham Emergency Government War Headquarters 259

FOREWORD

This book was commissioned as a sequel of sorts to *Secret Underground Cities*, my history of Second World War underground architecture in the United Kingdom. My original intention was to show that, just as the underground factories, bunkers and ammunition depots of the Second World War had evolved piecemeal out of earlier underground structures, the network of cold war bunkers and command centres was just another step in this subterranean evolution, drawing largely upon an already established infrastructure. It soon became apparent that this was only partially true at best and that my remit must expand beyond its original rather limited horizon.

To fulfil this expanded remit ran the risk of merely rewriting Duncan Campbell's seminal work on the folly of British nuclear war plans (*War Plan UK*, Burnett Books, 1982), an astonishingly accurate exposé of the truth about civil defence in Britain published some twenty years ago when the truth was more carefully guarded and manipulated than it is today. Campbell cites Peter Laurie's *Beneath the City Streets* (Allen Lane, 1970) as the spark that initiated his own enquiries, and I must claim a similar inspiration. The pages of *Beneath the City Streets* made credible the stories of huge and secret strategic telephone exchanges and other government installations buried deep below the Wiltshire countryside, that I thought incredible at the time, recounted in guarded terms some five years earlier by an old school friend, then a seventeen-year-old apprentice telephone engineer who claimed to have worked on their construction.

I hope that, given the easier access to pertinent state papers the lapse of nearly a quarter of a century has allowed, this book to some extent complements those earlier works. My preliminary working title was *The Passive Defence of the Western World During The Cold War* but my publishers, quite rightly, thought that too dry and academic. Nevertheless that is the vista it endeavours to encompass, ie.

> all those measures (to quote the *Civil Defence Act* of 1948) including any measure not amounting to actual combat for affording defence against any form of hostile attack by a foreign power.

Whether or not the function of the various early warning radars amounts to actual combat is a fine distinction, but the subject matter is too interesting to exclude.

Inevitably, research across so broad a front has required me to draw upon the works of many investigators whose knowledge in their specialist fields far exceed my own humble capabilities. To all of these I offer my heartfelt gratitude. In particular I must thank Mark Bennett, who has forgotten more than I shall ever know about the ROTOR radar system and who has given freely of the raw documents that are the fruits of countless hours research at the Public Record Office. The interpretation of this material within this work, and hence the errors, are my own.

It is an unfortunate fact that, due primarily to its often narrow focus, much of the finest historical research remains unpublished and the authors unacknowledged. Some of this work is published privately and never gets the full recognition it deserves. Two examples in this latter category stand out: Paul Stokes' *Drakelow Unearthed* is a prime example of local history at its best, and Steve Fox's two volumes (soon to be followed by a third) in his *Control Chain* series are models of meticulous research into Civil Defence, Local Authority Emergency Planning and the implementation of emergency regional government. I have drawn heavily upon both these authors' work and acknowledge my debt to them.

Much credit, too, is due to Keith Ward, whose knowledge of the secret infrastructure of Civil Defence is encyclopaedic, and whose ability to interpret the footprint of cold war architecture from aerial photography is uncanny. Many other individuals and organizations have helped in larger or smaller ways and I offer my thanks to them as well. Mike Kenner provided some startling information on chemical weapons trials in Westwood Quarry, while Christopher Date, archivist of the British Museum, facilitated access to the museum's archive, revealing much information regarding early cold war plans for the evacuation of art treasures to Westwood and elsewhere. I must thank the staffs of numerous County Records Offices throughout Britain who have answered my manifold queries, and to over four hundred local authority Emergency Planning Officers who replied most willingly to my requests for information about, and permission to visit, their emergency bunkers. A special thanks must go to Peter Streets, Emergency Planning Officer for the City of Coventry whose help has been exceptional and whose contacts and influence have opened many doors for myself and subsequent researchers in this field.

Finally, I must thank Nick Catford, who has provided most of the photographs that illustrate this book and whose reports upon visits to many of the sites mentioned have provided the basis of much of my narrative.

A note on sources - many thousands of primary and secondary sources have been consulted during the preparation of this book. Due to their variable nature a comprehensive bibliography would be of questionable value, but readers seeking a deeper understanding of some of the issues raised pertaining to U.S policy are advised to seek out the various publications of the Brookings Institute, the Federation of American Scientists, and the U.S Department of Defense Legacy Resource Management Program. Publications produced by all these bodies include extensive bibliographies and provide excellent jumping-off points for further research. Similarly, the published historical documents of Emergency Preparedness Canada give an excellent introduction to the Canadian perspective. Material relating to Britain's emergency war plans (much of it, unfortunately still restricted) can be found in the Public Record Office at Kew. Investigation of the following classes, among many others, will prove rewarding: Cabinet Office records CAB/21, Home Office files in HO/225, 226 and 227, War Office files WO/32, and Treasury files in class T/227. Documents relating to London's deep-level shelters can be found in WORK/28 and CM/8, while the files of the Machinery of Government in War Working Party can be found in DEFE/7. Detailed plans for the ROTOR radar project are scattered throughout the AIR classes, but the Operating Record Books of the various stations are in AIR/28 and AIR/29.

GLOSSARY

3CI	Command, Control, Communication and Intelligence
AA	Anti-Aircraft
AAOR	Anti-Aircraft Operations Room
ABM	Anti-Ballistic Missile
AC	Alternating Current
ACDS	Assistant Chief of Defence Staff
ACHDF	Assistant Chief of Home Defence Force
ADCC	Air Defence Control Center
ADIS	Airborne Defence Information System
ADMP	Air Defence Master Plan
AEW&C	Airborne Early Warning & Control
AFB	Air Force Base
AJWR	Alternate Joint War Room
ALRI	Automatic Long Range Input
ARP	Air Raid Precautions
AT&T	American Telephone & Telegraph
ATC	Air Traffic Control
AUTOVON	Automatic Voice Network
BAS	Bomb Alarm System
BMEWS	Ballistic Missile Early Warning System
BUICC	Back Up Interceptor Control Center
CD	Civil Defence
CEW	Centimetric Early Warning
CFP	Combined Filter Plot
CH	Chain Home
CHEL	Chain Home Extra Low
CND	Campaign for Nuclear Disarmament
CONAD	Continental Air Defense
COS	Chiefs of Staff
CRP	Crisis Relocation & Planning
CTDS	Code Translation Data Services
CWS	Carrier Warning System
DC	Direct Current
DCDS	Deputy Chief of Defence Staff
DCMO	Defense Crisis Management Organization
DCSA	Defense Communication Services Agency
DEW	Distant Early Warning
DFTS	Defence Fixed Telecommunications Service
DoD	Department of Defense
DSP	Defense Support Program
EGWHISC	Emergency Government War Headquarters Inter-Services Committee
EGWHQ	Emergency Government War Headquarters
EMO	Emergency Measures Organization
EMP	Electro-Magnetic Pulse
EPC	Emergency Planning Canada
FEMA	Federal Emergency Management Agency
GCI	Ground Control Intercept
GDA	Gun Defended Area

GHQ	General Headquarters
GPO	General Post Office
GSM	General Situation Map
HE	High Explosive
ICBM	Inter-Continental Ballistic Missile
IFF	Identification Friend or Foe
JSTPS	Joint Strategic Target Planning Staff
MAD	Mutually Assured Destruction
MCS	Master Control Station
MIT	Massachusetts Institute of Technology
MoD	Ministry of Defence
MOWB	Ministry of Works & Buildings
NAOC	National Airborne Operations Center
NARS	North Atlantic Radio System
NATO	North Atlantic Treaty Organization
NDFRS	Nuclear Detection and Fallout Reporting System
NEACP	National Emergency Airborne Command Post
NORAD	North American Air Defence
NSD	National Security Directive
NWS	North Warning System
PJBD	Permanent Joint Board on Defense
PJHQ	Permanent Joint Headquarters
PPI	Plan Position Indicator
PSA	Property Services Agency
RADEF	Radiation Defense
RAFFTS	RAF Fixed Telecomm System
RCAF	Royal Canadian Air Force
RGHQ	Regional Government Headquarters
ROC	Royal Observer Corps
ROF	Royal Ordnance Factory
RSG	Regional Seat of Government
RTS	Radar Tracking System
SAC	Strategic Air Command
SACEUR	Supreme Allied Commander Europe
SACLANT	Supreme Allied Commander Atlantic
SAGE	Semi-Automatic Ground Environment
SALT	Strategic Arms Limitation Talks
SLEWC	Standby Local Early Warning & Control
SOC	Sector Operations Centre
S-RC	Sub-Regional Control
SSPAR	Solid-State Phased-Array
TCTS	Trans-Canada Telephone System
TR	Tactical Reconnaissance
UHF	Ultra-High Frequency
UKADGE	United Kingdom Air Defence Ground Environment
UKCAOC	United Kingdom Combined Air Operations Centre
UKLF	United Kingdom Land Forces
UKWMO	United Kingdom Warning and Monitoring Organization
USAF	United States Air Force
VHF	Very High Frequency
WRAF	Women's Royal Air Force

INTRODUCTION

Throughout the second half of the twentieth century the world stood poised on the edge of nuclear annihilation. Since the end of the Second World War, hundreds if not thousands of books and learned articles have sought to explain the origins of the cold war and to ask why two nations, the USA and the Soviet Union, that had so much to gain from victory in Europe, decided instead to squander the greater part of their combined national wealth on a war that never was. But for our purposes all this is irrelevant: for fifty years the cold war was an undisputed fact, and that is all that matters. It influenced the lives of everyone who lived through it and left its mark in steel and concrete upon the face of the world. These concrete symbols of mutual distrust, the archaeology of war, are what interest us in this volume.

Some qualification is necessary here. The military hardware of nuclear war does not concern us much, for the bombs and bombers, missiles, submarines, ships and silos and airbases have all been written about before. These are things that could not be hidden and by their very nature intruded themselves upon daily life. Huge US airbases in Britain were all too visible and the newspapers and aeronautical press followed avidly every development in aircraft, missile and tank technology. Popular awareness of current events has become more sophisticated since the Second World War, when every propaganda-laden government announcement was met with unquestioning acceptance. When, in June 1980, a computer glitch at NORAD Headquarters underneath Cheyenne Mountain announced the arrival of phantom Soviet Missiles over Washington and the Third World War was just the flick of a switch away, across the Atlantic Ocean, four thousand miles away, the runway lights at RAF Fairford flashed on, eighteen KC135 tankers rumbled down the runway *en route* to refuel the retaliatory B52s that were already airborne in a distant western sky and half of Gloucestershire knew within minutes that something was up with the Americans.

Since the Second World War the United States has become, arguably, the most warlike nation in the world. Her whole economic, industrial and political structure is deeply imbued with preparation for a war yet to come; she seeks out and plots the destruction of enemies of her own imagination. How should it be that a country with a pacifist, non-interventionist history, that had never been subject to invasion (other than a little local difficulty with Mexico) had no ambitions of Empire and had previously never forced her will upon any other nation, should suddenly become so engrossed with military preparation?

The answer is simple - Pearl Harbor and Berlin. During the inter-war years the USA saw the tremendous growth in its economy and in its international trade weakened by recession, recovery from which was threatened by a war in Europe. America needed expanding markets to absorb the output of its rapidly developing industries. The war further expanded the industrial base, industrial efficiency so output increased exponentially and the nation enjoyed the benefits of near full employment. As victors in a European war that had

1

bankrupted Great Britain, the only country that might have vied for economic dominance of the post-war world, the United States was admirably placed to maintain its ascendancy. As the self-styled saviour of European democracy and the world's great creditor nation, America held, by virtue of her unlimited financial resources, the key to European reconstruction and thus to her own security.

At the end of the Second World War Russia and the United States found themselves in military occupation of most of Europe and possessed of unexpected international power. The Soviet Union, historically wracked by paranoid insecurity through centuries of sporadic incursions by its neighbours, was suddenly in a position to secure its borders by virtue of a buffer zone of occupied, satellite states that would later be her unwilling acolytes in the Soviet bloc.

The presence of two new, politically naive military powers in Europe, and furthermore two powers with radically different political ideologies and plans for the future of Europe that were in polar opposition could mean nothing but trouble. Capitalist America, hell-bent on economic expansion, came head-to-head with a Soviet Union determined to consolidate communism within an extended home-base protected by a belt of satellite states persuaded, or where necessary coerced, to accept a similar political ideology. The inevitable tensions between such opposites came to a head with the Berlin crisis of 1948. The geo-political problems that arose from the defeat of Germany in 1945 were brought about by the clash of arms, and the threat of further armed conflict to achieve a final resolution blighted the world for the rest of the century.

So, America had found her enemy in a faraway country of which she knew little. But why should a semi-feudal, industrially and economically backward country half a world away that no other nation on earth either admired or cared about, be a threat to the American homeland? The answer is - 'Pearl Harbor'. The Japanese attack on the US naval base at Pearl Harbor on 7 December 1941, the day which Franklin D. Roosevelt all too chillingly predicted would 'live in infamy for ever', sent a shock-wave through the United States administration that continues to have repercussions today. Naive in the ways of war, America was unprepared for Japan's bolt-from-the-blue, or at least took no heed of such warnings as were given, and suffered catastrophic losses in consequence. This shock embedded in the US psyche a fear of sudden, unprovoked attack that became an over-arching national paranoia. Post-war, in the American military mind the Soviet Union became the aggressor that would fulfil the paranoid nightmare and henceforth the whole of America's scientific, military and industrial complex would be geared towards a cataclysmic east-west nuclear war that most saw as inevitable.

The most curious, contrary feature of America's nuclear war plans was that despite the thousands of billions of dollars wasted upon ever more powerful weapons of mass destruction and ever more sophisticated platforms to deliver them to their targets, these plans were riddled with a base, defeatist fatalism that such a war could not be won. For fifty years, while one group of Pentagon planners plotted a war to defend the philosophical construct of democratic capitalism, others were planning the early warning systems that would monitor, as they quaked, impotent and defenceless, in their command centres, the approach of Soviet missiles, unstoppable by any human agency, that guaranteed their own destruction. Others were designing the bunkers that would hide the few who would survive and later re-emerge to rule a world so utterly destroyed that the concept of democratic capitalism would be an irrelevancy for generations.

A consequence of America's economic dominance over her erstwhile wartime allies was that in exchange for economic aid they were compelled to accept the status of America's front line against the Soviet hordes. This was offered not necessarily as an overt ultimatum but, more insidiously, couched in terms of 'mutual defence for the common good'. Western Europe was slowly drawn into the US web and all the world was polarized by American propaganda, fuelled by paranoia, between the American dream of free market capitalism or the repression of Soviet communism. The United States ensured that the Soviet Union was held at arm's length by a policy of 'forward defence'. America's listening posts, her early warning systems, her forward fighter and bomber bases were spread across Canada, the North Atlantic islands, Great Britain, France, Germany and Italy. When General de Gaulle, always suspicious of the motives of America and perfidious Albion, withdrew French troops from NATO in 1966, most of the US elements of the French-based NATO forces transferred to the United Kingdom, accentuating Britain's role as America's unsinkable aircraft carrier and increasing still further her exposure as a target for Soviet missiles. When the bombs and missiles fell it would be on British soil.

This huge concentration of American military assets in the United Kingdom is the reason that her countryside and cities are littered with bunkers built to protect key elements of the nation's military and administrative establishment. There are great, complex bunkers for central government deep underground that have cost tens of millions of pounds to build and millions more each year to maintain; there are bunkers for regional government controllers who might or might not lead the post-holocaust national recovery; there are bunkers for the County Councils from which they would enact the local plans they often as not had never prepared; there are bunkers for water-board engineers who would ensure that every survivor had two litres of fresh water daily; bunkers for electricity board engineers who would ensure that the street lamps worked even if the buildings that lined those streets were swept away; there are bunkers large and small for the thousands of Royal Observer volunteers who thought they were protecting their own neighbours and community but were in fact just cogs in the vast machine that protected the American homeland; and there were bunkers for the radar stations built to give timely warning to the fighters and guns supposed to protect Britain's airborne nuclear deterrent but in fact just protecting the US bomber bases in East Anglia and the great US early warning station on Fylingdales Moor.

This book is about that other aspect of nuclear war, the secret, invisible infrastructure, the networks of underground control bunkers and radar stations stretching across continental North America and Great Britain, whose existence has never been more than rumour. This network radiates outwards like ripples in a pond from the ultimate American bunkers built beneath mountains in Virginia and Colorado, and includes concentric arcs of early warning stations, foisted unwillingly upon the government of Canada, that stretch across the arctic wastes of her northern provinces waiting for a surprise trans-polar attack. Beyond these, even more powerful early warning radars in Alaska, Greenland and Great Britain search the skies for thousands of miles beyond the horizon, looking for the tiny pinprick that would herald the start of a Soviet missile assault. Below these, in the passive defence hierarchy, are the civil and military bunkers built to protect the governments and people of the host countries, principally the United Kingdom, who have accepted these early warning radars and US forward defence bases and have thus made themselves Soviet targets in their own right.

Within a fifteen-mile radius of the house in which I live there are some thirty nuclear bunkers, including six underground ROC posts, a UKWMO Sector control bunker, the Emergency National Seat of Government, three military communications bunkers, a Regional War Room from 1955, an underground telephone repeater station, at least eight local authority bunkers and at least three belonging to the pre-privatization water boards, a ROTOR radar station, an underground radar Sector Control Room, and three Civil Defence control bunkers dating from 1957. This pattern is repeated throughout the country, and in the pages that follow I hope to explain their evolution, and the evolution of the great American command bunkers and early warning radar chains that they ultimately supported.

1

THE AMERICAN 'BIG BUNKERS'

All wars in the modern period up to and including the Second World War were essentially wars of attrition. Unlike the classic conflicts of earlier centuries, the participants in these wars included more than just the armed forces on opposing sides; they encompassed the whole industrial infrastructure, workforces, and civil populations of the countries involved. They included, too, a more intangible element; the national will to continue the struggle against all odds. The very nature of attrition warfare ensures that it is prolonged and both materially and socially destructive; dragging on maybe for several years as the manufacturing bases of the belligerents are eroded, or, as in the case of Germany at the end of the Second World War, until popular support for the war dissolves and central government is destabilized.

With but one startling exception, the preliminary phases of all modern wars have tended to develop gradually over several weeks or months, with often a minor diplomatic disagreement leading to a little local problem that ripples outwards and grows in intensity as larger states become involved and international defence treaties are invoked. Sometimes the threat of overwhelming action by a third party has broken the cycle of escalation, but the possible failure of such intervention carries the risk of either a humiliating diplomatic climb-down or further and deeper embroilment. This slow, spiralling sequence of belligerency was apparent in both the great wars of the twentieth century and, until jolted out of their traditional reactionism by the hydrogen bomb, seemed to set the pattern expected by most military planners for the next war too.

Traditionally, as the weight of enemy assault against the homeland, its industries, and seats of government increased, the level of protection provided for the most vulnerable of these establishments was increased in response. By 1941, as the Germans concentrated their attack upon the RAF and the British aircraft industry, many key factories and plants were dispersed about the countryside or found new homes deep underground. Similarly, as the London blitz intensified, somewhat primitive underground bunkers were built to protect the war cabinet and basements under key ministries were strengthened. The fear was always, however, that the vulnerable twigs and branches upon which the larger trunk of government and society depended would be killed off first: the airfields disabled one by one, the factories and workers' homes slowly destroyed, roads, railways and communications gradually disabled, until government had no assets left with which to prosecute the war. Bombs on the Second World War scale, however, even the largest, were inaccurate and relatively innocuous against point targets and personnel. There was never any real fear that even the most carefully calculated and executed attack could ever end a war by wiping out the entire national leadership at a stroke. If an aggressor nation was suddenly to collapse, it would be through the capitulation of its leaders or as a result of their

5

patent inability to rule in the face of popular disillusion or revolt.

The exception to the general rule of gradual escalation was the surprise attack on Pearl Harbor by the Japanese navy on 7 December 1941, an event which so shocked the military hierarchy of the United States that its repercussions were to be the major influence upon US strategic thinking for half a century. Since 1941 the United States government has been gripped by a paranoid fear of a 'bolt-from-the-blue' that still haunts it today; a paranoia which reached its apotheosis in the 1960s and engendered all the key elements of the cold war: the arms race, morbid fear of a bomber gap and then a missile gap, and the concepts of tripwire response, massive retaliation and mutual assured destruction.

In retrospect the origins and long-term consequences of the cold war may be explained by examining this paranoid US perspective. In the decade following the end of the Second World War America was afraid both of a surprise, trans-polar attack by Russian manned bombers against her own homeland or by crippling attacks against her security interests in Europe. The possibility of conflict between the western allies and the Soviet Union, that had been suppressed by an uneasy wartime alliance, became a reality following the Berlin crisis of 1948 which saw the breakdown of the inter-allied agreements which should have moulded the future peace of Europe. At first the prospect of war was remote, due in great part to the United States' overwhelming superiority in armament manufacture and technology, and to its possession of the atomic bomb. But the explosion of the first Russian atomic bomb in 1949 dispelled this complacency and the realization in 1957 that the Soviet Union had not only developed a hydrogen bomb but also a credible missile system to deliver it half way around the globe revived the nightmare vision of another Pearl Harbor. These developments by the supposed 'Evil Empire' of the USSR drove the United States to a frenzy of passive and active defence construction. The offensive weapons development programme is largely beyond the scope of this book, but we will now look in some detail at the measures taken, from 1950, to build a secure and survivable, nuclear-bomb-proof network of bunkers to protect the US administration and its major military command, control and communications centres. Six major underground command and control centres were built, including the NORAD centre at Cheyenne Mountain, described in Chapter 2. These were supplemented by two alternative airborne command centres, 'Night Watch', the National Airborne Operations Centre (NAOC), and 'Looking Glass', the E6B Airborne Command Post, which was commissioned as an airborne alternative for the Commander in Chief of Strategic Air Command. There was also a short-lived National Command Centre Afloat, but the credibility of a relatively vulnerable shipboard operations centre was doubtful from the start and the project was subsequently abandoned.

RAVEN ROCK MOUNTAIN –
THE ALTERNATE JOINT COMMNICATIONS CENTRE
Just as the United States was drawn into the Second World War following the Japanese attack upon Pearl Harbor, plans were being made to draw together all the War Department offices under one roof. Constructed in Arlington County,

Virginia, between 1941 and 1942, the revolutionary new building, known by virtue of its floor plan as the Pentagon, was at the time the largest office building in the world. The thirty-four-acre site, with a useable area of nearly four million square feet spread over five floors, provided space for a staff of 30,000, and at the end of the war it became home to the newly formed US Department of Defense. By 1948 however, as a consequence of President Truman's declaration that the USSR was 'a clear and present threat to the USA', worries grew regarding the vulnerability of the Pentagon to aerial attack from Russian bombers due to its enormous size and highly conspicuous signature from the air.

Following the explosion of the first Russian atomic bomb in 1949 the construction of a hardened headquarters for the National Command Authorities and the Joint Communications Service became imperative. After some debate as to whether the new facility should be a full peacetime replacement for the Pentagon or simply an emergency relocation centre, it was decided that it should function as an alternative, backup facility, on a scale sufficient to house some 2,000 senior executive and support staff, or about ten percent of the peacetime Pentagon complement. Known officially as the Alternate Joint Communications Centre, the Raven Rock facility was primarily a *communications* centre, although within it was housed the most important of all the strategic defence command centres – the Alternate National Military Command Centre – or the Pentagon at War. A number of factors were taken into account when finding a suitable location for the new complex: as well as meeting rigidly defined geological criteria, the site had, for example, to be far enough from Washington to be safe from the expected atomic onslaught on that city, but yet be close enough to enable key staff to relocate within

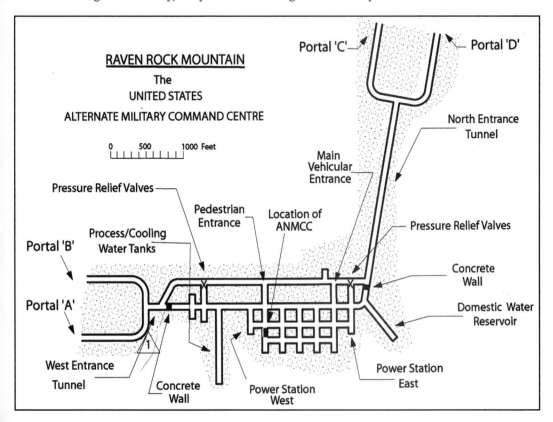

the short time span predicated by the 'bolt from the blue' hypothesis.

Eventually a suitable site was found below Raven Rock Mountain, six miles north of Camp David on the Pennsylvania/Maryland border and about eighty miles from Washington. Construction was authorized in May 1950 and was completed early in 1953, ready for operational inauguration on 30 June.

The underground control centre was built within chambers constructed over two thousand feet below the summit of Raven Rock, and two thousand feet laterally from the mountain's edge. Two pairs of tunnels, 500 feet apart, give access to the subterranean nucleus from the north-west and north-east faces of the mountain, each pair merging to form single roadways six hundred feet inside the mountain. After a further thousand feet or more the access roads meet the five main, parallel chambers that form the heart of the complex. Two subsidiary lateral roadways join the centres and ends of the five chambers, while shorter tunnels house the site's two power stations (each of which contain three 1-Megawatt generators), and water reservoirs. Within each of the five, damp, bare rock chambers a series of three-storey steel buildings were erected to provide operations centres for the three defence services and for the numerous ancillary facilities. As a reaction to the explosion of Russia's first *useable* nuclear weapon in 1958 a major extension was made to the Raven Rock facility which it was hoped would further harden the site against the more powerful weapons then envisaged, and also provide accommodation for the more advanced and sophisticated communications equipment that was coming into service. A new outer bypass tunnel was excavated around the perimeter of the underground complex joining the western and eastern access tunnels. At the same time the original access tunnels were blocked with thirty-foot concrete plugs just beyond the point at which the new tunnel intersected them, and two new underground entrances to the main chamber complex, protected by huge blast doors, were made at right-angles to the bypass tunnel. With the aid of pressure release valves at each end, this bypass tunnel ensured that the blast from a nearby nuclear explosion would pass right through the mountain from the west to the east portals without affecting the main complex. Two chambers excavated in conjunction with these new works provided space for additional communications equipment, including a new Automatic Message Processing System and dormitory space for an additional 1,000 staff. It is thought that the opportunity was taken during this 1960 programme to equip a private suite for the President and his immediate family.

Initially the Army, Navy and Air Force Operations Centres were run independently and were unmanned under normal peacetime conditions, although a full-time Army staff maintained the essential site services. At the warning of imminent war Pentagon Staff would be evacuated to their pre-allocated underground desks, and would from there determine the future history of the world. Changes brought about in 1959 under the Eisenhower presidency led to a rationalization of the three independent service control centres and their inevitable inter-service jealousies, resulting in the formation of the Alternate Joint War Room, which was essentially a tri-service strategic command, control, communications and intelligence centre from which World War Three would be directed. Under the new system, which became fully operational in early 1961, the AJWR was permanently manned by a tri-service Alternate Command Battle Element and an Army communications staff. At the core of the AJWR was a central operations room and briefing room, supported by a range of communications and data processing suites.

Less than a year later the newly promulgated Department of Defence Directive 5100.30 codified the pivotal role of the National Military Command System in ensuring the survival of the United States. Key elements in this plan were measures to ensure the survival of the person of the President or his constitutional successors (detailed later in this chapter), and the provision of a secure, hardened and effective command, control, communications and intelligence (3CI) system that could ensure the execution of the Presidential war directives. Under this plan the existing 3C1 command centre at the Pentagon and Raven Rock were reorganized and supplemented by two new elements - the National Emergency Airborne Command Post and the Minimal Essential Emergency Communications Network. The five principal constituents of the 1962 plan were:

The National Military Command Centre – located within the Pentagon, which would, in peacetime or on the brink of war, be the central decision-making forum where the Joint Chiefs of Staff would meet their political master, the Secretary of Defense, to determine the nation's defence strategy.

The Alternate National Military Command Centre – at Raven Rock Mountain. The old AJWR renamed, this would become the combat operations centre for the Joint Chiefs of Staff, senior military personnel and the Defense Secretariat in event of war, and would also act as a secure crisis management centre during civil insurrection or any other catastrophic civil emergency that threatened the continuity of government.

The National Emergency Airborne Command Post (NEACP), – First proposed in December 1959, the NEACP was perceived as a means of countering the risk of a Soviet surprise first-strike wiping out the Raven Rock bunker, which it was thought could not survive the power and accuracy of the new Russian ICBMs then coming into service.

Night Watch, - The Airborne Operations Centre, a flying war-room based upon a Boeing 747-200 airframe. To ensure constant availability, four aircraft were converted, one of which was always ready for take-off from Offut Air Force Base in Nebraska at fifteen minutes' notice.

In response to increasing fears that Offut AFB was too vulnerable to Soviet missiles targeted on Washington, the NEACP mission was transferred to Andrews AFB in Maryland in 1982, and at about the same time it was renamed the National Airborne Operations Centre. It is usual for one of the 'Night Watch' aircraft to shadow the Presidential aircraft 'Air Force One' (which can be any one of a large number of aircraft that the President may choose to use), whenever the President travels either within the US or abroad. 'Night Watch' will normally land at an alternative airfield to that used by 'Air Force One', but which is no more than fifteen minutes flight-time away.

The official mission of the NAOC is:

> to serve as the National Airborne Operations Centre for the National Command Authorities. In case of national emergency or destruction of ground control centres, the aircraft provides a modern, highly survivable command, control and communications centre to direct US forces, execute emergency war orders, and co-ordinate actions by civil authorities.

The main deck of the 747 is divided into six principal sections; the National Command Authority bureau, a conference room, briefing room and a rest room, a communications section, and Operations Team work area. Within this compact area a total crew of 114 personnel including the Joint Services Operations Staffs might seal the fate of nations. Although the recently upgraded aircraft are EMP shielded and have sophisticated thermal and radiation shielding, they suffer from two serious drawbacks. Firstly, even with in-flight refuelling, they can remain airborne for no more than seventy-two hours, for after that period of constant running the engine lubricating oil rapidly breaks down; and secondly, despite the advanced on-board satellite data transfer equipment which should allow flexible communication with the whole range of US strategic and tactical satellite systems, they still rely heavily on communication with Raven Rock and other ground stations. The need to refuel presupposes the survival of tanker aircraft (which do not have long flight endurance) and of the airfields from which to fly them.

> The Minimal Essential Emergency Communications Network – which consisted of a highly redundant, hardened network of VHF radio, microwave and land-line links. These, together with the Ground Wave Emergency Network, provided reliable and survivable communications between the most critical 3Cl centres. These channels were supplemented by other world-wide communications systems including the Switched Circuit Automatic Network, which was later developed into the AUTOVON (Automatic Voice Network) system and remained in service until the early 1990s, when it was largely replaced by the Defense Switched Network. Hardened bunkers were built throughout North America, in the UK, and across Europe to house AUTOVON repeater equipment, and many, like that at Ipswich in Suffolk, have only recently been abandoned.

For thirty years from 1962 until 1992 the AJCC was on constant alert, monitoring situation reports and warning status reports from the NORAD HQ at Cheyenne Mountain, the White House Situation Room and Strategic Air Command HQ at Offut Air Force Base, while a skeleton staff shadowed the Pentagon National Military Command Centre. The twenty-four-hour alert ceased on 1 February 1992, but the communication and risk assessment function continues at Raven Rock into the twenty-first century. During the mid-1960s it became apparent that even the hard rock of Raven Rock Mountain would not be safe against the ever more accurate and powerful Soviet ICBMs, and much attention was given to finding an even more secure and invulnerable solution. The years following the Cuban missile crisis were marked by a considerable slackening in East-West tension, and much of the impetus for change was lost. Plans for the National Emergency Airborne Command Post came to fruition and Raven Rock, under the aegis of US Army Information Systems Command assumed day-to-day responsibility for its communication support, but little else developed.

The Cuban crisis marked the coming-of-age of nuclear strategy: before Cuba nuclear threats and nuclear brinkmanship were little more than a game between East and West; threats were made and bunkers built, but the consequences were never really calculated. The late realization of what could result from the terrible concurrence of Cuba and the emergence of the nuclear-armed ICBM as a mature weapon, was perhaps the steepest learning curve in history and brought strategists on both sides of the ideological divide to their senses with great abruptness. Until that time the military inertia characterized by Lloyd George's comment in 1915 that 'policy seemed to be that of preparing, not for the next war, but for the last one or the last but one' seemed to rule universally. Although nuclear weapons existed, they were rattled like nineteenth century sabres, or at best, and certainly in the early, naive days of the atom bomb (if not in the ICBM era) strategies for their use were those that governed the use of conventional bombs during the Second World War. The Cuban crisis forced the Soviet Union and America to come to terms both with each other and with the traumatic realities of nuclear war. The result was dramatic and could have signalled the end of the cold war, but for the continued paranoia of the United States.

From the mid-1960s increasing east-west tolerance, if not harmony, led to a welcome reduction in preparation for Armageddon. In financial terms, the first victim of this dropping-of-the-guard was public protection, always the most insoluble problem in war planning. In the United States, as in Britain, the early 1970s witnessed the nadir of civil defence expenditure, and thereafter the emphasis turned towards the primary importance of early-warning and strategic communications. With the new vision of nuclear reality came the realization that all the old ideas of survivability, the legacy of Second World War civil defence 'rescue and recovery' policy, was a vacuous irrelevancy. Faced with an inability to ensure the safety of the civil population and the continuity its social structures, sections of the embunkered government previously allocated to these impossible tasks eroded away, leaving just a central nucleus charged with the task of maintaining the more intangible but constitutionally vital fiction of 'continuity of government'.

By the early 1980s electronic communication technology had still not advanced sufficiently to allow the massive 1960s atom-bomb bunkers to be replaced by the current scheme of hugely redundant networks of small communication nodes; a twenty-first century concept that essentially offers security through multiplicity, ie: more targets than there are enemy warheads to destroy them. So, the big bunkers, including Raven Rock, remain even after the official end of the cold war, although they have evolved into predominantly strategic communications hubs. Meanwhile the control function has devolved to a range of smaller, more ephemeral sites.

The tendency of US strategic planners to focus upon the vulnerability of even the deepest bunker to a direct hit from an ICBM has tended to distract attention from the prime asset of the big bunkers: the massive level of protection they provide against fallout and radiation for relatively large groups of personnel. This unbalanced focus is symptomatic of the whole paranoid strategy of the United States and indicates a unique ability to believe in two opposing rationales simultaneously. Despite their absolute and justified confidence in their own technological superiority, the US military authorities were convinced that Soviet missiles were more accurate and more powerful than their own, and these irrational assumptions have been the bedrock upon which every defence strategy since 1948 has been built. *Tripwire* was supposed to launch all the US missiles in a last, mad paroxysm of war, before the hail of Soviet rockets, detected at launch by the vast array of surveillance radars scattered worldwide over the territory of her allies, destroyed them in their silos.

Yet the more rational voices in the US administration gave ample evidence that the supposed Russian numerical advantage in missiles was chimerical. They knew the inadequacies of Russian guidance systems and targeting technology, and historical analysis told them that no projection that professed the infallibility of a weapons technology that no one ever dared use could be given any credibility at all. The unspectacular performance of many of the so-called 'smart' weapons like the 'Patriot' anti-missile missile, used in the conflicts of the late twentieth century, and the equally unspectacular performances by successive US ABM systems, illustrate, despite the exaggerated claims made at the time, the disparity between wish and fulfilment on the automated battlefield.

The presumption that the Soviet Union possessed more than enough missiles and warheads, of pinpoint accuracy, to destroy every US command and control bunker and every US missile, armed but impotent in its launch tube, has, to the American military psyche, rendered the need for *fallout* protection of secondary importance. All would be destroyed and the fallout clouds would drift over dead men's dust.

Through the 1970s a different, more realistic, philosophy of war emerged, and the concepts of limited nuclear conflict and 'strategic withholds' came in to vogue. In the latter years of the twentieth century it was realized that nuclear war, should it come, would perhaps not be so clinically terminal as the war-games of the 1960s had predicted, and that it would be survivable by a significant proportion of the population.

Thus, protection against the threat from fallout once again became an important factor in planning for national recovery, at least for those government officials who were predestined to lead the recovery. At the highest levels of government, the 'withhold' principle, which has never been officially acknowledged, involved the specific de-targeting of key Soviet and Western command and control bunkers, so that at the end of a limited nuclear exchange national leaders would survive to negotiate a peace settlement.

Though of diminished importance as an executive control centre, Raven Rock continues to operate as a multi-force Military Branch Operations Centre and provides home for two critical communications systems: the Defense

Information Systems Agency Regional Telecommunications Management & Control Centre, and the Global Control & Command System computer together with the Global Command Support system. These systems jointly monitor the worldwide military situation, process commands, assess risks and suggest solutions after analyzing the available US military assets.

MOUNT WEATHER

Whereas Raven Rock mountain was the alternative national military control centre, Mount Weather, or the 'High Point Special Facility' was built to fulfil the role of an alternate seat of civil government in nuclear war. The final cost of the project at 1998 prices, adjusted for inflation, was in excess of $1 billion. Mount Weather lies on the border of Clarke County, seventy miles from Washington, and was purchased by the government in the inter-war years for use as a weather station. In 1936 the 434-acre site was taken over by the US Bureau of Mines as a research site, so when tunnelling for the new underground complex began in 1954 the increased activity attracted little unwonted attention.

Later that year the tunnelling work was taken over by the Army Corps of Engineers under the code-name 'Operation Highpoint'. By the end of 1958 the 200,000-square-foot labyrinth of tunnels was excavated and construction of twenty-nine three-storey office buildings within the tunnels was nearing completion. Like the NORAD centre at Cheyenne Mountain, the roof of Mount Weather is reinforced with many thousands of ten-foot-long steel bolts which bind the hard rock strata together. The main entrance is protected by a guillotine gate and a 20′ x 10′ blast door that is five feet thick, weighs thirty-four tons and reputedly takes fifteen minutes to open or close. Support facilities for the 2,000 staff working within the tunnels include a hospital, crematorium, recreation rooms and dormitories. Refrigerated food supplies, drinking and process water reservoirs and fuel reserves for the centre's underground power station would enable Mount Weather to operate for a minimum of thirty days in shut-down mode. During peacetime operation a nearby surface complex houses an additional support staff of 240 personnel. Mount Weather's ultimate purpose is to ensure the 'continuity of government', a concept that means, in practice, the survival of the President, or his prescribed successor, and the maintenance of his ability to direct the military and civil processes of state. This concept was further extended to include measures for government continuity in times of civil insurrection or disaster, as well as total war, as was made clear in a speech by President Nixon in 1969, when he commented that:

> our national security is dependent upon our ability to assure continuity of government at every level, in any national-emergency type situation that might conceivably confront the nation.

The line of succession to the Presidency, as revised by the *Presidential Succession Act* of 1947, is in the order: President, Vice President, Speaker of the House of Representatives, President pro tempore of the Senate, and then successively through selected members of the Cabinet. To maximize the probable survival of at least one member of this hierarchy in time of war, senior government officials were divided into three groups, one of which would remain in Washington as long as this was tenable, one would go to Mount Weather, and the third would evacuate to another continuity of government bunker, either Raven Rock, Cheyenne Mountain, Greenbrier or Mount Pony. The locations and status of all personnel designated to succeed the President were continuously tracked and monitored, in peace and war, by a special staff at Mount Weather.

Mount Weather was similar in initial concept to the Canadian government's 'Diefenbunker' and the Spring Quarry complex at Corsham which housed what was effectively an alternative wartime Whitehall. As well as a Presidential staff, Mount Weather would have been the wartime home of at least nine Federal Departments crucial to the national reconstruction effort after a nuclear war. These included: the departments of Agriculture, Commerce, Health Education & Welfare, Housing and Urban Development, Labour, Transportation; the State Department, Interior Department, and the Treasury. Most of the important Federal Agencies and Private Corporations were also represented, including the Federal Communications Commission, Selective Service Commission, Federal Power Commission, Civil Service Commission, the Veterans Administration, the US Post Office and the Federal Reserve. Special provision was also made for the nine members of the Supreme Court.

From 1961 until its replacement in 1970 by a satellite-based warning system, Mount Weather was also the monitoring centre for the Bomb Alarm System, which consisted of a network of sensors mounted on telegraph poles near ninety-nine cities and military bases throughout the United States. The sensors would be triggered by the intense flash and thermal pulse of a nuclear bomb-burst and would illuminate tiny red indicators on a large-scale map display. Bomb blast information monitored at Mount Weather was relayed to similar displays at NORAD headquarters and at the ANMCC at Raven Rock. Rather surprisingly, the greater part of the Bomb Alarm System relied upon commercial overhead telephone lines for data transmission and was consequently prone to power failures and false warnings. During the Cuban missile crisis at least one panic rumour of nuclear attack was safely suppressed when the BAS failed to indicate a detonation at the rumoured point of impact. Reports were more unpredictable, however, during the great North Western power failure of 1965 when excess electricity demand resulted in many power stations tripping-out on overload, and thereby causing widespread blackouts.

Although the alert system correctly reported the power failures at twenty-two sensor locations, it also erroneously reported nuclear detonations at Salt Lake City and Charlotte, West Virginia. Those false indications triggered a full-scale national security alert and it took several days to discover that the warnings were triggered by faulty wiring within the display console.

Since the end of the cold war Mount Weather has justified its existence by adopting the role of National Emergency Co-ordinating Centre of the Federal Emergency Management Agency (FEMA) all-hazards control and monitoring organization. Although now an overtly peacetime, civil contingency control centre, Mount Weather still retains within its infrastructure all the systems and functions needed to return instantly to a war alert status. A peacetime staff of

900 personnel man six major disaster operations facilities:

1. The National Processing Service Centre
2. The Satellite Teleregistration Centre
3. The Disaster Finance Office
4. The Disaster Information Systems Clearing House
5. The Disaster Personnel Operations Division
6. The Agency Logistics Division

Under ordinary conditions FEMA's two main disaster recovery data processing systems, known as the Contingency Impact Analysis System and the Resource Interruption Management System, provide continuous training and exercise facilities using sophisticated simulation techniques. Under emergency conditions these systems rapidly evaluate dangers threatening the State and ensure the optimum allocation of assets available to the various government agencies. The site now monitors all types of emergencies in the United States, from floods and hurricanes to civil riots, public utility failures and earthquakes. Like all the large continuity of government bunkers, Mount Weather has numerous connections to all the emergency communications systems and to the military and civil trunk telephone network. An indication of the scale of the telephone exchange capabilities of the complex can be gauged from the fact that it was able to absorb the entire telephone switching load of the huge Denton telephone exchange when the latter was put out of action by severe snowstorms in January 1997.

THE GREENBRIER CONGRESSIONAL BUNKER

Perhaps the most surprising feature of the huge nuclear bunker under the Greenbrier Hotel in White Sulphur Springs, West Virginia, is the fact that it was so successfully kept secret from the hotel's tens of thousands of visitors and 1,600 staff for over thirty years, until notoriously exposed by an investigative reporter from the *Washington Post* in 1992.

One of America's premiere hotels, the Greenbrier, built by the Chesapeake & Ohio Railway Company in the 1920s, had traditionally been a favourite haunt of Presidents and foreign dignitaries since long before the war. During the Second World War the estate was requisitioned for use as a military hospital, but by the 1950s it had recovered its splendour and regained its reputation for excellence. It is probable that its wartime military associations and prominent familiarity among the higher echelons of government influenced its choice as the location for the most luxurious of all the 'continuity of government' bunkers: - the congressional nuclear retreat, code-named 'Greek Island'.

The 112,000-square-foot bunker, built during 1959-62, was designed to accommodate both the House of Representatives and the Senate, along with a nucleus support staff amounting to some 1,200 personnel.

The massive building task was undertaken under the disguise of an extension to the hotel now known as the West Virginia Wing. And indeed the subterfuge was so complete that the largest room in the bunker, the vast Senate Chamber, was openly used by the hotel as an exhibition hall for three decades before its true purpose was discovered, the twenty-eight-ton blast doors that would seal

15

the area if the bunker was activated being disguised behind false panelling within the approach corridor.

Construction of the two-storey, underground, reinforced concrete bunker involved the excavation of a seventy-foot-deep cavity and the pouring of some fifty thousand tons of concrete to form the foundations, walls, and bomb-proof roof slab, all of which have a minimum thickness of three feet. Entrance to the bunker is gained via four access points on the first floor. The 450-foot-long main west entrance tunnel, which is hidden in a wooded cutting behind the hotel, allows discreet access for personnel and vehicles completely independent of the main hotel building. Large enough to drive a truck through, this tunnel is also used for provisions storage and carries service pipes from the air-conditioning plant to a surface cooling tower which conveniently but erroneously gives the impression of being part of the hotel ventilation system. Of the other three entrances, two, as described above, are within the West Virginia Wing, their massive, twenty-eight-ton steel doors disguised behind panelling. The fourth entrance point is a small service door in a ventilation airway.

Most of the second floor of the building is taken up by an assembly hall and by dormitories, eighteen in all, each with steel bunks for sixty of the bunker's inhabitants. Part of the floor also contains three 14,000-gallon fuel tanks for the powerhouse and three 25,000-gallon reserve water tanks. These, together with a stockpile of refrigerated and dried food supplies, ensure that the Greenbrier bunker can, under emergency conditions, be operated in secure closed-down mode for a minimum of forty days. To supplement its internal water reserves, the site has its own deep well and pumping equipment some three-quarters of a mile away.

The first floor houses a second assembly chamber (normally open to view as the Greenbrier exhibition hall) and most of the bunker's service plant and utilities. A surprisingly spacious powerhouse contains three Fairbanks Morris 675 Kw diesel alternators, any one of which is capable of sustaining the full load of the building under emergency conditions, as well as boilers and refrigeration equipment for the bunker's sophisticated air-conditioning and ventilation systems. Lavish catering facilities were provided for personnel forced to spend prolonged periods in the bunker. A 17,500-square-foot dining room, complete with elegant black and white tiled floor and huge 'picture window' murals to alleviate the potential gloom of life underground, could seat 400 of the bunker's inhabitants at a single sitting, seated around elegant little café-style circular tables.

This floor also contained a large lecture theatre and television briefing room from which the nation's leaders might broadcast messages of hope to what, if anything, remained of the nation's people. Other facilities included a well-equipped medical centre with X-ray apparatus, a dental laboratory, pharmacy and intensive care unit. A nearby chamber was fitted out as a strong room to house important current and historical Documents of State. This room also doubled as a rather sinister armoury for close defence weapons for use within the secure zone. Plans for the area defence of the bunker envisaged the government again requisitioning the entire Greenbrier estate in time of dire emergency, with the hotel building used to house security personnel and a plethora of less essential support staff. Under peacetime conditions a team of thirty permanent maintenance staff looked after the bunker and, to cover their activity and integrate their obvious presence into the day-to-day running of the hotel, a subterfuge reminiscent of the best 'conspiracy theory' fiction was employed. When the bunker was first built, a notional company, 'Forsythe Associates', was formed with an overt contract to maintain the very extensive audio-visual and communication systems in the Greenbrier Hotel. Staff and visitors at the hotel thought that the thirty or so Forsythe employees worked for the Greenbrier, but, whilst a few hours of each week may have been occupied mending hotel televisions, their real occupation was maintaining the secret congressional bunker below.

One of the most striking features of the Greenbrier bunker in comparison with other continuity of government sites is its air of comfort and luxury. Whereas, for example, the Raven Rock complex exudes an air of 1960s utilitarianism, with dripping rock-walled tunnels containing sombre steel buildings, the Greenbrier is beautifully carpeted throughout like a modern corporate headquarters of the 1960s. All the main rooms were fitted with concealed ceiling lights and the private quarters for senior staff were tastefully furnished and decorated. Even the dormitories for the lesser mortals, though only provided with steel bunks (with proper sprung mattresses, not palliases as in most of the British bunkers), had fitted carpets and vanity barriers between each pair of bunks, to protect both the feet and sensibilities of the occupants.

Mount Pony – the Federal Reserve Bunker

The tendency of modern historians when analysing the major conflicts of the late nineteenth and twentieth centuries is to subscribe to the view that their common origin is rooted upon economic nationalism. Since the industrial revolution and the growth in international trade that it engendered, it has been imperative, both for international prestige and to sustain economic growth, that the great nations of the world should capture markets abroad and secure supplies of raw material wherever they may lie. Economic growth, based on industrial expansion, and military might are mutually self-sustaining. A strong industrial base provides the weapons of war and weapons of war provide the means to capture and protect markets and raw materials and to force weaker competitors out of those markets. Industrialization was the driving force of the imperial system. The success of all this, however, depends upon an internationally acceptable economic system, the enforceability of contracts and the sustained credibility of *money*.

Money has become the great motivating force in modern society and the collapse of the monetary system resulting from global war would inevitably hasten the collapse of social order and jeopardize the prospect of post-war reconstruction. The pivotal importance of money was recognized by Germany during the Second World War, when, in an attempt to destabilize the British economy by creating rampant inflation, plans were laid to print and circulate millions of counterfeit banknotes. It was realized too, that rapid, post-war European recovery could only be achieved by stabilizing the currencies of those countries that had been occupied by the German army. To this end, in 1944, the De La Rue company printed a huge stockpile of legitimate currency for several occupied mid-European countries. Until the end of the war this stockpile was stored in Clubhouse Quarry, one of a number of disused stone quarries converted for various government purposes one hundred feet below the village of Corsham in Wiltshire. Similarly, the American government printed some 400 tons of French Francs to replace the German-occupation currency following the liberation of France. Half of this was destined to be stored in Algeria for distribution through the south of the country, while that for the northern districts was to be stored in England. Spring Quarry at Corsham, a wartime underground aircraft engine factory that was later to become the British Emergency Government War Headquarters, was proposed as a suitable storage site, and when this was discounted Dartmoor prison was put forward as an alternative. By the time the notes were ready, however, the war had ended and they were shipped directly to France.

The importance of economic continuity in the broadest sense, and the survival of a monetary system in its narrowest, i.e. exchangeable currency bills, has not been lost in the war plan for World War Three. Whilst civil defence measures for the protection of the civilian population was paid little more than lip service throughout North America, in both Canada and the United States 'business continuity programmes' were well established by the mid 1950s.

1. **Mount Pony Federal Reserve Bunker, Culpeper, Virginia.** An aerial view of the three-level Mount Pony bunker, where billions of dollar bills were stored throughout the Cold War, sufficient to replenish the circulating currency of all the States north of the Mississippi. *Author's collection*

2. **Mount Pony Federal Reserve Bunker, Culpeper, Virginia.** Entrance doors to the currency vault. *Author's collection*

Bomb-proof vaults were built to house the business records of all the large corporations; the Standard Oil Company, for example, is purported to have built an underground nuclear shelter over three hundred feet below ground one of its office blocks. Even in the United Kingdom, whose economy was stretched to breaking point by the Second World War, a new vital document secure storage industry developed, often using underground wartime facilities constructed at government expense and rendered redundant at the war's end. Among the first to flourish in this field was Wansdyke Security Ltd, which developed a Second World War underground naval ammunition store in Goblins Pit quarry at Corsham and later extended into two much larger de-requisitioned government quarries at Monkton Farleigh and Westwood. The latter quarry was ideal for the purpose, having been converted at enormous expense in 1942 into a high security repository for treasures evacuated from the British Museum.

Probably the largest such repository in the United States was the Federal Reserve bunker commissioned in December 1969 at Mount Pony, near Culpeper, Virginia. This enormous, 400-foot-long semi-underground bunker, located only seventy miles from Washington, doubled as a standby continuity of government facility, with all the usual services to sustain a staff of 540 for thirty days. The entrance front of the reinforced concrete structure, which is built into a gentle sloping hillside, is exposed, and windows in this façade are fitted with lead-lined radiation-proof sliding steel shutters which can quickly seal the openings under emergency conditions. The bunker consists of three floors: the lower, or access floor is served by three lorry-loading bays and contains offices, maintenance workshops, a plant room, cafeteria and the main storage vault. The middle floor was a 30,000-square-foot computer suite and included a dedicated, forty-seven-ton, air-conditioning plant. Standby generators and other service machinery are housed on the upper floor.

Although having a 'continuity of government' role, the prime function of the bunker was to ensure the continuity of the 'American Dream' – the maintenance, in extreme adversity, of democratic capitalism. From 1969 until 1988 the main 23,500-square-foot vault on the lower floor contained several billion dollars worth of US currency bills, shrink-wrapped and stacked on pallets, ready for distribution north of the Mississippi river in the aftermath of nuclear war. The Mount Pony bunker also functioned as a secure server centre on behalf of the Reserve Bank of Richmond, which operated seven computers on the site that between them processed and maintained records of all American electronic fund transfer transactions.

Having been gradually run down since 1988, the Mount Pony bunker was offered for sale in 1997, and in November of that year, with the aid of a £5.5 million grant from the David and Lucile Packard Foundation, it was purchased by the Library of Congress to house its motion picture, television and recorded sound archive. A further grant of $4.5 million from the Packard foundation has financed continuing renovation and development work.

CIVIL DEFENCE POLICY IN THE USA

The common perception on both sides of the Atlantic is that governments and military leaders have spent lavishly to ensure their own survival after the nuclear war that would be of their own making, but that measures to protect the civil population have been conspicuously absent. In the United States the civil defence debate came to prominence on two occasions: first, under the Kennedy administration during the period 1960-62, when for the only time during the cold war nuclear annihilation was a fleeting but frightening reality, and secondly, during the Reagan period when the western powers played the game of nuclear brinkmanship with the crumbling ruin of the USSR. Up until 1962 civil defence in the USA, (which since the Bull report of 1947 had been considered essentially a private concern, dependant upon the American philosophy of community and individual self-help rather than government intervention) was a matter of *insurance* rather than *strategy*.

If war was to come despite the best efforts of government, then some measure of help would be there to alleviate the suffering. By the late 1970s and until the end of the cold war civil defence, or at least the overt symbols of civil defence, became a military concern – a matter of nuclear strategy. The widespread existence of public shelters and bomb-proof bunkers for local authorities and public utilities would became a symbol of preparedness; they showed that the country was ready to wage war and was determined to survive that war. A national shelter programme was an overt challenge to the enemy: 'We are prepared for war. Are you?' The problem with this approach was that many analysts saw the provision of civilian shelters as provocative and destabilizing, and it was widely held that the converse – a positively vulnerable populace – was a *good thing for world peace*. A critical Federal Emergency Measures Agency (FEMA) report published in 1979 described this doctrine of vulnerability as 'a factor in keeping US Civil Defence at a minimal level'.

Throughout the Truman era the greatest fear was of total and immediate destruction of the industrial areas of the USA by the blast effect of atomic bombs, and contemporary civil defence proposals centred upon the evacuation of industry and industrial workers away from the vulnerable cities. This was soon realized to be a logistic impossibility, and the widespread effect of atomic fallout, not properly appreciated until the Bikini trials of 1954, reinforced the futility of evacuation. Gloomy forecasts made in 1956 indicated that the provision of fallout shelters to protect the population of the 315 most vulnerable target areas in the United States would cost $32 billion. As east-west tension rose to its peak during the Berlin and Cuba crises, The Senate authorized a public shelter budget of $316 million, but this measure was emasculated by Congress and only paltry sums were ever made available in subsequent years.

Following the dramatic end of the Cuban crisis, which was in reality the safety valve that emphatically ended the 'hot' period of the cold war, interest in fallout shelters quickly waned. Immediately prior to the Cuban missile crisis there had been an upsurge in private shelter construction; in 1961/2 America was awash with government and privately sponsored pamphlets recommending the virtues of this or that fallout shelter and a rash of commercial shelter-building companies emerged. But by November 1962 the balloon had burst. In Cork County, Illinois, for example, where over a quarter of a million of the state-sponsored 'Family Fallout Shelter' pamphlets were distributed, only nineteen people out of a population of 3,500,000 had applied for government grants under the shelter incentive programme to build household shelters. Meanwhile, over 240 million shelter places had been assigned or identified in public or large corporate buildings and marked by the ubiquitous but now fading yellow shelter signs that are still common in many US cities. This scheme progressed with little enthusiasm, however, and with a minuscule budget little was done other than identify and record suitable locations. Many of these sites were in fact very unsuitable, ranging from underground car parks, basements of structurally dubious buildings, pipe tunnels and the service areas of corporate office blocks.

By 1978 President Carter's woefully inept handling of nuclear affairs had led to the re-emergence of the civil defence debate after a decade of fragile quiescence. Presidential Directive 41 pinpointed enhanced civil defence measures as a discreet component of the deterrent, and a direct challenge to the increased Soviet expenditure on shelter provision reported by US intelligence sources. The nature of this challenge was put thus by Samuel Huntington, the Director of the Harvard University Centre for International Affairs:

> In the event of a confrontation with the Soviet Union in which American Society was considerably more vulnerable than Soviet Society, the credibility of the US nuclear deterrent with respect to Soviet military and diplomatic pressure on western Europe would be greatly reduced in the eyes of both the Soviets and the west Europeans.

As western perceptions of the probable course of nuclear conflict developed, the 'short-sharp war' scenario gave way to a process of gradual escalation, preceded by a prolonged warning period; a model that gave renewed credibility to mass evacuation. The euphemistically named Crisis Relocation Planning policy (CRP) developed by FEMA in the late 1970s remained in force until 1985. Under this scheme FEMA expected, given seven days' warning, to evacuate 145 million people from the main target areas. Under the Reagan administration, CRP policy was supplemented by an enormous programme of shelter building for key industrial workers based upon the Soviet model, and a parallel programme of hardening the public utility infrastructure and protecting the most critical industrial plants. The object of this policy was to enable the best prospects for post-war recovery and demonstrate to the Soviet Union that the preconditions for both national and social recovery were firmly established in the USA. NSDD 26, promulgated in 1982, proposed a seven-year, $4.2 billion budget to implement these plans, but this was blocked by Congress each year and sunk without trace following the financial crisis of 1986.

Somewhat belatedly, western governments came to realize that the 1960s concept of 'continuity of government' was inadequate without an underlying hierarchy of protected administration at all levels to oversee the national recovery. The situation was succinctly stated by a FEMA official in 1981, who commented that:

> In the past, in too many instances, continuity of government was limited to succession to the Presidency. Now that didn't make sense to me. It doesn't make a great deal of sense to have a President if you don't have the rest of the structure, so we have expanded the continuity of government programme to include the rest of the Federal Government, and also State and local government.

FEMA regional headquarters did exist prior to 1981, but a 1986 study indicated that these were generally unsatisfactory and that only three States had made adequate preparations. FEMA considered that a network of Regional Operating Centres was essential for the restoration of post-attack society and advocated a $1.5 billion building programme to be completed between 1988 and 1992 that would equip 600 new bunkers at all levels. The sudden end of the cold war obviated the need for this requirement, but by 1992 there existed six FEMA regional bunkers and a limited number of lower order protected administrative centres.

Since the mid-1960s six main, underground FEMA Regional Operations Centres have been built at Olney, Maryland; Thomasville, Georgia; Denton, Texas; Denver, Colorado; and Bothell, on the outskirts of Seattle, Washington. All are hardened, two-storey bunkers with accommodation for about 300 staff, built to a similar overall design although adapted to local conditions. The underground bunker at Bothell, a typical example, was built in 1968 on an out-of-town site, close enough to the urban centre to be easily accessible but in a location hopefully safe from a direct hit on the centre of the built-up area. Its primary function was to monitor fallout patterns across the states of Alaska, Idaho, Oregon and Washington.

The provision of emergency centres at City level was more patchy and the standard varied considerably. In Cincinnati a half-hearted gesture was made to convert part of the subway system into a blast and fallout-proof headquarters for sections of Federal, County and City government, but the project was never completed. For nearly forty years some two miles of subway tunnel had lain derelict below the centre of Cincinnati, the relic of a failed transport venture begun just after the end of the First World War that ran out of money and into legal difficulties ten years later, after struggling with innumerable engineering setbacks. Parts of this tunnel system were partially sealed off and sub-divided into office space in the late 1950s to provide a bunker of sorts, but was never used.

In contrast to the majority of local authority bunkers, the emergency operations centre built at Dallas is a fine example of civic emergency planning. Built beneath the old Health & Science Museum in Fair Park, Dallas, in 1960/61, the city bunker cost $120,000, half of which was found from Federal funds. Access to the single-level bunker is via two stairwells, each protected by horizontal, ten-inch-thick, concrete and steel trapdoors operated by hydraulic rams. The stairwells are outside the secure perimeter of the bunker proper, which is protected by further sets of steel blast doors, behind which are air-locks and decontamination showers. Almost a quarter of the total floor space is taken up by a machine room which contains two standby generators and a complex air-conditioning and filtration plant. The main central section is taken up by an Operations Room and communications room, which includes links to the RADEF (radiation defence) monitoring system and the US Emergency Broadcasting System. Separate offices are provided for Civil Defence, Fire, Police, Sanitation and other key municipal services.

2

NORTH AMERICAN RADAR

Although the threat of direct attack upon continental North America during the Second World War was only slight, a number of perimeter radar installations were established on the Atlantic and Pacific coasts of Canada and in Alaska. These acted both as navigational aids and, like the station on Tigalda Island in the Aleutians, gave early warning of possible Japanese attack. Somewhat prematurely in the light of subsequent events, most of these stations, many of them remote and inaccessible, were abandoned at the end of hostilities in 1945.

The increasing tension of the cold war, highlighted by events in Berlin during 1948, indicated a need for warning radar to detect Russian aircraft approaching from Siberia and by the end of the year a single refurbished station in the far north-west was on full-time alert, with four others on limited duty. Realization that the USSR was in possession of long-range, piston-engined bombers capable of delivering atomic weapons to inland targets made a North American early warning screen imperative and by the middle of 1950 forty-four radar stations were operational, using obsolete wartime equipment, to protect the industrial areas of the Great Lakes, Washington and California. By the end of 1952 most of the equipment at these stations had been upgraded, under the code-name Operation LASHUP, and a further eighty-five stations brought into service to provide blanket coverage of the United States mainland. Beyond this blanket, a great umbrella of radar early warning stations, four concentric arcs, the Alaska Radars, the Pinetree Line, the Mid-Canada Line and the Distant Early Warning Line, stretching from the Aleutian Islands to Newfoundland, gave some limited security to an increasingly paranoid United States administration. Ten years later this umbrella would be augmented by an even greater shield, the Ballistic Missile Early Warning System, with its arms outstretched from Alaska, across the North Atlantic through Greenland to the bleakness of Fylingdales Moor in Yorkshire. An increasingly ominous feature of American Air Defence, then as now, was that its hardware, and hence its prime targets, were concentrated on the territory of foreign sovereign states.

THE PINETREE LINE

Constructed to protect the eastern heartland of the United States, although sited on Canadian soil, the Pinetree Line, located very approximately along the 50th parallel, was the offspring of an agreement concluded in 1951 between the United States and Canada. Military co-operation for the mutual defence of continental North America had its origins in an earlier agreement reached in August 1940 between US President Roosevelt and Prime Minister Mackenzie King of Canada which led to the formation of the Permanent Joint Board on Defense. The PJBD was the springboard for a number of joint ventures and by 1946 it was already considering plans for an extensive radar defence network for

North America. The scheme as first envisaged was, however, far too ambitious and expensive, so initially the two countries went ahead with limited national networks, Canada concentrating on radar coverage over the Quebec and Ontario regions, while the United States concentrated on the eastern and western seaboard.

Negotiations for an air defence scheme for North America, put forward by the USAF and entitled 'A Plan for Extension of the Continental Air Defense System', were first opened between the US Continental Air Command and the Royal Canadian Air Force (RCAF) in October 1950. The sense of urgency was such that by the end of the following month a detailed programme had been developed calling for the construction of thirty-two radar sites and one Air Defense Control Centre. The title of the plan 'An Extension of the Continental Air Defense System' reflects the fact that despite it being the progeny of the PJBD it was essentially a United States inspired expansion of an existing Canadian scheme for an eleven-station radar system. The PJBD plan would include a further twenty-two heavy radar stations, built on Canadian soil but orientated to protect the industrial and administrative centres of the northern United States. The cost of this scheme was estimated at $191,806,000, a figure which did not include much of the electronic equipment which had yet to be fully developed.

This financial cost, coupled with the manpower problems associated with so vast a construction task undertaken in such inhospitable and sparsely populated areas, was beyond the resources of the Canadian economy and consequently most of the financial burden fell upon the United States. Further discussions held at the Pentagon early in March 1951 established an electronic equipment requirement costing a further $47,490,000. The following month it was agreed that the United States would man, equip and finance the entire cost of the seventeen authorized radar stations east of the Ontario/Quebec border, and would also finance a further five sites which would be operated by RCAF personnel. The remaining eleven stations which comprised the original Canadian national plan, all in Quebec, were to be built and manned by the RCAF. A hopelessly optimistic construction schedule was announced which called for the completion of the entire chain by July 1952; this as a response to United States intelligence reports which suggested that the USSR would have long-range, high-speed bombers capable of striking anywhere in North America within eighteen months.

The first stage of the Pinetree plan as originally conceived consisted of thirty-three prime radar sites and six short-range gap-fillers stretching from Newfoundland to Vancouver Island. The first section of the line extended from southern Ontario to the Atlantic coast and was completed by 1954. As the rationale of US defence strategy move from protection of the nation's industrial capacity and civil population towards that of protecting the Strategic Air Command bases, a realignment of radar coverage was required which entailed the expansion of the Pinetree Line in the prairie provinces, northern Ontario and Quebec. Construction of this second phase was undertaken and financed wholly by the Canadian government and was completed in 1962.

Six manned gap-filler radars were built by the USAF in Labrador in 1957 to increase the low altitude cover in that area, which was considered particularly vulnerable to infiltration. The equipment employed consisted of lightweight AN/FPS-14 search radars with a range of approximately sixty-five miles built by the Bendix Corporation. A northward extension of the original Pinetree Line was authorized in August 1958, which saw the building of two new heavy GCI stations at Moosonee and Chibougamau, together with six short-range, unmanned gap-fillers at La Tuque, Lac-du-Loup, Manton River, Biscotasing, Timmins and Belle Terre.

The target date for completion of the $37,216,000 expansion programme was March 1962, set to coincide with the commissioning of the Ottowa SAGE Sector. The advent of supersonic jet aircraft rendered obsolete the systems of radar reporting and control which utilized manual plotting and tracking and voice-telling over land-lines as practised in both the United States and Britain. In the UK these developments led to the abandonment of the only recently completed ROTOR radar system, while in the United States the solution was a computerized data-handling system known as the Semi-Automatic Ground Environment (SAGE), which was eventually extended to the entire air surveillance network controlled by NORAD, except for the Alaska radars.

SAGE AND BUICC

Under the 1948 plan, (Operation LASHUP), the network of eighty-four home radar stations were controlled from eleven semi-hardened, surface Command & Control Centres, designed by the architects Holabird, Root and Burgee, and constructed between 1950 and 1952. Investigations conducted by the Atomic Energy Commission indicated that a building with a square footprint would be best able to withstand the anticipated blast overpressure. The commission also concluded that due to the accepted inaccuracy of current atomic weapons the probability of a direct hit, or even a near miss, was very low and that a design based around a framework of fourteen-inch-square reinforced concrete beams infilled with air-spaced eight-inch and four-inch concrete panels would give adequate protection. The control buildings were of two storeys, with detached, single-storey concrete powerhouses nearby.

1948 PLAN COMMAND & CONTROL CENTRES
- Duluth, Minnesota
- George, Southern California
- Griffiss, New York
- Hamilton, San Francisco
- Kirtland, New Mexico
- McChord, Washington
- Robin's, Georgia
- Selfridge, Michigan
- Stewart, New York
- Tinker, Oklahoma

These Sector Control Centres were co-ordinated from the Air Defense Command Combat Operations Centre at Ent AFB, Colorado, which was commissioned in 1954. Like ROTOR, its British equivalent, the LASHUP network relied upon land-line voice and telex reporting and the manual display of track information on vertical and horizontal situation boards supplemented at some centres by photographic projection of radar images. Internally the American operations rooms resembled their RAF counterparts, with central map wells surrounded by tiered balconies for directing and intelligence staffs.

LASHUP was an interim measure only and plans were developed for its replacement, hopefully by 1954, by an automatic data transmission system which would incorporate the existing Control Centres with five new centres to be built at Andrews AFB (Washington), Fort Knox (Kentucky), Larson AFB (Washington), Richards-Gebaur AFB (Missouri) and Truax AFB (Wisconsin). Research indicated that even under favourable conditions LASHUP would detect and stop only ten percent of a large Soviet air assault and that the only way to improve upon this would be by the use of high-speed computerised data transmission to provide a large-scale, real-time composite radar picture of the air battle.

By 1951, the Massachusetts Institute of Technology (MIT), which had been deeply involved in two earlier computer development projects, ENIAC, for the Manhattan Project, and WHIRLWIND, for the Office of Naval Research, was co-ordinating a joint services programme to develop a digital air-defence computer referred to as the LINCOLN project. Plans for the new air defence network incorporating the LINCOLN computer system (now known as the Semi-Automatic Ground Environment, or SAGE scheme) were fully developed by 1954. The system would use digital processing but still retain only voice transmission, and implementation was expected to be completed by 1958.

The construction timetable inevitably slipped as air defence requirements evolved in the face of an increasing threat from the ICBM and the corresponding diminution of that posed by manned bombers. The final schedule called for eight sector level Combat Centres, similar in concept to the British ROTOR Sector Operations Centres, and thirty-four sub-sector Direction Centres. A number of 1948-period Command & Control stations were adapted to fit the new requirements, and large new SAGE annexes were constructed at these sites to house advanced IBM computers. All were to be operational by the autumn of 1962. Construction work began in 1955 and by the end of the following year Direction Centres at McGuire (New Jersey), Stewart (New York), Fort Lee (Virginia), Topsham (Maine), and Fort Custer (Michigan), were complete.

It had been intended to collocate the majority of the Combat Centres with Direction Centres, but this plan was eventually implemented at only Richards-Gebaur, Syracuse, and Truax AFBs. These centres were also complete by the autumn of 1956, and because of tight budgetary restraints and doubts regarding their ultimate effectiveness, they were, in fact, the only SAGE Combat Centres to be built. Similar financial considerations had thwarted an earlier Air Defence Command scheme which had envisaged all the Combat and Direction centres as underground structures, but a DoD analysis of potential Soviet targets in the United States indicated that the most prominent Strategic Air Command bases were most vulnerable and should therefore attract the higher funding. The purpose-built SAGE Directions Centres were designed by the architectural partnership of Burns & Roe, and were four-storey buildings 150-feet square and seventy-five feet high, with single-storey detached power-houses of similar design, 110 feet square and twenty-one feet high. Four Worthington diesel-driven alternators provided backup power. Specifications issued in the *SAGE Operations Plan* of 1955 called for the buildings to be 'designed to be shock resistant and contamination proof'. To meet these criteria, the building framework consisted of twenty-eight-inch square reinforced concrete pillars with mushroom capitals and twelve-inch concrete infill panels, and much of the equipment within the bunker was spring-mounted. Radiation-proofing features incorporated in the SAGE centres were first developed for the protection of New York's main telephone exchange in the early 1950s.

The basement of each control centre contained two AN/FSQ-7 computers, developed by MIT and built by IBM. Each machine contained 58,000 thermionic valves, weighed 275 tons, consumed three Megawatts of power, and had rather less processing power than the average laptop PC of the late 1990s. IBM was contracted to build sixty AN/FSQ-7 (Whirlwind II) computers at a cost of $30 million each, and this contract would provide half of the corporation's revenue during the 1950s. The technological benefits of the contract to IBM was largely instrumental in forging the corporation's dominant lead in the microcomputer market during the following four decades. As the SAGE system expanded smaller computers, weighing in at only a quarter of a ton each, were installed at each radar station to process the raw radar data prior to transmission to the centres.

Although the technology seemed to meet the ADC requirements, the DoD had lost control of the cost of the SAGE project by early 1957 and all further work was suspended for several months until various contractual problems were resolved and a more rational budget developed. Towards the end of the year work resumed on the construction of a limited number of outstanding Direction Centres at Malmstrom, Minot, Luke, Beale, Stead, Norton, K I Sawyer, and Larson AFBs, with completion scheduled for early 1958. The first centre to become operational was at McGuire AFB, New Jersey, in August 1958 for the protection of the New York Air Defence Sector.

During the next two years many of the first generation manual stations were closed down and the sector boundaries realigned. Shortly after the first twenty stations became fully operational it was realized that most of the Combat Centres were built on or near highly vulnerable Strategic Air Command bomber bases. This came to light at a particularly difficult time for the US administration and triggered a panic proposal to construct ten Super Combat Centres, buried 300-500 feet below ground. Whilst this was technically feasible due to the availability of much smaller computers following the advent of the solid-state transistor, the cost would have been astronomical and the plan was quickly shelved. Indeed, by this time the threat from Soviet ICBMs was seen to have completely eclipsed the SAGE system and all remaining works were permanently abandoned.

At its peak the NORAD Air Defence organization consisted of twenty-three Sectors:

NORAD SECTOR	DIRECTION CENTRE
BANGOR	Topsham AFB
BOSTON	Stewart AFB
SYRACUSE	Syracuse AFB
NEW YORK	McGuire AFB
WASHINGTON	Fort Lee, Virginia
MONTGOMERY	Gunter AFB
DETROIT	Custer AFB
SAULT St MARIE	K I Sawyer AFB
CHICAGO	Truax AFB
DULUTH	Duluth AFB
SIOUX CITY	Sioux City AFB
OKLAHOMA	Richards-Gebaur AFB
GRAND FORKS	Grand Forks AFB
MINOT	Minot AFB
GREAT FALLS	Malmstrom AFB
PHOENIX	Luke AFB, Arizona
RENO	Stead AFB, Nevada
SAN FRANCISCO	Beale AFB
LOS ANGELES	Norton AFB
PORTLAND	Camp Adair, Oregon
SEATLE	McCord AFB
SPOKANE	Larson AFB
CANADA	Goose Bay (integrated into SAGE system but never automated)

When activated, ADC long-range radars would pick up unidentified aircraft and transmit track information via telephone line to their parent Direction Centre where the information would be correlated with tracks from closer-range gap-filler radars. This composite picture would be relayed to the SAGE Identification Room where track information would be compared with filed flight-plans. Any inconsistencies that mismatched by more than one minute would be notified to the SAGE Weapons Room where computers would generate the necessary interception options for the Weapons Director, possibly by the deployment of fighter aircraft or the recently introduced NIKE and BOMARC missiles. If fighter interception was selected then relevant enemy track information would be transmitted by datalink to the aircraft radar.

By the time it was fully implemented SAGE was already nearing functional obsolescence. A series of reports produced in the early 1960s outlined its shortcomings:

- The system could just cope with a moderate enemy attack under the most favourable conditions.
- The radar could not discriminate sufficiently to counter enemy chaff or radio counter-measures.
- Neither the long-range nor gap-filler radars could reliably detect incoming bombers flying below 10,000 feet.
- The data processing systems would be swamped by any more than fifty tracks.

In response to the ICBM threat the Direction Centres at Minot and Grand Forks AFBs were replaced in 1963 by underground 'Standing Alert' Command & Control Centres, and over the following two years several other SAGE centres were closed down. The best responses to the ICBM were seen to be dispersal and redundancy, and to facilitate this ADC looked again at the eighty-five 1948/9 period, pre-SAGE, Command and Control sites that they still retained in mothballs. Most of these buildings had the added advantage of not being located on or near SAC air bases. ADC proposed to recommission many of these sites using smaller, modern Burroughs digital computers, naming them initially NORAD Automated Control Centres, and later Back Up Interceptor Control Centres (BUICC).

BUICC was introduced in three phases from 1962/3 when the first group of twenty-seven former Control Centres were brought on line using manual transmission procedures. These stations could assume immediate control of their Sector should the SAGE centre be put out of action. Although BUICC was originally intended as an emergency back up for SAGE it did in fact largely replace it. By 1963, when phase-one was virtually complete, only sixteen of the twenty-three SAGE centres were still operational. Phase-two centres could process information from adjacent Sectors, and included in their construction greater radiation protection with two-feet of concrete cladding added to the exterior walls of the original structures and steel plate lining for the interiors. Phase three, which continued through 1968, involved the extension of several sites to twice their original size and the addition of further radiation protection. These centres offered the greatest flexibility of operation and could integrate information from up to ten adjacent Sectors. 1970 saw the completion of the BUICC programme, with twelve sites completed to BUICC-III standards and just six SAGE centres remaining. These survived until July 1984 when they, and most of the BUICC system, were displaced by new and very powerful phased array radars at eight locations forming the US/Canadian Joint Surveillance System.

PINE TREE LINE EXPANSION

Stations on the Pinetree Line were generally equipped with the ubiquitous, medium-range FPS-3 search radar in main and standby configuration, together with an FPS-6 or TPS-502 height finder, all protected from the elements by fifteen-metre-diameter rubberized radomes. During the 1960s most stations were upgraded with new FPS-26 height finders and FPS-27 frequency-diversity search radars which had much greater imunity from jamming, and included a more advanced IFF (Identification, Friend or Foe) system. A few sites were

30

designated as either dedicated 'Early Warning' or 'Ground Control Intercept' (GCI) stations; the former being equipped with radar configured to detect intruding enemy aircraft, while the latter, acting on information transmitted from the EW stations, vectored defending fighters on to the enemy. Most stations on the Pinetree Line, however, were equipped for a dual EW/GCI role. Building of the domestic sites was a major operation as facilities had to be provided for a staff of up to 400 personnel, until the advent of SAGE in the mid 1960s progressively reduced this requirement. Under SAGE, control of the air battle was transferred from the individual GCI stations to Sector Direction Centres where digitized information from all the long-range detection radars within the Sector could be processed and displayed as a unified air picture.

Early in 1960 the RCAF planned the construction of forty-five additional gap-filler radars in the eastern provinces, but before construction was far advanced technical improvements and a swingeing cut in the Canadian defence budget led to its abandonment in 1964. Few if any of the gap-fillers were completed and none became operational, although contracts for the construction of twenty-five were awarded and substantial preliminary works were completed at at least nineteen sites. One incidental feature of many of the gap-filler sites planned for the heavily forested areas was that the seventy-foot-high radar masts were to incorporate a fire-watchers platform, built to replace existing fire-towers which had to be demolished because they would interfere with the radar returns.

Overall control of the Pinetree Line was vested in the Air Officer Commanding US Air Defense Command, and below him four Sector Commanders exercised operational control over all radar and weapons system within his designated sector. The four operational sectors, each with an Air Defense Control Centre where the overall battle picture could be displayed, were:

64th Air Division ADCC	Fort Pepperell, Newfoundland
No. 1 Sector ADCC	Lac St. Denis, Quebec
No. 2 Sector ADCC	St. Margarets, New Brunswick
No. 3 Sector ADCC	Vancouver, British Columbia

Construction of the Pinetree stations was a major civil engineering undertaking, although this was as nothing compared with the building of the Distant Early Warning Line deep in the arctic region of Canada. Few of the Pinetree sites were remote from existing road or rail access, but the high and often precarious hilltop sites selected for the radar towers and operations rooms created their own problems. In most cases the station domestic and service sites were some distance from the technical areas in more easily accessible valley locations. The exposed positions of the scanner heads rendered them vulnerable to the typically extreme weather conditions of the region and it was to counter the disruptive effects of high winds that they were enclosed in rubber radomes, the internal pressure of which was adjusted automatically depending on the external wind speed and atmospheric pressure. On several memorable occasions, however, the forces of nature proved irresistible, as at Goose Bay early on the evening of 31

March 1955, when winds of over 105 mph ripped the CPS-5D back-up search radar completely clear of its mounting, and at Holberg in February 1957 when a much heavier FPS-3 radar was completely destroyed by 145 mph winds. Often radar and communication towers would collapse under the weight of accumulated ice that could build up to 10″ thickness on girders and cables.

Three standard designs of station (with local variations) were used on the Pinetree Line; designated types 'B', 'C' and 'II'. Types 'B' and 'C', which were GCI stations of Royal Canadian Air Force design, differed only in that at the type 'B' sites the radar towers consisted of three free-standing steel lattice towers, while at type 'C' the main search radar was mounted on the roof of the operations building with height finders on separate towers.

Type 'II' sites were Early Warning stations built to a USAF design with the radar masts separate from the operations building. Rather surprisingly in view of their critical function, none of the station buildings were underground or even blast-proof, the type 'B' and 'C' operations buildings being of asbestos-clad steel-frame construction while type 'II' was wooden-framed.

Stations constructed under the extension programme cost approximately $6.5 million each; the breakdown of costs for the Gypsumville site is typical:

Clearing land	$20,000
Roadways, hard standings and drainage	$298,500
Fencing site	$39,800
Laying new railway spur	$4,000
Fuel storage and handling facility	$72,000
Sewage treatment plant	$258,000
Water storage, treatment and distribution	$372,000
Ducted heating system	$230,000
Electrical installations	$380.000
Gate houses	£25,000
Admin block and hospital	$130,000
Mess building	$275,000
Single accommodation block	$316,000
Mobile equipment/Unit supply building	$128,000
Construction engineering/ Fire Hall	$111,000
Chapel	$87,000
Central heat and power plant	$650,000
90 x mobile homes for staff accommodation	$1,044,000
FPS-26 Radar tower	$300,000
Foundations (only) for FPS-6 tower	$20,000
FPS-27 Search radar tower	$800,000
Telephone exchange building	$134,000
SAGE Annexe	$265,000
Radio communications building	$175,000
Landscaping	$20,000
TOTAL	**$6,544,300**

PINETREE LINE RADARS

Station	Province	Date of Commission	Date of Closure
Alsaska	SK	1962	August 1987
Armstrong	ON	1954	October 1974
Baldy Hughs	BC	1955	April 1988
Barrington	NS	1957	August 1990
Beausejour	MB	1951	August 1986
Beaverbank	NS	1954	April 1964
Beaverlodge	AB	1953	April 1988
Cartwright	LAB	1953	June 1968
Chibougamau	QC	1962	April 1987
Cold Lake	AB	1954	August 1990
Comox	BC	1954	June 1958
Dana	SK	1962	June 1987
Edgar	ON	1952	April 1964
Falconbridge	ON	1952	November 1986
Foymount	ON	1952	October 1974
Frobisher Bay	NWT	1953	November 1961
Gander	NF	1953	August 1990
Goose Bay	LAB	1953	July 1988
Gypsumville	MB	1962	July 1987
Holberg	BC	1954	January 1991
Hopedale	LAB	1953	June 1968
Kamloops	BC	1958	April 1988
Lac St, Denis	QC	1952	August 1986
Lowther	ON	1957	April 1987
Moisie	QC	1953	August 1988
Mont Apica	QC	1952	August 1990
Moosonee	ON	1961	April 1975
Pagwa	ON	1953	October 1966
Parent	QC	1953	April 1964
Penhold	AB	1963	August 1986
Puntzi Mountain	BC	1952	October 1966
Ramore	ON	1953	October 1974
Resolution Island	NWT	1954	November 1961
Saglek	LAB	1953	June 1971
Senneterre	QC	1953	April 1988
Sioux Lookout	ON	1952	July 1987
Stephenville	NF	1953	October 1969
St Anthony	NF	1953	June 1968
St Johns	NF	1954	October 1961
St Margarets	NB	1953	April 1988
St Sylvestre	QC	1955	April 1964
Sydney	NS	1954	January 1991
Tofino	BC	1955	December 1957
Yorkton	SK	1963	August 1986

THE MID-CANADA LINE

Pressure on the Canadian Government to build the Mid-Canada line came early in 1953 from powerful voices within the United States military establishment and from the Eisenhower administration, which was concerned that the Pinetree Line, then under construction, would not give the United States sufficiently early warning of trans-polar attack from Russia. The Canadian/American Military Study Group was asked to report on

> those aspects of the North American Air Defence System, and the early warning system in particular, which are of mutual concern to the two countries.

By July the group had agreed upon the construction of a second early warning line to complement the Pinetree radars, which would run from Alaska to Newfoundland along the 55th parallel.

Based upon research undertaken some years earlier at McGill University, the Mid-Canada line was planned as a Doppler-radar fence, consisting of two parallel, staggered lines of radar stations some five to ten miles apart, with stations at sixty-mile intervals. The radars were not of the conventional rotating search type, but consisted of pairs of transmitters and receivers set up at adjacent sites with an unmodulated standing radio wave pattern between them. Should an aircraft pass through this wave field phase-alterations in the wave path due to reflected signals would be registered. By correlating detections from the two parallel radar fences approximations of speed and heading could be determined. The nominal operating range of the system was between altitudes of 500 and 65,000 feet. Detection of aircraft passing through the Mid-Canada line as unidentified intruders depended upon the checking of all detections against authorized flight plans and, to enable this system to work effectively, the airspace around the line was designated the 'Mid-Identification Zone'. Any aircraft entering this zone without having filed a proper flight plan was forced to land at one of several specially built emergency aerodromes to obtain clearance. The Mid-Canada line was essentially a trip-wire mechanism that would transmit early warning of intrusion to the Pinetree and other search and intercept radars.

The approved plan, estimated at $120,000,000, called for ninety unmanned Doppler stations spread along the 2,700 miles of wilderness between the coastlines of Labrador and British Columbia, and for eight Sector Control Stations, which would be located at Dawson Creek, Stoney Mountain, Cranberry Portage, Bird (Manitoba), Winisk, Great Whale River, Knob Lake and Hopedale. The last named centre was actually located within the Hopedale Pinetree Control Centre and reported penetrations to Goose Bay. Intercepts from a remote Doppler station were transmitted to its parent Sector Control centre where it was checked against recorded flight plan information, and where there was an anomaly this information would be passed southwards to one of the larger NORAD centres, Dawson Creek for example, reported to Spokane in Washington and Great Falls, Montana, as well as Canada NORAD at North Bay. All ninety-eight sites were connected by microwave links (with relays at each Detector station), while the 'Polevault' tropospheric scatter radio system connected the eastern Sector stations to the

Pinetree and Distant Early Warning Lines and provided southward communication to the NORAD centres. At the western end of the line commercial landlines and the military microwave network provided communication to the south. The Stoney Mountain, Cranberry Portage and Knob Lake Sector Control Centres were also equipped with conventional heavy surveillance radars to track aircraft for identification purposes. Although unmanned, the Detector stations were provided with dormitories and cooking facilities for the maintenance crews who would be despatched from the nearest Sector Control Centre in event of an equipment failure. Most of this equipment was duplicated with automatic switchover from the failed unit and all vital functions were remotely monitored by telemetry at the Sector Control. All sites had three diesel generators installed, each one capable of taking the full station load.

The 55th parallel runs through some of the most rugged bush terrain of Canada's sub-artic tundra region, pocked with thousands of lakes, mostly impassable for much of the year due to the autumn freeze and spring thaw, and still, in the early 1950s, largely uncharted territory. The first task was to carry out an engineering assessment of the proposed route, to see if the project was technically viable. In December 1953 a series of tractor trains set out to investigate the area in a manner strikingly similar to a polar expedition, and based on their findings it was decided to first survey a fifteen-mile-wide strip along the route by aerial photography and then to produce maps to the scale of one inch to the mile. By the autumn of 1954 all the preliminary work was complete and, once formal approval from both governments was received, the Trans Canada Telephone System (TCTS) was appointed Management Contractor and the engineering task began. Base camps were established and tractor-trains and helicopter air lifts put in place to transport the 200,000 tons of equipment into some of the most remote and inhospitable places on earth. Transport and site access and problems encountered due to the terrain at the eastern end of the line were primarily responsible for the final increase in costs to $224,566,830, which was almost double the original estimate.

Construction of the four western Control Centres was completed by April 1957 with all their Detector stations on-line, and by the following January the entire system was operational. Within seven years, however, its operational usefulness had come to an end, brought about by the advent of high-speed jet aircraft and unsupportable operating costs, which were much higher than projected before the line was built. An RCAF performance analysis of the Mid-Canada Line, implemented to determine whether the running costs justified the operational benefits, found that almost invariably by the time fighters were scrambled due to an MCL warning, the targets had already been acquired by the Pinetree radars. Under pressure from the Canadian government the western half of the line was closed down in January 1964, but the American authorities, concerned about their eastern industrial heartland, pressed for the retention of the eastern section until April 1965 when they too accepted that it was no longer viable.

THE DISTANT EARLY WARNING (DEW) LINE

Still insecure in the face of what is now perceived as its largely erroneous assessment of the Soviet threat, and despite the protection offered by the Mid-

Canada and Pinetree radar defences, the United States sought and received support from the Canadian government to build a further, even more distant, early warning radar chain on the very edge of Canada's polar ice cap. This, the Distant Early Warning Line, which cost the US taxpayers $347,000,000, probably ranks as the most challenging military construction task ever undertaken.

The DEW line ran 10° north of the Mid-Canada line along the 66th parallel from north-west Alaska to the eastern shore of Baffin Island, through vast tracks of snowbound waste inhabited by no more than a few hundred Inuit Eskimo. Initially sixty-three stations were built about 160 km apart. A later extension, known as DEW East, incorporating long-hop tropospheric scatter radio stations, continued the line through Greenland and Iceland to the Faeroes and Shetland Isles, so by 1961 there was continuous radar coverage on the edge of the arctic circle from the Aleutian Islands to Scotland. Of four additional auxiliary stations built in Greenland between 1958 and 1960, two, built on the high icecap, were constructed as modular units on 'rafts' supported on hydraulic legs which were extended by a metre each year as the ice subsided.

Aerial surveys undertaken in 1955 enabled the identification of suitable areas of high ground which were at the required 160 km interval. When selecting sites consideration was given to the proximity of natural gravel deposits that would be needed as raw material for concrete used in construction. Many of these sites in the central region were completely inaccessible except by air, so small bulldozers were parachuted in to enable primitive airfields to be levelled in order that larger plant and construction equipment could then be flown in. Once the airfields were complete there were 2,800 supply flights using huge Globemaster cargo aircraft, over sixty of which were damaged or destroyed whilst landing in the atrocious arctic conditions, with the loss of thirty lives. Later, commercial airlines made over 45,000 flights delivering 120,300 tons of supplies. In Alaska hundreds of tractor trains each towing as many as twenty cargo sledges supplied the construction sites during the winter months, while during the sea lifts of 1955 and 1956 fleets of 120 ships made their way down the Mackenzie River to sites in western Canada and through the Foxe Channel between the eastern mainland and Baffin Island. Many ships were badly damaged by ice during these operations.

During its thirty-year life span some stations closed and others opened, so an accurate chronology is impossible, but by 31 July1957 the first planned series of fifty-eight stations was fully commissioned. There were six long-range 'main' stations approximately 800 km apart at Barter Island and Point Barrow in Alaska and at Cape Parry, Cambridge, Hall Beach and Cape Dyer in the North West Territory. Each of these was responsible for between four and ten 'auxilliary' stations fitted with short-range radars and each was in southward communication with NORAD controls via tropospheric scatter propagation. In 1974 troposcatter was replaced by the US 'Anik' communications satellite. Primary radar was the Raytheon FPS-19 which had back-to-back seventeen metre rotating heads enclosed in weatherproof radomes, while FPS-23s served in the gap-filler stations. All sites were also provided with Doppler radars for low-level detection. A further thirty-one unmanned Doppler 'intermediate' stations were built, but these were so unreliable that warnings from them were routinely ignored at their parent stations and they were abandoned in 1963.

By July 1961 the entire North American continent was protected by a vast curtain of radar cover that extended in width and breadth from the sub-arctic DEW line southwards through the populated areas of Canada and the USA. Fleets of radar picket ships extended this cover for hundreds of miles beyond the eastern and western coastlines. In July 1961, to augment the 'over-the-pole' surveillance capability, Airborne Warning & Control aircraft (AW&C) were transferred northwards from the Argentina-Azores area to join picket ships already stationed along the Greenland-Iceland-UK barrier. Picket ships also patrolled to the west of the United States beyond the Aleutian islands, forming the final link in a continuous radar chain that eventually extended from Hawaii to the mainland of Europe.

The naval radar picket fleet consisted of sixteen Second World War Liberty Ships converted between 1954 and 1959 to carry purpose-built SPS-17A radars. This, the 'Guardian' class radar fleet, consisted of:

USS *Guardian*	USS *Lookout*	USS *Skywatcher*
USS *Searcher*	USS *Scanner*	USS *Locator*
USS *Picket*	USS *Interceptor*	USS *Investigator*
USS *Outpost*	USS *Protector*	USS *Vigil*
USS *Interdictor*	USS *Interpreter*	USS *Tracer*
USS *Watchman*		

THE NORTH WARNING SYSTEM

For over two decades the DEW line functioned efficiently, although at considerable expense due to the high re-supply and servicing costs of such remote locations, and unlike most of the other North American radar systems it was not substantially upgraded until towards the end of its life. The reason for this is that by the late 1960s the threat of attack from manned Russian strategic bombers, its principal *raison d'être*, had virtually evaporated as the technology of annihilation became dependent upon the Inter-Continental Ballistic Missile. By the end of 1979, however, a different philosophy of global war was developing which renewed western fears of Soviet aggression. Russia, like the United States, was developing a new generation of very advanced, high speed, low or high altitude manned bombers like the upgraded 'Backfire' and 'Blackjack', capable of air-launching nuclear cruise missiles.

In response to this threat and at the instigation of the Reagan administration, the North American Air Defence Modernization Agreement was concluded between the US and Canada in March 1985, which led to the modernization of the DEW line and its transition into the current North Warning System. This scheme involved the construction of fifteen new long-range, FPS-117 phased-array radars at existing DEW Line locations, together with three similar radars at previously abandoned Pinegap sites on the east Labrador Coast at Saglek, Cape Kiglapait, and Cartwright. Forty Unisys type FPS-124 short-range unattended gap-filler radars were also installed at ex DEW line stations, those in

Canada coming into Commission in 1992 and the last three, at Wainright, Lonely and Bullen Point in Alaska towards the end of 1994.

The table below shows the locations and closure dates of the most important DEW line stations, and the dates of their transition to NWS operation:

NAME	TERRITORY	DEW closed	NWS established	NWS radar type
COLD BAY	Alaska	6/1969		
NIKOLSKI	Alaska	6/1969		
DRIFTWOOD BAY	Alaska	6/1969		
CAPE SARICHEF	Alaska	6/1969		
PORT MOLLER	Alaska	6/1969		
PORT HEIDEN	Alaska	6/1969		
CAPE LISBURNE	Alaska	7/1963		
POINT LAY	Alaska		1989/90	LRR
WAINWRIGHT	Alaska	4/1995	1994	SRR
CAPE SABINE		7/1963		
ICY CAPE		7/1963		
PEARD BAY		7/1963		
POINT BARROW	Alaska		1989/90	LRR
LONELY	Alaska	10/1990	1994	SRR
OLIKTOK	Alaska		1989/90	LRR
BULLEN POINT	Alaska	4/1995	1994	SRR
CAPE SIMPSON	Alaska	7/1963		
KOGRU	Alaska	7/1963		
MCINTYRE	Alaska	7/1963		
BROWNLOW POINT	Alaska	7/1963		
BARTER ISLAND	Alaska		11/1990	LRR
STOKE POINT	Alaska		7/1991	SRR
DEMARCATION BAY	Alaska		7/1963	
SHINGLE POINT	Alaska	6/1989	6/1989	LRR
STORM HILLS	Yukon		11/1990	SRR
TUKTOYAKTUK	NWT	9/1993	9/1990	SRR
LIVERPOOL BAY	NWT		11/1990	SRR
NICHOLSON PENINSULA	NWT	9/1993	10/1990	SRR
HORTON RIVER	NWT		6/1991	SRR
CAPE PARRY	NWT	8/1989	8/1989	LRR
CLINTON POINT	NWT	3/1993		
KEATS POINT	NWT		7/1991	SRR
CROKER RIVER	NWT		8/1991	SRR
CAPE YOUNG	NWT	8/1993		
HARDING RIVER	NWT		9/1991	SRR
BERNARD HARBOUR	NWT		9/1991	SRR
LADY FRANKLIN POINT	NWT	6/1989	6/1989	LRR
BRYON BAY	NWT	8/1993		
EDINBURGH ISLAND	NWT		10/1991	SRR

Cape Peel West	NWT		10/1991	SRR
Cambridge Bay	NWT	9/1989	9/1989	LRR
Sturt Point	NWT		10/1991	SRR
Jenny Lind Island	NWT	1992	10/1990	SRR
Hat Island	NWT		9/1991	SRR
Gladman Point	NWT	1992	10/1990	SRR
Gjoa Haven	NWT		10/1990	SRR
Shepherd Bay	NWT	7/1989	7/1989	LRR
Simpson Lake	NWT		9/1991	SRR
Pelly Bay	NWT	1992	9/1991	SRR
Mackar Inlet	NWT	1992		
Cape McLoughlin	NWT		7/1992	SRR
Lailor River	NWT		8/1992	SRR
Hall Beach	NWT	9/1989	9/1989	LRR
Rowley Island	NWT		8/1991	SRR
Bray Island	NWT		8/1991	SRR
Longstaff Bluff	NWT	1991	11/1990	SRR
Nudluardjuk Lake	NWT		10/1991	SRR
Dewar Lakes	NWT	7/1989	7/1989	LRR
Kangok Fjord	NWT		9/1992	SRR
Cape Hooper	NWT	1991	12/1990	SRR
Broughton Island	NWT	1991	12/1990	SRR
Cape Dyer	NWT	8/1989	8/1989	LRR
Sisimut	Greenland	1990/91		
	Greenland icecap	1990/91		
	Greenland icecap	1990/91		
Kulusuk	Greenland	1990/91		

East Coast North Warning System stations that were not components of the DEW line:

NAME	TERRITORY	Previous site use	Date of construction	NWS radar type
Cape Mercy	NWT		7/1992	SRR
Brevoort Island	NWT	Polevault	10/1988	LRR
Loks Island	NWT		8/1992	SRR
Resolution Island	NWT	Pinetree	9/1991	SRR
Cape Kakiviak	Labrador		7/1992	SRR
Saglek	Labrador	Pinetree	11/1988	SRR
Cape Kiglapait	Labrador		8/1992	LRR
Big Bay	Labrador		9/1992	SRR
Tukialik	Labrador		10/1992	SRR
Cartwright	Labrador	Pinetree	11/1988	LRR

ALASKA RADAR

The period immediately following the Berlin crisis of 1948 saw a number of important US military bases at Anchorage and Fairbanks in western Alaska completely unprotected by radar cover and vulnerable to surprise attack from the USSR. In response to this threat five temporary radar stations were set up on the coast, later supplemented by a chain of radar picket ships stationed along the length of the Aleutian islands. A plan to build thirty-seven permanent stations in two arcs, one inland and the other following the coastline, was later reduced to ten due to budgetary restrictions, although four earlier installations were upgraded and re-equipped to augment the coastal coverage. The coastal stations, including that at Tin City, which had the distinction of being the American radar installation closest to the USSR, acted as early warning radars, while the seven sites on the inner arc were ground-control-intercept (GCI) stations.

Unlike the Pinetree and Distant Early Warning Lines, the Alaska radar system was never incorporated in the Semi Automatic Ground Environment (SAGE) computerized data handling system and continued to function with manual track reporting until the introduction of 'Seek Igloo' phased-array radar in the early 1980s. Until that time the surveillance radars were connected to the NORAD Regional Control Centre at Elmendorf Airforce Base at Anchorage via two manual control centres at King Salmon and Murphy Dome near Fairbanks.

Development of 'Seek Igloo' began in 1977 and the complete system including the AN/FPS-117 radar and its associated computerized data-handling, digital-transmission and display equipment was accepted for service in 1983. FPS-117 is a long-range (250 mile), low-power phased-array, three-dimensional radar which scans horizontally by rotation, but uses a solid-state electronic system for vertical scans. The ability to alternate randomly between eighteen channels gives a high degree of immunity to jamming, and an operating frequency range of 1215-1400 Mhz provides for high discrimination for the detection of small targets. There was some doubt, however, that it would be totally effective against cruise missiles. The revamped Alaska Radar consists of thirteen stations; the main sites are fitted with minimally attended FPS-117 radars, and auxiliary sites with shorter range, unattended FPS-124 equipment. An earlier, valve-based, phased-array radar was built on the Aleutian island of Shemya in 1977. By 1988 the principal function of this site, code-named 'Cobra Dane', was to monitor test launches of Soviet ballistic missiles.

Alaska was also the home of two 3,000-kilometre-range over-the-horizon backscatter radars, similar to other installations in New England and elsewhere in the United States. The backscatter system, which utilized pairs of enormous transmitting and receiving 'billboard' antennae nearly a mile in length and many miles apart, was not suitable for use on the North Warning Line due to the atmospheric electromagnetic peculiarities of the polar region. Transmitter and receiver units reporting to the Anchorage Operations Centre were erected at Gulkana and Tok, respectively, while a similar system was erected on the Aleutian island of Amchitka to monitor airspace over the Sea of Okhotsk.

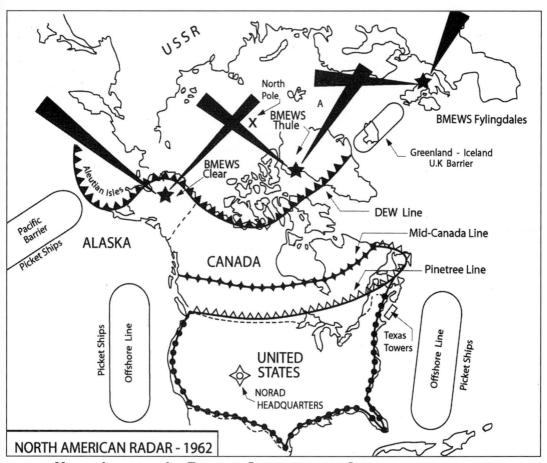

NORTH AMERICAN AIR DEFENCE COMMUNICATION SYSTEMS

The atrociously difficult terrain made the construction and manning of conventional HF/VHF radio or microwave relay stations across the arctic waste of northern Canada practically impossible, so some other reliable means of communication between the new radar chains and their control centres to the south had to be found. The initial answer, as we have seen, was tropospheric scatter radio; a system by which enormously powerful radio transmissions were bounced off the troposphere and onwards to a far distant ground station using huge dish or 'billboard' antennae. Only a tiny fraction of the transmitted radio energy was reflected back, so very careful alignment of the antennae and maintenance of the electronic equipment was required.

Construction of the main troposcatter system across northern Canada, codenamed POLEVAULT, started in 1954 on the section linking Frobisher Bay to Gander in Newfoundland which became operational in January 1955. This line was extended the following year to Cape Dyer at the eastern extremity of the DEW Line. The troposcatter system was supplemented by a submarine cable stretching from Thule in Greenland to Newfoundland via Cape Dyer in 1959, but this was plagued with problems, being cut by trawlers and icebergs on numerous occasions from the day it was brought into service. A new high-power tropospheric link was established between Thule and Cape Dyer in 1960 and by way of the DEW line at Hall Beach in 1964. The need for a more reliable digital

41

data transfer system with the onset of SAGE led to the gradual shut-down of POLEVAULT from 1963 and to its complete replacement by satellite communication in the early 1970s, when most of the plant was sold to the Bell Telephone Company for commercial use.

A similar system codenamed WHITE ALICE served the Alaska radar network from 1956 until it was superseded by satellite in the early 1970s. The original scheme, which was built by the Western Electric Company at a cost of $140,000,000, consisted of twenty-five stations. New stations were gradually added and in 1960 it was extended westward through the Aleutian islands and eastwards to join the DEW Line at Barter Island. Following the construction of the pivotally important Ballistic Missile Early Warning radar at Clear, Alaska, in 1960 new microwave communication links were established southwards to NORAD headquarters and between the Fairbanks and Anchorage centres.

The building of the Ballistic Missile Early warning radars at Thule in Greenland and Fylingdales Moor in Yorkshire between 1960 and 1962, together with a series of new radar stations through Greenland, Iceland and the Faeroes which effectively continued the DEW Line across the North Atlantic, called for a new chain of high-powered tropospheric scatter radio stations to link these sites to the NORAD headquarters in Colorado. This communication chain, known as the North Atlantic Radio System (NARS), consisted of the following five stations built in 1960/61:

Keflavik	South West Iceland	Provided link to DEW line sites in Greenland
Hofn	South East Iceland	
Faeroes		
Mormond Hill	North East Scotland	Provided communications for Buchan radar
Fylingdales Moor	Yorkshire	Provided communications for BMEWS radar and connections to US military communications within UK via link to RAF Martlesham Heath

Most stations had 60′ antennae and 10 Kw transmitters except for those making the Iceland-Greenland link which required 120′ antennae and 50 Kw transmitters. Tropospheric scatter over these ranges was reasonably reliable but required the utmost vigilance to maintain the unstable valve-based electronics, and by the mid-1970s, with the increasing need to pass high volumes of digital data, the future viability of the system was called into question. Upgrading the obsolete transmitters with modern solid-state electronics in 1978 restored the system's reliability, but in 1992, following the transition to satellite communications, the entire chain was closed down. Three years earlier the Fylingdales NARS facility was terminated when the area it occupied was required for the new, phased-array BMEWS equipment.

3. **Texas Tower No. 2.** An aerial view from the landward side. The radar scanners are protected by pressurised rubber radomes. Note the tropospheric scatter dishes attached to the side of the platform, and the Chinook helicopter on the helipad. *Author's collection*

THE 'TEXAS TOWERS'

During the early 1950s the US administration became increasingly fearful of the vulnerability of the industrial and administrative regions of the north-east seaboard to surprise attack from Russian bombers approaching from the Atlantic, despite the protection offered by the broad belt of radar stations that spanned the North American continent. To overcome the perceived weaknesses of the existing radar cover, it was proposed to develop a comprehensive coastal system consisting of radar picket-ships, airborne early warning and control aircraft (AEW&C), and, most spectacularly, a chain of five static radar stations, resembling oil-drilling platforms, standing on the ocean floor one hundred miles offshore. These stations – aptly named 'Texas Towers' after the drilling rigs common in the Gulf of Mexico – would extend the east-coast contiguous coverage some five hundred miles out into the Atlantic, giving an extra thirty minutes early warning of attack.

Design of the platforms and oceanographic investigations into their siting was put in hand by the US Navy Bureau of Yards and the Massachusetts Institute of Technology (MIT) Lincoln Laboratory early in 1952. Selecting locations for the Texas Towers was simplified by the fact that for over one hundred miles offshore the North American continental shelf was no more than fifty to one hundred feet deep, and five shoals were quickly identified as suitable:

Station	Name	Location	Depth	Nearest Landfall
TT 1	Cashes Ledge	42°53" N - 68°57" W	36'	100 miles east of New Hampshire
TT 2	Georges Shoal	41°44" N - 67°47" W	56'	100 miles east of Cape Cod
TT 3	Nantucket Shoal	40°45" N - 69°19" W	80'	South-east of Rhode Island
TT 4	Unnamed Shoal	39°48" N - 72°40" W	185'	84 miles SE of New York City
TT 5	Brown's Bank	42°47" N - 65°37" W	84'	75 miles south of Nova Scotia

Following a report by the Judge Advocate who ruled that there would be no legal impediment to establishing the radar towers outside territorial waters, the USAF authorized a construction programme which was to be completed by 1955. The Bureau of Yards specification called for structures that could withstand waves of thirty-five foot and winds of 125 mph. Primary core-drilling work was contracted to the de-Long Concrete Company and the Raymond Concrete Pile Company in July 1954, and contracts for technical feasibility and final design were awarded to two private civil engineering firms in October. The approved designs were for five identical platforms taking the form of equilateral triangles about a half-acre in extent with truncated ends, each side being 210' long. The superstructures were divided into three decks, the lower of which housed service plant, maintenance workshops and stores, the middle deck consisted of crew accommodation, catering and welfare facilities, and the upper deck supported the radar control rooms, which took up rather more than half the total area, and were surmounted by the rotating radar heads. The rest of the upper decks were used as a helicopter landing pads. Each tower was supported on three tubular steel legs, inside which were concentric steel tubes used as storage tanks for fuel, lubricating oil and fresh water.

Texas Tower 2 at Georges Shoal was the first to be built, principally because it was the most urgently required and also because the location was the least technically demanding. Construction of the 6,500-ton platform was contracted to the Bethlehem Steel Company at its yard at Quincy, Massachusetts, and it was completed and ready for launching in June 1955. Numerous difficulties were encountered, but these were overcome and towing began on 12 July, the platform arriving at Georges Shoal two days later. Temporary legs were positioned on the shoal and the superstructure jacked into position above them while the 160' long permanent caisson legs were assembled below. The bottom forty-eight foot was set deep in the shoal, about sixty-foot was submerged, and the remaining sixty-foot carried the platform high above the ocean waves. Texas Tower 2 was handed over to the USAF on 2 December 1955, although installation of the radar and communications equipment was not completed for some time and the station did not go on line until 7 May 1956. A long period of testing and familiarization then ensued, until full operational status was achieved in April 1958, some six years after the station's requirement was first mooted.

Late in November 1955 contracts for Texas Towers 3 and 4 were awarded to J Rich Steers Inc of New York, but by this time technical advances and cuts in the defence budget led the USAF to reconsider the need for the remaining towers TT1 and TT5, a debate that culminated, in December, in their permanent deletion from the air defence programme. Construction of the remaining towers continued throughout 1956/57, and TT3 was launched during the night of 7 August and erected at Nantucket Shoal later that month. TT4 had been launched a couple of months earlier and fitting out of both towers with their technical equipment began in November. The two towers became fully functional as manual ground control intercept stations in April 1959 and were integrated into the SAGE system exactly one year later. The total cost of the towers, including equipment, amounted to $13,000,000 each and operating costs were $1,500,000 per year.

Radar equipment aboard each tower consisted of two FPS-6 long-range height finders and one FPS-3A search set (later modified to FPD-20A standards), each contained within a fifty-five foot diameter pressurized-rubber arctic radome to protect the vulnerable rotating elements from the extreme weather conditions. At a ground-based station these radars would be spaced a minimum of 150′ apart but due to the restricted area of the Texas Towers other measures had to be taken to avoid interference. The FPS-3A scanner was mounted above the two height-finders, which were synchronized in such a way as to be always looking away from each other.

Initially it was envisaged that the towers would house only the necessary radar scanning heads and support plant, with all control functions exercised from shore-based parent stations via submarine communications cables. This concept minimized the crew requirements for each platform, and consequently the overall dimensions. Unfortunately, however, it was realized in July 1954, as the increasing cost of the project became apparent, that funds, (at first estimated at $1,000,000 per tower but later revised upwards to twice that figure), would not be available for the submarine cable, and that at that time no alternative means of reliable remote data transmission was available. Thus, until the end of the decade when steps were made to integrate the Texas Towers into the Semi-Automatic Ground Environment (SAGE) radar system, only manual control was exercised aboard the towers using a range of GPA-37 consoles to vector the intercepting aircraft.

Data communication was by means of type FRC-56 tropospheric scatter radio, using three twenty-eight foot diameter parabolic antennae mounted on the landward side of each tower; two dishes being used in parallel for transmission and all three for reception. The principle of tropospheric scatter was that more or less directional radio signals could be transmitted over the horizon by bouncing them of the troposhere (a region of dense air) some 30,000 feet above the earth's surface. Reliable transmission of manual data over a 200-mile range was possible in this way and it was hoped that digitally encoded information necessary for SAGE integration could be passed with equal reliability, but this was not to be. Early in 1960 plans for major upgrades to the towers' radar equipment were shelved on grounds of cost but certain ECCM components were incorporated to bring the existing radars up to FPS-67 standards, and FST-2 equipment was installed for SAGE automation. Several proposals were investigated to improve tower-to-shore communications, including a re-examination of the submarine cable solution, and also a plan put forward by the MITRE corporation to refine the existing system and include a Code Translation Data Services (CTDS) element. Simultaneously AT&T were asked to take over the existing tropospheric scatter system and get it working properly, but in the meantime the towers reverted to manual operation.

Towards the end of 1960 all talk of stringing new submarine cables, adding CTDS or utilizing other electronic improvements was abandoned, (partly through lack of space aboard the cramped towers), and the cheaper option of handing over the entire communications to AT&T management was approved. Improvements made by AT&T in the fields of antennae alignment, operator training and plant maintenance led to significant improvements in performance that enabled tropospheric scatter to be employed successfully within SAGE.

From the start the Texas Towers were burdened with a multitude of technical problems other than those associated with communications, which were eventually to prove, quite literally, their final downfall. The platforms were never stable, rocked as they were by wind and ocean, and subject to vibration from the rotating and oscillating mass of the radar scanners. The eleven 250 Kva diesel generators in each powerhouse and the complexity of air-conditioning and other service plant added to the vibration that resonated through the tuning-fork-like structures, and often generated spurious currents that created false indications on the radar screens. These electrical effects were exacerbated in summertime by curious temperature inversion phenomena that could black out the screens entirely.

Because of the much deeper water in which TT4 was located, the adverse effects were particularly pronounced aboard this tower. These difficulties became evident at an early stage and a series of cross-leg struts were incorporated during manufacture to improve stability, but while under tow in July 1954 some of these struts were torn off. Makeshift repairs were made on site but TT4 was effectively erected in a condition somewhat short of its design strength. The tower wobbled alarmingly in high wind and seas, and towards the end of 1958 an underwater inspection revealed that a number of the cross-bracings had sheared off or worked loose. These faults tended to redirect the load onto other sections of the support structure which themselves became overloaded and began to show stress failures. Remedial work undertaken during the spring of 1959 rectified the problems to some extent, but this was soon undone by a series of four severe storms that struck the platform during the winter of 1959/60.

An investigation revealed irreparable damage to the underwater sections of the tower legs, and a great deal of strengthening was done above water to recover some of the original stability. This work was completed by August 1960, but on 12 September the tower was struck by hurricane 'Donna', experiencing 132 mph winds and fifty-foot waves. In the light of metrological forecasts, all personnel had been evacuated two days previously as a precautionary measure. TT4 survived the storm but much of the superstructure was destroyed and below the waterline most of the remaining cross-bracing was ripped off, reducing the stability of the structure by forty-five per cent. Temporary abandonment was inevitable until permanent repairs could be made in the following spring. In the interim a twenty-eight-man strong maintenance team boarded the rig to make temporary repairs, but on 15 January a further storm hit the stricken platform and at twenty minutes past seven that evening one of the three support legs snapped; the remaining two, unable to bear the strain, quickly collapsed and the 6,500-ton platform plunged to the seabed carrying with it all twenty-eight hands on board.

Following the collapse of TT4 the remaining two towers were rigorously inspected and found to be sound, but all confidence in them was lost. Commenting in March 1961, Lt General Robert M Lee, US Air Defence Commander, stated:

At this time there is no valid reason for abandonment of Texas Towers No. 2 and 3. However, in view of the inherent danger and the current inability to evacuate safely during normal conditions, this headquarters, in conjunction with headquarters NORAD, will continue to consider the operational requirement for these towers. There is a possibility that, after the ALRI (Automatic Long Range Input) system becomes operational in AEW&C aircraft, sufficient reliable coverage may be achieved so that the contribution of Texas Towers 2 and 3 to the air defence system will be reduced. In this event, shutdown of the towers, with a resultant elimination of the inherent risk, and saving in money and manpower, may be possible. On the basis of technical advice now available there is no concern for the stability of the towers, but should the result of the engineering survey indicate the existence of any deficiencies, immediate action will be taken to discontinue their operation.

In fact the predicted technological developments in AWE&C aircraft came on line within three years, and ALRI-equipped aircraft from Otis Air Force Base rendered TT2 and 3 redundant.

Until ALRI became available, however, measures were taken to make rapid evacuation of the towers feasible, these taking the form of watertight escape capsules able to house seven men and with food and oxygen for fifteen days. Built by the Electric Boats Division of General Dynamics, two of these capsules were installed on each tower in October 1962. Routine evacuation of all except a seven-man emergency crew was ordered whenever winds exceeded fifty mph or waves over thirty-five foot were predicted. The emergency crew was required because, as the towers stood in international waters, if they were fully evacuated they would probably be boarded by crews from the Russian surveillance trawlers that were always in the area, who would then claim salvage rights. Emergency crews, too, would be evacuated if winds exceeded seventy knots and coastguard vessels would patrol the area to dissuade Russian salvage attempts.

Throughout 1962/63 over 120 operational days were lost due to adverse weather. In a summer storm in 1962 a protective radome was swept away from TT3, while the following winter the radome of one of the height finders collapsed, seriously damaging the sensors. Meanwhile, wave action was scouring away the rock around the support legs of both towers. Early in 1963 the ALRI Atlantic Fleet AEW&C aircraft became operational and in January abandonment of the remaining towers was authorized.

TT2 was decommissioned on 15 January and, after all the salvageable technical equipment was removed, the hulk was sold for scrap. The scrap men intended to dynamite the legs and then float the remaining 6,000-ton platform ashore, but, to their consternation, the huge superstructure simply keeled over and sank to the ocean floor. Taking no chances with TT3, the scrap men used the same technique but first filled the lower deck with millions of litres of polyurethane foam to ensure buoyancy. Like her sister, TT3 plummeted below the waves, but, to the relief of all concerned, bobbed up to the surface like a cork a few seconds later.

3

NORAD AND THE
CHEYENNE MOUNTAIN COMPLEX

Although the Canadian/US Joint Defence Board served as a basis for post-war co-operative defence planning between Canada and the United States that sufficed through the early 1950s, it was apparent that, to ensure the comprehensive air defence of the North American continent, a fully integrated command structure was called for under centralized operational control. Discussions about how this was to be achieved began in 1954 and towards the end of the year a detailed study was inaugurated under the auspices of General Earle Partridge, the Commander in Chief of the newly formed US Continental Air Defense Command (CONAD). An acceptable scheme was developed over the following two years, and the integration of both nations' air defence resources was announced in August 1957. The new organization was to be known as the North American Air Defense Command (NORAD). Operations began from an overground headquarters complex within Ent Air Force Base, Colorado on 12 September 1957, some eight months before the formal ratification of the agreement by the two governments on 12 May 1958.

With the increasing threat from high-yield nuclear weapons it was soon obvious that the existing surface accommodation at Ent AFB was too vulnerable and in April 1958 the CinC NORAD put forward to the Joint Chiefs of Staff an outline proposal for a hardened, underground Combat Operations Centre in a remote location deep below the granite peak of Cheyenne Mountain, near Colorado Springs. Preliminary investigations of this and other potentially suitable sites had already been undertaken and expert opinion was that the Colorado Springs location could be developed at a cost acceptable by the US Treasury. Approval for the underground operations centre and an adjacent, new headquarters complex was given early in March 1959, with construction scheduled to begin in May 1961. Building this tremendously complex establishment was to take nearly six years, at a cost of $142.4 million.

Earthworks began for the 196,000 sq ft Cheyenne Mountain facility on 16 June 1961 and were virtually complete a year later, except for an area of poor roof at the intersection of two principal corridors. Overcoming the geological problem in that location involved the construction of a large reinforced concrete dome; a protracted task which was not completed until May 1964 and added $2.7 million to the cost of the project. To ensure the stability of the rock walls of the tunnels, over 115,000 steel rock-bolts bind the strata, and two men armed with large spanners are employed on constant duty to ensure that the bolts remain tight. The layout of the underground workings is a regular grid of wide accommodation chambers accessed by a single entrance tunnel nearly one mile in length which passes right through the mountain some 1,750 feet below its peak. The Combat Centre is to one side of this tunnel, sealed from it by

4. **NORAD Headquarters, Cheyenne Mountain, Colorado.** North entrance to the underground complex. *NORAD*

5. **NORAD Headquarters, Cheyenne Mountain, Colorado.** One of the thirty-ton blast doors sealing the command centre from the main access tunnel. *NORAD*

pneumatically operated double blast doors, each weighing thirty tons, which are set flush in the tunnel wall. This arrangement ensures that the blast wave from a nearby nuclear explosion would pass right through the tunnel and vent at the far end, thus bypassing the Combat Centre. Similar arrangements to deflect blast pressure were adopted on a smaller scale at the Canadian Government bunker at Ottawa and in the design of the lift-head buildings at the British Government's emergency war headquarters at Corsham in Wiltshire.

Within the Cheyenne Mountain complex the major functional units are housed in fifteen three-story steel buildings, which, together with the majority of the service plant and smaller buildings, are mounted on 1,300 huge coil springs, each three feet in diameter and four feet long. By insulating the buildings from the mountain bed-rock in this way, it was hoped to protect them and the delicate computer equipment within them from the seismic ground movement resulting from a nuclear ground-burst 'near-miss'. Flexible spring mounting of equipment is a common feature of many American cold-war structures including the bunkers and relay stations associated with the 'L4' defence communication network, in many of which even the toilet pans are mounted on springs.

In 1958, when plans for Cheyenne Mountain were first put forward, it was envisaged that the principal threat to national security would come from manned Russian bombers carrying, at first, kiloton yield atomic bombs, and then later, megaton hydrogen bombs. Its prime initial function was to co-ordinate continental air defences, including fighter aircraft and the BOMARC and NIKE ground-to-air missile batteries using data provided principally from the Canadian and Alaskan radar chains (the Alaska Radar, Pinetree Line, Mid-Canada Line, and Distant Early Warning Line). Even before construction had begun, however, the Inter-Continental Ballistic Missile (ICBM) had emerged as the greater threat, and against this weapon there was no active defence. The only responses to the ICBM were to take cover and to reply in kind, but to do this effectively it was necessary to detect Soviet missiles at far greater range than the existing radars could provide. During the late 1950s, just as the primary phase of the DEW line was nearing completion, development work began on the Ballistic Missile Early Warning System, the first station, at Thule, Greenland, becoming active just as work started at the Mountain. By 1966, when the NORAD Combined Operations Centre was transferred from Ent AFB to Cheyenne Mountain, the complete BMEWS network had been operational for two years and early warning of Soviet strategic missile attack, based upon data received from BMEWS, became the most important mission of Cheyenne Mountain.

For a brief period during the mid-1970s, even as the first, tentative Strategic Arms Limitation Talks (SALT) were getting under way and the bleak concept of massive retaliation was giving way to 'flexible response', the US administration made the deliberately provocative decision to continue development of the NIKE-X anti-ballistic missile (ABM) programme. The authorized budget for this over-ambitious and technically flawed programme was a staggering $759,100,000. The first two ABM weapons sites for what eventually became known as the Safeguard System were constructed in Montana and North

Dakota in 1970. The Soviet Union argued that ABM defences further destabilized the existing weapons imbalance, an argument strengthened by the fact that the US Defence Department had earlier ensured that increased expenditure upon ABM development was contingent upon parallel increases in public shelter building and the proliferation of hardened government command and control bunkers. The first SALT agreement, ratified on 3 August 1972, limited ABM deployment to just two sites, one for the defence of the capital and one for the defence of the ICBM launch sites. The withdrawal of protection from the populated areas of the United States by abandoning the greater part of the ABM programme implied that civil vulnerability under conditions of Mutual Assured Destruction was a beneficial option. This philosophy was also used by the United States government to justify its policy of minimal Civil Defense expenditure and public shelter provision. Control of the short-lived ABM system was exercised from the Ballistic Missile Defense Centre in Cheyenne Mountain until it was disbanded in February 1976. During its operational period the centre acted as the command link between NORAD, the Continental Air Defense Command Operations Centre and the Safeguard Missile Defense Centre at Grand Forks, North Dakota.

Other sensitive defence facilities gradually transferred to the underground complex at Cheyenne Mountain included the Space Surveillance Centre, which moved to the mountain from Hanscom Field, Massachusetts, in the early 1960s. Its mission was to detect, track, identify and record all man-made objects and activity in space. By the mid to late 1970s the United States had become increasingly reliant upon satellite technology, both as a means of military communication and as a source of national prestige. Fears that the Soviet Union was developing offensive anti-satellite systems led to the establishment of a counter-offensive Space Defense Operations Centre at Colorado Springs in 1979. Through the following decade the space and missile warning roles of Cheyenne Mountain were absorbed by the Combat Operations staff of the recently created Air Force Space Command, and in 1994 the Space Surveillance Centre and the Space Defense Operations Centre were combined to form the Space Control Centre. In recent years much of the emphasis of this unit has been upon the protection of space shuttle missions.

By the mid-1960s the Cheyenne Mountain complex housed the most sophisticated and potent concentration of electronic computing power in the world, but as early as May 1966, only a month after the centre became operational, there were already fears that the rapid technological developments in electronics would render much of it obsolescent, if not obsolete, within five years. Three years later the Air Force issued the 'Cheyenne Mountain Complex Improvement Programme', (the 427M programme), which scheduled the new computer systems that would be required in 1971 to upgrade the NORAD Control System and the Space Computational Centre. The underground accommodation at Cheyenne Mountain was considerably enlarged in 1970 to provide space for additional generators and air-conditioning equipment to support the two new Honeywell Force-Support computers which formed the core of the 427M project.

Although secure from external 'hacking', the Cheyenne Mountain computers proved, despite the most rigorous testing and evaluation, not to be immune to potentially catastrophic operational and component malfunction. On at least two occasions these malfunctions did not 'fail-safe' and, had the international situation been just slightly less stable, then the result could have been an inadvertent US first-strike nuclear launch. On 9 November 1979, during an exercise to test the US response to an all-out missile attack, simulated attack data was, during a three-minute period, inadvertently fed to the live operational side of the 427M system, which processed it as evidence of a real Russian attack and transmitted this information to missile warning consoles in the Command Centre and to the Alternative National Command Centre at Mount Weather. For some eight minutes, while controllers in Cheyenne Mountain wrestled with a mass of conflicting information, the world stood on the very edge of nuclear annihilation. Just six months later, on 2 June 1980, a similar false attack warning was transmitted to Strategic Air Command and the Alternate National Command Centre as a result of a component failure in the Cheyenne Mountain computer system.

Coincident with the implementation of the 427M project came a distinct thaw in East-West relationships and, except for the commissioning of several very advanced phased-array radar stations, development of which had been inaugurated many years earlier, for a decade defence expenditure substantially declined. 'Mutual vulnerability' – the strategic philosophy that led to the virtual abandonment of the Safeguard ABM system in 1976 – also enabled the US Secretary of State for Defense to put forward further savings in defence expenditure amounting, in 1974, to over $1 billion. Delays in upgrading the air defence radar systems and the NORAD-assigned interceptor aircraft forces resulted in such depletion that by the end of the decade the entire system was at risk of failure through obsolescence. In partial justification of these cutbacks it was announced that, in view of the greatly reduced likelihood of global war, the revised mission of NORAD was only to ensure continental air sovereignty in time of peace.

The serious weakness of the system as it stood in 1979 was thrown into sharp relief as tensions with the Soviet Union emerged once again following the invasion of Afghanistan and the breakdown of the SALT II negotiations. During the early 1980s a massive increase in defence expenditure was authorized by the Reagan administration, a significant proportion of which was absorbed in the implementation of the USAF Air Defence Master Plan (ADMP), which recommended a further reorganisation of NORAD and its defence assets. Among the principle features of the ADMP was a reorientation away from 'air defence' towards *aerospace defense*, with the establishment of the United States Space Command in September 1985; the replacement of the ageing DEW line by the North Warning System; deployment of Over The Horizon Backscatter Radar; and the accelerated introduction of Airborne Early Warning & Control (AWACS) aircraft. Special emphasis was given towards the establishment of five Forward Operating Locations in northern Canada to counter the threat of Soviet air-launched cruise missiles.

Before the full programme of improvements was completed, however, the cold war came to an abrupt end. This allowed the cripplingly expensive North Warning System to be completed prematurely and in a somewhat truncated form, and also resulted in the abandonment of three of the four proposed backscatter radars; the fourth, at Bangor, Maine, was itself progressively run down and finally relegated to cold storage in the mid 1990s. Other major upgrades continued, however; replacement of the ageing BMEWS radars with modern phased-array scanners started in 1987, and a programme of space-based early warning and surveillance systems is still ongoing.

Inside the mountain work began in 1981 on a comprehensive $968 million upgrade of the computer and communications network scheduled for completion in 1987. The Cheyenne Mountain Upgrade Programme included the replacement of the five most pivotal existing sub-systems, including the Communications System segment, which processes most of the NORAD internal and external automated communications; the Surviveable Communications Integration System, which provides multiple redundant communication services between the centre and the missile warning sensors; the Command Centre Processing and Display System, which processes and displays ballistic missile warning data on huge situation maps within the complex; the 'Granite Sentry' sub-system which processes and displays all air-breathing target air defence and command post data, and the Space Defense Operations Centre. The new works scheme was expanded in 1989 to included an Alternate Processing and Correlation Centre to be built at Offut Air Force Base in Nebraska, which would take over the function of the Cheyenne Mountain complex if the systems there should fail.

Unfortunately this programme was badly planned and managed from its inception, the principal fault being that each segment was designed in isolation with too little regard to the various elements running as an integrated system. As parts of the project were completed it was found that they were incompatible with one another and in many cases less efficient than the systems they were designed to replace. Often there was so little confidence in the new systems that they were run for years in parallel with the existing equipment. After one particular element of the upgraded Integrated Tactical Warning and Assessment module was commissioned it was discovered that, whereas the computer programme was intended to integrate independent missile threat reports from more than one sensor site to increase confidence in the veracity of the threat, what in fact happened was that the computers interpreted the multiple incoming reports as extraneous duplicates and rejected them.

These manifold problems inevitably retarded the project and in 1989, two years after the programme's notional completion date, it was reported that work was now seven years behind schedule and that it was already $342 million over budget. A revised completion date of December 1995 was projected but this passed with still much to be done and a further three-year requirement was forecast with a projected total budget of $1,864,000,000. The Defense Appropriations Sub Committee of the US House of Representatives was warned, however, that this last figure was still only a projection and would probably rise much higher.

It is the function of all defence agencies, whatever their avowedly passive stance, to seek out enemies of the state, and, despite the apparent end of the cold war and the justification offered by the United States that increased expenditure upon the NORAD headquarters at Cheyenne Mountain is now required to combat the insidious threat proffered by the lone drug-smuggler, one basic, unaltered assumption is still paramount – only Russia has the systems and platforms to launch a concerted nuclear attack upon the American continent. With increasing globalization of the defence market it is inevitable that during the first decade of the twenty-first century many more countries – some of them unstable and threatening to western democracy, will acquire sophisticated and potent cruise missiles, but to be effective these weapons require prohibitively expensive 'first-stage carriers'. At present Russia still controls vast and viable fleets of such long-range bombers and nuclear submarines, and, despite the patent and visible closing of the ideological divide, the very existence of these first-stage carriers maintains Russia high on the US target list.

During its forty-year life span, the Cheyenne Mountain Combat Centre, as first conceived in the 1960s, has, at the start of the twenty-first century, evolved into the Cheyenne Mountain Operations Centre, a hugely sophisticated underground complex capable of detecting, assessing and co-ordinating responses to any airborne or space-based threat to the United States or its overseas forces from anywhere in the world. A peacetime staff of 1,100 men and women man the complex, and under attack conditions the entire site can be secured and made self-sufficient in power, food and water for thirty days with an emergency staff of 800.

Within the complex a series of separate control centres, each reporting to the Command Director in the main Command Centre, monitor events within their specialist spheres. The Space Control Centre maintains a database of over eight thousand objects orbiting in space, constantly determining whether they are benign or malignant and ensures that collisions with the Space Shuttle and other US space missions is avoided. The Missile Warning Centre, using data from BMEWS and other space and land-based sensors, provides early warning of long-range strategic missile attacks upon the American homeland, or of shorter-range tactical or 'theatre' attacks upon American forces overseas. The detection of Iraqi 'Scud' missiles and defensive deployment of 'Patriot' anti-missile batteries during the Gulf War are examples of theatre operations controlled from Cheyenne Mountain, many thousands of miles from the point of conflict.

The detection of intrusion into North American airspace by manned bombers or cruise missiles is controlled from the Battle Management Centre, which also co-ordinates counter-force air defences. Developing a cohesive, minute-by-minute picture of the potential threats to the security of North America from the disparate array of data collected within the various operations centres is the remit of the Combined Intelligence Watch Centre. Here electronic data regarding space and strategic air activity is correlated with geopolitical intelligence gleaned by the worldwide resources of the US intelligence services to provide a reliable, current assessment of the security status of the United States.

Hardened microwave links, underground coaxial cables and optic fibres link the mountain to the continental radar control centres, the United States Strategic Air Command Headquarters, the Canadian Air Force HQ in Ottawa, numerous important military bases within the US and throughout the world, and to the White House, the Pentagon, the Alternate National Command Centre and numerous other underground 'continuity of government' facilities. The Command Director is in direct 'hot-line' telephone connection with the US and Canadian national command and central government nuclei; this is of fundamental importance, for the Cheyenne Mountain Complex is essentially a warning and control centre. It has no executive function and cannot, for example, launch a retaliatory missile strike without the approval of its political masters.

STRATEGIC AIR COMMAND
Now that the major players in the US war plan have been described we can understand the process of target acquisition, identification and evaluation:

- Early warning of missile attack has been received and assessed by NORAD at Cheyenne Mountain.
- The alternative military command centre at Raven Rock has resolved the optimum response.
- The embunkered central government nucleus at Mount Weather has, after consultation with its NATO allies, sanctioned implementation of the military response and returned the initiative to Raven Rock for action.
- The executive decision has now to be translated to action on the ground: ie. the transmission of launch orders for a retaliatory attack by Strategic Air Command, from its hardened underground command bunker at Offut Air Force Base, Nebraska.

Strategic Air Command was formed in March 1946 to provide a credible strategic deterrence against forces that might threaten the security of the United States. The Command mission, defined by General Carl Spaatz, was:

> to be prepared to conduct long-range offensive operations in any part of the world either independently or in co-operation with land and naval forces: to conduct maximum range reconnaissance over land or sea either independently or in co-operation with land or naval forces, to provide combat units capable of intense and sustained combat operations employing the latest and most advanced weapons.

Command HQ was initially established at the former Continental Air Forces HQ at Bolling Field, but moved to Andrews Field, Maryland, on 21 October 1946. The old Second World War air base at Offut was transferred to Strategic Air Command in November 1948, and shortly afterwards the Command Headquarters were transferred, for the second time in two years, to a converted Martin Nebraska bomber factory on the airfield perimeter. It was quickly realized that this exposed building was extremely vulnerable and plans were prepared at an early stage for its replacement by a secure underground bunker. Budgetary restrictions prevented much progress on this project for several years and it was not until April 1955 that the $8,662,464 building programme was finally authorized. Construction was finished by the end of the following year and in January 1957 most of the previously dispersed SAC components were concentrated in the new HQ at Offut.

The new headquarters bunker was a multi-floor reinforced concrete structure built in a man-made excavation about forty feet deep, using construction techniques similar to those used for the Canadian central government bunker and, on a smaller scale, for the British underground 'ROTOR' radar stations. As the Dulles concepts of Massive Retaliation and Mutually Assured Destruction matured around 1960, it became increasingly apparent that the targets of nuclear enemies were primarily the enemy's nuclear weapons, and subsequently all defensive systems on both sides of the nuclear divide were orientated towards protection of those weapons systems. By 1961 the primary *raison d'être* of all the command and control bunkers in the federal arc, all the North American radar systems and BMEWS, and all the US forward bases throughout the world, was to protect the arsenal of Strategic Air Command and its headquarters at Offut.

Co-located at Offut in support of SAC were two vital intelligence and planning units; No.544 Reconnaissance Wing, which joined SAC in November 1950, and the Joint Strategic Target Planning Staff (JSTPF), which was formed in 1960. The mission of the JSTPS was to co-ordinate targeting of the US nuclear triad, i.e the nuclear submarine fleet, the SAC nuclear bombers and the ICBMs, in a unified war plan, or Single Integrated Operations Plan (SlOP). Location at Offut enabled the JSTPS to take full advantage of SAC's extensive communications systems and existing war planning capabilities. The role of No.544 Reconnaissance Technical Wing (renamed 544 TR Group in 1958 and 544 Aerospace Reconnaissance Technical Wing in January 1963) was to provide the bulk of the intelligence material required for the SlOP, for contingency planning and for attack warning and defence analysis.

4

THE BALLISTIC MISSILE EARLY
WARNING SYSTEM

In the summer of 1963 the British public were led to believe that they could in
future sleep easier in their beds, because a fabulous new radar system of
astonishing power had been built on Fylingdales Moor in North Yorkshire to
protect them from the evil machinations of the empire that lurked menacingly
beyond the eastern horizon. This radar, which was a keystone of the Ballistic
Missile Early Warning System (BMEWS), would give a whole four minutes'
warning of annihilation by Russian nuclear missiles; time, we were told, to
arrange our affairs, retreat to our bunkers (that were never built) and ride out
the nuclear winter. For nearly thirty years this myth has remained the common
perception in the public mind about the three gigantic, sinister, pale blue
'golfballs' that loomed upon the moorland north of Scarborough. Such a
perception, however, was far from the truth.

Fylingdales is in fact the outermost radar shield that protects the central
government of the United States and is in many ways the lynch pin upon which
the entire US 'continuity of government' programme hinges. Although at first
sight just another of the concentric arcs of radar stations that began with the
Pinetree Line and extended through Canada to the Dew Line (until its
replacement by the North Warning System), the BMEWS radar system is
fundamentally different from its compatriots. While the North Warning System,
et al, function essentially in an air defence role – to detect intruders and alert
defending forces that can intercept and stop the enemy – BMEWS can do no
more than announce the imminent arrival of the destroyer of worlds. It is the
ultimate harbinger of doom, for nothing on earth, as a string of failed ABM
technologies have proved, can prevent an ICBM from reaching its target once
launched upon its trajectory. BMEWS' sole role is to give the US government
time, if every system functions as it should, to assess the threat, activate its
limited retaliatory options and run for cover.

Planning for BMEWS began in 1957 following the launch of the first 'Sputnik'
satellite on 3 November, which confirmed American intelligence reports that
Russia had developed a long-range missile capable of delivering megaton nuclear
warheads to any location in the USA.

The ICBM completely changed the nature of future war and aroused the
darkest fears among America's strategic planners. Throughout the late 1950s
they had assumed that a Soviet attack would start without warning; an
assumption based upon the nightmare that the humiliation of Pearl Harbor
could be repeated in a future, more devastating, war. To counter that possibility,
America's own retaliatory rockets were buried deep in hardened silos, and her
command and control bunkers, both civil and military, were also given deep
underground protection. But what was safe against the atomic bomb was not

necessarily safe against the new generation of hydrogen bomb and the military planners were sceptical that the underground command posts and government bunkers, the locations of which were undoubtedly known to the Russians, could survive a direct hit. Fear that the entire command organization could be wiped out by the first salvo of Soviet rockets before the order for a retaliatory launch could be given gave rise to the tripwire 'launch on warning' strategy. Under this policy the United States would launch its entire fleet of ballistic missiles immediately upon detection of a Soviet missile launch and before the first enemy warhead impacted upon American soil.

For this strategy to be effective, two structures needed to be in place:

- A radar system capable of providing sufficient warning of attack to allow the threat to be assessed, a response to be authorized by the Executive and the missiles to be launched.
- An extended and defined line of succession to the Presidency and a series of dispersed, hardened bunkers to protect this select executive staff.

The purpose of this second provision is to ensure the 'continuity of government', a constitutional fiction axiomatic in western minds to the prosecution of nuclear war. As long as the power of the President is vested in one man in the line of succession and that man survives, then democratic government is deemed to have survived too, and the State remains intact and undefeated. If fear of massive retaliation and the inevitability of 'Mutually Assured Destruction' (MAD) failed to keep the peace, then the 'tripwire' and 'continuity of government' policies might ensure national survival... of a sort.

The BMEWS infrastructure consisted of three sites strung across the North Atlantic and continental North America, equipped with long-range radar powerful enough to track Russian missiles by detecting them in their initial launch phase. The three stations covered all potential trans-polar missile approach corridors and had detection ranges of 2,800-3,000 miles. After a three-year development programme the first station was opened at Thule, Greenland, in the autumn of 1960 and the second, at Clear, Alaska, eighteen months later. Thule and Clear were both 'search' stations, fitted with General Electric FPS-50 detection radar and huge, fifty metre by 120 metre 'billboard' antennae. Each radar had a peak power output of ten megawatts, and the provision of such power to the remote Greenland site was a major obstacle, overcome by permanently mooring a US Navy ship nearby which was in effect a floating 34,500 Kva power station.

The third radar station, which would be located in the North West Atlantic region, either in Iceland or, more probably, northern Britain, would have a slightly different role. Whilst still monitoring the trans-polar corridors, BMEWS-3 would also track Intermediate Range Ballistic Missiles launched from Russia or other Warsaw Pact countries targeted upon US or other NATO military assets in western Europe.

A decision regarding the location of the third site was deferred for some months while various sites in Iceland, Scotland and north Yorkshire were examined. Prestwick in Ayrshire was under consideration for some time and in

December 1959 it looked increasingly as though an alternative site near Dounray in the north of Scotland would be chosen. On 29 January 1960, however, it was announced that the third and final BMEWS station would be built on four and a half square miles of land provided by the Ministry of Defence on Fylingdales Moor in Yorkshire. Three weeks later, on 16 February, an announcement by George Ward, Secretary of State for Air, stated that:

> The station will be commanded and operated by the RAF. The information it obtains will be available simultaneously to operations centres in the UK and the USA. SACEUR will receive the warning generated by the system; and the UK will also have access to information provided by the other stations. The United States will provide and install the radars and pay for the communications required to link the station to the rest of the system. The UK will provide the land, erect the buildings and provide communications required to link the station with our own authorities. For the first five years technical spares will be provided by the US government and on-site maintenance will be borne by the UK. Capital cost to this country is expected to be about £8 million, and to the US about £35 million.

Replying to press questions, Mr Ward would not be drawn upon the inadequate UK warning period, beyond commenting that:

> It was hoped to achieve a good deal more than four minutes... enough to get a substantial part of our bomber force into the air.

How this was to be achieved when even the quick-reaction V-bomber force was on a minimum fifteen-minute standby, and the 'Thor' missile, which entered service later that year, required some forty-five minutes to fuel up, freezing its vital guidance components and making it unusable for several days if not launched immediately, was not made clear. The government was also evasive about which way the radar looked and would not comment upon whether or not it could detect submarine-launched missiles approaching from the west. This was a pertinent question, for at that time the possibility that the Soviet Union might launch a sneak attack from missile submarines just a few hundred miles off the US coastline was exercising the minds of America's strategic planners. Such an attack would, at a stroke, negate the small advantage gained by BMEWS. The possibility of such an attack led, in the 1980s, to the construction of the PAVE PAWS ground radars in California, Texas, Massachusetts and Georgia to monitor the US ocean approaches; but even these radars, which complemented a series of Defense Support Programme (DSP) early warning satellites launched a decade earlier, could not guarantee more than a few minutes' warning of sea-launched missiles.

Some increase in warning time was achieved by bypassing the NORAD centre and transmitting DSP warning data directly to the Pentagon or the Alternate National Defense Control Centre, but, while this significantly increased the US 'launch on warning' capability, it also increased the risk of a disastrous first-strike response following a launch on false warning.

Since its inception Fylingdales has acquired a number of subsidiary defence functions. In 1964 an Electronic Counter Counter Measures tower was added and in 1968, following the opening of the Space Surveillance Centre at Cheyenne Mountain, Fylingdales took on the 'Spacetrack' role, which involved the detection, monitoring, and analysis of all man-made items in space, whether satellites, payloads or merely space debris. This is a role of utmost importance as it enables the early detection of spy satellites and guards against the terrible consequences of falling space debris being erroneously interpreted as an enemy missile warhead on its re-entry trajectory.

Construction of the Fylingdales station was completed in 1963. The prime contractor for the project was RCA, but the surveillance radar systems were manufactured by the General Electric Corporation, which subcontracted the design and erection of the antennae to D S Kennedy & Co. Each of the three 'golfball' radomes, designated BMEWS 3-00, 3-01 and 3-02, contained an eighty-four foot diameter FPS-49 parabolic antenna emitting split beams approximately one degree in width. Two radars tracked horizontally through a 30° arc, one searching for targets at an elevation of 2.5° and the other at 5°. If a target was acquired by both radars it could be supposed that it was a rocket in its boost phase, and information from the detection radars would then be sent to the third, tracking radar at Fylingdales and to the tracking stations at Thule and Clear, which would compute the missile's trajectory and point of impact. Data from the BMEWS radars was transmitted to NORAD HQ at Cheyenne Mountain via the North Atlantic Radio System until this was supplanted by satellite communications between 1990 and 1992.

Construction was made more difficult due to the challenging geology of Fylingdales Moor. Each of the 112-ton radar dishes is supported by massive concrete piles that had to be sunk through over fifty feet of peat before solid bedrock was reached. The base of each radar tower was enclosed by a 120-foot square, three-storey, steel-framed control building which housed, on the ground floor, all the switchgear and service equipment for each tracking unit. The first floor housed the klystron cabinets and monitoring equipment, whilst the upper floor contained the radar waveguides and mixing chambers. All three tracker buildings were linked together by a 1,500-yard-long, blast and radiation proof, concrete-lined, steel-plate access tunnel that afforded absolute security by means of huge air-lock blast doors and security guard houses at each end. There were no other access points to the radar buildings, and this feature, together with an air-conditioning system that maintained a slight overpressure within the whole complex, ensured not only physical security against external attack or sabotage, but also ensured against the ingress of airborne irradiated particles. The twenty-foot-high tunnel, which was large enough to allow lorry access to equipment loading docks within the buildings, connected to the rear of 3-01 and 3-03, and ran through the middle of an extension to the rear of the central block, 3-02.

The extension to the rear of the central tracker building was the operational heart of the Fylingdales complex and housed the Main Computer Room, Control Switching Room, the Missile Warning Operations Centre and the

Central Systems Monitoring Room. All the principal computer systems were duplicated and ran in parallel so that outputs from the two systems could be compared to ensure that false missile warnings were not generated by systems malfunctions. The earliest computer system installed at Fylingdales was an IBM 7090 Missile Impact Prediction analyser; this remained in service until 1982 when it was replaced by an upgraded Data Cyber 170 series 700 computer.

After nearly thirty years the old RCA equipment was becoming obsolete and in 1987, as the first stage of a major upgrade programme, BMEWS Site No.1 at Thule was dismantled and replaced by a phased-array radar. The famous Fylingdales golfballs were dismantled in the early 1990s when the old FPS-49 system there was replaced by a new Raytheon solid-state, phased-array radar (SSPAR). This has similar performance characteristics to the old system, but is much more secure against interference and can scan 360° in azimuth. The SSPAR, which entered service in October 1992, consists of an ominous, 120-foot-high, three-sided, truncated pyramid with eighty-four foot wide faces, each containing arrays of 2,560 individual circularly polarized receive/transmit modules. Like the older AN/FPS-49 equipment, the entire phased-array AN/FPS-115 system was built as a heterogeneous whole. The radar signal generators, control rooms, operations rooms and a huge internal power station containing a triplicate power plant are all contained within the Fylingdales pyramid, which today is as surreal a landmark on the Yorkshire moors as the golfballs ever were.

5

COLD WAR BUNKERS IN CANADA

Although Canada was unaffected by enemy bombing during the Second World War she had in place by 1946 a comprehensive civil defence structure developed during the war years that was similar in many ways to that of Great Britain and which remained virtually unchanged until 1954. That year an inquiry initiated by the incoming Liberal government cast doubt upon the efficacy of the existing Second World War measures which, though they may have had some vestigial effect against attack by atomic bombs, were patently obsolete in the H-bomb era. Although a non-belligerent state, except as far as membership of NATO compelled belligerency in the cause of mutual defence, Canada was exposed to serious risks from fallout clouds drifting from the large industrial and administrative areas of the United States that were close to her southern border, should they be attacked by the USSR.

Early in 1957 a report was issued by the government-sponsored 'Inter Departmental Working Group on War Measures' that recommended the establishment of a joint structure to ensure the continuity of government and the passive defence of the civil population. Plans for the continuity of government were broadly based and encompassed the maintenance of viable communication links, the preservation of essential records, and measures to ensure the preservation of law and order, the economy and the western system of capitalist democracy. The report also called for a hierarchical network of blast and fallout proof bunkers at Federal, Provincial and local level to protect key government staff who were to implement the plans for national survival during the attack and post-attack phases of nuclear war. The report went on to say that:

If provision is not made in peacetime for emergency relocation sites, these governments may be unable to function when war starts. There will be no time then to improvise the necessary facilities outside the present capitals. It is therefore recommended that steps should be taken now to develop an emergency government headquarters in the vicinity of Ottawa, a regional emergency headquarters in each province that would include both federal and provincial components as well as an army component, and possibly a number of sector headquarters in each province. The various headquarters will be interconnected by an integrated, government communications network so designed as to permit the exercise of either decentralised or centralised control.

Previously civil defence had been a community-funded responsibility based upon Second World War preconceptions, but it was soon realized that recovery from the destruction and dislocation of a nuclear war would be beyond the resources of the local communities and that henceforth civil defence should be federally funded.

63

In June 1957 John Diefenbaker's Progressive Conservative government formed the Emergency Measures Organization, (EMO) which was charged with implementing the Working Group plans. EMO was at first placed under the umbrella of the Department of Health and Welfare, but in October 1959 responsibility was transferred to the Department of Defense. The Canadian Army took charge of communication, public warning and the detection and analysis of nuclear explosions, paralleling the function of UKWMO in the United Kingdom. The Army also agreed to construct the underground Federal Government Emergency War Headquarters at Carp, near Ottawa, and a series of smaller Regional bunkers.

PUBLIC WARNING

It was presumed in the Canadian war plan that at the outbreak of a nuclear war the first attack would be against the USA, either upon her industrial and administrative homeland or upon US defence bases abroad. The first tactical warning would originate from NORAD headquarters at Cheyenne Mountain and be relayed via the Canadian national bunker at Carp to the provincial centres. Based upon this assumption a number of exercises, code-named TOCSIN, were conducted in the early 1960s. Subsequent analysis of these exercises caused EMO to conclude that:

> If an enemy attack followed a counter force pattern against American Strategic Air Command bases, the Continuity of Government system as it existed between 1960 and 1963 would probably have been adequate, since damage to Canada would be less than in other forms of attack.

To locate and determine the pattern of nuclear detonations on Canadian soil the Army established the Nuclear Detonation and Fallout Reporting System (NDFRS). This organization functioned in a similar manner to the UKWMO in the United Kingdom. The NDFRS maintained a concentration of Nuclear Detonation Reporting Posts around major military and industrial target areas, supplemented by a further 2,000 posts scattered across the more sparsely populated areas of the country. Information from the reporting posts was monitored by group filter centres, which then transmitted the collated fallout and blast reports to Army prediction centres at the Provincial and Federal bunkers. The Canadian Army established a dedicated national teletype network, the National Survival Attack Warning System, to maintain communications for the NDFRS. The first public warning of attack would, until 1960, be the sounding of the existing Second World War ARP siren system which consisted of some 350 sirens located in the major conurbations. In response to the heightening international tension this system was extended to 1,360 sirens by 1962.

THE FEDERAL AND REGIONAL EMERGENCY GOVERNMENT HEADQUARTERS

To ensure the greatest probability of democratic government surviving a total war, if only in an emasculated form, all western countries developed systems of decentralized emergency government with zonal or community based elements, regional headquarters and a central government nucleus, each with a protected bunker for key staff. Under the Canadian system the central or Federal bunker would house the Governor General, the Prime Minister and a group of senior departmental ministers, with larger departmental staffs accommodated in relocation centres elsewhere. In the early recovery phase the Central Government bunker would issue only policy guidelines; its main function was simply one of maintaining morale, to demonstrate that Canada as a nation state continued to exist and that the Canadian government was still in control.

Day-to-day management of the remaining national resources, and the maintenance of some semblance of social order, would be the responsibility of the regional level bunkers. The areas of responsibility of these regional emergency administrative centres more or less corresponded to the geographical boundaries of the Provinces, except that the Alberta bunker included within its sphere the Yukon and North West Territories. Due to the size and population densities of Ontario and Quebec it was intended to have sub-regional bunkers between the zonal and regional level but this proposal was later abandoned. Each regional bunker was to be the reporting point for between one and eight zone-level bunkers, but most of these were never built, and in any event their function was never fully defined. By October 1964 only two zone bunkers, both in British Columbia, had been completed, but consideration was being given to completion of a further thirteen of the thirty-four originally proposed. Three years later still only nine zone bunkers, each with a target complement of 100 personnel, had been built. Similarly, the lowest level of control, the proposed network of local government emergency headquarters, was never completed, only 160 of the planned 350 being commissioned.

The Provincial emergency headquarters, built under the code-name BRIDGE, were to function as both secure accommodation for Federal and Provincial officials in each federal region and as army emergency communications centres, with both peacetime and wartime roles. During wartime they would accommodate the relevant elements of civilian government together with Canadian Army command, communication and warning units. The peacetime role was primarily to provide accommodation for the Canadian Forces Communication System and the National Survival Attack Warning System.

Following the abandonment, early in 1960, of an interim plan to provide temporary accommodation in ten existing government buildings while the permanent bunkers were under construction, financial approval was granted in May to go ahead immediately with a limited programme of just six of the permanent structures. Reflecting their peacetime use, sites for these bunkers were surveyed at six army bases at Nanaimo, Penhold, Shilo, Camp Borden, Valcartier and Delbert. All six sites became operational between May and November 1964. In the less vulnerable regions of Saskatchewan, New Brunswick, Newfoundland and Prince Edward Island it was initially intended to make radical conversions of existing government buildings but this was never accomplished. Temporary sheltered accommodation was, however, eventually provided in the basements of federal buildings in Regina, Camp Gagetown, Charlottetown, and St John.

Each permanent, reinforced concrete bunker consisted of two main buildings;

a 70,000-square-foot, two-storey receiver building, which was the main structure, and a smaller, 18,000-square-foot remote transmitter building, each covered by substantial earth mounds. Although this form of construction offered only moderate blast protection, the radiation protection factor was in excess of 1000, post-attack radiation being considered the greater hazard and greatest deterrence to rapid recovery. Two designs of building were employed; typified by those at Borden and Nanaimo, which although similar in general layout differed slightly in dimensions. The upper floor of the regional bunkers housed the domestic facilities, including dormitories, catering facilities and a sick bay, while the lower floor contained the main operations room, communications centre and service plant.

THE 'DIEFENBUNKER'

Planning and construction of the Central Government Emergency War Headquarters, codenamed EASE (Experimental Army Signal Establishment) began in late 1957 and, like the Regional Headquarters, was the responsibility of the Canadian Army. Initial plans for a vast, deep underground bunker near Calabogie, to the west of Ottawa, were progressively scaled down as the financial repercussions were assessed, and more moderate plans for a cluster of four smaller, earth-mounded buildings were considered. The cost of this plan, too, was found to be prohibitive and the final design, consisting of a single 350-foot-square, four-storey semi-underground structure near Carp, with a smaller, two-storey transmitter station at Richardson, was decided upon. Technical design work was a joint military/civilian effort with the Foundation Company of Canada acting as consulting engineers. Excavations for the 100-foot-deep foundations finally got under way during the summer of 1959 and building was completed by December 1961.

The design parameters called for a structure that could be built with reasonable economy, would have moderate blast protection (ie safe against a five megaton bomb with ground zero 1.1 miles away) but that would have a radiation protection factor in excess of 1000, and that would be proof against the disruption caused by the ground wave emanating from a nearby nuclear explosion. It was decided that to meet these requirements it would be necessary to bury the building in dry, sandy soil, and the location of such terrain in a primarily hard rock region very much dictated the siting of the bunker. To further minimize the ground wave effect, the bunker's reinforced concrete shell was built on a five-foot-thick layer of coarse gravel and was surrounded on all sides by a gravel envelope. External service connections such as water, sewage and electrical cables were connected via flexible couplings that would flex with any movement of the building within its envelope. As in most of the US bunkers and communication centres, special sprung mountings were provided for sensitive electronic equipment as well as for more mundane items like toilet pans and wash basins.

The building design called for immense strength coupled with the maximum functional floor area, and to provide this special care was taken in the design of the concrete pillars that supported the floors. These were built to a slender design but had flared capitals and bases to spread the load. Similar care was taken to ensure that the five thousand tons of steel bars that reinforced the concrete shell were properly earthed to avoid spurious electrical interference. The locations of all openings in the walls and floors, from main doorways down to the smallest mounting bracket or pipe or cable duct, were carefully surveyed and cast *in situ* to ensure that no post-construction cutting or drilling was required that might sever a reinforcing rod and thus destroy the earth continuity. When completed the five-foot-thick concrete roof was covered with ten feet of earth, landscaped to a gentle slope to deflect blast. Although not built deep within a mountain like the major US bunkers, a similar style of blast protection was employed for the main entrance to the Diefenbunker. A long, open-ended tubular approach tunnel, twelve feet in diameter, was constructed at a right angle to the main entrance in such a manner that the blast wave from an explosion would pass right through it without impinging upon the steel blast doors that protected the entrance air lock. Two emergency exit routes were also provided, consisting of shafts sealed at the bottom with lightweight doors and filled with loose sand, which would have to be dug away before escape was possible.

A unique feature of the Carp bunker was that it was designed to automatically shut down and seal itself off from outside air if any one of a number of detection systems sensed the effect of a nuclear explosion over nearby Ottawa. High-speed solenoids operated by compressed nitrogen would close and lock the ventilation inlet valves in less than half a second if the detection systems were triggered by gamma radiation, blast overpressure or the infra-red heat wave from a detonation. Once closed down the air-conditioning system could maintain a viable atmosphere within the building using recirculated air for a minimum of three days. Thereafter, when external radiation levels had diminished, the bunker's filtration system could provide uncontaminated air for an indefinite period. During peacetime operation electricity was drawn from the Ontario grid, but incorporated within the bunker on the second floor was a powerhouse containing four 327 KW diesel generators together with a forty-day reserve of fuel. An internal 32,000-gallon reserve of drinking water was also provided, supplemented by pumping equipment that could draw unlimited supplies of pure, uncontaminated water from springs 130 feet underground.

Conditions within the bunker, although not luxurious, were far from austere; floors in the domestic areas were either carpeted or tiled and most rooms had concealed lighting and a subdued colour scheme. The lower floor was principally a storage area, but also contained the fuel and water storage tanks and pumping equipment, together with water treatment plant, waste compactors and a small morgue. Much of the second floor was put over to domestic facilities including a kitchen and dining room area that could seat 300 personnel. The main powerhouse, containing the four diesel generators, was also on this floor. The third floor was the nerve centre of the bunker and was dominated by the communications centre and a central operations room that was the hub of the National Attack Warning System. Adjacent to the operations centre was a private suite of rooms for the Prime Minister, while on the uppermost, or entrance, level was private accommodation for the Governor General and offices for the various government departments represented in the bunker. At the end of a short tunnel leading from the lower level of the Carp bunker a huge safe-door seals the entrance to a 400-square-foot vault, built deep underground as an extension to the main structure, which in the event of global war would have been the last repository for the gold reserves and essential records of the Bank of Canada.

PUBLIC SHELTER & SURVIVAL – THE DECLINE OF CIVIL DEFENCE

Until the late 1950s when the threat posed by the ICBM turned strategic war planning on its head, Canada subscribed to the same policy of civil evacuation accepted by the USA and to a lesser extent by Great Britain. This policy was based upon assumptions formed during the height of the Second World War blitz, modified only by experience gained from the atomic bombs dropped on Japan. It was assumed that the North American Air Defence System would give three hours' notice of impending attack by manned Soviet bombers, which was judged sufficient time to evacuate all the major Canadian cities that were considered to be prime targets. With the advent of the ICBM, this warning time was reduced to just fifteen minutes. With evacuation out of the question, any requirement for the Canadian government to provide large communal shelters, which it could in any case not afford, was obviated. Instead, government proposed that the best protection would be by means of individual home shelters, built at private expense. Although there was much public opposition to this plan, the example of Switzerland, where such provision was mandatory, showed that such a scheme was viable. Federal government was consistently unwilling to subsidize private shelter construction, or, despite a concerted press campaign, to incorporate public shelters in the Montreal Metro or the Ontario Subway, although later it did agree, following the US example, to survey government buildings to assess their potential for adaptation as fallout shelters.

After the psychological shock of the Cuban missile crisis there was a rapid de-escalation of international tension and a parallel decline in the influence and importance of EMO. This decline in status was coincident with a transfer of responsibility from the Privy Council Office to the Ministry of Defense Production in 1963. Early in the following year a far from radical modification to the EMO war plan was announced, which included five major proposals:

1. The Attack Warning System would be completed.
2. The Emergency Broadcasting Facility would be completed, with remote emergency transmitters in hardened bunkers.
3. The ten Regional bunkers would be completed.
4. Strategic stockpiles of medical supplies would be established.
5. Basic public shelter system similar to that proposed in the United States would be established, consisting principally of identified basements in suitable Federal buildings. These would not be provided with ventilation or sanitation facilities.

By 1966 the threat of war had receded and all the old preconceptions which assumed that nuclear war would be sudden and unannounced were replaced by the concept of progressive escalation. Within EMO there was a distinct shift of emphasis towards 'wartime planning with a peacetime application', and in the 1967 budget government announced a drastic reduction in Civil Defence expenditure. A new, five-year 'Canada Survival Plan' was put forward which included the refurbishment of the by now obsolescent Diefenbunker and construction of the four outstanding Regional bunkers proposed three years earlier. While a certain amount of work was completed at the Central Government bunker, financial constraints prevented any progress on the Regional bunkers and, although the budget for this work was nominally deferred to the following year for several successive years, it was eventually formally abandoned in 1975.

More dramatic changes were to result from the Phoenix Report, which was a document issued as a conclusion to the CEMO conference of 1969. This proposed a national survival and recovery plan that went beyond a simple response to nuclear attack, widening the remit of the Canada Emergency Measures Organization to include response to 'anything that tends to create instability in our social, political or economic culture'. Despite an overt drift towards civil disaster planning, EMO's principal aim was still to deal with the effects of nuclear war, and the published priorities of the organization were:

1. The maintenance of national sovereignty.
2. Defence of North America in conjunction with the USA.
3. Maintenance of defence responsibilities within NATO.
4. Peacekeeping activities.

By the late 1970s, with its budget cut by some eighty per cent and renamed 'Emergency Planning Canada' (EPC), the old Emergency Measures Organization had become a true civil emergency/wartime contingency organization. With the threat of war diminishing to a level of irrelevancy, the vast majority of its slender resources were orientated towards civil emergencies. By 1978 nuclear war planning in Canada had sunk to a sorry state; the National Survival and Attack Warning Systems were under nominal care and maintenance, but were marginal and rapidly deteriorating, and the viability of the National and Regional bunkers which were also suffering from serious neglect, was doubtful.

This state of affairs was brought to an abrupt reversal at the end of the decade by developments in Europe and East Asia. The deployment of Russian SS20 missiles against targets in western Europe and the provocative deployment of US Pershing and cruise missiles in Britain and elsewhere, together with the Soviet invasion of Afghanistan, saw the end of détente with the USSR and a revival of superpower brinkmanship. Joint US/Canadian war plans were hurriedly drawn up and allocated more realistic budgets. Whilst Canadian government propaganda emphasized the peacetime function of EPC, actual priority was once again given to planning for war. An assessment of the existing emergency infrastructure made in 1983 revealed that, despite the cutbacks of the previous ten years, most of the bunkers were still viable, but that the mechanical plant, much of which had not been run for many years, was in poor condition and the communications equipment had deteriorated badly. When the bunkers were first fitted out the risk to electronic equipment from electro-magnetic pulse (EMP) was not fully appreciated, and it was felt that much of the equipment within the bunkers was not sufficiently protected. It was also discovered that the government essential records procedure, which was intended to ensure that copies of all the most important central government archives were maintained at the Carp bunker, had not been adhered to. Between 1985 and 1987 updated maintenance agreements were concluded with the Canadian Army and new operating and manning procedures agreed. Once again consideration was given to the completion of the outstanding regional bunkers and preliminary plans were prepared for at least one of these as part of a Maritime Forest Complex near Fredericton, but by the end of 1983 this proposal was shelved. When the EPC bunker network was finally closed down in 1992 it was essentially the same as it had been in 1968.

As the Soviet Union collapsed towards the end of the 1980s the role of EPC was refocused on civil emergencies, and in August 1988 it was decided to transfer the HQ function progressively from the somewhat austere bunker at Carp to a modern, unprotected office suite in Jackson Building, Ottawa. The Diefenbunker and the six regional bunkers were finally closed down in 1995 and disposed of by the government with rather unseemly haste. As a symbolic gesture to wash away Canada's cold war history, the government proposed the complete destruction of the Carp bunker, but popular pressure led to its preservation and it is now restored as a national heritage site.

6

THE 'ROTOR' RADAR SYSTEM

Following the increasingly widespread introduction of radar during the Second World War, the United Kingdom Control and Reporting System became the main organization through which the active and passive air defence of the nation was alerted and controlled. Early pre-war radar equipment was capable of detecting approaching aircraft at medium altitude with varying degrees of accuracy, but its low level of discrimination made it useless as a ground control radar for directing friendly fighters. It was not until 1941 that suitable Ground Control Intercept (GCI) radar was developed and by this time the two functions of *reporting* and *control* had developed as two separate organizations under different command. This separation was to hinder development of a truly effective, comprehensive radar system until the early 1960s. The Control and Reporting system expanded enormously through the war, but, due to the high financial and manpower demands that it imposed on the nation's resources, it underwent a rapid contraction as the German bomber threat receded. In May 1944 there were 208 warning stations and thirty-three Ground Control Intercept stations, twenty of which had already been reduced to care and maintenance status. Most of the Chain Home stations in the north-west were closed down through 1945 and by July a further eighteen east coast stations were reduced to care and maintenance and all western radar cover between St David's Head and Cape Wrath was withdrawn.

Thus, by 1948, when tension with the USSR and difficulties in Berlin and eastern Europe once again made Britain potentially vulnerable to air attack, an operational system still existed but only within a limited area of the south and east coasts. Elsewhere most of the stations had been closed down, some stripped of their equipment, some under minimal care and maintenance, but the majority just abandoned to decay and vandalism.

In the immediate post-war period two reports were to determine the shape of UK air defences for the following twenty years. The first of these, a Chiefs of Staff paper prepared over a twelve-month period and issued in July 1945 under the title 'Air Defence of Great Britain during the ten years following the defeat of Germany', made the following assumptions and recommendations:

1. Only an essential peacetime nucleus should be retained but the bulk of the radar control and reporting system should be capable of expansion to a full war footing within two years.
2. No. 11 Group, Fighter Command should remain at full strength, and Nos. 10, 12 and 13 Groups should be reduced to half-strength.
3. Full radar cover should be maintained over vital manufacturing and administrative areas (the wartime Gun Defended Areas or GDAs) within No. 11 Group but elsewhere stations should be reduced to care and maintenance although expandable to full war capacity within six months to two years.
4. 'Control' and 'Reporting' radar stations should be integrated into single

'Master Radar Stations', which would also receive reports direct from the Royal Observer Corps.

This plan was not acceptable to the Cabinet, which highlighted its ineffectiveness in the event of a sudden attack and it proposed instead that the vulnerable areas of the UK should be divided into a 'defended' zone where cover could be extended at short notice, and a 'shadow' zone, where the radar would not be maintained at operational status but could be activated within two years. Existing anti-aircraft cover, amounting to over eight thousand medium and heavy guns, would be retained in the defended areas. These guns would protect the ports, industrial centres, military depots and London as the Seat of Government. Within the shadow area anti-aircraft cover would be withdrawn, but the gun sites would be retained and their immediate surroundings protected from development.

Towards the end of the year a critical report was published by Group Captain J Cherry entitled *A memorandum on the Radar Reporting and Control Aspect of the Air Defence Organisation*. The Cherry Report drew attention to the major weaknesses of the existing system, the errors and delays associated with the manual voice-telling system, the complexity of the existing communications links and the consequent need for excessive re-plotting of tracks, and the fact that there were far too many 'gap-filler' radar stations providing too much information of dubious value. Whilst recognizing that Britain's current political and financial situation was not propitious, Cherry outlined his specifications for an ideal air defence system:

1. With the prospect of high-speed supersonic bombers capable of speeds in excess of 700 mph at heights of over 80,000 feet, radars were required with ranges of 190 miles at sea level and 330 miles at 60,000 feet.
2. An improved IFF (Identification Friend or Foe) system.
3. Radar displays should be in the form of large-scale Plan Position Indicators (PPIs) capable of simultaneously displaying track, altitude, number and identity of aircraft, derived from several radars up to one hundred miles apart.
4. Groups of radar stations in any one sector should report to unified control and reporting centres, which would effectively be combined filter rooms, sector operating centres, GCI stations and anti-aircraft operations rooms (AAORs), merged into a single Sector Control Centre housed in an underground building.

Cherry presumed that the filtering, sorting and automatic transmission of plots from disparate radar stations would be accomplished by new technology not yet developed. As an interim measure it was suggested that the most important GCI stations in track preparation areas should become Master Radar Stations and assume responsibility of the earlier Sector Operations Centre. Master stations would communicate with all the CH, CHEL, and other GCI stations in their areas as well as the relevant fighter airfields and AAORs. AAORs would be fitted with tactical control radar that would enable the guns to be used safely while friendly fighters were in the air. Each master station would have a sea-approach and overland plotting table, and combined plots from these would be transferred to the General Situation Map (GSM) and broadcast to Group HQ and adjoining GCIs and AAORs. It was hoped that as the technical developments came to fruition the Master GCIs would be capable of automatic transmission of the composite air picture or GSM to all clients. All GCI stations would be refitted to perform a reporting *and* control role. The report suggested that about seventeen Master GCI stations would be required.

Unfortunately the Cherry report made little impression upon the incoming Labour government, which, strapped for cash, preferred to spend what little it had on civil projects, reconstruction and the drive for exports. Apart from a modest increase for guided weapons research (and concealed expenditure upon nuclear weapons), the 1946 and 1947 Defence White Papers proposed little more than maintenance of the status quo.

Following the Berlin crisis of the previous year the Air Council in 1949 approved the 'Short Term Plan' for the improvement of UK passive air defence, which involved the overhaul of many existing Second World War radar stations and the construction of a few new ones, together with the provision of extensive new domestic sites to house the extended staff that would be needed. The primary object of the Short Term Plan was to provide the best possible radar defence for Greater London at bearable cost and within the limited time span of two years. It became clear, however, that in view of the trend in international relations, the vulnerability of existing stations and the inadequacies of the wartime radar equipment called for a much more extensive radar defence programme for the greater part of the UK as a matter of great urgency.

Accordingly, in 1950 a much more comprehensive scheme, code-named ROTOR, was developed jointly by the Air Staff and the Ministry of Supply. Under this scheme parliamentary approval was given for the re-equipment and modernization of the existing East Coast and English Channel system and for the extension of this cover, with limited capability, to the whole of Great Britain other than the Hebrides and Shetland Islands. At first ROTOR was envisaged as a stop-gap solution which would suffice until more powerful, high-discrimination centimetric radar, then only at an early research stage, became available around the end of 1957. However, unexpected developments in the technical field led to ROTOR evolving as a much more comprehensive system than originally envisaged. This programme developed in three stages identified as ROTOR 1, 2 and 3, which are described in outline below.

ROTOR 1

The ROTOR 1 plan called for the installation of improved equipment, known as 'Stage 1 Radar', currently still under development, but in view of the perceived seriousness of the international situation it was agreed to proceed, as an emergency measure, with the overhaul and restoration of the existing Second World War vintage Chain Home stations until the new equipment became available. It was also decided to retain some of the older Chain Home sites to augment the new Stage 1 stations. At the time ROTOR 1 was the largest defence capital project ever undertaken in the UK. Building work alone was estimated at £24 million, with a further £8.5 million earmarked for new electronic equipment and £19 million for communications equipment, most of which was to be provided by the GPO. The prime contractor for radar equipment was the Marconi Company. Completion of the Stage 1 ROTOR plan was called for 'by the end of 1952 if possible, and in any event not later than mid-1953'. A chilling addendum to the official outline plan, circulated in March 1951, noted that:

> Although preparedness of the system for a war occurring before these dates is outside the scope of Operation ROTOR, it is prudent to plan the operation in such a way that cover for the most vital and vulnerable areas in the country is provided first.

The level of cover required in the most vulnerable area from Portland Bill to Flamborough Head and northward to the Moray Firth amounted to duplicated control cover from 5,000 feet, duplicate reporting cover from 2,000 feet, and continuous single surface and very low cover out over the sea approaches. In the South and West control and reporting coverage was to be limited to medium and high altitude only. The north of Scotland and the Isles of Orkney were to have only minimal Chain Home cover. To attain this level of coverage the Air Staff called for the restoration of twenty-eight Chain Home stations nationwide, utilizing existing equipment, and the construction of fourteen new Chain Early Warning (CEW) and Chain Home Extra Low (CHEL) stations equipped with Stage 1 radar. There were also to be eight new Ground Control Intercept (GCI) stations equipped with Stage 1 radar.

The area of the UK covered by ROTOR was divided into six geographical sectors, each controlled from a Sector Operations Centre. Overall control of the active air defences of the United Kingdom was exercised from the underground Fighter Command headquarters operations room at Bentley Priory, through the sector commanders in their respective centres. A Sector Commander would control the air battle within his sector and co-ordinate the anti-aircraft guns and fighter aircraft allotted to him. The operations room of the SOC would display information co-ordinated from the radar reporting stations, the VHF fixer organization, the Royal Observer Corps and other supplementary sources, including continental radar. The original ROTOR scheme proposed that track information from individual reporting stations would be combined and manually plotted at a number of Combined Filter Plotting Centres (CFPs) located at a limited number of key CEW and GCI stations, but this requirement was later withdrawn.

Information from the radar reporting stations was told off by land-line to the SOC operations rooms, GCI stations, and the Anti-Aircraft Operations Rooms (AAORs), where it was plotted manually on the operations tables together with information received from other sources. Information regarding airfield conditions and squadron readiness within each sector was displayed on a 'Tote' board in the SOC operations room. This decentralized system of track-telling and reporting by land-line required the laying, by the GPO, of many thousands of miles of telephone cable, and delays in completing this task, occasioned by material shortages compounded with short-sighted government restrictions regarding the deployment of GPO labourers, was to dog the entire ROTOR project.

Tactical control of defending fighters when airborne was primarily exercised from the GCI stations although for broadcast control of fighters engaged against low-flying hostile aircraft certain CHEL and CEW stations were also provided with control capabilities.

ROTOR 1 STATIONS
(a) GCI

NAME	GRID REFERENCE	NAME	GRID REFERENCE
Anstruther	NO 568088	Gailes	NS 327361
Bawdsey (combined GCI/CH)	TM 347388	Langtoft	TF 155129
Boulmer	NU240125	Neatishead	TG 346184
Buchan	NK 113408	St Anne's	SD 348303
Calvo	NY 144545	St Twynell's	SR 944976
Charmy Down	ST 768702	Sandwich	TR 297575
Chenies	TQ 015997	Scarnish	NM 032456
Comberton	SO 968461	Seaton Snook	NZ 519280
Hack Green	SJ 647483	Skendleby	TF 438709
Hartland Point	SS 237277	Sopley	SZ 163977
Holmpton	TA 367225	Treleaver	SW 766174
Hope Cove	SX 716374	Trewan Sands	SH 322754
		Wartling	TQ 662088

(b) CEW STATIONS

Beachy Head	TV 590959	Portland	SY 696735
Bempton	TA 192736	St Margaret's	TR 370451
Cold Hesledon	NZ 417468	Trimingham	TG 290385
Inverbervie	NO 841734	Ventnor (combined) CEW/CH)	SZ 565784

(c) CHAIN HOME STATIONS

Castle Rock	IC 796346	Ringstead	SY 751817
Danby Beacon	NZ 732097	Rye	TQ 968232
Douglas Wood	NO 488415	Sango	NC 417675
Drone Hill	NT 845665	School Hill	NO 908982
Drytree	SW 723218	Sennen	SW 376246
Dunkirk	TR 076595	Staxton Wold	TA 023778
Folly	SM 858195	Stenigot	TF 256827
Hayscastle Cross	SM 920256	Stoke Holy Cross	TG 257028
High Street	TM 411720	Swingate	TR 335429
Hill Head	NJ 947616	Trelanvean	SW 762193
Netherbutton	HY 610440	Trerew	SW 812585
Pevensey	TQ 644073	West Beckham	TG 142389
Poling	TQ 043052	West Prawle	SX 771374

(d) Chain Home Extra Low stations

Crosslaw	NT 880680	Goldsborough	NZ 830138
Fairlight	TQ 862113	Hopton	TM 540990
Foreness	TR 385710	Truleigh Hill	TQ 224109

(e) Sector Operations Centres

Barnton Quarry	NT 203748	Kelvedon Hatch	TQ 561995
Bawburgh	TG 165080	Longley Lane	SD 541365
Box	ST 850690	Shipton	SE 542618

At the end of the first year of construction it was reported that good progress had been made, but there was some slippage of the timetable. Target completion dates for the various outstanding elements of ROTOR 1 were divided into four phases:

1. Completion of the Chain Home restoration programme, using existing Second World War equipment, by March 1952.
2. Completion of all the CEW and CHEL stations by the end of 1952.
3. Completion of all the underground GCI stations by mid 1953
4. Completion of the remaining surface GCI stations and underground Sector Operations Centres by the winter of 1953/4, with decentralized filtering ready by the summer of 1954.

Decentralized filtering, which would allow processed tracks from more than one radar to be displayed on one Plan Position Indicator together with injected label information, called for modifications to the existing PPI indicators, principally by the introduction of fixed-coil displays. Development of these fixed-coil displays proved troublesome and delayed completion of the GCI stations.

Air Council policy, announced in early 1950, required that all radar stations built at exposed locations on the east and south coasts between Portland Bill and the Moray Firth should be provided with underground operations rooms. Four of the six new Sector Operations Centres were also to be built underground, while of the two remaining centres, both of which used existing Sector Stations which were a legacy of the recent war, one, at Box in Wiltshire, was already deep underground in a converted limestone quarry. Contrary to the common perception that the underground ROTOR bunkers were built to withstand the effects of a 20Kt nuclear detonation at a range of 400 yards, the operations buildings were in fact only designed to be proof against pattern bombing from 26,000 feet with conventional Russian 2,200lb armour-piercing bombs. At some GCI stations in vulnerable locations but not in the critical coastal areas, semi-buried operations centres were to be built, designed to give protection against five-inch HVAR rockets or near misses by 1000 lb bombs. Hack Green and Hope Cove are examples of this latter type of station. Above-ground GCI buildings elsewhere were to be proof against near misses from 500 lb bombs.

Standard designs of operations buildings for the various different functions were drawn up at an early stage:

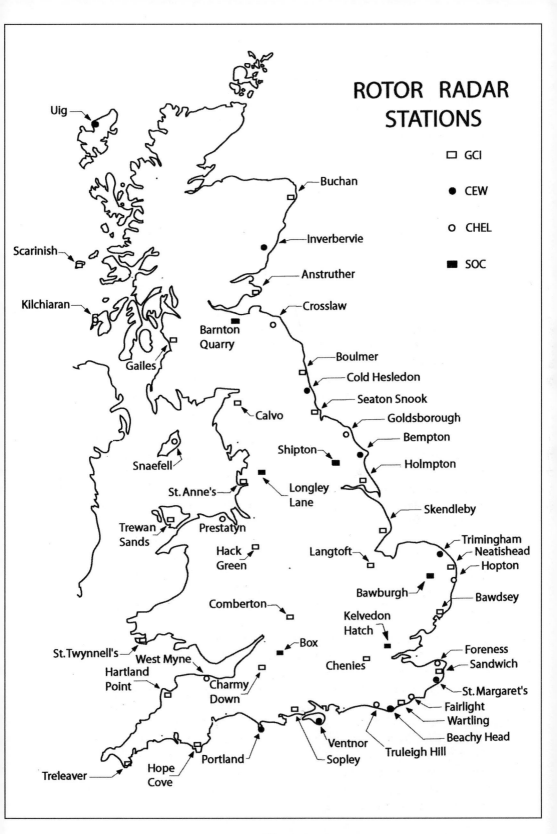

ROTOR RADAR STATIONS

□ GCI

● CEW

○ CHEL

■ SOC

Uig

Scarinish

Kilchiaran

Gailes

Buchan

Inverbervie

Anstruther

Crosslaw

Barnton Quarry

Boulmer

Cold Hesledon

Seaton Snook

Calvo

Goldsborough

Bempton

Shipton

Holmpton

Snaefell

Longley Lane

St. Anne's

Skendleby

Trewan Sands

Prestatyn

Hack Green

Langtoft

Trimingham

Neatishead

Hopton

Bawburgh

Bawdsey

Comberton

Kelvedon Hatch

Box

St. Twynnell's

West Myne

Chenies

Foreness

Sandwich

Hartland Point

Charmy Down

St. Margaret's

Fairlight

Wartling

Beachy Head

Treleaver

Hope Cove

Portland

Sopley

Ventnor

Truleigh Hill

77

R1 - standard underground Centimetric Early Warning station.
R2 - standard underground Chain Home Extra Low station.
R3 - standard underground Ground Control Intercept station.
R4 - standard underground Sector Operation Centre.
R5 - design for a surface GCI station, later abandoned.
R6 - standard semi-underground Ground Control Intercept station.
R7 - underground 'well' used for type 7 radar.
R8 - standard non-hardened, 'Seco' surface Ground Control
Intercept station.
R9 - converted 'Happidrome' GCI building (design later abandoned).

April 1953 saw specifications issued for three new building types:

R10 - above-ground CEW station for ROTOR 3 stations. Similar
internal layout to underground R1.
R11 - above-ground CHEL station for ROTOR 3 stations. Similar
internal layout to underground R2.

Details of the internal layouts of the various control bunkers can be seen on the plans below. The design and construction of all the underground bunkers is very similar, with detail differences to suit local conditions and requirements. Most of the single-level R1 and R2 bunkers are buried about forty feet underground and consist of reinforced concrete shells with ten-foot-thick walls and roofs that are a minimum of fourteen feet thick. Within the main bunker a central spine corridor divides the operational areas (radar room, plotting room, etc) on the left-hand side from the domestic and service quarters on the right. Access to the underground area is usually through an innocuous surface guardhouse that

6. **Typical 'ROTOR' Guardhouse.** Bungalow-like structures such as this example, at Patrington, control access to the underground radar operations centre. The flat-roofed rectangular extension to the rear of the main building covers a vertical shaft to the bunker. *Nick Catford*

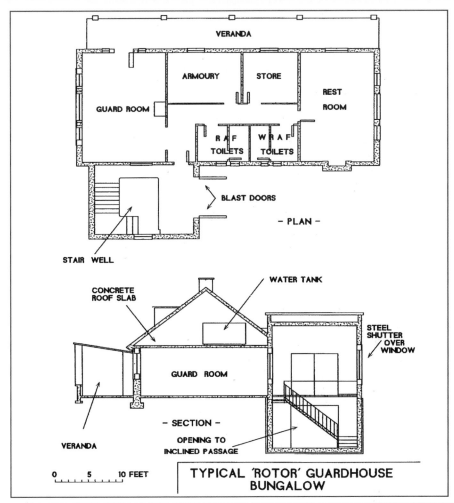

VERANDA

ARMOURY

STORE

REST ROOM

GUARD ROOM

R A F TOILETS

W R A F TOILETS

– PLAN –

BLAST DOORS

STAIR WELL

CONCRETE ROOF SLAB

WATER TANK

STEEL SHUTTER OVER WINDOW

GUARD ROOM

– SECTION –

VERANDA

OPENING TO INCLINED PASSAGE

0   5   10 FEET

TYPICAL 'ROTOR' GUARDHOUSE BUNGALOW

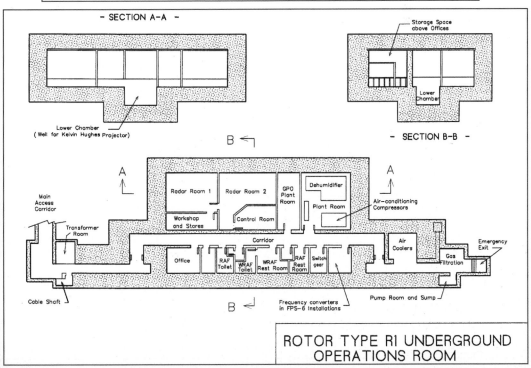

– SECTION A-A –

Storage Space above Offices

Lower Chamber

– SECTION B-B –

Lower Chamber
(Well for Kelvin Hughes Projector)

B

A   A

Main Access Corridor

Transformer Room

Radar Room 1

Radar Room 2

GPO Plant Room

Dehumidifier

Plant Room

Air-conditioning Compressors

Workshop and Stores

Control Room

Corridor

Air Coolers

Emergency Exit

Office

RAF Toilet

WRAF Toilet

WRAF Rest Room

RAF Rest Room

Switch gear

Gas Filtration

Cable Shaft

Frequency converters in FPS-6 Installations

Pump Room and Sump

B

ROTOR TYPE R1 UNDERGROUND OPERATIONS ROOM

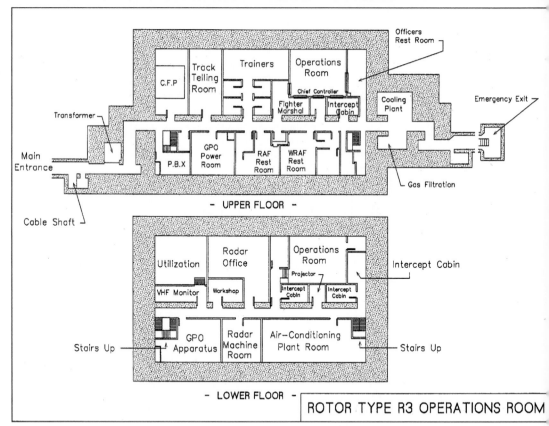

Officers Rest Room

C.F.P

Track Telling Room

Trainers

Operations Room

Chief Controller

Fighter Marshal

Intercept Cabin

Cooling Plant

Emergency Exit

Transformer

P.B.X

GPO Power Room

RAF Rest Room

WRAF Rest Room

Gas Filtration

Main Entrance

Cable Shaft

– UPPER FLOOR –

Utilization

Radar Office

Operations Room

Intercept Cabin

VHF Monitor

Workshop

Projector

Intercept Cabin

Intercept Cabin

Stairs Up

GPO Apparatus

Radar Machine Room

Air–Conditioning Plant Room

Stairs Up

– LOWER FLOOR –

ROTOR TYPE R3 OPERATIONS ROOM

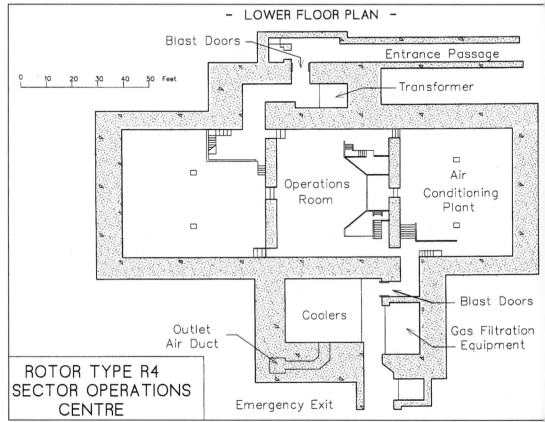

– LOWER FLOOR PLAN –

Blast Doors

Entrance Passage

Transformer

0 10 20 30 40 50 Feet

Operations Room

Air Conditioning Plant

Coolers

Blast Doors

Outlet Air Duct

Gas Filtration Equipment

ROTOR TYPE R4 SECTOR OPERATIONS CENTRE

Emergency Exit

looks very much like a residential bungalow. The pitched roof and dormer windows are, however, an architectural conceit, for below the tiles the bungalow has a two-foot-thick, flat concrete slab roof. Within, a heavy blast door protects the top of a double flight of stairs, with heavy lifting gear above the stair-well for manoeuvring heavy equipment into and out of the bunker below. At the bottom of the stairs more blast doors secure access to a sloping tunnel about two hundred feet long, lined with steel ring-girders, that descends a further twenty feet where it meets more blast doors and a series of dog-leg bends before joining the spine corridor. At the far end of the corridor there are more blast doors and dog-legs, giving access to a vertical shaft containing a zig-zag arrangement of steel stairways that lead to an emergency exit hatch on the surface. This shaft also acts as a ventilation airway. Air-conditioning and gas filtration equipment occupies a chamber between the shaft and the emergency exit blast doors.

The multi-floor R3 and R4 buildings are buried to a similar depth, but because of the extra height of the additional floors the overhead cover is less, and at some locations earth mounds have been used to increase this cover. Inside these larger bunkers stairs at each end of the central corridors on each level give access above or below. Large, refrigerated air-conditioning plants are installed on the lower floors of the R3 and R4 bunkers. The ventilation equipment is adjacent to the air filters in the R1 and R2 types. The semi-buried R6 is broadly similar to the R3 pattern except that most of the upper floor is above ground and the whole structure, though still massive, is less substantially built, normally of concrete just two feet thick. The bunkers had no integral emergency generators and relied instead upon semi-hardened power houses built either a short distance from the main structure or much further away on the supporting domestic site.

The visible evidence of a typical ROTOR station would consist of a six-acre plot, surrounded by a high wire fence with a small bungalow-like guardhouse with an empire-style veranda, usually quite close to the main gates. Five or six brick radar plinths surmounted by scanning heads would be dotted about the site, and where a Type 80 radar was installed there would be a large, windowless brick building that housed the modulating gear. At some distance from the guardhouse there would be another brick building, somewhat smaller than a radar plinth, with a steel cowl on top; this was the emergency exit and ventilation shaft. Most of the R3 GCI stations had a separate and rather conspicuous ventilation tower directly above the underground control room. During construction, the scale of the operation must have been obvious even to the casual observer, for a huge depression, at least sixty feet deep and two hundred feet in diameter had to be excavated before building could begin. Once excavated, the pit would be lined with thousands of tons of sand that acted as a shock-absorber, protecting the concrete structure against the seismic shock of a nearby ground-burst bomb. Before construction of the reinforced concrete shell could begin the hole was given a waterproof lining to prevent the ingress of seepage water.

The vast scale of the construction job can be gauged from the fact that the entire output from several steel-rolling mills was required to provide the reinforcing bars for the concrete bunkers; the R6 type alone consumed some 4,000 tons of steel, as the following extract from an Air Ministry progress report illustrates:

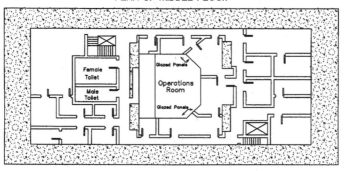

- PLAN OF TOP FLOOR -

Glazed Panels

Tote

Operations Room

Glazed Panels

RAF Rest Room

Officers Rest Room

Kitchen

Male Toilet

Female Toilet

RAF Rest Room

- PLAN OF MIDDLE FLOOR -

Female Toilet

Male Toilet

Operations Room

Glazed Panels

Glazed Panels

0   10   20   30   40   50 Feet

ROTOR TYPE R4 SECTOR OPERATIONS CENTRE

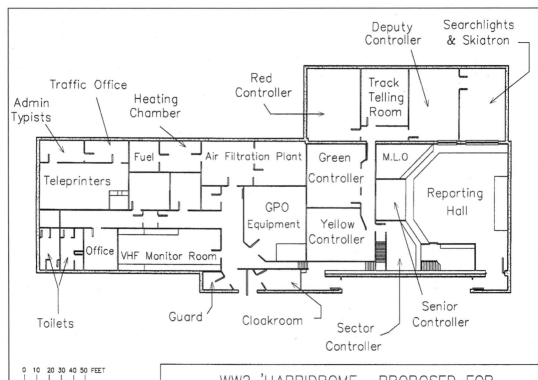

Deputy Controller

Searchlights & Skiatron

Red Controller

Track Telling Room

Traffic Office

Heating Chamber

Admin Typists

Fuel

Air Filtration Plant

Green Controller

M.L.O

Teleprinters

Reporting Hall

GPO Equipment

Yellow Controller

Office

VHF Monitor Room

Toilets

Guard

Cloakroom

Sector Controller

Senior Controller

0 10 20 30 40 50 FEET

WW2 'HAPPIDROME' —PROPOSED FOR CONVERSION TO 'ROTOR' R9 OPERATIONS CENTRE

All siting and land clearance has been completed with the exception of the proposed 'readiness' GCI station for the protection of Glasgow and the Clyde and of the recently added station to be provided on an island to the N.W of Glasgow. This has raised complicated problems and is still under examination. Building work is in progress at all but a few stations for which Works Contract action has only recently been concluded. In fact only 2 contracts remain to be let (Calvo and the GCI station planned for the Glasgow area). Works progress to date is satisfactory except as reported below.

Serious difficulties have been experienced over the supply of more than 4,000 tons of reinforcing steel for the 'readiness' GCI (semi-submerged R6) operations blocks where work has only recently started or is about to start. The recently agreed economies have undoubtedly eased the situation in that the requirement for reinforcing steel has been about halved. After making all the necessary representations for the full 4,000 tons, rolling mills have recently been nominated to supply sufficient reinforcing steel for those semi-submerged stations retained in the plan.

Building and fitting out of the stations progressed reasonably well through the winter of 1951/2, but when the time came to install the radar and telecommunications equipment in mid-1952 problems began to arise, as a further extract from the progress report shows:

Building work on the four new SOCs is proceeding satisfactorily and they are expected to be ready for GPO installation to start in April 1952. The GPO advise us that they are unlikely to complete their work before July/August 1953. This means that the associated radar stations will be completed before their respective SOCs.

The highest priority is being given to the completion of the SOC buildings. The earlier this is done the more quickly can the GPO begin their installation work, although the most serious bottleneck is the shortage of GPO equipment.

Partly due to difficulties with the power supplies to several stations following the decision to fit American FPS-3 radar as a temporary measure, but mainly due to a national shortage of materials, severe delays arose in the air-conditioning and ventilation contract. This in turn led to complaints from Marconi and the GPO about the intolerably high humidity and levels of dust experienced in the areas where they were trying to install delicate electronic equipment. These problems arose at a particularly inauspicious time for the Air Ministry, and, with Parliament pressing for cuts in the defence budget, the chairman of the ROTOR progress committee felt compelled to comment that:

It is perhaps worthy of mention to record a small but significant deflation in the atmosphere of urgency previously associated with ROTOR. It is thought that this may be due to a change in public outlook occasioned by

Press knowledge that war now appears less imminent, supported, as it is, by further knowledge of national economies, cuts in capital expenditure and a retardation of the re-armament programme. In this atmosphere the fulfilment of so complex and condensed a programme as ROTOR will become increasingly difficult.

The decision to refurbish the radar reporting and control system with what was essentially re-engineered Second World War equipment resulted from an assessment by the Marconi Company that no new equipment of the required performance could be developed and manufactured in the two-year time span contemplated. From the very start, therefore, ROTOR was seen as an interim measure only and it was accepted that its replacement by an as yet undeveloped centimetric radar (referred to as 'Stage II radar') would be necessary by 1957. Since the earliest implementation of the original ROTOR 1 scheme, several factors arose that questioned its viability, to the extent that in February 1952 Fighter Command noted that:

> The fact of the matter is that, with the introduction of 'ROTOR' equipment having the performance estimated for it, the significant deficiencies which make the present day system almost useless for the successful defence of the United Kingdom against attack by modern aircraft will remain.

This statement continued with the following broad outline of the deficiencies:

> There is insufficient range of early warning to enable interception of a high speed bomber to be made before its arrival over the areas (including London) of the majority of the Priority 1 targets.
> The ability to estimate the size of raids at long range is completely inadequate. Thus deception against the system is simple.
> In order to obtain the cover required a large number of stations are needed and several equipments have to be sited at each station to give continuity of tracking. Thus one of the greatest failures of the present system, ie the Filter problem, with its associated telling and plotting weaknesses, has not been eliminated.
> The system depends on metric equipment to provide high cover (above 25,000') and this equipment is extremely susceptible to jamming.
> The 'ROTOR' system does not provide complete coverage over all the approaches to the Priority 1 targets, nor over all the areas of the UK outside the Priority 1 target system.

To compound the technical shortcomings of the Stage 1 radar, production schedules slipped by about eighteen months. As an insurance against further delays in the delivery of Stage 1 equipment holding up the entire ROTOR project, arrangements were made to purchase twelve sets of American FPS-3 25 cm radar with which to equip certain CEW sites. Delivery was expected by the end of 1952 and it was considered that temporary installation of this equipment would not seriously hinder the main works. Construction of the first two underground stations, Truleigh Hill (CHEL) and Portland (CEW) was complete and fitting out with air-conditioning and power supply equipment had begun by January 1952, so Portland was selected as a 'guinea pig' station for the installation of FPS-3.

Unfortunately delays in the erection of aerials at the Portland site resulted in a change in priorities. St Margaret's instead became the prototype station, even though the underground operations building was still incomplete and control and communications equipment had to be housed in a temporary hut. Beachy Head was the first underground operations building to be equipped with the American radar, becoming operational on 15 May 1953. Many of the twelve stations earmarked for FPS-3 were still unfinished in February 1952, as the following table shows:

Priority	Name	Building Type	Initial Installation (Temporary or permanent ops building)	Target Operational Date for FPS-3
1	St Margaret's	R1	Temporary hut	16/3/53
2	Trimingham	R1	Temporary hut	04/5/53
3	Bawdsey	R3	Temporary hut	04/5/53
4	Boulmer	R3	Temporary hut	04/5/53
5	Sandwich	R3	Temporary hut	04/5/53
6	Buchan	R3	Temporary hut	04/5/53
7	Beachy Head	R1	Permanent underground	15/5/53
8	Gailes	R8	Temporary hut	31/5/53
9	Bempton	R1	Permanent underground	15/6/53
10	Anstruther	R3	Temporary hut	30/6/53
11	Chenies	R8	Temporary hut	15/7/53
12	Portland	R1	Permanent underground	31/7/53

The FPS-3 equipment installed at Gailes was originally destined for the Ventnor CEW site until the latter was dropped from the scheme in favour of Gailes in January 1953 following representations from Fighter Command.

In the meantime an experimental ten centimetre long-range early-warning radar, developed outside of the Stage 1 ROTOR programme, had proved very successful in preliminary trials. Although it did not fully meet the Air Staff Operational Requirement for the new radar required by 1957, it looked to be vastly superior to the Stage I equipment currently entering service under operation ROTOR. Its range in the Early Warning role was 210 miles with solid cover down to fifteen miles between the radar horizon and 50,000 feet, and its resolution was twenty times as good as that of the existing high-cover equipment. High resolution meant that the size of an approaching enemy force could be accurately assessed. Solid cover coupled with high resolution enabled filtering, with its attendant telling and plotting delays, to be eliminated over the sea approaches and much reduced over land. The most significant anticipated benefit of the new radar, known as 'Stage $1\frac{1}{2}$' or 'Type 80', was that, with the introduction of an automatic plotting system, which was possible with Type 80 but not with Stage 1 ROTOR, the composition and accuracy of the General

Situation Map would be greatly improved. The financial benefits, too, would be enormous: the introduction of Type 80 would enable the abandonment of most, if not all, of the Chain Home stations and the removal of sixty-seven Stage 1 radars from the primary programme. This represented an immediate capital saving of £1,600,000 and a reduction in annual running costs of £1,500,000. For these savings to be realized, however, installation of the new equipment had to begin within twelve months.

Despite the limitations of the Type 80 it was decided to go ahead with early installation in a limited number of ROTOR stations on account of its significant superiority over the Stage 1 radar. Meetings were held at Fighter Command Headquarters towards the end of 1951 to decide the most effective way to implement this decision. An important consideration was that delivery of Type 80 sets could not begin until the middle of 1954 and that the hopefully revolutionary Stage II radar would not be available until at least 1958. Type 80 would, therefore, have to provide cover for the pivotal five-year period during which the high-altitude, high-performance bomber was perceived to be the major emerging threat. An assessment circulated by Fighter Command AOC-in-C in December 1951 noted that:

> For a 500 knot bomber flying between 40,000 and 50,000 ft, the Order To Scramble must be given before the bomber is within fifteen minutes flying time, or 125 miles, from the coast. An additional five minutes are required for the appreciation to be made by the Controller and a further $3^{1}/_{2}$ minutes to allow for the delays from the time of first detection to display on the General Situation Map. These time allowances total $23^{1}/_{2}$ minutes which represent a distance of approximately 200 miles of early warning. The average range of early warning to be expected from [existing] ROTOR or the present CH stations is 130 miles. During the same five-year phase the ROTOR control equipment, while still suffering from poor resolution, has nevertheless sufficient performance to allow the 500 knot aircraft to be intercepted.
>
> It will, therefore, be seen that the overriding requirement to enable interception to be made is the extension of Early Warning from the ROTOR figure of 130 miles to a minimum of 200 nautical miles.

To overcome the shortcomings of the Stage 1 radar, the Air Council approved the early introduction of Type 80 equipment in July 1952 under the code name 'Operation ROTOR 2'. Installation was expected to begin in October 1954 and be completed in 1958, with first priority given to the Centimetric Early Warning stations. At the same time the Air Council also approved the ordering of an experimental Automatic Air Defence Information System (ADIS), together with seventy-seven projection Plan Position Indicators (PPIs), and thirty high speed photographic projection displays. The large scale displays would enable a large number of fighter controllers to exercise broadcast control over many fighters simultaneously in event of massed enemy raids. Operations rooms in Type 80-equipped stations were altered to accommodate horizontal Kelvin Hughes photographic projection displays in place of the earlier 'grease-pencil-and-tally' manual plotting tables. At Portland a deep well was constructed below the false floor of the operations room to house the Kelvin Hughes projector, but this was never installed as the station was never equipped with Type 80 radar.

ROTOR 2 - INSTALLATION OF TYPE 80 MK1 RADAR

Name	Target Date for Type 80	Target Date for Fixed Coil Display	Target Date for Type 1498 Display
Trimingham	10/2/55	10/2/55	10/2/55
St Margaret's	8/9/55	8/9/55	8/9/55
Beachy Head	8/8/55	8/8/55	8/8/55
Bempton	20/9/55	20/9/55	20/9/55
Ventnor	31/12/54	31/12/54	31/12/54
Buchan	25/4/56	Fitted as original equipment	25/4/56
Boulmer	7/2/56	Fitted as original equipment	7/2/56

It was realized that Type 80 was difficult to jam and had very good resolution, which, except for the fact that it had no height-finding capability, also rendered it highly suitable in the GCI role. Therefore it was recommended that it should, as a second priority, be installed in GCI stations in the most vulnerable areas. Initially Type 80 was to replace the existing Type 14 Mks. 7 and 8 at Buchan and Boulmer. Twenty GCI stations were earmarked for conversion at a later date, using a further refinement of the ten centimetre radar known as Type 81, although delays in its development, manufacture and delivery forced major deviations from this plan.

Even after the completion of ROTOR 1 and 2, a number of the deficiencies mentioned in the Fighter Command paper of February 1952 remained, and recommendations for the resolution of these problems formed the basis of Operation ROTOR 3. The principal components of ROTOR 3 consisted of:

1. Provision of radar cover in the north and west of the British Isles which were currently exposed to attack, particularly the Glasgow, Liverpool, Bristol and Belfast areas.
2. Provision of low and surface-level cover over the sea approaches to Glasgow, Liverpool and Bristol, the absence of which prevented effective action against low flying enemy aircraft.

Early Warning cover over the north and north-west approaches was to be provided by two new Caledonian Sector CEW stations at Uig and Saxa Vord, equipped with Type 80 Mk 2. These stations would not be immediately fitted with auxiliary control radar, but cabling was to be installed in preparation for this dual function and the stations categorized as 'operational readiness'. Operations rooms were to be of a new, standard design, above-ground building similar in internal layout to the R1 underground bunker, designated Type R10. GCI cover would be provided by a station at Killard Point, fitted initially with Stage 1 radar but later upgraded to Type 80. The Killard Point operations building was to be a standard semi-permanent 'Seco' R8 structure. Five new CHEL stations equipped with Stage 1 radar to enable detection, tracking, and interception of low flying aircraft approaching the major western ports were proposed at Kilchiaran, Murlough Bay, Snaefell, Prestatyn and West Myne, together with additional CHEL equipment installed in existing GCI stations at Gailles, St Twynells and Hartland Point. The new CHEL operations buildings were to be unprotected above-ground buildings designated R11 and similar in internal layout to the underground R2 bunkers. A hand-written addendum to the Fighter Command 'Outline Plan' notes that:

> There is no present requirement for the CHEL (200' tower) at St Twynells. The need for additional low cover will be reconsidered should the threat of Global War increase.

It was hoped that ROTOR 3 would be complete by August 1957 and, to ensure that current government restriction on the use of steel and other materials did not delay construction, all technical aspects were classified as 'Super Priority'. Indeed, such was its strategic importance that the whole ROTOR operation was to take precedence over all other government projects except atomic research and guided missile development. Emergency mobile radars were maintained for use should a sudden international emergency erupt before the completion of the ROTOR 3 stations.

ROTOR 3 STATIONS

Name	Type	Building	Grid Reference	Target Completion
Killard Point	GCI	R8	IJ 605435	August 1957
Kilchiaran	CHEL	R11	NR 207616	April 1956
Murlough Bay	CHEL	R11	ID 213407	April 1956
Prestatyn	CHEL	R11	SJ 079819	April 1956
Saxa Vord	CEW	R10	HP 632167	August 1955
Snaefell	CHEL	R11	SC 398881	April 1956
Uig	CEW	R10	NB 047390	August 1955
West Myne	CHEL	R11	SS 927485	April 1956

As Type 80 was further engineered and its use expanded, it was found that the Mk 3 version, which had been developed as a GCI radar, had a better range and performance than earlier Mk 1 versions currently equipping the CEW stations. This created something of a blurring of the distinction between the GCI and CEW functions and offered a compelling justification for finally abandoning the traditional distinction between the *Control* and *Reporting* stations. Between 1951 and 1953 considerable progress was made in the technology of radar data transmission, leading to the development of digital transfer of information between remote stations and their Sector Operation Centres over GPO land-lines using bi-stable relays to produce the digital pulse. By 1956 these developments, together with the introduction of the Kelvin Hughes photographic projection display, paved the way for the Comprehensive Radar Station.

The rather better than expected performance of Type 80 may have represented a technological bonus, but a contemporary technical development, the Carcinitron Valve, was to effectively negate that advantage, sealing the fate of ROTOR and questioning the viability of the Comprehensive Radar Stations before the concept was even off the ground. The Carcinitron was an electronically tuneable wideband valve which, once fully developed, proved highly suitable for jamming Type 80/81 radars, which had previously been reasonably immune from interference.

If electronic technology overtook ROTOR, then nuclear physics and the see-saw of international affairs ensured its final passing. Following the abandonment in April 1955 of two 'readiness' ROTOR GCI stations at Calvo and Charmy Down at a capital write-off of £400,000 the Chief of Air Staff was questioned by parliament regarding the current state of UK air defence policy, as outlined in the 1954 Chiefs of Staff paper entitled 'UK Defence Policy'. His reply amounted to a résumé of the changing nature of the air threat since 1945, and, so far as it directly effects the ROTOR programme, it is outlined below.

Following the American use of the atomic bomb against Japan in 1945 it was inevitable that, given time, the USSR would produce its own weapon despite the attempts by the United States to contain atomic proliferation. The rapid progress made by the USSR that resulted in their first atomic detonation in September 1949 came as something of a surprise. Yet the atomic bomb was not seen as a decisive weapon; a thousand-fold more powerful than the largest conventional bomb, but a quantitative improvement only, not a qualitative revolution. The relatively small-yield atomic bombs then envisaged were still seen as point-target weapons to be countered by point defences, as was the status quo. Evidence at the time suggested that the sort of protection against the atomic bomb, delivered by manned bombers, would be the same as against conventional bombs. The 'A' bomb was survivable, and in any event, the USSR was not to have a strategic bomber (the Myasishchev M4 Bison) capable of carrying its atomic bomb until 1956. In terms of radar protection, an atomic attack would require solid air cover at low and medium altitudes over land, and ROTOR had achieved that.

The nature of the risk as perceived by the Air Staff changed little even after the United States detonated its first thermonuclear weapon ('H' bomb) in October 1952. It was realized that the 'H' bomb represented a true difference in kind rather than quantity – a weapon of unimaginable horror – but despite this the western democracies still felt pretty secure, confident of the unbridgeable gap between the USA and the USSR in the thermonuclear arms race. The 'H' bomb inevitably hastened the end of Anti-Aircraft Command, because strategic bombers carrying thermonuclear weapons would have to be destroyed far beyond friendly shores and way beyond the range of anti-aircraft gunfire. Tactically too, AA guns were redundant for, given the massive destructive power of the 'H' bomb, point-defence was no longer a viable concept. The eventual demise of AA Command had, indeed, been on the defence agenda since at least 1953 as the inability of heavy and medium anti-aircraft guns to keep up with the forthcoming generation of high-flying sub-sonic and supersonic aircraft became manifest.

Suddenly, however, theorizing gave way to reality when, to the amazement of US defence planners, the USSR successfully detonated its own 'H' bomb in August 1953, less than a year after the Americans. At a stroke, the West had lost its strategic dominance and all the old defence assumptions, including the British concept of the 'main defended area' and the protection of key elements of UK industry, population and administration, were rendered obsolete overnight. For the United Kingdom, with point-defence untenable in the face of the Soviet 'H' bomb, the merely old became obsolete. Other elements, too, colluded to create a new western defence philosophy. Financial constraints throughout the early 1950s had forced reductions in all the western defence budgets with corresponding decreases in the strength of the ground forces. Meanwhile the Soviet conventional forces had multiplied to the extent that, when war broke out again in Europe, as the American administration was sure it would, conventional defence would be quickly overrun and the only response would have to be the Hydrogen bomb. Thus was born the 'Tripwire' policy and the concepts of massive retaliation and the three-day war. With the 'H' bomb, a future war would be over before Soviet ground forces reached the channel, and either their bombers would have been destroyed hundreds of miles beyond the UK shoreline or the nation's entire industrial and administrative infrastructure would have been wiped out. Under these changed circumstances the existing ROTOR radar defence system had no role, or could not guarantee to fulfil whatever vestigal role it still maintained. The Chiefs of Staff therefore considered that, mindful of the limitations of ROTOR, a reduction in its scope – firstly the closure of Charmy Down and Calvo, and soon after of several other stations – was an appropriate response. At the same time the front-line fighter force was reduced by twenty percent, and fifty out of eighty-two airfields were closed down. Within a few years the concept of 'deterrence' had taken the lead role in the defence of the western hemisphere, and in Britain the role of Fighter Command was no longer to guarantee the safety of the nation, root and branch, but simply to protect the deterrent force bases - the 'V' bomber airfields.

THE '1958' PLAN

ROTOR 1 was finally completed and the thirty-nine new stations (thirty-four of them underground) were officially transferred to Fighter Command in April 1956. By that time some stations had already been closed, operations ROTOR 2 and 3 were in progress, but the Type 80, upon which much depended, was already under threat and a thorough review of the Control and Reporting system was in hand. The outcome of this review was the interim '1958 PLAN', targeted, appropriately enough, for completion in 1958, which envisaged a UK air defence ground environment divided into nine sectors, each with a 'comprehensive' radar station (combined CEW/GCI using Types 80/81 radars), supported by a Satellite Control Station and a dedicated CEW station. The project was divided into three phases:-

1. The conversion of eight existing GCI stations into Comprehensive Radar Stations, and the construction of one new Comprehensive station at Farrid Head.
2. Conversion of a further nineteen existing ROTOR stations into Satellite control stations or Type 80-equiped CEW stations.
3. The introduction of fully automatic, computerised data handling systems.

PROPOSED ORGANIZATION OF THE '1958' PROJECT:

Sector	Comprehensive	Satelite GCI	CEW Station
1	Buchan		Saxa Vord
2	Boulmer	Anstruther	
3	Patrington	Seaton Snook	Bempton
4	Neatishead	Skendleby	Trimingham
5	Bawdsey	Sandwich	St Margaret's
6	Wartling	Sopley	Beachy Head
7	Hope Cove	St Twynells	Treleaver
8	Killard Point	St Annes *and* Scarinish	
9	Farrid Head		Uig

Although a partial implementation of the 1958 plan went ahead, its potential financial burden and the failure of technical development to keep up with its notional requirements led to progressive cutbacks. During 1957 several more stations including Hope Cove and St Twynells were dropped from the scheme and abandoned. At a meeting of the Air Council on 8 January 1959 it was recorded that the first part of phase one of the plan, (i.e. the conversion of eight GCI stations into Master Radar Stations) had been completed. This had already resulted in the closure of the six Sector Operations centres which were now redundant. It was clear, however, that the remaining work in phase one, which amounted to the re-arrangement of console positions in the Master Radar Stations to suit the new operational requirements, would not be completed until mid-1962.

The Air Council agreed that future progress on the 1958 plan should be halted, considering its already precarious reliance on Type 80 radar and the fact that the proposed systems would be incapable of integration with the 'Bloodhound' surface-to-air missile (which was now nearing acceptance by the RAF) and its impotence in the face of the new threat posed by Inter-Continental Ballistic Missiles. Between 1957 and 1959, then, a large number of heavily protected underground control bunkers, including six three-level Sector Operations Centres, many R3 CEW stations and several underground and semi-buried GCI stations were made redundant. This was of crucial importance to other aspects of government nuclear defence planning, as we shall see elsewhere.

Meanwhile, in January 1959 the Air Council proposed a new scheme, code-named 'PLAN AHEAD' which was essentially a modification of the 1958 plan that took into account the development of yet another new and hopefully even more jam-proof series of radars, the Types 84 and 85. As well as providing enhanced early warning and fighter control capabilities, the Type 85, in conjunction with Type 82 radars at the Bloodhound missile bases, would allow tactical control of the surface-to-air guided missiles from the Master Radar Stations. The initial requirement for PLAN AHEAD consisted of five Radar Tracking Stations (RTS)s, and two Master Control Centres (MCS)s. These stations would be equipped with a new, and as yet non-existent, generation of computers to provide automatic data handling, extraction and processing, with high-speed data links between the stations and the Air Defence Operations Centre.

When presented with this proposal the Secretary of State for Air accepted that 'the proposed re-equipment appears to be essential to maintain the defence of the deterrent, but the cost is substantial'. He questioned whether operational economies could be made and whether the second Master Control Centre was essential. In reply the Chief of Air Staff stated that if manual tracking could be completely replaced with computerised tracking by mid-1964 then 500 men might be dispensed with, resulting in a substantial saving. He also noted that although one MCS might do the job satisfactorily, should an equipment failure render it unserviceable at a critical moment there would be no standby capability.

By August 1959 a minimum configuration was decided upon, consisting of three RTSs, at Neatishead, Staxton Wold and Bramscote. The first MCS was to be established at Bawburgh. To protect against the loss of an MCS, each RTS was to have limited control capacity built in. A little later, the existing site at Boulmer was substituted for Bramscote. Given adequate priorities, it was considered that this minimum system could be completed by 1962, to coincide with the commissioning of Bloodhound, which was scheduled for initial deployment at North Coates late in 1961. Phase two of the scheme, should it go ahead, was to include two further RTSs at Buchan and Killard Point. In the meantime Type 80 radars were to be maintained at Saxa Vord, Patrington and Buchan to give extended coverage to the north of the main PLAN AHEAD area.

Planning was well advanced by September 1960 and in the following March contracts were negotiated for reconstruction of the control bunkers at Neatishead and Bawburgh to a new R12 specification. Then suddenly, for motives both political and economic, the Cabinet, heavily influenced by Prime Minister Harold Macmillan, put the entire project on hold. The immense cost of PLAN AHEAD was again brought into question and the Air Ministry was requested to justify this cost, given the diminishing value of air defence radar in the era of the Inter-Continental Ballistic Missile. Even if the justification was accepted, PLAN AHEAD would only be allowed to go ahead if it could be integrated into a new joint Air Defence/Civil Air Traffic Control system. The rapid advances in commercial jet aircraft and civil aviation in general, as well as increases in military air traffic, had made a fast, flexible and integrated radar system imperative.

In reply the Air Staff stressed the strategic role of air defence radar, arguing the requirement for timely early warning of Soviet aircraft equipped with modern, powerful jamming apparatus designed to disable the Ballistic Missile Early Warning System, and particularly the BMEWS station at Fylingdales Moor in Yorkshire, construction of which had just been agreed in February 1960, following a two-year negotiation with the United States government. The Chief of Air Staff admitted the futility of point defence, going so far as to state that

> since the defence of the deterrent has been abandoned in 1960, air defence was now limited to prevention of intrusion and jamming.

It was also argued that, given the catastrophic consequences of a wrong evaluation in a period when use of the 'H' bomb could be initiated by a hair-trigger tripwire, an adequate air defence radar would facilitate the formation of an accurate air picture in times of tension, allowing sufficient time for central government to make an appropriate political or military response.

Having nearly sunk under the weight of political bureaucracy, a much modified version of PLAN AHEAD re-surfaced under the code-name LINESMAN/MEDIATOR. This was the joint civil/military system insisted upon by Harold Macmillan, 'LINESMAN' being the air defence element. It was insisted that, much against the wishes of Fighter Command, the proposed Master Control Station be relocated from Bawburgh to the Southern Air Traffic Control Centre at West Drayton. This meant that the contract to build an extension to the existing R3 Rotor bunker at Bawburgh, in effect building a second, identical bunker adjacent to it and linking them by a central corridor, had to be retracted at considerable cost. Construction was well in hand at Neatishead by mid-1962, with completion expected in September 1964. Early that year, however, as a result of delays in every aspect of the task, the entire LINESMAN project was rescheduled, with completion of the first phase (the Master Radar Stations) due in October 1968.

Despite continued opposition from Fighter Command, which argued that a joint ATC/Air Defence centre in West Drayton would be too vulnerable because it could not be built as a hardened underground structure, and that the necessary broad-band radio links to the radar stations would be too exposed to jamming, construction of the 'L1' centre began at the end of 1965. The site was ready for fitting out with its control and computer systems eighteen months later, but it was soon realized that the massively complex data-handling requirements were at the very limit of current programming technology. Delay followed delay and the shortage of suitably skilled computer programmers threatened the future of the project. After two years of minimal progress AVM Moulton, AOC of RAF 90 Group, put forward a report in December 1969 arguing that the project was too unwieldy as it stood and should be drastically simplified if it was to have any chance of survival. Moulton suggested that West Drayton should be classified as a Tactical Control Centre, relinquishing all its fighter and missile control functions to the radar stations, and that all the non-essential elements of LINESMAN such as ground-to-air data links should be abandoned until the available technology was more refined. He recommended that in the meantime the RAF should revert to voice control of interceptors. Moulton's proposals, which in effect called for a reduction in the overall UK air defence cover, received tacit acceptance, coming, somewhat propitiously, at a time when the nuclear threat was receding and the concept of 'Flexible Response' was overtaking the tripwire policy.

Most of the hardware to equip West Drayton for its more limited role was in place by December 1970, but hopes to commission the centre in December 1974 were put in doubt by further arguments about its ultimate utility. Eventually, however, the decision was made to complete the L1 building, and on 31 March 1974 LINESMAN in its truncated form was declared operational. At this time steps were taken to ensure a closer integration of the United Kingdom Air Defence Ground Environment (UKADGE) into the larger NATO Air Defence Ground Environment (NADGE) by means of digital data links with continental early warning radar systems.

By the early 1970s the LINESMAN system consisted of the following stations:

STATION	RADAR EQUIPMENT	NOTES
RADAR TRACKING STATIONS		
Boulmer	Type 84 & Type 85	Also Standby Local Early Warning Control (SLEWC)
Neatishead	Type 84 & Type 85	Also SLEWC
Staxton Wold	Type 84 & Type 85	
Killard Point (Bishops Court)	ATC radar, which it was intended should be supplemented by redundant Type 84 from Bawdsey, but installation was delayed due to continued requirement for Bawdsey following the fire at Neatishead.	
MASTER RADAR STATIONS		
Buchan	Type 80, and FPS-6	
Patrington	Type 80	
Bawdsey	Type 80 and Type 84	Type 84 later transferred to Bishops Court
NATO RADAR STATIONS UNDER RAF CONTROL		
Faeroes		
Saxa Vord		SLEWC Capability

Bawdsey and Patrington were closed in 1973 as the SLEWC data-handling facilities at Neatishead and Boulmer became operational.

In 1979 a new Air Staff Requirement (ASR 888) called for an enhanced command and communication system to replace LINESMAN which was already seriously outdated. Contracts for the replacement system, known as the Improved United Kingdom Air Defence Ground Environment (IUKADGE), were signed in 1981 and completion was expected by 1986, although software development problems delayed this for a further six years. In recent years advances in microchip technology have seen the emergence of computing power undreamed of even a decade earlier and this has allowed the United Kingdom to develop, during the last years of the twentieth century, what is probably the most sophisticated air surveillance and control system in the world. Key to the current system are two Control and Reporting Centres (CRC) at Buchan and Neatishead, which report to the underground UK Combined Air Operations Centre (UKCAOC), located at the RAF Strike Command Headquarters at High Wycombe. The radar reporting station at Boulmer functions as a standby CRC. Buchan and Neatishead control airspace north and south of Newcastle respectively, receiving information from both civil and military radars within their geographical regions. Principal air defence reporting radars are located at Benbecula in the Outer Hebrides, Saxa Vord in the Shetland Isles, Portreath in Cornwall and Staxton Wold in North Yorkshire. Both Neatishead and Buchan CRCs also incorporate a reporting element.

ROTOR RADAR STATIONS

Anstruther (Fife)
This two-level underground R3 GCI bunker near St Andrew's, Fife, opened in June 1953 although it is probable that the station did not become fully operational until 1956. Anstruther closed in 1958 and later that year it became the Scottish Northern Zone Regional Seat of Government. Following major upgrades in the late 1960s and again some ten years later, the bunker continued to function as Scotland's northern Regional Government Headquarters until the end of emergency government planning in Scotland in 1993. The following year Anstruther was opened to the public as a tourist attraction.

Barnton Quarry (Edinburgh)
One of six underground Sector Operations centres, the three-storey R4 building at Barnton Quarry controlled the Caledonian Sector and was built on the site of a Second World War Sector Operations Centre. It was hoped that the centre would be fully functional by the summer of 1954, but this target could not be met and operational status was not achieved until January 1956. Within two years technological advances had rendered the hugely expensive Barnton Quarry complex, and the other five Sector Operations Centres, redundant, although Barnton Quarry limped along as the Air Defence Notification Centre North until September 1958.

By the end of the decade the bunker was in possession of the Scottish Office which adapted it as the Scottish Central Emergency Government Headquarters. This status was maintained until 1983 when a reorganization of Emergency Regional Government resulted in the closure of Barnton Quarry and its replacement as Scottish Central Control by the former Eastern Zone Headquarters at Kirknewton.

The following year the disused complex passed to Lothian Regional Council who, finding the site a liability, sold it in 1987. Since then it has passed through

TABLE OF ROTOR 1 RADAR STATIONS

Station	Type		Surface or U/ground	Target Service Date	Radar Type									PPI		H/R Display		'A' Scope	Projectors	
					13	14	54	79	11	7	FP S3	80 E/W	80 GCI	60a	64	61	65	61a	Type 32	Phillips PPI
Truleigh Hill	CHEL	R2	U/ground	16/8/52[1]	1									6				1		
Fairlight	CHEL	R2	U/ground	30/8/52	1									6				1		
Hopton	CHEL	R2	U/ground	13/9/52			1							6				1		
Foreness	CHEL	R2	U/ground	20/9/52			1							6				1		
Goldsborough	CHEL	R2	U/ground	4/10/52			1							6				1		
Crosslaw	CHEL	R2	U/ground	11/10/52			1							6				1		
Portland	CEW	R1	U/ground	18/10/52	3	2				1	1			9		3		1	2	
Ventnor	CEW	R1	U/ground	1/11/52	3	2				1	1	1		9		3		1		
Beachy Head	CEW	R1	U/ground	8/11/52	2	2				1	1			9		2		1		
St. Margaret's	CEW	R1	U/ground	22/11/52	2	2				1	1			9		2		1		
Trimingham	CEW	R1	U/ground	29/11/52	3	2				1	1			9		3		1		
Bempton	CEW	R1	U/ground	13/12/52	3	2				1	1			9		3		1		
Inverbervie	CEW	R1	U/ground	20/12/52	3	2				1	1			9		3		1		
Cold Hesledon	CEW	R1	U/ground	31/12/52	2	2				1	1			9		2		1		
Bawdsey	GCI	R3	U/ground	28/2/53	6	2				1	1		1		23	6	6	1	2	
Holmpton	GCI	R3	U/ground	20/3/53	5	2				1	1		1		21	5	6	1		1
Wartling	GCI	R3	U/ground	10/4/53	5	2				1	1		1		19	5	6			1
Sopley	GCI	R3	U/ground	24/4/53	5	2				1	1		1		19	5	6			1
Sandwich	GCI	R3	U/ground	8/5/53	5	2	1			1	1		1		19	5	6			1
Neatishead	GCI	R3	U/ground	22/5/53	5	2			1	1	1		1		19	5	6			1
Seaton Snook	GCI	R3	U/ground	5/6/53	5	2				1	1		1		20	5	6			
Buchan	GCI	R3	U/ground	19/6/53	6	2				1	1		1		23	6	6	1	2	1
Anstruther	GCI	R3	U/ground	26/6/53	6	2				1	1	1	1		23	6	6	1	2	
Langtoft	GCI	R6	Semi-sunk	10/7/53	5	2				1	1		1		20	5	6			
Skendleby	GCI	R3	U/ground	17/7/53	5	2				1	1		1		22	5	6			
Hack Green	GCI	R6	Semi-sunk	31/7/53	6	2				1	1		1		19	6	6		2	
Hope Cove	GCI	R6	Semi-sunk	7/8/53	6	2			1	1	1		1		24	6	6		2	
Boulmer	GCI	R3	U/ground	21/8/53	6	2				1	1		1		23	6	6	1	2	
Treleaver	GCI	R6	Semi-sunk	4/9/53	6	2				1	1		1		22	6	6	1	2	
St Twynell's	GCI	R6	Semi-sunk	18/9/53	6	2				1	1		1		20	6	6		2	
Calvo	GCI	R8	Surface	2/10/53	4	2				1	1		1		15	4	6			1
Comberton	GCI	R9		9/10/53	5	2				1	1		1		20	5	6		2	
Trewan Sands	GCI	**		23/10/53	5	2				1	1		1		20	5	6		2	
Chenies	GCI	R8	Surface	6/11/53	4	2				1	1		1		14	4	6			1
Charmy Down	GCI	R8	Surface	20/11/53	4	2				1	1		1		15	4	6			
Scarnish	GCI	R8	Surface	4/12/53	5	2			1	1	1		1		20	5	6			1
Hartland Point	GCI	**		18/12/52	4	2				1	1		1		15	4	6			
Gailes	GCI	R8	Surface	31/12/53	5	2				1	1		1		19	5	6			
St Anne's	GCI	R8	Surface	31/12/53	5	2				1	1		1		20	5	6		2	1

NOTES: (1) Target service dates do not include the installation of FPS-3 or Type 80 radar both of which were extensions to ROTOR 1.

the hands of several property developers who have been singularly unsuccessful in developing the property which is now in very poor condition. Most of the plant has been stolen or destroyed and a very serious fire, set by vandals, has largely wrecked much of the interior of the bunker.

Bawburgh (Norfolk)

An R4, three-level underground Sector Operations centre, opened 1954. It was intended that Bawburgh would become a Master Control Station under the LINESMAN/MEDIATOR plan, which would have involved the construction of an extension effectively doubling the size of the bunker. This plan was withdrawn in 1962 following the decision to relocate control of the cut-down LINESMAN system to the SATCC at West Drayton.

Bawburgh was subsequently acquired by the Home Office and by 1970 was operating as one of three S-RC's in the Eastern Region, and in 1980 was upgraded to become RGHQ 4.1. Following the end of emergency regional government in the United Kingdom, the Bawburgh bunker was sold into the private sector and it is now owned by Highpoint Communications, who use the surface compound as a transmitter site. The underground areas are apparently disused.

Bawdsey (Suffolk)

Bawdsey has the longest radar associations of any RAF site in the United Kingdom, the site having been chosen in 1935 by the Tizard Committee for experiments into the development of the RAF's first effective radar system. By 1937 Bawdsey had emerged as the first fully fledged radar site in Britain. Continuously extending its capabilities throughout the war years, it was first a Chain Home Low, then a Chain Home and later also a Coastal Defence radar station.

The Bawdsey site was approved as a GCI station under the ROTOR plan in 1950 with construction of the underground, two-level R3 bunker scheduled to start the following year. It was hoped to install the radar equipment during the midwinter of 1951/52, but this was not to be. The R3 building was constructed by scooping a huge depression in the gently sloping cliff edge, building the concrete shell (a fifty-feet-high 'box' with walls ten feet thick), and then filling the hole in around it and covering the structure with fifteen feet of soil. Some years later, in 1974, a further ten feet of earth cover was added to enhance the blast and radiation protection.

The underground control room was finally commissioned in 1954, although the interim equipment of American AN/FPS-3 radar had been operational since the previous February, control being exercised from a temporary wooden hut on the surface.

Bawdsey's radars were gradually improved over the next decade, a Type 80 Mk III (*Green Garlic*) being installed in 1958 followed by Type 84 in 1962 as part of the LINESMAN/MEDIATOR project. That year Bawdsey was designated a Master Radar Station which, with Patrington, controlled the 'Bloodhound' surface-to-air guided missiles. Although the station was demoted to a satellite of Neatishead following the reorganization of 1964, this situation was reversed two years later when Neatishead was disabled by a serious fire in the underground control room there. Ten years later Neatishead resumed the master function, and in 1975 Bawdsey was mothballed under care and maintenance. Over the next couple of years most of the remaining ROTOR equipment was dismantled, but in 1979 the station was reactivated as a 'Bloodhound II' site, with the R3 utilized as the missile control room. This continued until 1990.

Meanwhile, in 1985, the underground R3 was designated as the RAF Strike Command Interim Alternate War Headquarters, a function that it retained until close-down in 1991. Bawdsey was to remain an MoD site, though disused and with the underground bunker firmly sealed, for nearly a decade before being finally offered for sale. The guardhouse, emergency exit shaft and the Type 84 modulator building still survive on site, along with a rare R7 plinth for a Type 7 radar at a remote location on Alderton Marshes.

Beachy Head (East Sussex)
A Centimetric Early Warning station with an underground R1 operations block commissioned in May 1953, following successful tests of the temporary FPS-3 radar that was to suffice until Type 80 became available. The station closed in April 1958 and in recent years the guardhouse/access bungalow has been demolished and all shafts into the underground bunker sealed.

Bempton (Yorkshire)
A Centimetric Early Warning station, scheduled for construction during the winter of 1953 but finally commissioned, with Type 80 Mk1 radar, in 1956. Bempton was allocated as a satellite to the re-designated Comprehensive Radar at Patrington under the 1958 scheme. Since closure the site has reverted to a local landowner and has been subject to extensive vandalism above and below ground. Much of the underground R1 Control Centre has been gutted by fire.

Boulmer
Originally opened as a ROTOR GCI station, with an underground R3 bunker in 1954, Boulmer has been constantly upgraded and today acts as a standby Control and Reporting Centre in the United Kingdom Air Surveillance and Control System (UKASACS) supporting Neatishead and Buchan.

Box (RAF Hawthorn, Corsham)
The Southern and Western air defence sectors, which protected the south-western and north-western approaches to the United Kingdom respectively, were, because of their relative invulnerability, afforded a lower priority in the allocation of assets and funding. Consequently the Air Ministry, under pressure from the Treasury, pressed into service existing structures to house their sector control centres rather than provide new R4 buildings.

The location selected for the Southern Sector Operations Centre was the old No.10 Group Fighter Command operations room in Brown's Quarry at Box, near Corsham in Wiltshire. This was part of a huge ramification of underground government facilities built 100 feet below ground in the long-disused Corsham stone quarries. Between 1935 and 1944 approximately 3.5 million square feet of underground space was developed straddling an area north and south of Brunel's Box railway tunnel. Development of the northern section began in 1935 on an area that was to become Tunnel Quarry, Corsham Central Ammunition Depot, Sub Depot No. 1. The western end of Tunnel Quarry was later developed as an RAF communications centre (South West Control), and in January 1941 a series of headings connecting to the northern boundary of Tunnel Quarry was opened as No. 10 Group Operations Centre. After July 1943 access to the operations centre was by means of an electric lift; prior to that RAF personnel had to walk underground via the ammunition depot slope shafts.

Because its various rooms had to be shoehorned into the random layout of support pillars left in the old quarry to support the roof, the layout was very different from the standard wartime operations room. Nevertheless, the engineers were able to construct one massive chamber over forty feet high which formed the plotting room. Two glass-fronted mezzanine floors, or balconies, looked down upon the plotting table, while behind the main operations room another large chamber was adapted as a filter room.

At the end of hostilities No. 10 Group was absorbed by 12 Group and the facilities at Box were no longer required for active service. Between 1946 and January 1948 the existing equipment was adapted for a training role and the Box control centre became the Fighter Command Control and Reporting School.

Training ceased in 1948 and, after a few years disuse, with little new construction work required and with an existing, though obsolete, radar infrastructure, the conversion of the wartime control room in a ROTOR Sector Operations Centre was quickly accomplished and the centre was declared operational in January 1952. The Box SOC lost its ROTOR function in February 1958, but retained a Home Office/ROC element for some years as a matter of convenience, while the sector ROC headquarters remained underground at Corsham. In later years some degree of ROC continuity was maintained with the establishment of a Nuclear Reporting Cell which supported the Central Government Emergency War Headquarters in an adjacent quarry.

From the mid-1970s the Brown's Quarry SOC has been the home of the Controller, Defence Communications Network (CDCN). The main operations room, however, fell into disuse due to decay in its wooden internal structure many years ago.

Buchan

Buchan is one of the few ex-ROTOR radar stations that has seen continuity of service (although in a variety of guises) until the present day. Construction of the underground R3 bunker began in late 1952 and it was commissioned in September 1954, although the station had been operational since the previous autumn from a temporary surface operations room. A Type 80 radar was installed in August 1956, replacing an earlier, American-built AN/FPS-3 unit which sufficed as interim measure. The Type 80 was to remain in place until 1993, although supplemented since 1973 by a Marconi Type S259, and a few years later also by an Argentinean Westinghouse TPS-43, one of the spoils of the

Falkland conflict.

The underground bunker was completely rebuilt and refitted during the years 1979-82 and shortly afterwards became a key element of IUKADGE with the installation of the most up-to-date Type 92 radar.

Calvo (Solway Firth)

GCI 'readiness' station with R8 'SECO' surface control room. Scheduled for completion in October 1953, but delayed in construction and deleted from the ROTOR programme before it was completed.

Charmy Down (Bath)

The Charmy Down site, situated on a disused Second World War airfield two miles north of Bath, was designated a 'readiness' GCI station and was not given a high priority in the funding schedule. Work started on its construction in May 1953, but progressed slowly and the station was still incomplete when it was abandoned in April 1955 after some £200,000 had been spent on it. Nothing remains of the lightweight 'SECO' prefabricated control building other than a large, overgrown slab of concrete with numerous drain holes and cable ducts. Five red brick radar plinths remain, surmounted by steel-girder turntable bases, together with a raised platform for a mobile radar and a powerhouse building, stripped bare of all its equipment.

Chenies (Buckinghamshire)

A GCI station provided with unprotected 'SECO' R8 control building, opened in November 1953. After closure, the Chenies site remained RAF property and until recently was a Strike Command communications station. At the time of writing the station is deserted and subject to vandalism.

Cold Hesledon (County Durham)

Centimetric Early Warning station with underground R1 bunker. Scheduled for completion in December 1952, but probably not fully operational until 1954. An early closure, the guardhouse entrance building has been demolished although the surface site is still used as a transmission station and the compound is kept securely fenced.

Comberton

GCI 'readiness' station on the site of a wartime radar station, with R9 (converted Second World War 'Happidrome') surface control room. Scheduled for completion in October 1953, but delayed in construction and deleted from the ROTOR programme before it was completed.

Crosslaw

The Chain Home Extra Low station at Crosslaw was provided with a single-level R2 underground bunker, completed in September 1952 and handed over to the RAF for operations the following January. The site has been derelict for many years and is in private ownership.

Fairlight (East Sussex)

Chain Home Extra Low station with underground, single-level R2 bunker, scheduled for completion August 1952. The station was involved in the high-speed 'Winkel' passive detection system before closure in 1968. Demolished by the local authority in 1970 and the site cleared.

Foreness

Chain Home Extra Low station with underground R2 single-level bunker. Demolished after closure; no trace now remaining.

Gailes

GCI station with R8 'SECO' surface control room on site of earlier HF station that was operational until 1951. Scheduled for completion in October 1953, but delays in construction meant that, following the installation of American FPS-3 centimetric radar in May, control was exercised for several months from a temporary wooden hut until the R8 was completed. It is probable that the station was deleted from the ROTOR programme before the FPS-3 was replaced, although the records for this station, like most of the 'readiness' sites, are incomplete. A Civil Aviation Authority ATC radar now occupies the site.

Goldsborough (North Yorkshire)

The underground R2 operations block at this Chain Home Extra Low radar station was built in late 1951 and commissioned the following year following the delayed installation of the electronic equipment. As a result of the technical superiority of the Type 80 Mk 3 radar, Goldsborough was declared redundant in 1957 and scheduled for closure, but before this could be implemented the underground control bunker was destroyed by fire.

Now privately owned, the site has been cleared and the badly damaged underground areas sealed, although plans are afoot to re-open it temporarily in order that a full survey may be undertaken.

Hack Green (Cheshire)

The semi-buried R6 bunker at Hack Green near Nantwich in Cheshire was scheduled for completion in April 1952, but building work on the site, a former Second World War GCI station, did not begin until January 1953. The station became operational the following year, but by the end of 1958 it was closed as an air defence GCI radar, a casualty of the '1958' plan.

One consequence of the Second World War was the rapid post-war growth of civil aviation, particularly commercial aviation. This was due in part to the advances in airframes and engines made under pressure of war and also to the immense surplus of useful aircraft and trained pilots. With the skies filling with aircraft flying higher, and in other than VFR conditions, some organization of the skies was necessary, involving the establishment of airways, upper air routes and controlled airspace, and particularly of a system to control the crossing of predominantly east-west military traffic with north-south commercial traffic. Civil Air Traffic Control developed from the early 1950s, and in those early days it was little more than an offshoot of the military system. Most civil control centres were ex-military establishments, or had joint civil-military staffs. In March 1959 Hack Green became one such site, its old radars modified for UKATC service. The station was refitted with a Marconi 246 A/H radar in 1962 which sufficed for a few years, but by 1966 advances elsewhere had rendered Hack Green redundant and the station was closed down.

The site remained disused and abandoned for ten years; then, in 1976, it was purchased by the Home Office and plans were prepared for its conversion into a regional government bunker. Progress was somewhat desultory however, and physical building work did not begin until 1980. After four years work, which involved the complete remodelling of the interior of the bunker, reconstruction of the entrances, the provision of a new external emergency power station, and the expenditure of some £22 million, the bunker re-emerged in 1984 as RGHQ 10.2. Within ten years this role, too, became redundant and in 1994 Hack Green was offered for sale. It is now a cold war museum.

Hartland Point (Somerset)

Another of the west coast 'readiness' GCI stations and one of the few to be completed. Provided with an R8 'SECO' control building, the station was operated by RAF No. 405 Signals Unit from 1956 to 1970; thereafter its function was transformed and the station was redesignated RAF Hartland Point. The site is still active and secure. There is evidence of disused mounting plinths for six radars, including a T13 on the cliff edge.

Holmpton (Yorkshire)

A GCI station near the remote village of Patrington on the Spurn peninsula. The underground R3 operations centre opened in March 1953. Under the '1958' Plan, Holmpton became a Master Radar Station following the abolition of the Sector Operations Centres, reporting direct to the Air Defence Operations Centre. After closure in 1973, when the SLEWC facilities at Neatishead became operational, the radar equipment was removed, although the surface structures remain intact and the site used for RAF training. The underground areas are still in good condition, though unused. The site is scheduled for disposal in 2001.

Hope Cove

One of several GCI stations in the south-west provided with relatively lightly protected R6 two-level control bunkers, only the lower floor of which was partially below ground level. Even while final plans for its construction and fitting out were being made doubts were raised as to whether it could be afforded and whether it was really required operationally. Although scheduled for completion in August 1953 the building was still not completely fitted out by the following Spring. It would appear that the station was active for less than two years, between January 1956 and September 1957, after which it became, briefly, the RAF Fighter Control School. Thirteen months later the site was closed completely and relinquished by the RAF.

The Hope Cove bunker was immediately transferred to the Home Office for

7. **Hope Cove 'R6' Control Bunker.** This semi-underground bunker was built as a ROTOR GCI operations building but was later adapted as a Regional Seat of Government, and subsequently as a Regional Government Headquarters. Note the large concrete air duct at the left-hand end and the separate, single storey powerhouse. *Nick Catford*

conversion into a Regional Seat of Government (RSG7), which would control the south-west of England in event of nuclear war. The R6 building was not large enough to house the full RSG complement, so the Home Office extended and refurbished the old Second World War 'Happidrome' operations building that remained virtually intact a short distance from the bunker. This building was linked via a covered walkway to the original west entrance of the R6 building and was primarily used as domestic accommodation for the staff. A large new kitchen and dining room were added to the western end, while the older structure was adapted to provide sleeping accommodation. A new external power station was also built at this time.

After the last reorganization of emergency Regional Government in the 1980s the reduced staffing levels required at the bunker in its new guise as RGHQ 7.2 resulted in the abandonment of the happidrome. In 1989, in the quaint phraseology of the Home Office, 'enabling works, abandonment, and rationalization of services' were instituted, and the happidrome was demolished. The RGHQ was closed down rather quietly in the early 1990s and sold, still in excellent condition, in 2000. Most of the external ROTOR structures are long gone except for the derelict shell of the Type 80 modulator building which is now used as a fodder store.

Hopton (Norfolk)

A Chain Home Extra Low station with underground R2 operations bunker, completed in September 1952 but not handed over to the RAF until the following June as the result of a serious fire in the air-conditioning plant during commissioning tests. Long closed, the surface site was retained by the MoD until 1999. Access to the underground areas was sealed prior to disposal.

Inverbervie (Aberdeenshire)

Centimetric Early Warning station with underground R1 Control Centre. After the closure the underground bunker became the emergency wartime Armed Forces Headquarters for Scotland. Closed in 1993 and offered for public tender in 1997.

Kelvedon Hatch (Essex)

A typical, purpose-built underground R4 structure, differing from the otherwise similar control centres at Shipton and Bawburgh in that the access tunnel entered the lower floor of the bunker rather than the top because the bunker was built into a hillside. A standard ROTOR guardhouse protects the entrance passage, which slopes slightly uphill into the Operations Centre.

Before the ROC/UKWMO was provided with its own hardened bunker network in the early 1960s, their Sector Controls were usually co-located with the RAF Sectors to which they reported. As a matter of convenience (because of the existing Home Office presence), after closure in 1957 the Kelvedon Hatch SOC, along with several others, continued to function as a Royal Observer Corps Sector HQ until its transfer to the new ROC Group HQ bunker at Horsham.

In the meantime, however, the Home Office's retained interest in Kelvedon Hatch resulted, in 1962, in its selection as a Sub-Regional Control in the Emergency Regional Government organization, and later as the Regional Government Headquarters (RGHQ) for the London region. Details of this later incarnation can be found elsewhere in this volume.

8. **Inverbervie Former Rotor Control Room.** Following abandonment of the ROTOR radar system the underground bunker at Inverbervie was taken over by the U.S Navy for use as an oceanic monitoring station, and this view shows the control room reconstructed for that purpose. After 1978 the Americans moved out and the bunker became the British Army's standby emergency control centre for Scotland. *Nick Catford*

NO SMOKING

Kilchiaran (Islay)

One of eight ROTOR 3 stations, the Chain Home Extra Low radar at Kilchiaran, Islay, was opened in April 1956 on the site of a Second World War CHL station, and closed just four years later after a very short operational life. The control centre was housed in an above-ground R11 building, an un-hardened structure similar in layout to the underground R2 bunker. This, and many of the Second World War buildings, remain intact on the site which is now used as a BT microwave communications link.

Killard Point (County Down)

Western Approachess 'readiness' GCI station with surface R8 'SECO' control room, opened in December 1957. Scheduled as a Comprehensive Radar under the 1958 plan, Killard Point was to have been refitted with the Type 84 set from Bawdsey, but this plan was upset by the fire at Neatishead. Killard Point eventually took on a civilian ATC role under the name of Bishops Court radar.

Langtoft (Peterborough)

Located on the site of an earlier Second World War radar at Langtoft, near Peterborough, the ROTOR Ground Control Intercept station was opened in July 1953 and closed in 1958. The semi-underground, two-storey R6 building which, like those at Hack Green, Bolt Head and elsewhere, has the upper floor unprotected by any earth mounding, was sold in 1965 following several years under minimal care and maintenance. The building is now in commercial use and is in very poor condition.

Longley Lane (Preston)

Stations in the Western Sector were the last to be built and before construction was fully under way the ROTOR project had very much run out of steam. As with the Southern Sector HQ at Box, the Air Ministry elected on grounds of cost to utilize an existing structure for the SOC and chose the former Second World War Sector Operations Centre at Longley Lane, at Goosnargh near Preston. This site consisted of three semi-underground bunkers, an operations room, filter room and communications centre. The operations room was the largest of these and was the one adapted for ROTOR. After a slow start, the Longley Lane SOC had a limited operational capability because, due to the contraction of the later stages of ROTOR, few data sources fed into it. The centre closed in September 1957 and thereafter it was occupied and gradually extended by the Royal Observer Corps, becoming a pivotal element in that organization. The post-ROTOR history of this site is detailed elsewhere in this volume.

Murlough Bay

A 'Readiness' GCI station, it was intended that Murlough Bay should utilize a modified Second World War 'Happidrome' as a control room, but this plan was later abandoned in favour of a 'SECO' R8 structure. It is unlikely that the site was ever brought to operational standard.

Neatishead (Norfolk)

The GCI station at Neatishead was provided with a two-level R3 underground control bunker and was scheduled for opening in May 1953. Under the '1958' plan the Neatishead station was earmarked as a Comprehensive Radar, with Skendleby and Trimingham as its satellites. When the 1958 Plan resolved into 'Plan Ahead' the station was re-designated as one of five Radar Tracking Stations and a major reconstruction scheme was drawn up which mirrored that proposed for Bawburgh. National politics and worries over the cost of the project curtailed most of the on-going work associated with 'Plan Ahead' in 1960 and resulted in the abandonment of the proposed Bawburgh improvements. Work resumed at Neatishead, however, in 1962 under the umbrella of the LINESMAN/MEDIATOR plan and was expected to be complete within two years. This target was delayed by a serious fire in the unfinished underground bunker in 1966 and the structure was not ready for handover until 1968. Neatishead finally emerged in the early 1970s as a Radar Tracking Station equipped with both Type 84 and Type 85 radars. Since then the station has continued to develop and now, as one of two main Control and Reporting Centres (CRCs), controls all the UK airspace south of Newcastle. Neatishead also works closely with CRCs in Holland, Germany and France.

Portland

The underground R1 control room for the Portland CEW station was one of the earliest completed and probably the most spectacular. Major building works on the underground operations room were complete by the beginning of 1952, allowing installation of the air-conditioning and filtration plant to begin. Delays in delivery of the radar equipment, and more particularly of the antennae elements, retarded the commissioning date to July of the following year.

Portland was an early recipient of FPS-3 radar, which was to have been installed as an interim measure only, and a small powerhouse was built on the surface to house rotary converters to meet the particular power requirements of this American equipment. Building works had already been completed in preparation for the Kelvin Hughes horizontal projector and its associated processing equipment below the floor of the main operations room, but this was not installed because Portland was never supplied with the Type 80 radar that was supposed to have replaced FPS-3.

The Portland control bunker is a semi-submerged structure built in the bottom of the sixty-foot deep moat that surrounds the island's Verne prison. After completion of the concrete shell it was covered by a thirty-foot layer of rubble and earth, presumably bulldozed over the cliff-like edges of the moat. This area was later landscaped and separated from the rest of the moat by a high concrete wall. The presence of the underground bunker explains the apparent shallowness of the seaward end of the moat compared with the greater part of its length. Having constructed the main part of the bunker with such apparent economy, the most extraordinarily expensive mode of access was provided from the guardhouse which is located on high ground to the south of the moat.

The principal access is via an electric lift in a vertical shaft. The lift, which is

10. **RAF Portland.** The lower lift landing at the bottom of the seventy-foot vertical access shaft. *Author's collection*

9. **RAF Portland.** Decommissioned, abandoned and sealed up over forty years ago, the underground ROTOR operations room at Portland is the only surviving example of its type. *Nick Catford*

11. **RAF Portland (right).** The main entrance tunnel into the bunker, viewed from the bottom of the lift that descends from the entrance guardhouse. The main operations centre is to the right of the tunnel at the far end. *Author's collection*

12. **RAF Portland (below).** Air-conditioning plant in the underground bunker. This equipment maintained a reasonable working environment for the radar operators and provided cooling air for the valve-operated electronic apparatus. *Author's collection*

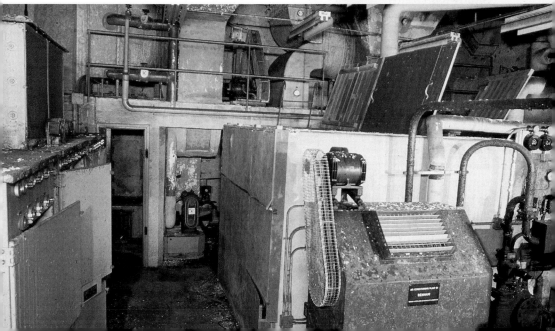

surrounded by a spiral steel stairway, descends for seventy feet; the lower landing opens onto the end of a steel ring-girdered tunnel some one hundred yards long that slopes gently to a further twenty feet in depth before turning through a series of dog-leg angles then a sharp right turn before entering the main central corridor of the bunker.

At the far end of the spine corridor another series of dog-legs leads to a second vertical shaft that doubles as a ventilation inlet and emergency escape route. A zig-zag steel stairway climbs this shaft to a small surface building near the cliff edge that also contains an electrical sub-station.

Whilst having the same internal layout, the surface guardhouse at Portland differs from the standard ROTOR bungalow in that it is curved in plan, flat-roofed and built in local stone. A small extension to the rear contains the lift-head gear.

Portland ROTOR, like its sisters at Cold Hesledon and Inverbervie, were downgraded to CHEL feeder status at an early stage and closed around 1958. The site was transferred to the Royal Navy, which established a radio station on the surface and latterly used the compound for police dog training. Although still MoD property, the site has been disused since 1998. The underground bunker remained unused, still in its pre-Type 80 state, following the demise of ROTOR and is remarkably unchanged despite some fire damage in the radar room caused by vandals in recent years. The main control room with its cramped balcony is still intact, as is the power supply room, the underground substation and the air-conditioning and filtration plants.

Prestatyn

A ROTOR 3 Chain Home Extra Low station built to protect the Western Approaches, with surface-built R11 control room, similar to underground R2 in layout. After closure the building was used for some time as a rifle range. Now semi-derelict but still standing on the hill above Prestatyn.

Sandwich (Kent)

Otherwise known as RAF Ash, the Sandwich GCI station was opened in May 1953 and the R3 underground control bunker became operational three months later. The lower floor of the bunker is completely underground while the top floor is only slightly below ground, the whole structure being covered by a sloping earth mound. Towards the end of the 1950s the original two-level operations room was altered by the addition of a suspended floor, to provide two operations rooms. By 1961 plans were under preparation for a major refit of the Sandwich station as a satellite radar as part of the LINESMAN/MEDIATOR plan. Its principal role would remain as a military GCI facility with ancillary functions including the reporting and estimation of surface shipping. This did not come about, however, and in 1962 the station was transferred to the Civil Aviation Authority and refitted with Marconi T264A radars for civilian ATC duties. At that time the CAA abandoned the underground control centre and greatly altered the access guardhouse.

The CAA relinquished ownership of Sandwich in 1986 and the site reverted to the Ministry of Defence. A major refurbishment was undertaken to convert the station into a reserve Sector Operations Centre for the new and highly flexible Improved United Kingdom Ground Environment air defence radar system, capable of absorbing the load of the recently completed South Sector Operations Centre at Neatishead. The R3 bunker was largely rebuilt at this time with a completely new entrance arrangement and an extensive new underground powerhouse and air-conditioning plant-room added.

The station was finally closed down in 1997 and is now a commercial high-security computer centre.

Saxa Vord

Construction of the ROTOR 3 station at Saxa Vord started in 1955 and it was hoped that the surface-built R10 control bunker (a semi-hardened structure similar in layout to the underground R1) would be ready, along with its associated Type 80 radar, during the early months of 1956. Completion was delayed by atrocious weather conditions during the winter of 1955/56, with consequences more akin to events along the Canadian North Warning Line than in the United Kingdom. In January the recently erected Type 80 scanner was torn off its mountings and thrown over fifty yards down a hillside by gusts of up to 177 mph, which was more than double the wind speed to which the system had been tested.

Since 1957 the Saxa Vord site has been administered jointly by NATO and the RAF, and remains a very active part of IUKADGE.

Scarnish (Inner Hebrides)

GCI station on Tiree, provided with surface R8 control bunker.

Shipton (Yorkshire)

The three-level R4 underground Sector Operations centre built at Shipton-by-Beningbrough in North Yorkshire was commissioned towards the end of 1954. Like the five other SOCs its operational life was short, having been rendered obsolete and redundant in 1960 by the partial implementation of the '1958' plan which saw the conversion of eight existing GCI stations into Master Radar Stations, thus usurping the role of the former SOCs.

Between 1966 and 1968 the redundant bunker was taken over by the Home Office for incorporation into the Regional Government organization as S-RC 21, one of two Sub-Regional Controls responsible for northern England. After nearly a decade of sporadic maintenance, the bunker was completely rebuilt and extended during a five-year refurbishment programme started in 1976 that included the building of an additional storey on the roof of the existing bunker. This new floor, which housed new standby generators and additional reserve water tanks, extended slightly above ground level and was covered with a large earth mound.

Following the end of Emergency Regional Government the Shipton bunker was once again without a role and was sold into the private sector in 1996.

Seaton Snook (Northumberland)

Ground Control Intercept station with underground, two-level R3 bunker, scheduled for completion in June 1953. Commissioned late, the station was only operational from 1956 until 1958. For many years after closure the site became the yard of a construction company. Underground areas are sealed and surface buildings derelict.

Skendleby (Lincolnshire)

Located near the Lincolnshire village of Spilsby, one mile north-west of Skendleby, the site has was first developed as a radar station in 1941. The underground R3 GCI operations room was opened in 1953 and became redundant little more than five years later. The bunker is now easily discernible by the four prominent ventilation towers rising from the mound over the new plant room extension, and by the typical ROTOR guardhouse that remains intact above the entrance tunnel.

Between 1966 and 1968 the bunker was acquired by the Home Office and it was refitted to function as S-RC 3.1, one of two regional government emergency bunkers that would control the North Midlands in time of war. In 1985 the bunker was considerable rebuilt and upgraded to become Regional Government Headquarters 3.1. Major structural alterations were undertaken, including the insertion of an additional floor in the lower level, made possible by the removal of overhead ventilation ductwork and of the false floors which made available several feet of headroom previously taken up by cable ducts. The overhead cover was partially removed to enable the construction of a new upper level incorporating a plant room with two diesel generators; next to this is an enclosed water storage tank. This fourth floor was only partially underground, the exposed section being heavily mounded with soil.

The modernized internal arrangement of the lower floors bears no relationship to the original ROTOR layout, except that the air-conditioning plant room on the bottom floor is still in the original position, although the plant all dates from 1985 and is similar to that installed in the Chilmark RGHQ. Similarly, the kitchen and dining equipment in the middle floor domestic area is very much like that at Chilmark.

The Skendleby bunker was offered for sale in 1995 and is now in private hands.

Snaefell (Isle of Man)

A Chain Home Extra Low station commissioned under the ROTOR 3 plan. Target completion date for the R11 surface control room was April 1956, but there is no record of whether this was achieved or if the station ever attained full operational status. The site now houses a motorcycle museum.

Sopley (Hampshire)

A two-level, underground R3 control bunker scheduled for completion in April 1953 but completed late the following year. Although at first allocated as a GCI satellite to Wartling, Sopley, like the station at Hack Green, was a casualty of the '1958' plan but survived under similar circumstances for a further fifteen years.

After the end of ROTOR Sopley maintained two roles: between 1957 and 1965 as an ATC Training Unit (the Joint Air Traffic Control School), and as the home, from 1966, of the combined civil/military Southern Radar Control Centre. An air defence function remained, together with special tasks including the support of development flying from Farnborough and Boscombe Down research units.

Sopley closed in 1974 primarily as a result of the opening of the centralized ATC centre at West Drayton in March of that year.

By the end of the decade the underground control bunker was under Army control, having been adapted as the Emergency War Headquarters for UK Land Forces Command. For this role the bunker accommodated a staff of 100, with domestic facilities sufficient to maintain operations in 'shut-down' conditions for two weeks. The United Kingdom National Military Command Centre was located on the bottom floor together with the air-filtration and conditioning systems. The upper floor contained offices, dormitories and dining rooms, etc.

Land Forces vacated Sopley in 1988/9 and transferred to Corsham where plans were prepared but never implemented to lodge the headquarters in underground accommodation formerly occupied by the central government nuclear reporting cell.

The Sopley bunker was sold to a private purchaser in the early 1990s and is currently a high security store operated by BDM Logistics.

St Anne's (Blackpool)

The GCI station at St Anne's, near Blackpool, was scheduled for opening in November 1953 but the inevitable technical problems delayed this by several months. For financial reasons, and because of its relatively less vulnerable location, St Anne's was provided with a non-blast proof surface control room consisting of a large 'SECO' prefabricated hut.

By 1962 the station was fitted with Marconi 264A radars and took on an increasingly civilian role under the modified LINESMAN/MEDIATOR programme. Subsequently St Anne's was absorbed by the National Air Traffic Service.

St Margaret's (Kent)

The underground R1 bunker at the St Margaret's CEW station near Dover opened in November 1953 and was decommissioned in 1960. St Margaret's was chosen by default as the first station to be fitted with American FPS-3 radar as an interim measure in March 1953, despite the fact that the control equipment had to be housed in a temporary surface hut until the R1 was completed. Maintenance of the apparently disused site continued for over twenty years until 1982 when all the surface buildings were demolished, except for the guardhouse which was converted into a private home, and the bunker sealed.

St Twynell's (Milford Haven)

A semi-underground two-storey R6 GCI bunker, built in 1953 on a Second World War Chain Home Low radar side near Milford Haven. The control bunker, the brick-built radar transmitter building and the radar plinths remain though now in poor condition and used for agricultural purposes.

Treleaver (Cornwall)

A Ground Control Intercept station with two-level semi-underground R6 bunker, scheduled for completion September 1953, fully operational by 1956, and closed just two years later. After closure the site was purchased by the owner of the surrounding land and all the remaining buildings on site, including the R6, the Type 80 modulator building, and five radar plinths, are used for agricultural purposes. The R6 bunker is now an empty shell and has a large opening cut in its rear wall to allow the entry of farm vehicles.

Trewan Sands (Cornwall)

GCI 'readiness' station with R8 'SECO' surface control room. Scheduled for completion in October 1953. Work was still under way on this site in the autumn of that year, but construction was halted and the site deleted from the ROTOR programme before it was completed.

Trimingham (Norfolk)

The Trimingham ROTOR site has had a chequered history. Scheduled for completion in November 1952, the underground R1 operations building was finally finished late the following year although the electronic equipment had yet to be installed. Trimingham was selected as the first of the ROTOR stations to be equipped with Type 80 radar, which was assembled during the summer of 1954 and commissioned in April 1955.

By 1965 the Trimingham radars had fallen into disuse and by the end of the decade all the radar equipment had been dismantled, although the plinths that supported the rotating heads and the shell of the Type 80 transmitter building still survived. At that time or shortly after much of the surface land was sold and the guardhouse converted into a private residence.

During the 1980s revamp of the UK passive air defences, Trimingham was restored as an active site: land was re-acquired, new fences erected and the guardhouse largely remodelled to provide a two-storey administrative centre for the Type 91 '*Martello*' mobile radar that was stationed there on a semi-static basis. In 1996 the '*Martello*' equipment was replaced by a Plessey Type 93 static radar.

The underground control room has not been used since the early 1960s although it is still accessible to MoD staff.

Truleigh Hill

Construction of the underground R2 CHEL operations centre at Truleigh Hill, on the site of an earlier Second World War radar station, was completed in August 1952 and the station became operational a few months later. Following a working life of less than four years the Truleigh Hill radar was closed down in 1957 and the site sold in 1965.

The underground area was used for some years as a secure document storage facility, but is now disused, although still in reasonable condition. The surface compound is a privately run radio communications technical site.

Uig (Scotland)

A ROTOR 3 Centimetric Early Warning radar station with surface R10 bunker (similar in layout to underground R1). The site was designated as an 'operational readiness' station, not necessarily equipped with its full radar complement, but cabled in preparation. In latter years the site was home to an RAF Signals Unit, but its current status is unknown.

Ventnor

Located on Boniface Down on the Isle of Wight, Ventnor was a Chain Early Warning station with an underground R1 operations block, completed in November 1952 and commissioned in the spring of the following year. Following the demise of the ROTOR programme the Ventnor site was passed to the Civil Aviation Authority. For some years the underground areas were leased to the Isle of Wight Council, who held it as its standby emergency bunker, but it is unlikely that it was ever properly fitted out. The site reverted to the CAA for a couple of years and in 1991 the entrances to the bunker were sealed and the guardhouse demolished.

Wartling (East Sussex)

The GCI radar at Wartling was expected to be ready for operations from the underground R3 control room in April 1953, but technical problems delayed this by some eighteen months.

Sold in 1964, the guardhouse bungalow is now a private residence and the bunker below is derelict.

13. **Wartling Rotor Station.** The derelict remains of a Kelvin Hughes projector in its pit below the operations room floor in the underground control bunker. Unfortunately all the flooring in this bunker has been removed but its original level can readily be seen. *Nick Catford*

West Myne (North Somerset)

ROTOR 3 Chain Home Extra Low station built on the cliff edge on high land near Selworthy Beacon, west of Minehead in Somerset. The original plan called for an R11 surface control room at West Myne, but due to the scenically sensitive nature of Selworthy Beacon the actions of a number of pressure groups persuaded the Air Ministry to design a special, non-standard building for this station. This may not have been built, however, and there is evidence to suggest that West Myne was only ever used as a mobile site. There is little evidence on the ground of any substantive structures, other than a metalled roadway that crosses a field and ends nowhere, and a few concrete bases for buildings long demolished.

THE ANTI-AIRCRAFT OPERATIONS ROOMS

Early post-war ADGB planning envisaged an integrated system of air defence in which radar-controlled aerial interception of enemy aircraft was supported at local level by point-defence anti-aircraft gun batteries, also targeted with radar assistance. The futility of point-defence against the hydrogen bomb was soon realized, and by 1955 anti-aircraft gunnery had ceased to figure in the nuclear war plans.

Between 1950 and 1955, however, plans had been implemented to provide gunnery cover for some thirty-two strategically important districts, nominated 'Gun Defended Areas' (GDA)s. The nominated GDAs were broadly similar to those of the Second World War and included the large industrial and administrative cities (London, Birmingham, Manchester, etc); important naval and commercial docks and ports (Tyne, Tees, Liverpool, Portsmouth, etc), and strategically important military installations. Each area would be provided with a hardened central operations room that would control about half a dozen remote gun-sites within a radius of thirty miles or so, each equipped with batteries of automated 5.25" AA guns. In many areas existing Second World War

14. **Typical 1950s Anti-Aircraft Operations Room.** This example, at Ullenwood near Gloucester, controlled the guns of the Gloucester Gun Defended Area until decommissioned in 1954. Subsequently it has seen use as a Sub-Regional Control and as a local authority bunker. *Nick Catford*

15. **Ullenwood Anti-Aircraft Operations Room.** A view of the main operations room. Note the original curved perspex panels on the mezzanine viewing balcony. *Nick Catford*

gun-sites were re-used, as these locations had been specifically protected against development in post-war local authority regeneration schemes.

The Anti-Aircraft Operations Rooms (AAORs) were built to a standard design that bore a striking resemblance to all the other supposedly blast- and radiation-proof structures that appeared across Britain in the first wave of atomic-bomb-proof bunker building in the early 1950s. Constructed in reinforced concrete with walls two feet thick, the two-level bunkers were monolithic, windowless hulks about eighty feet square with blast-proof steel doors at the front and smaller emergency exits protected by blast doors at the rear. The only external features were two grilles protected by steel plates attached to the walls for power-house ventilation, an air intake above the air-filter room for main bunker ventilation, and a small chimney from the central heating furnace. Inside, the bulk of the space was taken up by a large two-storey operations well, typical of all Service operations rooms, with a balcony around three sides. This balcony was partitioned into offices and fitted with curved perspex glazing that gave an unobstructed view of the plotting table below. On each floor corridors ran around the external wall of the operations room giving access to the various offices. A small power-house on the bottom floor provided emergency electricity supply, while an adjacent room contained the ventilation plant. Some bunkers were provided with full, refrigerated air-conditioning, while others had simple forced-air ventilation. Rooms on the lower floor to the rear of the operations well housed radio communications and GPO telecommunications equipment. The upper floor housed sundry offices and a small canteen.

The major deviations from the standard design were determined by local topography. Normally the bunkers were constructed with the lower floor completely below ground and with both the main entrance and rear emergency exit on the exposed upper floor. In some locations, where perhaps the bunker has been built into a hillside, the entrance or exit may be on the lower floor. In four GDAs existing semi-hardened or fortified structures were adapted for use as AAORs. Amongst these is the Fort Fareham bunker which controlled guns in the Portsmouth and Southampton area. Here the operations room was arranged within a casemate of the old fort at the northern end of the barrack block.

Principally because the life span of the post-war Anti-Aircraft organization was so short, and that of the hardened bunkers even shorter (the Lansdown bunker, which controlled the Bristol guns, for example, was built in 1954 and vacated by AA Command in 1955), documentation regarding their construction and operation is sparse. It is not even certain that all the control rooms were completed by 1955, as construction was very much dependent upon a schedule of priority and available financial resources. Building of the more strategically important bunkers was complete by 1951, but thereafter the impetus of the programme declined.

After the dissolution of Anti-Aircraft Command in 1955 all the bunkers became redundant. By 1962 many had found new uses in the Civil Defence sphere, but many were simply abandoned. The following table lists the proposed locations and describes the current status of the AAOR's where this is known:

Barrow-in-Furness
Adapted as a Civil Defence Corps HQ in 1956 following the demise of AA Command. After 1968 the bunker was disused for several years until Barrow District Council took it over as its emergency headquarters; it was substantially upgraded in 1984.

Birkenshaw (Leeds)
The Leeds GDA bunker at Birkenshaw has been occupied as a Fire Brigade HQ since the early 1980s.

Brompton Road
During the Second World War two vertical lift shafts that gave access to the disused Brompton Road tube station were adapted as Anti-Aircraft Command 'Citadels' to control the guns of the Central London GDA. In the early 1950s the shafts, and parts of the original underground station, were upgraded to maintain the same function in the Atomic age. Floors were inserted in the shafts at vertical intervals and the lower of these floors was arranged as a conventional operations room, while new offices built on the original underground station platforms were used as communications and briefing rooms, etc.

The underground areas, now disused and abandoned, have reverted to London Underground, although the Ministry of Defence have retained the shaft head buildings.

Cardiff (Wenallt)
Until 1992 the Wenallt bunker was the British Telecom wartime emergency control centre for Wales. The building was considerably altered internally to fulfil

that role, and evidence of the extensive air-conditioning system that was installed at that time is still visible on the external elevation.

Conisbrough
Briefly an S-RC for the North-East region, this bunker, which controlled guns in the Sheffield area, has been abandoned and derelict for many years.

Craigiehall
During the 1980s the Forth GDA operations room at Craigiehall was the Armed Forces Emergency HQ for Scotland.

Dover
The Dover AAOR was housed in a section of 'Dumpy', the tunnel system below Dover castle.

East Kilbride (Torrance House)
Located in the grounds of Torrance House, now the Calderglen Country Park, the Clyde GDA operations room was reincarnated in 1961 as the Scottish western zone Regional Seat of Government. This function continued in different guises until 1983 when the Scottish east and west zones were merged and the headquarters transferred to the former Eastern Zone bunker at Kirknewton.

During this period an additional entrance was added and internally the operations well was floored over to increase the available floor space, and partitioned to provide additional office space. While disused in the early 1990s the AAOR was badly damaged by fire and is now used for rough storage by the Country Park.

Elvaston
Built to protect the industrial area of Derby, the Elvaston AAOR is now abandoned. There are substantial remains of an Anti-Aircraft gun battery close by.

Fort Bridgewood
Established on the site of a Victorian coastal defence battery, the Fort Bridgewood AAOR near Rochester controlled the guns protecting the naval dockyards of the Medway estuary. By 1960 the bunker had passed to the Civil Defence Corps who used it as a protected headquarters until stand-down. In 1975 the bunker was sold to a property developer and subsequently demolished. No trace now remains.

Fort Fareham
The AAOR at Fort Fareham was unusual in that it was an earlier building adapted for the role, rather than purpose-built. The control room was incorporated in an existing casemate at the northern end of the fort's barrack block. Currently disused, the site will is offered to let for light industrial use. The Fareham Borough Council emergency bunker formerly occupied an adjacent part of the fort.

Frodsham (Cheshire)

The Frodsham AAOR is one of the more interesting of the 1950s gun control rooms, as the location was chosen for experiments with a new tactical gun control radar known as 'Orange Yeoman', or Type 82. Before the system could be put into practice AA Command and the GDAs were abandoned, but the Type 82 radar remained at Frodsham for a further four years and the site maintained as a training establishment, principally in the use of Orange Yeoman with surface-to-air guided weapons. This facility was closed down at the end of 1959 and just over a year later the bunker was purchased by Cheshire County Council, initially as a Civil Defence Control for the Northwich area, and later as a County Emergency War Headquarters. Today the bunker still acts as the County Emergency Planning Centre.

Gaerloch

This remote bunker was acquired by the Highland Council for use as a standby for its main War Headquarters at Inverness. Considerable internal alterations were done to the front section of the bunker when it was adapted as a highways maintenance depot. No work was undertaken to convert it for the emergency role until 1988, when several rooms at the rear of the building were adapted and secured from the rest of the structure by blast doors.

Lansdown (Bath)

Construction of the Lansdown AAOR, which stands on the site of an earlier, Second World War gun battery on a ridge to the north-east of Bath with views across Bristol, Gloucestershire and the Severn estuary into Wales, was not completed until 1954.

After closure the following year the bunker remained disused until 1959 when it became the Royal Observer Corps No. 12 Group Headquarters. Discreet additions were made to the building by the Home Office in the early 1980s to house an additional plant room and filter room. Since 1992 the bunker and an

16. **Lansdown AAOR.** The railing around the roof is an ROC addition, its function being to protect ROC personnel inspecting monitoring equipment fitted to the roof of the bunker. *Author's collection*

17. **Lansdown AAOR.** This former AAOR was taken over by the ROC in 1959 and following the demise of that organization in 1992 it became the training HQ for Avon Fire Brigade. This photograph of the control room was taken during the Fire Brigade's tenure. Note the truncated balcony with the glazing removed, this is a feature of the 1959 ROC reconstruction. *Author's collection*

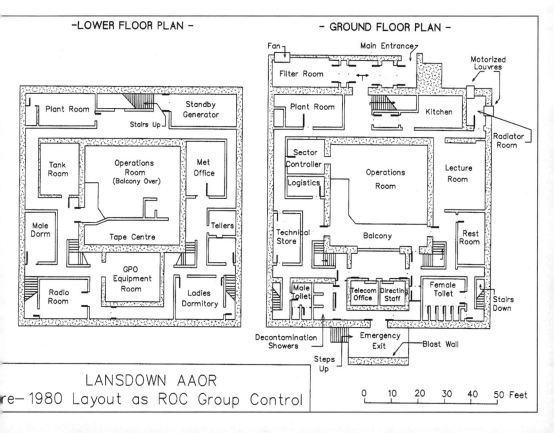

– LOWER FLOOR PLAN –

Plant Room
Standby Generator
Stairs Up
Tank Room
Operations Room (Balcony Over)
Met Office
Male Dorm
Tape Centre
Tellers
GPO Equipment Room
Radio Room
Ladies Dormitory

– GROUND FLOOR PLAN –

Fan
Main Entrance
Motorized Louvres
Filter Room
Plant Room
Kitchen
Radiator Room
Sector Controller
Logistics
Operations Room
Lecture Room
Technical Store
Balcony
Rest Room
Male Toilet
Telecom Office
Directing Staff
Female Toilet
Stairs Down
Decontamination Showers
Emergency Exit
Blast Wall
Steps Up

LANSDOWN AAOR
re— 1980 Layout as ROC Group Control

0   10   20   30   40   50 Feet

adjoining surface office complex have been owned by Avon Fire Brigade, who use it as their emergency services headquarters.

Lippit's Hill

Opened in 1953, the Lippit's Hill bunker controlled the guns of the London (North) GDA from its location just south of Epping Forest. After a short period of disuse, the bunker was acquired by the Metropolitan Police and converted into their North London Emergency War Headquarters in 1962.

When emergency war planning was wound up in 1989 the Lippit's Hill bunker was retained by the Home Office who now use it, and the surrounding land, as the National Police Training Centre. The bunker itself is used mainly for storage and is little changed internally from its earliest days, retaining many of the original features including the ventilation plant and the striking curved perspex windows overlooking the operations well.

Lisburn (Belfast)

The Belfast AAOR at Lisburn was, like the Lansdown bunker near Bath, taken over by the UKWMO, but not until 1963. It is now apparently disused.

Manchester

Situated in Middle Wood, Worsley, to the west of Manchester, this AAOR, which controlled the guns of the Manchester GDA, is set in a lightly sloping hillside and is thus constructed with most of both floors above ground level. The main entrance is on the lower floor but the emergency rear entrance is on the upper floor. Recently used as a short indoor shooting range, the bunker is now abandoned.

Merstham (Surrey)

The history of the South London AAOR at Merstham following the disbanding of Anti-Aircraft Command closely mirrors that of the North London bunker at Lippit's Hill. Acquired by the Home Office in 1962, the building was designated as the Metropolitan Police Southern War Room and retained that function until 1989. The Metropolitan Police maintained the site on care and maintenance for a further two years but in 1991 it was decommissioned and all the equipment removed. The bunker, which stood on a site close to Junction 8 on the M23, was recently scheduled for demolition.

Mistley (Essex)

The AAOR at Mistley, near Colchester in Essex, was built to control the guns of the Harwich GDA. In the early 1960s the bunker was taken over by the Essex Civil Defence Corps as a hardened control centre and in 1963 it became the Essex County standby emergency centre but was never properly fitted out. The property was sold in 1993 and three years later opened as a tourist attraction.

Pembroke

The AAOR that controlled the guns of the Pembroke Docks GDA was built in a converted gunpowder magazine within Llanion Barracks, Pembroke.

Plymouth

The AAOR for the Plymouth GDR is incorporated into Crown Hill Fort.

Swansea (West Cross)

One of the few AAORs to be built completely above ground with the entrance on the lower floor, the West Cross bunker became the West Glamorgan County War Headquarters in the mid-1960s. As a result of the 1986 local government reorganization, ownership was transferred to the City & County of Swansea Authority, who still use the bunker on a reduced scale. Although the operations well remains, complete with most of its curved perspex screens, the internal arrangement of the other rooms has been considerably rationalized. A new standby generator was installed in recent years after the original diesel engine suffered irreparable accidental damage.

Teeside

The AAOR, which is situated in Gosforth Park, was acquired for use as a county records repository in the early 1960s.

Tyneside

The Tyneside AAOR was near Kirklevington Hall, south of Middlesbrough, and has been converted into a private residence.

Ullenwood (Gloucester)

The AAOR at Ullenwood, which is situated to the north of the A436 between Gloucester and Cheltenham, controlled the guns of the Gloucester GDA. Like many of the former AAORs, the bunker passed to the County Civil Defence Corps in the late 1950s and briefly became a Group Headquarters in the southern region. By 1962 it had become the region's northern Sub-Regional Control (S-RC), sharing responsibility for the wartime government of south-west England with the Bolt Head bunker in Devon. As the Home Office regional government plans evolved Ullenwood was transformed successively into a Sub-Regional Headquarters and then a Regional Government Headquarters, relinquishing this role in 1985 when the new RGHQ at Chilmark was commissioned.

Abandoned by the Home Office, the bunker reverted to the local authority and acted for some years as the County Main Emergency Headquarters. With the end of local government war planning Ullenwood's role diminished, like so many cold war bunkers, to that of a mere storage facility, currently for counterfeit goods seized by the Trading Standards Authority.

Vange (Essex)

Located at Marsh Farm, Basildon, the Vange AAOR controlled seven gun sites that protected the North Thames GDA. An earlier, brick-built Second World War operations room stands derelict nearby. After a very short period as a Civil Defence Corps Centre soon after the stand-down of Anti-Aircraft Command in 1955, the bunker site was returned to the landowner from whom it was compulsorily purchased and was left derelict for many years. Proposals to restore the building as a local authority control, made at the height of the Thatcher bunker-building frenzy, came to nothing. Now in rather poor internal condition, though secure, the process of decay has been accelerated in recent years by the activities of paintball gamers.

Wawne (Humberside)
The Wawne AAOR controlled the guns of the Humberside GDA between 1952 and 1955. As with many of these bunkers that became redundant during the early atomic years, it was for a while used by the Civil Defence Corps until evolving into a true local authority wartime emergency control centre. This was a natural progression as the County Councils were, essentially, sponsors of the Civil Defence Corps and took over responsibility for Home Defence when the Corps was disbanded in 1968. The Wawne bunker became, first, the County Control for the East Riding of York and later the Humberside control until 1992. In recent years it has been used as a police training centre but is now empty and threatened with demolition.

Weymouth
The guns of the Portland GDA were controlled from a hardened AAOR high on the top of Ridgeway Hill north of Weymouth, above the railway tunnel and east of the A354. The bunker would have commanded panoramic views of Weymouth Bay, Chesil Beach, and the coastline for many miles in each direction, were it not for the fact that it is hidden at the bottom of an old chalk quarry and only its tall aerial mast nearby gives away its location.

After the demise of Anti-Aircraft Command the Operations Room was taken over by the Admiralty for use as a map, chart and aerial photograph library. The guardhouse is now the obvious clue to its location and may date from the Navy's period of tenure. The whole site is now privately owned; the guardhouse is a residential bungalow and the bunker appears to be in externally good order.

Wylde Green (West Midlands)
Construction of the Wylde Green AAOR in St Bernard's Rd, Sutton Coldfield, which was responsible for the Birmingham GDA, was completed in 1954, just in time for it to be declared redundant the following year. For the rest of the 1950s it was occupied in a desultory way by the Territorial Army, but in 1962 it found a new and prolonged lease of life as the Warwick County Council Civil Defence Headquarters and later as the county wartime emergency control bunker. Following the local authority reorganization of 1974 it was transferred to West Midlands Council and in 1986 to West Midlands Fire and Civil Defence Authority. Shortly after disposal in 2000 the building was demolished.

7

THE ROYAL OBSERVER CORPS AND UKWMO

Following the end of the Second World War the Royal Observer Corps, traditionally the eyes and ears of the RAF, was stood down on 12 May 1945. Throughout the war members of the Corps spent many long and fruitless hours listening for the sound of approaching German aircraft, at first unaided and then, in the south-east approach to London, with the help of great parabolic concrete sound mirrors, and later still with more sophisticated electronic listening devices. Sightings were transmitted by telephone from the remote Observer Posts to Group and Sector controls where they were co-ordinated with plots from the rudimentary early-warning radar system to give some degree of advanced warning of enemy attack.

Less than two months after stand-down, on 7 July 1945, the Chiefs of Staff Committee identified a continuing requirement for an Observer Corps, in modified form, to fulfil the conventional early warning role until a viable electronic network could be established. The re-formed Corps would later be required to augment the new radar control and reporting system. The COS paper recommended that:

> The raid reporting and control organization should contain means for the detection and recognition by ground observers. In the composition of the forces for the Air Defence of Great Britain there should be included the Royal Observer Corps, or a similar ground observer organization.

It was a further fifteen months, however, before this requirement was addressed, and eighteen months before active training of the new organization began in January 1947. With a largely undefined enemy, little equipment other than outdated remnants from the recent war, and subject to similarly outdated operational concepts from the same conflict, the ROC was ill prepared for its future task. In the larger sphere, too, its role was to be constrained by material shortages: most of the radar stations and control centres to which it previously reported were either dismantled or in terminal decay and there were few fighter squadrons remaining that could respond to its warnings. The Russian threat was largely ignored until the Berlin crisis of 1948 brought the ideological issues to prominence, and brought the B39s of the American 3rd Air Division back to the United Kingdom.

Awakening fears of Russian aggression stimulated the Chiefs of Staff to hesitant action as the 1940s drew to a close. Whereas the Defence White Papers of 1946 and 1947 proposed little more than a steady-as-she-goes policy, in 1949, against the background of Berlin and its sinister potential consequences, the Air Council approved the short-term-plan for improving the Air Defence of Great Britain. This scheme, which in many ways was technologically obsolete even before it was implemented, eventually emerged in the early 1950s as the ROTOR radar system. For the critical three years between 1949 and 1952, during which the first tangible steps were taken to refurbish Britain's ageing south and east coast radar defences, the role of the ROC became pivotal, despite its limited resources.

As the first ROTOR stations came into service it became obvious that closer integration of the ROC and the RAF control and reporting system was necessary, and on 20 February 1950 the Observer Corps was placed under the operational control of HQ Fighter Command. ROC Groups were allocated to each of the existing RAF Sectors:

METROPOLITAN SECTOR	
Group	
1	Maidstone
2	Horsham
17	Watford
18	Colchester
19	Beckenham

SOUTHERN SECTOR	
Group	
3	Winchester
4	Oxford
20	Truro
21	Exeter
22	Yeovil
23	Bristol
24	Gloucester
25	Cardiff
28/1	Carmarthen

WESTERN SECTOR	
Group	
7	Manchester
26	Wrexham
27	Shrewsbury
28/2	Caernarvon
29	Lancaster
32	Carlisle
33	Ayr

NORTHERN SECTOR	
Group	
8	Leeds
9 & 10	York
30	Durham

EASTERN SECTOR	
Group	
5	Coventry
6	Derby
11	Lincoln
12	Bedford
14	Bury St. Edmunds
15	Cambridge
16	Norwich

SCOTTISH SECTOR	
Group	
31	Edinburgh
34	Glasgow
35	Oban
36	Dunfermline
37	Dundee
38	Aberdeen
39	Inverness

These far from satisfactory arrangements were, however, based upon pre-war ADGB assumptions about the nature of enemy air attack, modified only to take account of the enhanced quantitative but not qualitative frightfulness of the atomic bomb. Ground observers armed with binoculars and crackling telephones were still the order of the day, and for the most part the motley collection of existing wartime headquarters, plotting rooms and observer posts were again pressed into action.

By the end of 1953 much of the ROTOR plan was operational and, although deeply flawed and already obsolescent, its inception proved to be a major turning point in Britain's early-warning defences. Sadly, the limited foresight that had historically characterized the British defence establishment still held sway in Whitehall and, despite the evidence available since 1948, the impact of high-speed jet aircraft and fast, high-altitude bombers upon the radar reporting system was yet to be fully appreciated. Although quite comprehensive plans were prepared and implemented for the future deployment of the Royal Observer Corps, these plans were essentially based upon a Second World War scenario of conventional warfare rather than the Third World War nightmare of total nuclear war.

Gradually the Group Headquarters were upgraded and the national network of Observer Corps field posts was rationalized and improved. Over 400 of those constructed hurriedly in the heat of war were re-sited to more suitable locations and rebuilt using standardized pre-fabricated concrete panels and sections. These 'Orlit' posts were generally built at ground level, but where required by local conditions they could be erected on six-foot-high concrete stilts. By the end of 1954, when the construction programme was completed, a further ninety-three 'Orlit' posts had been built in completely new locations. The winter of 1954 saw all six new ROTOR Sector Operations Centres (SOCs) operational and the entire ADGB and ROC organization restructured around these centres. The following table shows the reporting headquarters organization in the form that was to remain virtually unchanged from 1954 until 1963:

METROPOLITAN SECTOR
ROTOR SOC: Kelvedon Hatch

ROC Group	Group Headquarters
1	Beckenham
2	Horsham
4	Colchester
5	Watford

SOUTHERN SECTOR
ROTOR SOC: Brown's Quarry, Box

ROC Group	Group Headquarters
3	Oxford
9	Yeovil
12	Bristol
14	Winchester

EASTERN SECTOR
ROTOR SOC: Bawburgh

ROC Group	Group Headquarters
6	Norwich
7	Bedford
15	Lincoln

NORTHERN SECTOR
ROTOR SOC: Shipton

ROC Group	Group Headquarters
18	Leeds
20	York
23	Durham

WESTERN SECTOR
ROTOR SOC: Longley Lane, Preston

ROC Group	Group Headquarters
8	Coventry
16	Shrewsbury
19	Manchester
21	Lancaster
22	Carlisle

CALEDONIAN SECTOR
ROTOR SOC: Barnton Quarry, Edinburgh

ROC Group	Group Headquarters
24	Edinburgh
25	Ayr
26	Glasgow
27	Oban
28	Dundee
29	Aberdeen

No sooner had these arrangements been finalized than the whole system was thrown into disarray by the results of the Bikini Atoll atomic bomb tests, which had begun in March 1954 and were to end in 1958. These tests confirmed the suspected but hitherto largely disregarded consequences of nuclear fallout. The tests indicated that the blast effect of an atomic detonation was in many ways the lesser evil and that many thousands more would die slowly and horribly from the secondary effects, irradiated by lethal looming clouds of radioactive fallout drifting at the whim of the weather for tens or even hundreds of miles beyond the point of detonation. But at least those not evaporated at ground-zero or incinerated by the initial heat wave, could maintain some hope of survival if given sufficient warning. And henceforth *WARNING* became the keynote and the concept of evacuation was abandoned, with every town or city in the Kingdom, and even the remotest rural valley, equally likely to be cast in the shadow of the nuclear cloud. Nowhere was safe. The stark reality was, in the phraseology of the time, that 'if you're in the crater, you're in the crater,' but if you were not, then survival was feasible if accurate warning and prediction of fallout patterns enabled you to take adequate and timely shelter.

Government reaction to this sinister revelation was surprisingly rapid. In March 1954 meetings were arranged by the Chief of the Air Staff, Sir William

Dickson, and Sir Sidney Kirman, Director General of Civil Defence, to set up a discussion group comprising representatives of the Home Office, the Air Ministry, and RAF Fighter Command to look into the establishment of a joint fallout-reporting organization. Initially it was supposed that the new, government-sponsored but local-authority-administered Civil Defence Corps would undertake the reporting role, but this proposal met with opposition from the RAF and the Home Office. It was argued, quite rightly, that while the Civil Defence Corps was currently fighting a lost battle to establish a role and identity in the new world of atomic warfare, the existing Royal Observer Corps had not only a long history of expertise in a reporting role very similar to that which was now required, but also already maintained much of the infrastructure to support that role. The existence of a network of private ROC telephone lines and the fact that there already existed within the RAF Sector and Group Controls an experienced ROC staff lent weight to this argument. Detailed arrangements were left in the hands of R.F. Firth, Assistant Secretary to J3 Dept of the Home Office. Firth and his team at first expected that fallout reporting would remain a secondary function to the traditional role of aircraft reporting, but increasing awareness of the fallout threat quickly changed these priorities and by the beginning of 1956 the Home Office was pressing for fully hardened and radiation-proof accommodation for the ROC. The cost of this capital programme would, though, be a burden upon the RAF budget which was already stretched by the development costs of the V-bomber force, the ill-fated Blue Streak missile programme, ROTOR, new interceptors for Fighter Command and a host of secret nuclear weapons developments. The most that could be offered was an agreement to restore the wartime Warning Siren system and an increase in the total number of sirens to 6,000, the majority of which would be remotely controlled.

In the background the assumptions upon which future developments depended were changing more quickly, although neither the money nor the political will to implement these ideological developments were immediately forthcoming. By the spring of 1956 it was accepted that ROTOR was already obsolete; substantive work on the BMEWS was less than a year away and in April the first major Home Office fallout exercise, codenamed 'CLOVERLEAF', was conducted. Significantly, the ROC fallout reporting function was paramount in this exercise and the aircraft reporting role reduced to local, low-level activity only.

In May the first detailed plans for the soon to be ubiquitous ROC underground observation posts were finalised and the first prototype was completed at Farnham in September 1956. The prototype pattern was so successful that subsequently 1,559 similar posts were built with only minimal alteration to the original design, at a cost of approximately £1,250 each, equivalent at the time to the price of a modest terraced house. Observation posts were built approximately eight miles apart in a grid pattern that covered the whole country more or less evenly. Each four-man bunker consisted of a rectangular concrete box, approximately twenty foot long, seven foot wide and seven foot high internally, divided into two chambers, with concrete walls and

18. **ROC Underground Observation Post.** The large concrete block to the left is the entrance hatch, with a smaller ventilation shaft to the right. Note the large cylindrical 'Shadowgraph' ground zero indicator attached to the entrance hatch. *Nick Catford*

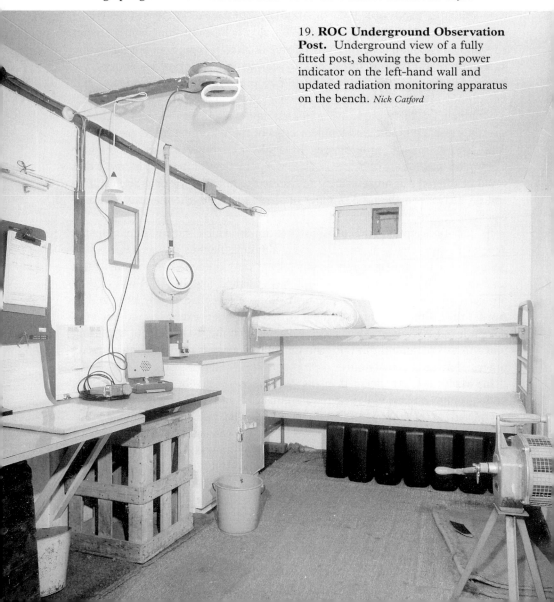

19. **ROC Underground Observation Post.** Underground view of a fully fitted post, showing the bomb power indicator on the left-hand wall and updated radiation monitoring apparatus on the bench. *Nick Catford*

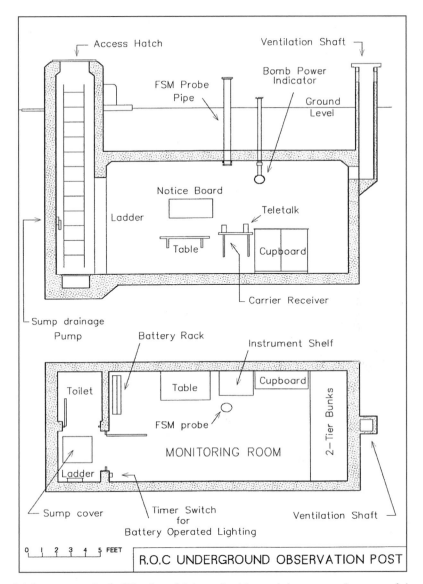

Access Hatch

Ventilation Shaft

FSM Probe Pipe

Bomb Power Indicator

Ground Level

Notice Board

Ladder

Teletalk

Table

Cupboard

Carrier Receiver

Sump drainage Pump

Battery Rack

Instrument Shelf

Toilet

Table

Cupboard

FSM probe

MONITORING ROOM

2–Tier Bunks

Ladder

Sump cover

Timer Switch for Battery Operated Lighting

Ventilation Shaft

0 1 2 3 4 5 FEET

R.O.C UNDERGROUND OBSERVATION POST

roof slab seven and a half inches thick, and with a minimum earth cover of three feet. The larger chamber consisted of a monitoring room containing two bunks, a desk, monitoring instruments, one storage cupboard and shelves to hold the post's battery power supply. The smaller chamber contained a chemical closet and a sump fitted with a semi-rotary pump by means of which seepage water could be pumped to the surface. Access was gained via a fifteen-foot-long vertical ladder in a narrow concrete shaft, heavily reinforced at the surface. The original design had vertical, double blast doors at the entrance, but this was changed on the 'production' models to a small horizontal steel hatch, which was more secure and offered a lower silhouette. The only other surface features were a small concrete ventilation shaft and connections for the various blast and fallout monitoring instruments. Food and water reserves held in the bunker could sustain the crew in a state of bearable discomfort for one week.

129

The Home Office pressed for an accelerated building programme for the underground posts, demanding 100 completions by the end of 1956 and a further 250 each year thereafter, with the last to be completed in 1962. By July 1958, when the first major exercises were conducted in which nuclear information was passed from ROC observation posts via Group and Sector operations centres to the Air Defence Operations Centre at Bentley Priory, some ninety-four underground posts were operational with a further 110 under construction.

The observers' task was to determine, with the use of a range of instruments that gradually increased in accuracy and sophistication with the passage of time, the location and power of nearby nuclear detonations and the local levels of radiation. Information was transmitted by telephone to Group Headquarters where, by triangulation and interpolation of measurements from a number of remote posts, the exact locations of bomb bursts could be determined and the direction of fallout clouds plotted and predicted. At first the only equipment available consisted of the Radiac Survey Meter No. 2, (which was a relatively insensitive instrument scaled to 300 Rontgens per hour and which required the observer to leave the post to obtain a reading), and the 'Shadowgraph' Ground Zero Indicator. This latter device consisted of a four-aperture pinhole camera mounted near the entrance hatch that could, by means of scorch marks on sensitized paper, give an indication of the direction of the thermal flash from a nuclear explosion. This instrument too required the observer to leave the relative safety of his bunker to retrive the indicator card.

1960 saw official recognition of the new role of the ROC and also saw the introduction of new equipment to help them fulfil this role. A directive issued on 7 September recognized the task of the ROC to be the reporting of nuclear burst, plotting and reporting of fallout drift and *in certain designated areas of Eastern England only* the reporting of low-level aircraft. Two improved monitoring instruments were introduced in 1960: the Fixed Survey Meter, which could, by means of a small-bore conduit, measure external radiation levels from inside the bunker, and largely replaced the inefficient Radiac No. 2; and the AWRE-designed Bomb Power Indicator, which was basically a bourdon-tube pressure gauge reading to 5 p.s.i and which, again by means of a small tube to the surface, could directly measure blast overpressure. Monitoring equipment was also installed at the Group and Sector operations centres and a few of the SOCs were provided with American-designed 'Bhangmeter' photoelectric bomb-burst indicators in addition to the standard instruments.

It was realized from as early as 1956 that for the network of underground observation posts to be effective the Group and Sector headquarters to which they reported would have to be equally secure. Two standard designs of protected Group Headquarters were drawn up; one, a two-storey, surface blockhouse in concrete and brick; the other a broadly similar design spread over two and a half floors constructed partially below ground level or else mounded with earth and approached via a flight of steps to the entrance on the upper level. The surface blockhouse pattern, which bears a more than passing resemblance to an oversize public convenience, was intended for the less vulnerable locations

20. ROC Group Headquarters. A typical 'Pagoda' style semi-underground type. This example, now demolished, was at Bedford. *Nick Catford*

21. ROC Group Headquarters. Surface pattern blockhouse. Originally built of brick-faced reinforced concrete, many of these structures, like this example at Ayr, were later clad in heavy gauge corrugated steel. *Nick Catford*

22. ROC Group Headquarters. Interior view looking down into the plotting room from the balcony of the Carmarthen Group Control bunker. *Nick Catford*

and cost £41,000 each. The rather more intimidating, semi-buried pattern, known by virtue of its curiously tiered design as the 'pagoda' style, cost, on average, £45,000 each. Thirty-one of these protected Group Controls were required (although not all were built) to replace all the existing controls, most if not all of which offered no radiation protection and little blast protection, but unfortunately the Treasury objected to the cost, which amounted to nearly £1,500,000.

As an economy measure it was decided in a few locations to adapt existing buildings and one of these; a conversion of the Bristol GDA Anti-Aircraft Operations Room at Lansdown on the outskirts of Bath, was the first of the modern ROC headquarters to be opened, for No. 12 Group, in August 1959. An identical conversion was undertaken on the Lisburn AAOR to serve No. 31 Group (Belfast) four years later. The Preston Group Headquarters, built to serve the newly formed No.21 Group, took over part of the former RAF Sector Operations Centre at Longley Lane, Goosnargh. This was the second post-war adaptation of the Longley Lane site within five years, for in the early 1950s it

23. UKWMO National Headquarters, Longley Lane, Preston. This view shows the ventilation towers for the new plant room extension built in the early 1980s when the bunker was substantially upgraded. *Nick Catford*

24. UKWMO National Headquarters, Longley Lane, Preston. An interior view of the newly refurbished operations room, seen from the balcony. *Nick Catford*

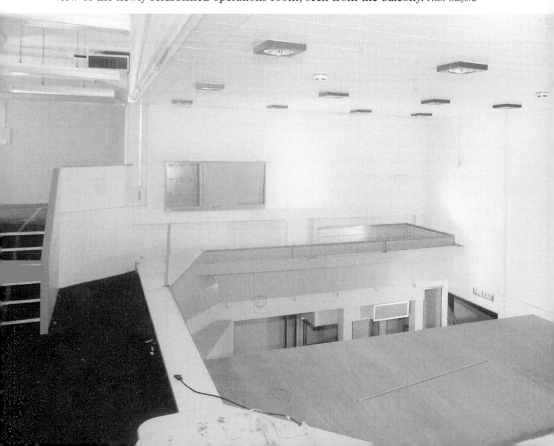

had been converted at enormous cost into the north-west Sector Operations Centre for the ROTOR project. The Second World War Sector Centres consisted of three main bunkers: an Operations Room, Communications Centre and Filter Block. At Longley Lane both the ROTOR bunker and the ROC Group Headquarters occupied the old Operations block, while the Filter Room, for a while, accommodated the Regional Armed Forces Headquarters. Meanwhile, at Inverness No. 30 Group occupied the old Caledonian Sector Operations Room at Raigmore from 1961. Ten years later the Filter Room was adapted as a war headquarters for the Highlands Council.

Against the backdrop of growing international tension, and following an agreed revision of the Group organization that saw a reduction from thirty-one to twenty-nine resulting from the integration of Bromley and Beckenham with Maidstone, and the loss of the Glasgow group, financial approval was given for the construction programme to go ahead in the middle of 1959. A semi-underground bunker in the grounds of Ashmore House, Maidstone, for No.1 Group was the first to be completed in 1960, quickly followed by the No. 15 Group HQ at Fiskerton near Lincoln in the same year. Construction continued at a rapid pace through 1962, when the majority were completed, and then tailed off following the post-Cuba deflation in tension. The last to be commissioned were No. 18 Group, Leeds, and No. 24 Group, Edinburgh, in April 1964, followed by No.10 Group at Oxford in 1965.

The majority of the protected Group Control bunkers built in the early 1960s complied with one of two standard patterns which were adapted slightly to meet local requirements. The surface pattern was a windowless, reinforced concrete structure, partially over two floors, often faced with brickwork. Entrance was gained to the lower, or main, floor via a recessed portico protecting two blast doors at right angles to the frontage. That on the left gave access to the air-conditioning filter room, while that on the right led to a central corridor which terminated, via a right-hand turn, at an emergency exit door at the far end of the building. Along the left-hand side of this corridor were ranged a decontamination suite, dressing room, a Chief Officers room, ladies toilets and male and female dormitories. The first room on the right contained the air-conditioning plant, including circulating fans, dehumidifiers, air washers and refrigerant compressors. Behind the plant room was a separate chamber housing a large diesel standby generator. At some, but not all, of the bunkers, the engine room was fitted with external blast doors.

Beyond the plant room was a two-storey operations room, distinguishable externally by a raised roof line. A balcony accessible from the upper floor surrounded three sides of the operations well. On the lower floor, behind a flight of stairs leading to the upper floor, was a GPO (British Telecom) equipment room, and beyond that a kitchen and canteen. The upper floor housed the upper section of the operations room and its balcony, an enclosed water tank and a communications centre.

The semi-underground bunkers were vertically inverted mirror images of the surface pattern, the major difference being that the central corridor and main suite of rooms was on the same level as the ops room balcony. The lower level,

134

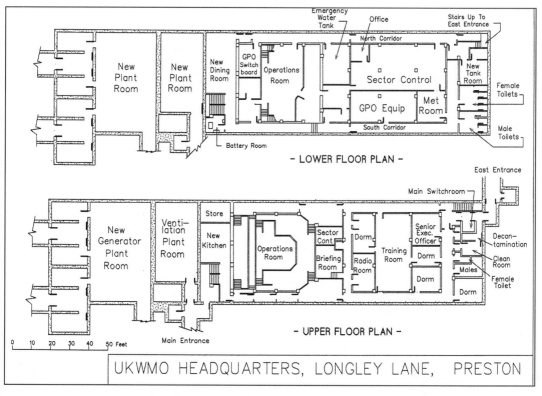

- LOWER FLOOR PLAN -

New Plant Room

New Plant Room

New Dining Room

Battery Room

GPO Switchboard

Operations Room

Emergency Water Tank

Office

North Corridor

GPO Equip

Sector Control

Met Room

South Corridor

New Tank Room

Stairs Up To East Entrance

Female Toilets

Male Toilets

- UPPER FLOOR PLAN -

New Generator Plant Room

Venti-lation Plant Room

Store

New Kitchen

Operations Room

Sector Cont

Briefing Room

Radio Room

Dorm

Training Room

Senior Exec. Officer

Dorm

Dorm

Dorm

Main Switchroom

East Entrance

Decon-tamination

Clean Room

Males

Female Toilet

Main Entrance

0 10 20 30 40 50 Feet

UKWMO HEADQUARTERS, LONGLEY LANE, PRESTON

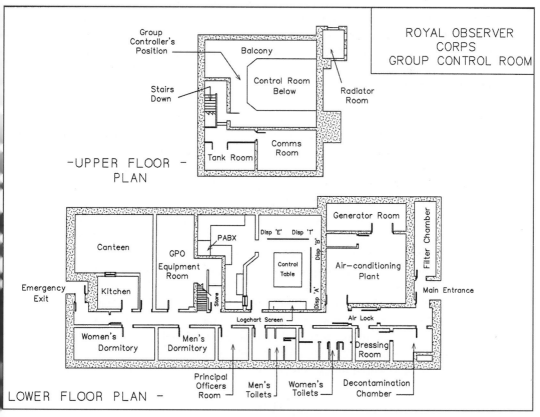

ROYAL OBSERVER CORPS GROUP CONTROL ROOM

-UPPER FLOOR - PLAN

Group Controller's Position

Balcony

Control Room Below

Stairs Down

Radiator Room

Tank Room

Comms Room

LOWER FLOOR PLAN -

Canteen

Kitchen

GPO Equipment Room

PABX

Disp 'E'   Disp 'T'

Disp 'B'

Control Table

Disp 'A'

Generator Room

Filter Chamber

Air-conditioning Plant

Emergency Exit

Store

Logchart Screen

Air Lock

Main Entrance

Women's Dormitory

Men's Dormitory

Principal Officers Room

Men's Toilets

Women's Toilets

Dressing Room

Decontamination Chamber

which was the only truly underground part of the bunker, consisted of only the floor of the operations well and the communications centre. The top floor which included the entrance portico was accessed via a broad flight of steps and contained only the air-conditioning filter room and decontamination centre.

Construction of the majority of the protected Group Headquarters coincided with three other important inter-dependent developments: the commissioning of the United States-sponsored BMEWS site at Fylingdales; development of the high-speed 'Carrier Warning System' for disseminating fallout information; and the creation of 'Nuclear Reporting Cells' at major military Command Headquarters. Whatever may have been public perception over the last four decades, the primary function of the Fylingdales Early Warning Station has been the protection of the United States homeland. Information from the giant golfballs was also relayed to US and NATO forces in Britain and Europe, but these Forces too were just forward defences for the embunkered political and military elite of the USA, safe in the bowels of Mount Weather and Raven Rock. As a secondary, corollary function, missile attack warning from Fylingdales was transmitted to UKWMO headquarters and thence to the UK civilian population. This is the origin of the 'Four Minute Warning'. Although of virtually no practical value to the population-at-large, Fylingdales and the four minute warning was of immense propaganda value to the British government at a time when pressure to either abandon nuclear weapons entirely or to establish a comprehensive public shelter policy, was mounting from all directions. Fylingdales was an immensely important *military* asset, financed primarily by the United States, that was consistently advertised by the government as the key element of a vast nuclear umbrella the prime object of which was the protection of the *civil* population. The widely publicized fact that, by 1962, ninety per cent of the running costs of UKWMO (which was promoted as the great voluntary organization that Fylingdales was built to serve) was financed by the Home Office (a steadfastly civilian Ministry), rather than the Ministry of Defence or the RAF reinforced the generally held misconception about BMEWS.

Although the ROC/UKWMO fallout warning network was much publicized, a parallel and much more secret organization was under development that was to continue to function for some years after the final winding up of the ROC in 1992. This secret sub-system was the network of 'Nuclear Reporting Cells' established first at RAF Command and Group Headquarters, and later at all the principal military and government headquarters. Staff at most of the Nuclear Reporting cells were RAF personnel trained by the ROC, but later many of these, except at Air Ministry Headquarters and at the Corsham Emergency Government War Headquarters (which would, *inter alia*, have included the function of Air Ministry Headquarters in time of war), were replaced by civilian volunteers.

To be effective, the high-speed radar warning system and the myriad other defence sub-systems that supported it required a data transmission network that was much faster and more efficient than that which existed in 1960, based, as it was, upon voice telling and unreliable common-carrier land-line links. New, dedicated military communications systems evolved which are beyond the scope of this volume, but we will look in some detail at the Home Office-designed 'Carrier Warning System' that was designed primarily for public warning. The CWS, codenamed HANDEL, consisted of some 20,000 modular warning units, or carrier receivers, installed at strategic locations nationwide in police and fire stations, factories, hospitals, local government, military and ROC headquarters, all of the 1559 ROC observation posts, and even, in remote areas, Post Offices, public houses or private homes. The first fateful warning of missile attack – Attack Warning Red – would be received at the Air Defence Operations Centre from Fylingdales or a NATO high command authority, or perhaps direct from Cheyenne Mountain, and distributed thence, via HANDEL to 252 Carrier Control Points, (usually located in the same central police stations that controlled the 7,000 emergency warning sirens). From these central points the alert would be re-transmitted to the 20,000 warning points throughout the country, which would in turn sound the final warning to the Nation by electric or manually operated sirens, or by the firing of maroons. These warnings would be backed-up by government radio and television broadcasts.

The warning receivers consisted of small amplifier units fitted with volume controls, loudspeakers and handsets connected to the commercial GPO (British Telecom) telephone lines, upon which the HANDEL signal was superimposed. These repeaters were never silent: during peacetime they emitted a constant, low-pitched ticking sound; when the warning came the ticking became a loud, high-pitched warbling note, interspersed with a staccato rattle which signalled a detailed fallout message or bomb burst report from the nearest police Carrier Control Point.

Instructions attached to the device explained its operation:

WAR EMERGENCY ACTION	
The receiver should be switched on and monitored continuously in a war emergency, when instructed by the Police or following a public announcement	
SIGNAL	**MEANING**
Warbling Note followed by a spoken message	ATTACK WARNING RED
High Pitched Pip tone followed by a spoken message	FALLOUT ATTACK BLACK Or ATTACK MESSAGE WHITE

HANDEL ticked away the cold war days for over thirty years, until the system was finally shut down on 10 July 1991. Throughout these years the volunteers of the Royal Observer Corps practiced their procedures weekly and acted out their scenarios for the end of the world; writing off friends and neighbours and workmates with quick entries in the exercise log-book, like these for Post 26/12 at Bradford-on-Avon, reporting to the Bristol Group Headquarters at Lansdown near Bath, in June 1985:

08.27 – Attack Warning Red

11.22 – Sitrep: Four bombs in Group. Two ground-burst and two air-burst in Exeter, Bridport, Wareham and Sherborne areas. Fallout already in the east, expected over whole Group by 14.00 hours approximately.

The little coastal town of Bridport seemed to attract more attention than the Bristol industrial conurbation, the Admiralty administration centres in Bath or the Corsham national government complex, all of which were within the 12 Group boundary. During exercise WARMON 2 in November 1985 Bridport was the centre of simulated CND opposition:

08.39 – Attack Warning Red

12.25 – Two bombs on Group, 12 in Sector. Fallout in north and middle of Group. No CND problems within Group. Some posts will be deployed later on mobile monitoring tasks.

15.40 - All Group now affected by fallout. Three bombs within Group, two ground-burst, one air-burst. CND problems at Bridport only. Seems to be going well.

The mid-1960s saw the end of the aircraft reporting role in East Anglia and, with the replacement of voice-telling by telex and high-speed teletype, the end of the traditional horizontal map table which was a vestige of the old aircraft reporting system. Huge, backlit transparent vertical situation maps, Type 'A' and 'B', replaced the latter and ROC plotters now manned the high-level balconies that overlooked them. Small swivelling blackboards were used to pass fallout information from the communications personnel on the balcony to the chart-tellers below. Changes in operational practice at this time were so radical that in May 1967 a Working Party was formed to determine the future organization of UKWMO and examine its communications requirements. It was realized that, whilst the Group organization worked very effectively, communications with the Sector Controls, which were the next tier above in the reporting hierarchy, were inefficient, inflexible and over-extended. The problem was that, whilst the Group Headquarters and Observation Posts had been planned as a cohesive whole, the Sector level was a hangover from the earlier, aircraft-reporting organization whose principal function was to assist RAF interceptors locate their targets. Most of the Sector Controls were in fact located in RAF premises, often some geographical distance from their Groups. It was recommended that key Group HQ bunkers should be expanded to allow co-location of the Sector Headquarters, and at the same time the Groups should be reorganized into five new Sectors: Metropolitan, Midland, Southern, Western and Caledonian.

In 1968 the atmosphere of relative international stability, coinciding with a dire financial crisis brought about by its own mismanagement, caused the cash-strapped Labour administration to announced massive cuts in the Home Defence budget, which saw the end of the Civil Defence Corps and the Auxiliary Fire Service, and deep cutbacks in the Territorial Army Voluntary Reserve. A ten per cent cut in the UKWMO budget – which at that time was perhaps the most publicly acceptable element of defence spending – resulted in the closure of 686 of the underground observation posts, the abolition of the Watford and Leeds Groups, and the reduction of the Truro and Oban Groups to satellite status. A secondary result was the shelving of the proposed Sector reorganization for five years.

Some new works were gradually put in hand during the early 1970s despite the financial stringencies and political apathy. Modifications to the Horsham bunker in 1972, and to the Craigiebarns HQ in Dundee in 1973, followed by Fiskerton in 1976, which allowed Midland Sector HQ to move out of RAF Uxbridge, saw the Sector reorganization completed. Southern Sector headquarters remained for a while longer in its very suitable underground accommodation in the old Brown's Quarry ROTOR sector operations room in the Corsham Quarries where it had been since 1953, before moving to the Group Headquarters at Lansdown. Western Sector HQ remained in residence at the Goosnargh Lane bunker in Preston, where it had been since transferring from RAF Barton Hall in 1966. The eighty-strong staff of each Sector control, which included a large proportion of Scientific Officers, occupied an important position in the UKWMO organization, for not only did they co-ordinate the activity of their respective Groups and pass filtered information to the Regional and Local Government Headquarters, but they also liaised at a high level with warning centres in adjoining NATO countries.

After a decade of near stagnation UKWMO witnessed a ten-year resurgence under the belligerent Conservative Government of Margaret Thatcher, followed by a rapid and terminal decline culminating in its abolition in July 1991. Always the most vulnerable aspect of any defensive system, the existing communications systems, in terms of both procedures and equipment, were highlighted by the 1981 Home Defence Review as the most important and yet the weakest link in the UKWMO arsenal. Huge sums were made available to sweep away the manual land-line switching apparatus and replace it all with solid state electronic MSX switching, and to radically overhaul the Government Emergency Communication Network. Fast, reliable and highly redundant communication links became the key element of Home Defence; with the flexibility of MSX virtually any node on the system could, in emergency, absorb the most central functions of government at any level. The first large-scale introduction of MSX into the UKWMO system was at Maidstone in 1984 and by the middle of the following year it had replaced teleprinters nationwide. By that time, too, the use of microwave links in the ECN was becoming general and by July 1988 the introduction of SX200 switching apparatus dispensed with the need for operator connections for land-line voice calls. Towards the end of the decade moves had also been made towards the automatic collection and processing of fallout and bomb detonation data, but little was implemented before the curtain finally fell on the ROC.

The increasingly high public profile of UKWMO during the 1980s, and its increasingly important role in co-operation with the Regional Government Headquarters and the Local Authority Emergency Centres, called for rather more modern and spacious peacetime accommodation than had hitherto existed. At many Group Headquarters striking new surface office complexes were built to house the enlarged specialist staff, but the plaster had hardly dried on the walls before they were rendered redundant in 1991. Often, the existence of these office blocks has made the otherwise forbidding bunker sites attractive propositions for their new, private sector owners. Others have found new uses in the public service; the surface complex at Lansdown – the peacetime HQ for No.12 Group – which commands wonderful views over three counties and across the Bristol Channel, is now the Control Centre for Avon and Somerset Fire Brigade. The old operations room now houses, in air-conditioned and deep-carpeted luxury, the force's 999 call centre.

GROUP HEADQUARTERS BUNKERS, FROM 1965 TO CLOSURE AND BEYOND:

METROPOLITAN SECTOR – Headquarters: Horsham
Group 1 - MAIDSTONE

Semi-underground bunker in the grounds of Fairlawns, a large house in Maidstone requisitioned in 1939 and used until 1953 as the Group Control HQ. At that time the ground floor and part of the basement were reconstructed to create an operations room. Between 1953 and 1961 the Maidstone Group was integrated with No. 19 Group (Beckenham), and Fairlawns was relegated to a training centre. Shortly after the opening of the new bunker, in June 1960 the situation was reversed and Maidstone was once again the headquarters location. After 1992 the house (renamed Ashmore House in memory of the Corps' founder) was redeveloped as offices and the bunker used as a secure document archive by a firm of solicitors.

Group 2 - HORSHAM

The two-storey surface bunker at Horsham was opened in April 1962. A matching brick-clad extension was added to the right-hand side of the building in the mid-1970s when Horsham became the headquarters of UKWMO Metropolitan Sector.

Group 3 - OXFORD

The Oxford bunker was the very last of the ROC Group controls to be opened, in May 1965. An adjacent office block of later construction formed the peacetime headquarters of UKMO. Had war broken out, this function would have transferred to the hardened, alternative wartime headquarters at Longley Lane, Preston.

Group 4 - COLCHESTER

Bunker demolished and land redeveloped shortly after stand-down.

Group 5 - WATFORD

Protected bunker opened in November 1961, but relegated in 1968 to training centre under control of Metropolitan sector HQ, Uxbridge. In 1973 the site was declared surplus and was put up for sale the following year.

Group 14 - WINCHESTER

A typical two-storey surface bunker in concrete with brick facing, opened in June 1961 on a site adjoining an earlier (1943) Second World War ROC operations centre at Abbots Rd, a mile or so north of the city centre. The earlier building was adapted as the Group peacetime administrative HQ. Both buildings are now empty and badly vandalized, plans for a variety of commercial uses having been made difficult by the building's Grade 2 listing.

Group 19 - BROMLEY
The Bromley Group was re-absorbed by Maidstone and ceased to exist before the protected accommodation programme got under way.

MIDLAND SECTOR - Headquarters: Fiskerton
Group 6 - NORWICH (OLD CATTON)
Typical semi-underground bunker, opened in September 1961 on the site of the former RAF base at Old Catton. After a period of neglect following the stand-down, the site was offered for sale by the Home Office in 1998.

Group 7 - BEDFORD
The semi-underground bunker in Bedford was opened in 1962 and closed in 1991. The Home Office maintained the site until 1998 when it was sold for residential redevelopment.

Group 8 - LAWFORD HEATH
Control of No. 8 Group moved from unprotected accommodation in Coventry to the new, semi-underground bunker at Lawford Heath near Rugby in November 1963. Following the 1991 stand-down the Lawford Heath bunker and its adjoining surface administration building were destined to become Regional Government Headquarters 9.2, to replace the existing, rather inadequate underground premises at Drakelow. Before much more than preliminary works could be completed, however, the RGHQ organization was itself wound up and the Rugby site abandoned.

After several years of neglect the two buildings were purchased by Satellite Media Services Ltd, who have developed the site into a high-tech commercial communications centre. The bunker has been much modified internally and externally and it is now difficult to discern the original interior arrangement, although the operations well has been retained in a much modified form. A covered way now links the bunker to the adjacent administration building.

Group 15 - FISKERTON
The semi-underground bunker was built in 1960 on land that was part of the former Fiskerton RAF base. Previously the Group Headquarters had been in unprotected premises at RAF Waddington. A modern administration block in pre-cast concrete panels stands nearby. Originally the emergency exit from the bunker was via a vertical ladder and a small hatch similar to those fitted to the observation posts, but this arrangement was replaced by a conventional doorway in the 1970s when the building was reconstructed as a Sector Control.

Closed in 1992, the bunker was purchased in 1998 by a Security company which now uses it and the adjacent office block for a variety of purposes.

Group 20 - YORK

A brick-built semi-underground bunker with the lower level protected by a substantial earth mound. A modern, single-storey administration block stands nearby. Located behind Shelley House on Acomb Road, York, this striking bunker was scheduled as an Ancient Monument by English Heritage in the year 2000, so its future is ensured.

SOUTHERN SECTOR – Headquarters: Lansdown
Group 9 - YEOVIL

The semi-underground bunker at Yeovil was built near the existing ROC centre off Hendford Hill on the south-west outskirts of the town in September 1961. A range of earlier hutted offices served as the peacetime administration centre.

Group 10 - EXETER

The two-storey surface bunker, opened in 1961, occupies a site which it shares with a Second World War Sector Operations Centre at Poltimore Park, close to the M5 motorway. Part of the earlier building in latter days served as the ROC administration block, whilst the remainder was used as a workshop for the repair of communications equipment.

Although badly effected by damp, the ROC bunker is still in fairly good order, but the earlier building, which in recent years has been stripped of its fittings for display elsewhere, is prone to flooding. Both buildings were sold by the Home Office in 2000, but the inflexible stance of the local planning authority has rendered their future use uncertain.

Group 11 - TRURO

Commissioned in May 1963, this uncompromising concrete two-storey bunker, its bleak elevation partially alleviated by local stone rendering, was, like that at Oban, closed as a result of the 1973 defence cutback. The building was retained until 1991 as a secondary training establishment for the Southern Sector. Following closure it was transferred to the RAF, which used it nominally as a seismic monitoring station. Although this role was reported to have ended on 31 December 1995, the property is still maintained and kept secure by RAF personnel, and locally there is considerable speculation about its current use.
A later, single-storey stone extension, built to house administrative staff, now functions as the Truro driving-test centre.

Group 12 - BRISTOL

No. 12 Group headquarters was among the first to be provided with protected accommodation, in August 1959. The Bristol bunker, actually located on the Lansdown escarpment overlooking the City of Bath, was one of two that were not purpose-built but used instead existing 1950s' Anti-Aircraft Operations Rooms, built as part of project ROTOR and abandoned following the dissolution of Anti-Aircraft Command in 1954. The group had moved from King's Square Avenue in Bristol to the former AAOR site at Lansdown the previous year and it is probable that it remained in temporary surface accommodation there pending completion of conversion work in the AAOR bunker.

Other than the removal of the balcony from one side of the operations well and foreshortening it on the other, and the removal of the curved glass panels, the layout of the building was changed little from its original design until 1980. Between 1978 and 1980 the bunker was partially upgraded and a modern administration block built alongside. Within the bunker parts of the upper floor were re-modelled to provide extra office space and at the rear the emergency exit was rebuilt and enclosed to provide a proper air-lock. A new extension at the rear was incorporated in the modified entrance arrangement, built to the same design of austere shuttered mass concrete to match the original structure. This extension houses a second standby emergency generator. The No. 1 power-house in the basement retains its original generator, built in 1952, which provides emergency power for the main bunker only. The new, upper power-house can be run in parallel with No. 1, or isolated to provide power only to the new surface offices.

Following closure, the bunker remained empty for two years until its purchase in 1994 by Avon County Council. The modern administration offices now form the Avon Fire Brigade Control Centre. The underground bunker is maintained and, while nominally the Fire Brigade conference and training centre, is used mainly for storage.

Group 13 - CARMARTHEN
A standard surface bunker, built in concrete and clad with heavy-duty square-section corrugated steel sheeting, it shares a site with the Carmarthen Territorial Army Centre. After the ROC stand-down the bunker was retained by the Carmarthen Civil Protection Unit until March 2000, when it was handed back to the Home Office for disposal. Nearby is a modern, two-storey administration block, markedly similar architecturally to the contemporary, single-storey office block at the No.12 Group HQ at Lansdown.

WESTERN SECTOR – Headquarters: Longley Lane, Preston
Group 16 - SHREWSBURY
Shorn of most of its appendages and with its red-brick-clad walls pierced by new window openings and adorned with floral window-boxes, the bunker, in a residential area of Shrewsbury, is no longer as conspicuous as in former years, and now serves as a veterinary surgery. The bunker, replacing an earlier, unprotected control centre in London Road, Shrewsbury, was opened in January 1962 and closed thirty years later.

Group 17 - BORAS (WREXHAM)
The Wrexham Group was absorbed by Caernarvon in 1953, but re-emerged in 1962 when the new, two-storey surface bunker was commissioned. A typical, prefabricated concrete administration building stands nearby. After stand-down the Boras bunker was considered as a possible location for the long-awaited but ultimately chimerical Regional Government Headquarters for North Wales. A

conversion project was proposed similar to that at Lawford Heath, but as at the latter location, the end of the cold war led to its abandonment.

The administration building now houses the offices of a construction company, whilst the bunker has been converted into a recording studio. Many of the original features remain, but the operations room has been altered beyond all recognition following the removal of the balcony and insertion of a false ceiling.

Group 18 - LEEDS

A semi-underground bunker, opened in April 1964 and closed just four years later, in 1968, following the Group re-organization that year. Between 1969 and 1995 the site was used as a training and social centre by the Royal Navy Voluntary Reserve. Subsequently the bunker and the surrounding estate was sold for commercial development and its future is uncertain. Due to its earlier closure date the Leeds centre retains many of the original features, including the vertical emergency exit arrangement, that have been lost during improvements and extensions at other sites.

Group 21 - PRESTON (LONGLEY LANE)

The Preston Group resulted from the 1960s' shake-up of the Royal Observer Corps and upon its formation took over the former ROTOR Sector Operations Centre at Longley Lane, Goosnargh, near Preston. The ROTOR building was itself an adaptation of an earlier Second World War RAF Sector Operations Centre; one of four that included Watnall, Craigiebarns and Kenton Bar. Each site consisted of three semi-buried bunkers: the Operations Room, Filter Room, and Communications Centre.

In the early years Longley Lane saw little change from its wartime configuration but from 1975 onwards it underwent a metamorphosis as it became increasingly important in the UKWMO hierarchy, becoming, first, the Western Sector Headquarters and later the alternate wartime supreme headquarters of UKWMO. Some idea of its importance may be gauged from the fact that by the late 1970s the bunker had also been designated as the reserve UK Air Defence Operations Centre.

Between 1975 and 1980 vast sums of public money were sunk into upgrading the bunker and in 1980 a government inquiry was instituted to discover how wisely this money had been spent. During this period the western end of the bunker was completely remodelled; a new kitchen and dining area was created and a very large extension built to house a state-of-the-art air-conditioning system and two new diesel standby generators. When work was completed the whole building was mounded over and landscaped, although it was impossible to disguise the large and rather sinister ventilation towers rising above the new plant room extension.

The peacetime administrative headquarters were housed in a purpose-built office block nearby on the same site.

The Second World War Filter Room, which is about 100 yards distant from the Operations Centre, is a smaller, two-storey bunker that served for many years as the Regional Armed Forces Emergency Headquarters. Although much altered internally for its latter role, the filter room still contains its original operations well and balcony, but much of what would previously have been office space has been converted into dormitories. The lower floor contained principally the kitchen and dining areas, dormitories and the air-conditioning plant. The upper floor contained the operations centre, more dormitories and a small emergency power station.

Both bunkers are now in private ownership following several years of neglect.

Group 22 - CARLISLE
Protected accommodation built at RAF Carlisle. Current status unknown.

Group 23 - DURHAM
The surface bunker, built in The Sands, just north of the city centre, was opened in June 1961 and is unique amongst the protected Group Controls. Unrecognizable as a bunker except for the blast-protected main door, it is topped by a matching brick office block, with a large Victorian house adjoining the property. The bunker is now incorporated in the office complex above.

Group 31 - LISBURN
The bunker, an adapted AAOR , at Lisburn, County Antrim, was one of the later protected headquarters and was opened in 1963. The conversion work carried out at Lisburn is identical to that undertaken for the No.12 Group HQ at Lansdown; indeed, the same architect's drawings were used for both projects.

CALEDONIAN SECTOR – Headquarters: Craigiebarns, Dundee
Group 24 - EDINBURGH (TURNHOUSE)
The semi-underground bunker, opened in 1964, occupied a location at the former RAF base at Turnhouse. Following closure, the bunker was demolished along with most of the other RAF buildings on the site (other than the hangars) and the area turned over to commercial use.

Group 25 - AYR
A surface bunker at Waterloo Road, Prestwick, built in brick and concrete but clad at some time in heavy corrugated steel sheeting. A prefabricated concrete administration block stands nearby. The air-conditioning system was upgraded shortly before closure in 1992. The bunker is in private ownership and is scheduled for demolition in 2001.

Group 26 - GLASGOW
Group 26 was never provided with protected accommodation and was disbanded in 1962, its observation posts being distributed between the Oban and Ayr groups.

Group 27 - OBAN
The two-storey surface bunker at Oban was opened in May 1962, but was a

casualty of the economies of the 1970s and closed following the absorption of No. 8 Group by Inverness in 1973. The bunker was retained by No. 30 Group as a standby communications centre however, a status that it retained until 1992.

Group 28 - DUNDEE

The Royal Observer Corps acquired Craigiebarns House, east of Dundee, in 1942 and it served as the former No. 37 Group (later, following the 1953 reorganisation, 28 Group) headquarters until the protected bunker was built in the grounds in April 1961. Thereafter the house provided a secure location for the Tayside Regional council bunker. The bunker was also the Caledonian Sector headquarters. In recent years Craigiebarns house has been redeveloped as residential flats and the bunker, which decayed rapidly after stand-down, has been demolished.

Group 29 - ABERDEEN

The standard, two-storey surface Bunker at Northfield in Aberdeen opened in May 1961 and closed at stand-down in 1991. Hutted accommodation nearby sufficed as a peacetime administration centre.

Group 30 - INVERNESS

The ROC took possession of the Operations Room bunker of the former Second World War Sector Operations Centre at Raigmore near Inverness, in 1947. Originally the Raigmore site was identical to the Longley Lane complex near Preston, and its post-war development was similar except that the works at Inverness were not so lavish. Shortly after closure the semi-underground bunker was demolished and the area redeveloped. A second Raigmore bunker, the wartime Filter Room, now houses the Highland Council emergency war headquarters.

8

CIVIL DEFENCE AND THE NUCLEAR BUNKER BUILDING PROGRAMMES IN THE UNITED KINGDOM

In this survey of nuclear preparedness in the United Kingdom we will examine six areas of bunker provision and two distinct historical periods. The six major themes are: buildings associated with the ROC and UKWMO Warning network; the Central Government War Headquarters; the Regional Seats of Government; the Civil Defence Corps and later the Local Authority bunkers; the Essential Industry bunkers, and the special, hardened facilities built by the most secretive of all British institutions, the General Post Office, to protect its most sensitive telephone exchanges. The two distinct periods identified throughout this study are the years of naive atomic war planning based upon the strategic principles of the Second World War that existed from the first Berlin crisis of 1948 until the Cuban crisis of 1962, and the period of fatalist brinkmanship that spanned the years from 1979 until the fall of Soviet communism. Between these periods there was a decade of uneasy lassitude, during which most of the obsolete, secret concrete edifices of the atomic years of the 1950s were either abandoned or put under a regime of care and maintenance that was, in effect, controlled decay. The progress and development of civil defence, and thus the bunker-building programmes, in the United Kingdom was fashioned by three forces: the fluctuating tensions of east-west diplomacy; the often parlous state of the British economy and the ideologies of the political party in power.

Before we examine the remaining concrete symbols that represent fifty years of nuclear paranoia, we should look briefly at the economic and political background of the period and the contemporary cultural values. Following the revitalization of Civil Defence in 1948 after the short-lived 1945 stand-down it was, for a brief period, fashioned upon Second World War lines as principally a rescue and recuperation organization. By the mid-1950s when the full terror of the megaton hydrogen bomb became apparent the organization underwent a degree of metamorphosis, but the official emphasis of nuclear policy was moving from the 'insurance' rationale towards deterrence. The overt government stance, however, remained unchanged, as was demonstrated by a Hansard entry in July 1957 which stated that:

> Even with the most powerful bomb, however, danger to life would result at any particular place only through some circumstances such as rain falling through the atomic cloud... I think I have made it clear that it would be exceptional to find serious danger to life from atomic fallout.

But the true situation was that Civil Defence as it existed in 1957 was totally ineffective, and, given the parlous state of the UK economy, was then, and would remain for the foreseeable future, both unviable and unaffordable. The following year the Conservative politician C M Woodhouse branded Civil Defence as 'a cold, callous, cruel fraud; a policy of mass suicide'. This assessment was indeed true, and had long been secretly accepted as such by the British government. While supporting the myth that Britain could survive nuclear war, (just as it had survived the German Blitz), by maintaining the Civil Defence Corps which throughout the Second World War had symbolised the British will to survive, the government was actually developing the infrastructure to support a completely different rationale for survival. This covert policy was an anglicized version of the US concept of 'maintenance of the machinery of government', or the rationale of State Survival. Such a concept is fatalistic in that it accepts that deterrence may fail and that 'insurance', ie the ability to mitigate the effects of war and drag survivors from the ashes, is impossible after all-out nuclear war. It proposes instead that a core of government at all levels must be given the ultimate protection in order that an alternative machinery of government should survive to direct the process of national survival and enhance the prospect of post-attack recovery. Long before Civil Defence was consigned to its final demise in 1968, plans for government survival were already being laid in the form of the Central Government War Headquarters at Corsham and the chain of Regional Seats of Government, which was more or less complete by 1962.

Unfortunately for the government, information about the RSGs entered the public domain in 1962, largely through the investigations of an organization known as 'Spies for Peace' which was a splinter group of the Campaign for Nuclear Disarmament. Politicians close to the CND camp were quick to capitalize on these disclosures and in December Frank Allaun warned that:

> If evidence of shelters for key personnel was confirmed, then it would cause tremendous resentment among the whole population.

While popular debate was to continue for the next four decades regarding the ethics of providing heavily protected bunkers for an elite minority while the masses were consigned to instant nuclear annihilation or a longer, lingering death from radiation, government interest in, and more importantly financial commitment to, Civil Defence diminished to insignifance after the shock of Cuba and maintained only a minimal priority until the ascendancy of Margaret Thatcher. The most obvious incarnation of this lack of enthusiasm was the final, almost embarrassing, abandonment of the Civil Defence Corp in 1968 that resulted primarily from the conclusions of the 1957 Defence White Paper. That paper revitalized the question, widely asked in the USA at that time, as to whether civil defence in the broadest sense was a weapon in the armoury of deterrence or a policy of strategic insurance. The view of the British government was that in its enfeebled form in the nuclear age it was of little deterrent value, (and if it did have any such value it would be merely provocative), and that as it could have no realistic rescue and recovery role it offered no insurance.

During the 1970s the emphasis of British nuclear planning was increasingly upon the early warning provided by UKWMO and the BMEWS system. Due to the compact size and dense population of the United Kingdom, evacuation or the provision of mass public shelters has never been feasible and for that reason the major emphasis of civil defence planning has always been upon warning and monitoring only. The largely American-financed BMEWS system provided an economical excuse for avoiding the question of public shelters, and simultaneously government propaganda stressed the value of privately financed family shelters, reflecting US values from the early 1960s. Most of the infrastructure changes made throughout these years reflected the government's need for economy, to dispense with what was clearly obsolete and to render more efficient what remained in the face of a diminishing but continually evolving threat.

By 1972 the UK, like the USA and Canada, saw a movement away from emergency planning for nuclear war towards a system biased towards civil contingency planning. Despite this, the Home Defence Planning Assumptions, published in 1973, included:

1. The security of the UK against *Internal* threat (this against the background of labour militancy at a level unknown since 1926).
2. Measures to mitigate the effects of *External* attack.
3. The provision of an alternate machinery of government to increase the prospect of national survival.
4. Measures to enhance the prospect of national recovery after attack.

The contrary threads of government emergency planning throughout the 1970s are clearly evident. Although this was a period of relative international harmony, the underlying tensions remained. The financially crippled government of the day nevertheless wanted to be seen to be doing something and clung to the chimera of BMEWS, suggesting that warning that one was going to die in three minutes (unless one made private provision) was an alternative to a viable public shelter policy. To mollify public distaste for nuclear brinkmanship, civil defence – now renamed 'Home Defence' – publicly stressed the civil contingency element of its role, thus allowing the Home Office to distance itself from war planning. In private central government still considered civil defence to be an effective weapon of deterrence, even though its overt exhibition might be unduly provocative.

The frightening resurgence of international tension arising from the invasion of Afghanistan, followed by the Cruise Missile problem in 1979, together with the growing evidence of renewed Soviet expansionism and US brinkmanship, once again legitimized overt discussion of civil preparedness for nuclear war in the United Kingdom. The better educated, more socially aware generation of the 1980s, less willing than their counterparts of the 1960s to accept unquestioningly government policy that effected their very survival, opened a vociferous and critical debate about nuclear strategy. Given America's seemingly provocative stance, the continued military allegiance between the US and Europe was also brought into question, particularly by the Campaign for Nuclear Disarmament which highlighted Britain's vulnerability as America's 'unsinkable aircraft carrier'. Home Office publications continued to emphasize the humanitarian role of government nuclear contingency planning, stressing the point that:

even the strongest supporter of unilateral disarmament can consistently give equal support for Civil Defence, since its purposes and effects are essentially humane.

The Conservative government's enhanced commitment to Civil Defence was made public in 1981 with the announcement of an increase in public home defence expenditure from £17.5 million to £45 million. Concurrent with this announcement, a statement from Willie Whitelaw that:

> Civil Preparedness is an important element of our defence strategy. To be seen to be prepared at home as well as capable of military deterrence and defence, will make war less likely

made it quite clear that within government the prime role of civil defence was seen as one of strategic deterrence rather than insurance. Funds were made available on an unprecedented scale for the construction of at least four completely new regional government headquarters and the upgrading and refurbishment of ten others, for the refitting of all the hardened UKWMO group and sector headquarters, and the construction (to a remarkably high standard) of hundreds of new bunkers for the numerous local authorities throughout the nation and for the Water Boards and other national utilities. There was, however, no provision for the protection of the civil population; Hansard, for 7 August 1980, records a comment by Willie Whitelaw that:

> The provision of public shelters through the government would be enormously costly and something which we could not contemplate.

E P Thompson, in the CND pamphlet 'Protest & Survive' (which parodied 'Protect & Survive', the much ridiculed Home Office guide to self-help protection), highlighted the aspect of government war planning that generated most public disquiet, and which had incensed Frank Allaun twenty years earlier, when he wrote of the 'bunkers deep under the Chilterns for senior politicians, civil servants and military'. Thompson was referring to the extensive, seven-storey, underground bunker complex at Northwood, constructed in the early 1980s as a multi-function military, NATO, and central government command, control and communications centre. Two years later George Morley, in an acute assessment of current Civil Defence planning, concluded that:

> the true purpose of Civil Defence is not to ensure the survival of as large a proportion of the population as possible but to ensure the survival of Government, whatever may befall the country.

This had long been obvious to the intelligent observer. The much-enhanced network of civil and military bunkers would ensure that this objective was met, but the civil element would have no rescue and recuperation mission; it would in future, as it had since 1968, only be of benefit to the sturdy survivors of the initial nuclear attack.

Before the entire and complex network of bunkers envisaged by the Thatcher régime was complete the cold war ended with the abrupt collapse of the Soviet

Union. By 1992 the majority of the local authority bunkers other than the County controls (which now serve as true, civil contingency emergency planning centres, residing with some embarrassment within their claustrophobic, blast and fallout protected basements) were abandoned, as was the entire UKWMO network. By the end of the decade all the regional government headquarters were gone too, sold into the private sector for a pittance, despite the countless millions of public funds that had been expended upon them. All that remain now are the hardened military command, control and communications bunkers like Northwood, Bentley Priory and the much publicized 'CCC' strategic communications bunker built in a disused underground ammunition depot near Corsham, along with the 1992 PINDAR crisis management centre, below the MOD extension in Whitehall, and the mothballed but still very secret Emergency Government War Headquarters at Spring Quarry, near Corsham in Wiltshire.

EMERGENCY REGIONAL GOVERNMENT OF THE UNITED KINGDOM UNDER NUCLEAR ATTACK

The early cold war measures adopted by the British government to ensure its own survival were based upon contingency plans first prepared in response to the unprecedented level of civil unrest that swept the country at the time of the 1926 general strike. It was realized at that time that concerted industrial action could quickly paralyse every aspect of the national communications systems and thereby leave central government at Whitehall isolated and impotent. Emergency powers were enacted that divided the nation into eleven geographical areas, to each of which was appointed a Civil Commissioner who could, in the event of a breakdown of effective control from Whitehall, assume certain limited powers of central government to ensure the maintenance of food supplies and essential services. This system was revived in a modified form in 1936 to ensure, on the national scale, the continuity of government in the event of overwhelming destruction by aerial bombardment in the European war that was now looming on the horizon and at the more local scale, to organize the structure of ARP and Civil Defence services in the regions. Under this system mainland Britain was divided into eleven regions, with London as a further, separate administrative region in its own right. Each region would be administered by a Regional Commissioner responsible for the day-to-day organization of the ARP and Civil Defence services, and who was also charged with the authority to assume much more wide-ranging powers of central government than his predecessor within his region, should any contingency prevent London exercising control throughout the country.

At the end of the Second World War most of the Civil Defence organization and regional government contingency plans were quickly swept aside by a government anxious to rid itself of the memories of the previous six years. By 1948 the bubble of optimism had burst; old and latent hostilities were revived and events in Berlin seemed to pave the route to inevitable war with the USSR. Despite the atomic bombs that were dropped upon Japan and incontrovertible evidence of Soviet possession of atomic weapons, western military strategists still assumed blindly that the next war would be much the same as the last and made their preparations accordingly. Although by 1952 the government had admitted that atomic bombs in the twenty Kiloton range, similar to those dropped on the Japanese cities, might be used against the United Kingdom, it was still envisaged that the next war would be a long war like the Second World War, lasting months or perhaps years. Attrition bombing and the continued and gradual destruction of the large industrial and administrative centres would be a central feature of this war, and thus a strong Civil Defence organization would be required to haul the injured from the ashes and provide succour and sustenance to the survivors. To meet the new demand, the recently dismantled wartime structure was reconstituted under the terms of the 1948 *Civil Defence Act*. The regional structure remained essentially the same, but London was divided into four administrative areas, each under the control of a sub-regional Commissioner, and a separate administration was established for Northern Ireland. The primary role of the Commissioner was still, as in the Second World War, one of directing the rescue and recovery function of the Civil Defence organization and ensuring the continuity of essential services, but increased emphasis was put upon his mandate to assume the authority of Central Government *in extremis*. As the Regional Commissioner was appointed from a list of prominent and competent local administrators he was not necessarily ideal for the potential central government role, and his primary purpose continued to be the organization of conventional Civil Defence measures within the region; the 'continuity of government' being very much a secondary issue. Following on the recommendation of the 1949 Home Office Working Party on War Rooms, it was decided that each region would be provided with a purpose-built hardened War Room, or bunker

> established outside the central key area of its Regional town, it must also be located in an area where adequate signal communications can be provided to keep the War Room in touch with other civil and military headquarters in the region and with the Central War Room in London.

Plans for the twelve mainland regional and four sub-regional London War Rooms were prepared in 1951. Construction began in the spring of 1953 and spanned the next three years; the last bunker, at Shirley in Birmingham, being completed in 1956. The chosen locations were:

Region 1:	Northern	Newcastle
Region 2:	North East	Leeds
Region 3:	North Midlands	Nottingham
Region 4:	Eastern	Cambridge
Region 5:	London	Mill Hill
		Wanstead Flats
		Chislehurst
		Cheam
Region 6:	Southern	Reading
Region 7:	South West	Flowers Hill, Bristol
Region 8:	Wales	Cardiff
Region 9:	Midlands	Shirley, Birmingham
Region 10:	North West	Manchester
Region 11:	Scotland	Kirknewton
Region 12:	South East	Tunbridge Wells

A standard design of two-storey, reinforced concrete structure, modified slightly to meet local conditions, was adopted for all the Regional bunkers, while smaller, single-storey buildings were designed for the London sub-regional centres. There appear to have been no dormitories provided for the London War Rooms, nor any large-scale reserves of food or water, which indicates that they, like the Regional structures, were not designed to operate for any length of time in a 'closed down' mode. Indeed, in the years before the danger of radioactive fallout was appreciated, there was no such requirement.

The Regional War Rooms were invariably built on existing government sites, many of which had their origins in the Second World War. Compared with the ad-hoc wartime accommodation, the 1950s War Rooms were very substantial structures, broadly similar to the Anti-Aircraft Operations Rooms (AAORs) which were built at the same time. The War Rooms were plain, rectangular buildings approximately ninety foot by seventy-five foot, with five-foot-thick reinforced concrete walls and roofs no less than seven feet thick. A single-storey annexe housed the heating, ventilation and air-conditioning plant. Three conspicuous concrete ventilation ducts on the roof of the annexe were the only irregular external features of these buildings. The internal layout was also broadly similar to the AAORs of the period, with a central, two-storey, thirty-three-foot square map-room and adjacent control centre, overlooked by perspex-glazed observation rooms on the upper floor and surrounded by a narrow corridor which gave access, on the lower floor, to the canteen, dormitories and other domestic services, and on the upper floor to the offices of various administrative departments. The walls of the central map room were themselves of substantial reinforced concrete construction and formed a hardened inner sanctum. Although later modifications were made, pedestrian access was originally possible only via two small, heavily constructed blast doors that opened onto dog-legged corridors fitted with internal air-lock doors, designed to minimize the effect of blast. Most of the War Rooms were built at ground level, though under certain ground conditions, as at Cardiff, the lower levels were partially buried.

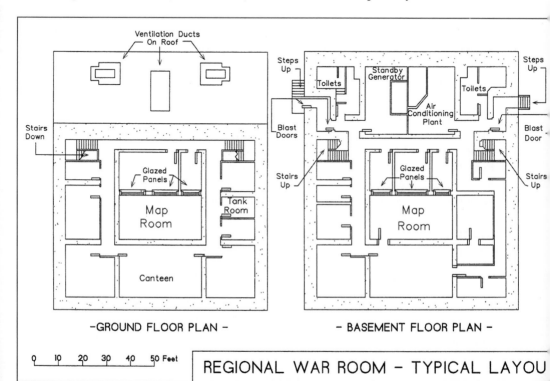

-GROUND FLOOR PLAN -   - BASEMENT FLOOR PLAN -

0 10 20 30 40 50 Feet

REGISTRATIONAL WAR ROOM - TYPICAL LAYOU

By the time the last of the War Rooms was nearing completion in 1956 their functional value was already being called into doubt. The implications of the hydrogen bomb and the spectre of radioactive fallout had dramatically altered the perceived image of war. There would no longer be a prolonged period of constant bombardment and gradual attrition; instead, the nuclear bomb would bring with it instant destruction of whole cities, national paralysis and industrial and social collapse. A short war, lasting no longer than perhaps a few days, would be followed by months or years of hopeless ruin, industrial decay and utter desolation. Civil Defence would be an anachronistic irrelevancy; the new requirement would be for a regional control system large enough, strong enough and sufficiently stable to oversee and guide the process of recovery through the months or years of hardship, recovery and national regeneration that lay ahead. With a staff of only forty-five personnel, limited communications facilities and no scope for expansion without radical reconstruction, the Regional War Rooms were totally unsuitable for the long-term task. Home Office plans for a series of sub-regional controls, which would have lightened the load of the Regional War Rooms and allowed closer liaison between the War Rooms and the lower-order Civil Defence controls, particularly in the more densely populated urban areas, were announced in 1955, but lack of funding prevented their implementation.

THE REGIONAL WAR ROOMS

Region No. 1: NEWCASTLE
Unlike all the other Regional War Rooms, which were new constructions built to a standard MOWB design, the Newcastle bunker utilized an existing underground structure dating from the previous war.

The bunker, at Kenton Bar, consisted of the old RAF No.13 Group Operations Room built in 1940. The operations room is approached via a long flight of stairs from an innocuous, un-hardened surface building. Disused since the 1960s the structure is still fairly sound and is currently being considered for preservation in the midst of a commercial development area.

Region No. 2: LEEDS
After 1960 the Leeds War Room was used by the City Council as its emergency control. Due to poor insulation the lower floor often flooded to a depth of two feet so the council used only the upper level.

Region No. 3: NOTTINGHAM
The Nottingham War Room, in Chalfont Drive, was extended to accommodate the extra staff required to fulfil its role as an RSG in the 1960s by the addition of an extra floor, seemingly supported on stilts above the original structure.

Region No. 4: CAMBRIDGE
Built on a government estate at Brooklands Avenue, the Cambridge War Room is one of two that continued to function in the Regional Government schemes until the end of emergency war planning in 1992. Details of its transformation to fulfil its role as a RSG are given elsewhere. By the 1980s the War Room was

nominally disused, its functions having been usurped by the new RGHQs at Bawburgh and Hertford, but in fact planning was well advanced for a thorough overhaul of the bunker in 1989 to fit it for a new but undefined role in future plans.

This scheme, which never came to fruition due to the abrupt end of the cold war, was to provide a vast network of small, relatively unsophisticated and highly redundant alternative communication cells from which both civil and military authority could be administered in time of future war. The Warren Row RSG was reactivated at this time for the same purpose and it is probable that the Truro ROC bunker, among others, was also earmarked for this purpose. Within the bunker, which is still in excellent condition, there is copious evidence of the unfinished improvement work, abandoned in 1991. The building is now disused and is the property of the Ministry of Fisheries and Food, who still occupy adjacent buildings.

Region No. 5: LONDON GROUP CONTROLS
Cheam: Bunker demolished and site redeveloped.
Wanstead: Bunker disused and scheduled for demolition.
Kemnal Manor: Bunker long abandoned, currently being redeveloped as a private residence.

Its replacement, Pear Tree House, is now also abandoned and will eventually be re-incorporated into the block of flats of which it forms a part.

25. **Wanstead London Sub-Regional Control Bunker.** *Nick Catford*

Mill Hill: Abandoned, overgrown, and scheduled for demolition.

Southall: A Second World War Civil Defence bunker re-activated in the 1960s and finally abandoned in 1983. Buried beneath Hanborough School in South Street, Southall, the bunker is in poor condition but contains many original artefacts and is likely to remain untouched for the foreseeable future.

Region No. 6: READING

The Reading War Room in White Knight's Park is now occupied by the University of Reading, who have made a number of internal alterations in recent years and have added two new emergency exits to comply with current Health and Safety regulations.

From the early 1960s when the Reading War Room ceased to have a primary executive function it served as a land-line communications centre for the RSG at Warren Row. The latter bunker, built in an underground Second World War aircraft component factory, was too small and structurally inadequate to operate successfully without external support.

Region No. 7: BRISTOL

The Bristol War Room is located in a government compound at Flowers Hill, just to the south of the A4, at the rear of a small trading estate in Brislington on the south-west outskirts of the city. Replaced by the two new S-RC bunkers at Hope Cove and Ullenwood in 1962, the Bristol War Room was relegated to a minor Civil Defence role overseeing the four Bristol Group controls until 1968. In later years the building was used as a county control by the new and highly unpopular County of Avon until the unmourned passing of that dire body some years ago.

26. **Brislington Regional War Room.** Its outline now softened by rampant Virginia creeper, this huge concrete monolith started life as a Regional War Room to control south-west England. Later relegated to the role of Bristol Corporation Civil Defence control it subsequently became, for a brief period in the early 1980s. the Avon County nuclear bunker. *Author's collection*

27. Brislington Regional War Room. Reactivated as the Avon County nuclear bunker for Operation SQUARE LEG in 1980, it was subsequently abandoned. Twenty-two years later the main operations room, seen here, is still littered with the paraphernalia of SQUARE LEG. *Author's collection*

28. Brislington Regional War Room. A view of the communications centre showing telephone operators' cubicles. *Author's collection*

The building is currently well maintained but subject to commercial proposals that may result in its demolition.

Region No. 8: CARDIFF
The Cardiff War Room, behind a BT training centre close to the M4 motorway at Coryton is now disused, although kept secure by British Telecom.

Region No. 9: BIRMINGHAM
The West Midlands War Room is located in Stratford Road, Shirley, on the southern outskirts of Birmingham, and has been owned by British Gas (now Transco) since the mid 1970s when they purchased it for use as an archive store.

Many of the internal features, including the generators, the remarkable curved perspex screens on the upper and lower floors of the operations well, and a curious 'dumb-waiter' used to transport documents between floors still remain. The only major alteration has been the insertion of a false floor that now spans the upper gallery of the operations well to provide additional storage space.

Region No. 10: MANCHESTER
The Regional War Room stands in the grounds of the Nuffield Hospital and is currently used by the Hospital Authority as a secure pharmaceutical store.

Region No. 11: SCOTLAND
Edinburgh (Kirknewton): A standard two-storey bunker with both levels completely above ground. Located in East Calder, the building became the Scottish Eastern Zone Control in 1962 and, following the rationalization of emergency planning in Scotland in 1983, the new Southern control, taking over the area of the former Western Zone HQ at Torrance House.

29. **Kirknewton Regional War Room.** In this exterior view the original, lighter coloured 1950s War Room is to the front, with the 1980s extension, built when the bunker was reconstructed as a Regional Government Headquarters, at the rear. *Nick Catford*

30. **Kirknewton RGHQ.** Interior view showing manual telephone switchboards in the communications centre. *Nick Catford*

Kirknewton also functioned as the Scottish Central War Headquarters from 1983 until purpose-built facilities were opened at Cultybraggan in 1990. The bunker was sold in the early 1990s and survived as a night club for a short while, until, like many cold war bunkers, being relegated to a storage facility.

Region No. 12: TUNBRIDGE WELLS

The Tunbridge War Room opened in 1953 and closed five years later in 1958 having been superseded by the RSG in tunnels below Dover Castle. Retained on care and maintenance, the bunker was reactivated in 1963 as a Sub-Regional Control, a role it maintained until 1972. Still retained by the Home Office, the bunker became the home of the first Police National Computer. In later years, after the PNC had moved to newer and more sophisticated premises, the Tunbridge War Room was relegated to duty as an archive repository. The building was demolished in 1997 to make way for the new Land Registry complex.

THE REGIONAL SEATS OF GOVERNMENT

Just one year later the entire system of wartime contingency planning was turned on its head as the full implications of total nuclear war became clearer. The requirement was no longer for a sustained Civil Defence rescue mission; the war would be over, quite literally, in a flash and survivors in the target areas, if there were survivors, would be beyond help. Communications would be destroyed and the previous system of delegated responsibility, from Central Government, through the Regions to the local authority and parish levels would be impossible to implement. Instead, to respond to the needs of a fragmented society, absolute

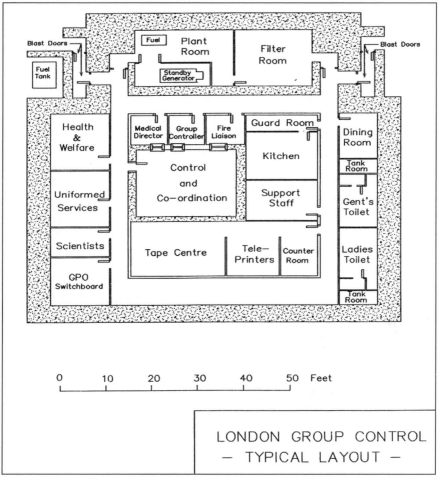

Fuel

Plant Room

Filter Room

Blast Doors

Blast Doors

Fuel Tank

Standby Generator

Health & Welfare

Medical Director

Group Controller

Fire Liaison

Guard Room

Dining Room

Kitchen

Tank Room

Control and Co-ordination

Uniformed Services

Support Staff

Gent's Toilet

Scientists

Tape Centre

Tele-Printers

Counter Room

Ladies Toilet

GPO Switchboard

Tank Room

0   10   20   30   40   50   Feet

LONDON GROUP CONTROL
— TYPICAL LAYOUT —

responsibility for the fate of the survivors in the less affected areas would be more completely delegated to the local authority Civil Defence organization, whose powers would be greatly enhanced. The local authority would continue to oversee the day-to-day minutiae of rehabilitation and stabilization within its immediate area for a prolonged period, until the general stability of the region was such that more direct control could be exercised by the Regional Commissioner and his staff.

The function of the Regional Commissioner was now redefined. Regional administration in the early post-war recovery stage would be limited to only the broadest policy level. Henceforth the Commissioner would be a central government, rather than local, appointee; his responsibility would now be primarily to Whitehall and his role was to assume the mantle of central government authority within his region should contact with London be lost. To fulfil this enlarged role, which was in effect to create a Whitehall in microcosm, a much larger staff was required in order to mirror all the Departments of State, with the exception of the Foreign Office, the Ministry of Defence and the Treasury. In the role of autocratic regional governor, the Regional Commissioner would have ultimate authority over the local military commanders and would be empowered to use their forces as he saw fit, either for defence against external enemies, to suppress internal dissent, or to implement sanctions. The existing war rooms were inadequate to meet the new requirements and in 1956 a Home Office working party issued specifications for a new form of Regional Government headquarters capable of sustaining an operational staff of over 300 for several months. The expanded role and closer co-operation with the military authorities of the proposed new bunkers was reflected in the designation 'Joint Civil-Military Headquarters' and the fact that, of the operational complement of 300, approximately one hundred would be military personnel. Further evidence of the increasingly intimate linkage between the civil and military elements of post-holocaust government is the fact that the original building specifications for the new Joint Headquarters, which were to be 'windowless concrete structures above ground, giving protection against fallout but not blast', called for them to be sited within the boundaries of existing military establishments.

By the end of 1957 swingeing budgetary cuts had led to a review, and subsequent cutback, of the bunker programme. The concept of new, purpose-built structures was abandoned and in 1958 it was proposed to adapt suitable existing buildings, where available, in the precautionary period leading up to all-out war. The London Sub-Regional War Rooms were to be retained, and four of the existing Regional War Rooms were earmarked for retention. Sites selected under the 1958 scheme were:

REGION	LOCATION
1	Catterick Barracks
2	Easingwold Civil Defence College (later, York Castle)
3	Nottingham War Room
4	Cambridge War Room
5	London Sub-Regional Headquarters
6	Reading War Room
7	Bolt Head ex 'Rotor' radar station
8	Brecon Barracks
9	Shrewsbury Barracks
10	Preston Barracks (Fullwood)
11	Scottish Region
12	Tunbridge Wells War Room

Little was accomplished under this plan, but in response to the quickening of international tension that culminated with the Cuban missile crisis, an ad-hoc emergency building programme was hastily initiated. Between late 1958 and the summer of 1961 a disparate assortment of existing government buildings were adapted to serve as regional bunkers. These structures were the legendary Regional Seats of Government or RSGs, the existence of which were spectacularly exposed by 'Spies for Peace', a splinter group of CND, in April 1963. Luckily, by 1961 the government had on its hands a range of redundant hardened structures suitable for adaptation, including several underground aircraft engine factories built at the height of the Blitz during the Second World War, a number of underground Air Ministry command centres of similar vintage, and a range of relatively modern underground or semi-underground control bunkers that were relics of the short-lived ROTOR radar network. The table below outlines the locations and origins of the early 1960s RSG network:

REGION No. 1 - NORTH
Gaza Block, Catterick Camp, Yorkshire.

REGION No. 2 – NORTH EAST
Imphal Barracks and York Castle.
Shipton ROTOR underground operations centre earmarked as a permanent replacement, but the RSG scheme was abandoned before this could be implemented.

REGION No. 3 – NORTH MIDLANDS
Nottingham War Room, Chalfont Drive, Nottingham.

REGION No. 4 – EASTERN
Cambridge War Room, Brookland Avenue, Cambridge.

REGION No. 5 – LONDON
The London War Rooms retained.

REGION No. 6 – SOUTHERN
Warren Row, near Henley on Thames, Second World War underground aircraft component factory.

REGION No. 7 – SOUTH WEST
Bolt Head, overlooking Salcombe Bay in Devon. Semi-underground ROTOR GCI radar station.

REGION No. 8 – WALES
Brecon Barracks.

REGION No. 9 – MIDLANDS
Drakelow near Kidderminster. Underground Second World War aircraft engine factory.

REGION No. 10 – NORTH WEST
Preston. (Fullwood Barracks).

SCOTLAND – NATIONAL HEADQUARTERS
Barnton Quarry, near Edinburgh. Semi-underground ROTOR radar operations centre.

SCOTLAND – WESTERN ZONE
Torrance House, former AAOR

SCOTLAND – NORTHERN ZONE
Anstruther. Underground, two-level ROTOR R3 pattern GCI radar operations room.

Scotland – EASTERN ZONE
Kirknewton, Regional War Room.

To render them suitable for their new role, the 1950s War Rooms at Nottingham and Cambridge were extended to more than double their original size to accommodate the RSG staff, which had, by 1963, expanded to 450. A notable feature of the two-storey, 140′ x100′ extension at Cambridge is that it is much more lightly built than the original structure, its external concrete walls being only twelve inches thick, reflecting the Home Office policy that the building need only be radiation-proof and not necessarily blast-proof. Whilst the redevelopment of the two war rooms took radically different forms, the final accommodation was similar, and a description of the finished work at Cambridge will illustrate the general layout. The upper floor consisted almost entirely of dormitories and catering facilities, while the lower floor consisted of a wide range of departmental offices and secondary air-conditioning and back-up power supply plant. The old building was reorganized to provide space on the lower floor for communications equipment, while the upper floor was given over to executive offices and a conference room.

The site of RSG-6 at Warren Row was a disused underground aircraft component factory, the construction of which began at the height of the Second World War blitz and latterly had been abandoned and placed under the care of the Ministry of Public Building and Works. The location, approximately fifty feet underground in a disused chalk mine, seemed attractive at first sight, but it was never satisfactory. Although substantially supported by brickwork erected when

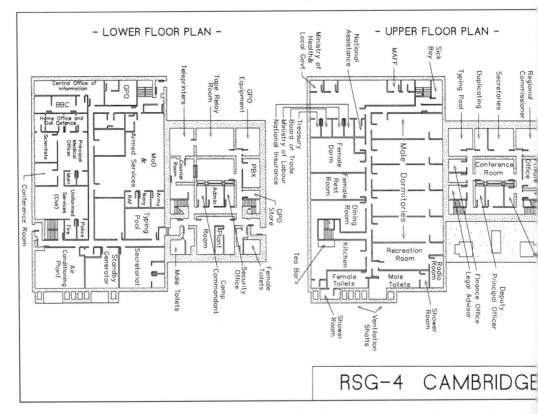

RSG-4 CAMBRIDGE

the quarry was developed as an aircraft factory, the rock formation was of dubious stability and the workings suffered badly from high humidity which proved virtually impossible to control for most of the year.

Hidden in a roadside copse on the edge of the tiny village of Warren Row, RSG-6 was, until commercialization in recent years made it more prominent, remarkably unchanged from its wartime appearance. All that is to be seen on the surface is an old brick boilerhouse with a suspiciously modern chimney, a tall aerial mask and a wooden hut full of sandbags. Underground, the 1000 feet of tunnel takes the form of an extended 'U', with a sloping entrance shaft at the end of each leg. Most of the tunnel is on one level with a clear roof height of about fifteen feet, but in places higher clearance has enabled an extra floor to be inserted, the upper levels occupied mainly by dormitories. Some forty-two offices and service chambers have been formed within the underground space, together with large drinking water storage tanks capable of holding an estimated two weeks' emergency reserve.

The existing, external boilerhouse was refurbished to serve the RSG, but a comprehensive new air-conditioning plant was installed underground in a side-passage that linked to the boilerhouse. Because of the limited space available within the tunnels it was necessary to locate most of the bunker's telecommunications equipment elsewhere and the old Regional War Room at White Knight's Park in Reading remained in service for this purpose.

Warren Row attained notoriety and secured an enduring place in the history of the anti-nuclear movement in April 1963 when a small group of anti-nuclear protestors, calling themselves 'Spies for Peace', broke into RSG-6 and, with the aid of documents discovered there, revealed to the world that the British

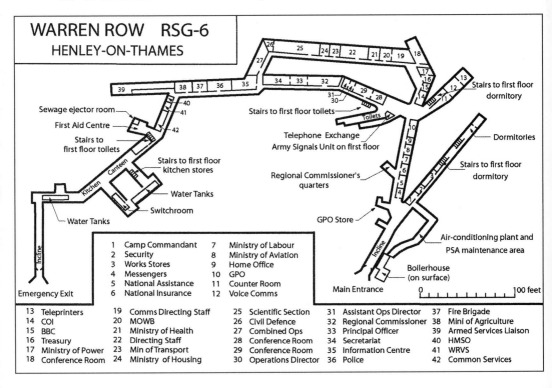

WARREN ROW RSG-6
HENLEY-ON-THAMES

Sewage ejector room
First Aid Centre
Stairs to first floor toilets
Kitchen   Canteen
Stairs to first floor kitchen stores
Water Tanks
Switchroom
Water Tanks
Incline
Emergency Exit

Stairs to first floor toilets
Telephone Exchange
Army Signals Unit on first floor
Regional Commissioner's quarters
GPO Store

Stairs to first floor dormitory
Dormitories
Stairs to first floor dormitory
Air-conditioning plant and PSA maintenance area
Boilerhouse (on surface)
Main Entrance
Incline

0   100 feet

1	Camp Commandant	7	Ministry of Labour
2	Security	8	Ministry of Aviation
3	Works Stores	9	Home Office
4	Messengers	10	GPO
5	National Assistance	11	Counter Room
6	National Insurance	12	Voice Comms

13	Teleprinters	19	Comms Directing Staff	25	Scientific Section	31	Assistant Ops Director	37	Fire Brigade
14	COI	20	MOWB	26	Civil Defence	32	Regional Commissioner	38	Mini of Agriculture
15	BBC	21	Ministry of Health	27	Combined Ops	33	Principal Officer	39	Armed Services Liaison
16	Treasury	22	Directing Staff	28	Conference Room	34	Secretariat	40	HMSO
17	Ministry of Power	23	Min of Transport	29	Conference Room	35	Information Centre	41	WRVS
18	Conference Room	24	Ministry of Housing	30	Operations Director	36	Police	42	Common Services

Government had constructed for its own protection a chain of secret underground bunkers in which the favoured few would sit out the looming nuclear war while the civilian population vaporized in the ensuing holocaust. This was a seminal moment for British society; the moment from which the nation, and in particular the intellectually aware, newly enfranchised younger generation, lost faith in the Establishment.

Spies for Peace circulated a pamphlet that spring, entitled 'Danger – Official Secret RSG-6', which encapsulated the distrust, fear, and feelings of a generation, and is reproduced below in full:

DANGER — OFFICIAL SECRET — RSG 6

This pamphlet is about a small group of people who have accepted thermonuclear war as a probability, and are consciously and carefully planning for it.

They are above the Army, the Police, the Ministries or Civil Defence. They are based in fourteen secret headquarters, each ruled by a Regional Commissioner with absolute power over millions of people. In the whole of Britain only about 5,000 men and women are involved: these chosen few are our shadow military government.

Their headquarters are called Regional Seats of Government. Our story mainly concerns RSG-6, which will rule much of Southern England. The people in RSG-6 are professors, top civil servants, air marshals and policemen. They are quietly waiting for the day the bomb drops, for that will be the day they take over... .

4000 copies printed and distributed in Britain and abroad. Sent to the national press, papers covering the Southern Region, local councillors and political parties. Sent to Bertrand Russell, Albert Schweitzer, Linus Pauling, and members of anti-war movements everywhere, we hope they will do something about it. Sent to Harold MacWilson, George Wigg, and the head of MI5, we hope it will make them cross. Sent to Michael Foot, Barbara Castle, Tony Greenwood, Frank Cousins and Gerald Nabarro,we shall be interested to see what they do.

Good Friday, 1963

Regional Seats of Government

The government have secretly established a network of Regional Seats of Government covering the whole country. RSG-12 lies far behind the Second World War gun emplacements in the Cliffs of Dover... . RSG-2 is in a converted fort on the outskirts of York... . RSG-4 is a concrete bunker underneath Government offices in Brooklands Avenue, Cambridge.

The locations and telephone numbers of the RSG's are as follows: (RSG-5 and RSG-11 are still being built):-

RSG-1	Catterick (2011, 2081)
RSG-2	York (59831, 59841)
RSG-3	Nottingham (291151)
RSG-4	Cambridge (59800)
RSG-6	Reading (61181, 62641)
RSG-7	Dartmouth (Kingsbridge 2611)
RSG-8	Brecon (861)
RSG-9	Kidderminster (3474)
RSG 10	Dover (2380)
RSG NI	Armagh (2230)
RSG Scotland	Edinburgh (Davidsons Main 1711)

The RSG system corresponds roughly to the Civil Defence areas, and its HQ (called CHAPLIN) is somewhere in London (ABBEY 1255). The RSGs are also linked to a military HQ at Aldershot (24431).

Where is RSG-6?

The post-nuclear government at Reading — RSG-6 — has some offices at the Regional Civil Defence Centre, among the Civil Service buildings at WHITE KNIGHTS PARK. But the real site of RSG-6 is in a subterranean bunker 8 miles out of Reading — in the aptly-named town of WARGRAVE, less than a mile off the main road from Reading to London (A4).

RSG-6 is disguised as the Home Office Underground Factory Warren Row. Under this name it is kept up without too much suspicion, and under this name it is maintained from a Ministry of Works office in Buckingham Avenue, Slough. It has in fact no manufacturing facilities whatever, except for duplicators and Photostats (red tape) and lavatories (bad smells).

The entrance to RSG-6 is a few yards across the road from the Red House pub, at the east end of Warren Row. It is surrounded and masked by a thick woods and low hills. All that can be seen from the road is a padlocked wooden gate and a gatekeeper's hut. There is no name outside, and no indication that it is a government establishment. It has been crudely but effectively disguised.

The surface buildings inside the gate consist of a couple of wooden storage sheds and a brick boiler house. But there is a concrete ramp wide enough to take motor vehicles, which runs down into the hillside as far as a pair of locked wooden doors (for keeping out H-blast, presumably). At some distance away there is an array of wireless aerials, whose cables disappear down a vertical shaft into the hilltop.

RSG-6 lies inside the hill, below the visible buildings and the wireless aerials — a comfortable, war-grave for the Southern Region military government.

What is RSG-6

RSG-6 is a standby headquarters with an operational staff of several hundred. In the event of war, it will take over the Government of the SOUTHERN REGION, which covers the counties of Oxfordshire, Berks, Hants, Dorset, and the Isle of Wight, and the county boroughs of Oxford, Reading, Portsmouth, Southampton and Bournemouth. It lies conveniently in the centre of a region with a population of three megadeaths.

RSG-6 is near the USAF Strategic Air Command and RAF Bomber Command underground headquarters at High Wycombe, the Army Tactical Command headquarters at Aldershot, and the Army Strategic Reserve's concrete bunker HQ near Salisbury. It is also just outside the blast area of a bomb up to sixty megaton size dropped on London.

Warren Row is a wholly self-contained community. It has its own facilities for generating electricity, pumping water and disposing of sewage. It has several months supply of fresh water, fuel oil and red tape. It has a canteen which can operate on a twenty-four hour basis. It even has a bar in which the lucky inhabitants can drink the world above them goodbye — open only during licensing hours, of course. There is dormitory accommodation for about 400 people, segregated by sex.

RSG-6 is the centre of a complicated communications network. It is connected to the ordinary telephone network (Littlewick Green 395), and by red telephone direct line to the underground switching centre at White Knights Park (Reading 61181/62641). It has a dozen teleprinters and a radio signals department with UHF and VHF wireless equipment, for use in the highly likely event of the telephone system being destroyed. Even the clocks in RSG-6 are labelled 'Zulu Time' — the international NATO system based on the US Strategic Air Command.

It is interesting to note that the GPO is now building thirty-six giant radio towers, in a network that will cover the entire country. One is London's Museum Tower, already a 300-ft concrete beanstalk off Tottenham Court Road. But a less publicised one lies just across the Thames from Warren Row among the beech woods of Stokenchurch, less than five miles from RSG-6. Most of these radio towers are close to one of the RSGs, and the system will be an integral part of the military communications. Total cost to the GPO subscriber? Tens of millions.

What is the Function of RSG-6?

RSG-6 is not a centre for Civil Defence. It is a centre for military government. It is the headquarters of the REGIONAL COMMISSIONER, who will have supreme power over the three million bodies in his region. In this headquarters the Regional Civil Defence Corps plays a minor and definitely subordinate part. RSG-6 is staffed by civil servants in the middle echelons, and by Service officers in the middle ranks. They all have been appointed.

Virtually every important Government department except the Church of England is represented and has been given its staff and offices. There are rooms for the Army, Navy, Air Force, Police, Fire Brigade and Civil Defence. Each of these is centralized under a Supremo, who has already been named in each case. There are offices for the Treasury (including the Big Five), the Central Office of Information, the GPO, the BBC (but not ITV!), the Board of Trade, and the Ministries of Health, Food, Supply, Transport and Power. Other departments which will undoubtedly be important after the bomb drops, and which also have offices in RSG-6, are the Ministry of Labour, the National Assistance Board, and the WVS.

The functions of the various departments are enlightening. The COI will be responsible for censorship, as well as for public announcements (to whom?). The Ministry of Labour will be responsible for conscription of special workers, as well as for labour relations (between whom?). The Ministry of Housing will deal with the disposal of the dead as well as the homeless. There are offices too for the departments without analogous peacetime functions. Thus the Scientific Unit will deal with bomb data and radiation risks, and HMSO will print proclamations against rioting. The whole thing is a perfect example of military government.

Who is in RSG-6?

If there were any doubt about the function of the Home Office Underground Factory Warren Row, the names of the people there would soon dispel it. The Camp Commandant, who looks after military administration, is Major G.D. Scales. His equivalent on the civilian side, the Principal officer, is S.L. Lees. Mr Lees is a Permanent Under Secretary at the Treasury, where he is Director of Organisation and Methods. On his secretariat are A.G. Hurrell (a Principal Officer at the Ministry of Education), I.H. Lightman (a Principal in the secretariat of the Ministry of Works), and L.H. Mann (a Senior Scientific Officer at the Ministry of Aviation).

Take a look at some of the other departments. Note particularly the rank of all concerned. There is not a single elected person among them. It is Colonels and Principal Officers who will rule after the bomb drops, not MPs or Councillors.

NAVY: Rear-Admiral F.E. Clemitson, (the Admiralty Regional Officer), with a large staff of Captains, Lieutenants, Commanders and Civil Officers, as well as ratings to polish the top brass.
ARMY: Major-General J.F. Metcalfe (General Officer Commanding Aldershot

District), with a staff of Officers and other ranks, including Lt. Col. J.D. Sale (Senior Staff Officer of Operations, Aldershot District).

AIR FORCE: Air Commodore J.B. Cowerd, with a number of officers, and some other ranks to whitewash the fallout.

POLICE: D. Osmond (Chief Constable of Hants) plus a staff of fifteen, including some Women Police Constables.

FIRE BRIGADE: E R Ashill (Regional Fire Officer, and Chief Fire Officer of Hampshire). P Mees (CFO for Berks and Reading), A.H. Johnstone (CFO for Surrey), and an all male staff of twenty-one.

CIVIL DEFENCE: Captain K.L. Harkness, RN (London Regional Director of Civil Defence) — one wonders who looks after London? Have the Londoners who have volunteered for CD been told where their boss is to hide out?

CENTRAL OFFICE OF INFORMATION: P.T. Ede (Chief Regional Officer of the COI). There is also a Special Information Unit, which will act as a co-ordinating centre for processing information from all the other departments. This will be run by J.N. Allen (a Principal Inspector at the Board of Inland Revenue) and J.S. Cassell (a Principal at the Overseas Department of the Ministry of Labour).

G.P.O: H.S. Thomsett (the Regional Engineer) and L.G. Hawker (Senior Assistant Telecommunications Controller, Home Counties).

HEALTH: C.J. Plumb (until recently a Principal Regional Officer at the Ministry of Health). On his staff is Dr H.L. Belcher (Surgeon Commander RN, Retrd) who is a specialist in venereal diseases. Also present are Dr Terence Geffen and Dr Charles Seeley (both Medical Officers of the MoH) and B.H. Street (a Senior Executive of the Executive Councils Division of the MoH).

FOOD: C. Dugelby (Chief Executive Officer of the SE Region of the Ministry of Agriculture, Fisheries and Food).

TRANSPORT: S.T. Benns (Clerk of the Metropolitan Traffic Area, Ministry of Transport). Marples' hole will be bigger then.

POWER: W.H. Willmot (a Principal Officer in the Coal Division of the Ministry of Power).

LABOUR: G.K. Pollard and W.A. Sutcliffe (both senior officers of the Southern Region of the Ministry of Labour).

The Old Boy Net in RSG-6

The largest civilian department in RSG-6 is the Scientific Section, which is run almost entirely by Oxford dons. Take a look at them, listed by faculty:

PHYSICS: G.K. Woodgate, MA, D.Phil, St. Peter's

                      J.M. Baker, MA, D.Phil, Merton

                      D.F. Shaw, MA, D.Phil, Keble

INORGANIC CHEMISTRY:

                      F.J.C. Rosotti, MA, BSc, D.Phil, St Edmund Hall

                      C.S.G Phillips, MA, PhD, Merton

PHYSICAL CHEMISTRY:

                      H.W. Thompson, CBE, MA, BSc, PhD, FRS, St John's

                      R.E. Richards, MA, D.Phil, FRS, Lincoln

Other universities are well represented, just to keep things fair, by such figures as Professor A.N. Black, MA, MI Mech.E, late of Exeter College Oxford (Professor of Engineering and Administrative Head of Engineering Department at Southampton University), and William Davey, BSc, PhD, FRIC, AM Inst. Pet, MBIM (Principal of the Portsmouth College of Technology).

In the Scientific Section at RSG-6 there are also a number of Scientific Officers of the War Office, Air Ministry, the Ministry of

Aviation and the Department of Scientific and Industrial Research. This section is obviously one of the most important in RSG-6.

It is comforting to know that the Scientific Section at RSG-4 is similarly run by the Oxbridge men of the Eastern Region — Cambridge dons, in this case. Among them are D.V. Bugg, MA, PhD, a Demonstrator in Physics, of Emmanuel; C.L. Smith, MA, PhD, Assistant Director of Research in Radiotherapeutics, St John's; and E.S. Shire, MA, Reader in Physics at King's. Mr. Shire is the Scientific Advisor to the Regional Civil Defence Corps. Incidentally, the Civil Defence section in RSG-4 is also run by someone from the London Region — J.P. Miller, the Assistant Regional Director, another lucky man who won't be in London when the bomb drops.

RSG-6 In Action

RSG-6 has been activated several times. One of these was for Exercise PARAPLUIE, which took place on a number of weekends in April, May and June 1962. This exercise was based on the assumption that seven bombs were dropped on England as follows: ten-megaton Bombs on NW and E London and Byfleet; a five-megaton Bomb on Birmingham; 100-kiloton Bombs near Oxford and Chetwode; and a teeny weeny fifty-kiloton Bomb on Aldershot. The Russians had exploded a sixty-megaton Bomb the previous autumn.

In the Southern Region troops were needed to help the police keep order. But soon after the Birmingham Bomb the radiation levels rose so high that all military personnel in the Region except for Dorset were ordered to go to ground for forty-eight hours. What happened to the civilian population does not bear thinking about. As for RSG-6, its communications fell into such a state of chaos that messages were transmitted up to two hours late, and there was total confusion about who messages had come from, and where they were going to. This happened during a purely imaginary exercise which assumed nuclear destruction on an absurdly small scale.

Things were even worse during Exercise FALLEX last September. 'Der Spiegel' revealed the chaos in Germany: the British Press wept crocodile tears about censorship over there, but has so far not said a word about the same exercise in Britain. We wonder if Fleet Street will ever report this pamphlet? FALLEX-62 was played under the observation of Sir Charles Cunningham, KCB, KBE, CB, CVO, Permanent Under Secretary of State at the Home Office, who reported direct to the Cabinet on what he saw in RSG-6. Sir Charles' salary is the maximum a civil servant can get, £6,950. He is one of the most powerful men in the country.

FALLEX-62 was a full scale rehearsal of the build-up to a nuclear war. After an imaginary increase of world tension, general mobilisation was ordered on 15 September 1962. Thousands of Reservists actually received practice call-up papers. The RSGs, RSG-6 amongst them, were manned on the same day.

On 17 September the hospitals were evacuated. On 18 September the Regional Commissioner assumed full governmental powers, and became the dictator of his region. On the same day an official evacuation of heavily populated areas began. Official evacuees included half the populations of Southampton and Portsmouth, and with unofficial evacuees they effectively choked all the main roads. On 20 September the ports were evacuated.

During this imaginary build up the Civil Defence Corps pretended to distribute the then unpublished Householders Handbook, which must have been very useful. We were told to get in fourteen days supply of food and water (where from?), and to stay under cover for seven days, (then what?). Large heavily populated areas like London were called Z-zones and then abandoned to their fate.

The imaginary nuclear war began on 21 September, which by an extraordinary coincidence was the day when all the preparations were complete. It started with an H-Bomb attack on a German NATO base, followed by similar attacks on Turkey, Italy, Britain and the USA.

FALLEX-62 was meant to test the military preparedness of NATO, but above all to examine in action the efficiency of the emergency plans for the civilian population (who, of course, were never told anything about it). It did that all right.

Within a few days Britain suffered widespread devastation, including fifteen megadeaths. The West German Minister of the Interior said afterwards that 'under the present circumstances nobody has a chance'. The 1963 White Paper on Defence tells another story: 'In general', the plans were 'basically sound and practicable.'

What are the facts? It was assumed that this country had been allowed six days of preparation, and that the dispersion and mobilisation schemes were complete before the war started. This is rather unlikely when nuclear war begins in earnest. It was assumed that the Civil Defence Corps was at wartime duty establishment. In fact, the Southern Region had barely half this figure. It was assumed that no major communication breakdown between the RSGs and with other centres would take place. They had learned the lessons of Parapluie in the spring, and changed the rules!

The medical services broke down completely. Every hospital in the Southern Region was destroyed or put out of action by fallout, the death of doctors or lack of supplies. The communications system broke down, and the roads were choked. Gloucester, Oxford and Plymouth were eliminated by small Bombs. London was paralysed: to go above ground was death. A lethal belt of radiation extended as far out as Windsor. (We trust the Heir to the Throne was not mutated.) Three quarters of the Police in the Southern Region were killed, injured or irradiated. Losses among the civilian population were proportionately even higher. Whoever won the war, we lost it.

In this nightmare world, the authorities still pursue their childish dreams. The RSGs still got in touch with their London boss by dialling ABBEY 1255 and asking for CHAPLIN. In the RSGs the heads of departments were known officially as 'players' (people like players) and unofficially as 'gauletiers'. (The games theory of war!)

But FALLEX-62 was not a complete waste of time. It gave Der Spiegel the chance to blow the gaff on the whole tragic farce of NATO. It proved once and for all the truth of the 1957 Defence White Paper that there is no defence against nuclear war.

And it convinced at least one occupant of at least one RSG that the deterrent is quite futile.'

DRAKELOW

Drakelow started life as one of a series of underground aircraft factories built in haste as a response to the threatened destruction of the British aero industry by intensive German bombing in 1940. Propelled into reality by the Minister of Aircraft Production, Lord Beaverbrook, with the full backing of Winston Churchill, the underground factory scheme, which also saw the construction of factories in disused London Underground tunnels, in a chalk mine at Warren Row, in a limestone underneath Dudley Zoo, and in the massive Spring Quarry complex at Corsham in Wiltshire, was a logistic and financial disaster. Despite infrastructure costs in excess of £20,000,000, productivity at the largest of these factories, Spring Quarry, was negligible, and the smaller underground factories were proportionately ineffectual.

Unlike most of the other underground factories which were adaptations of

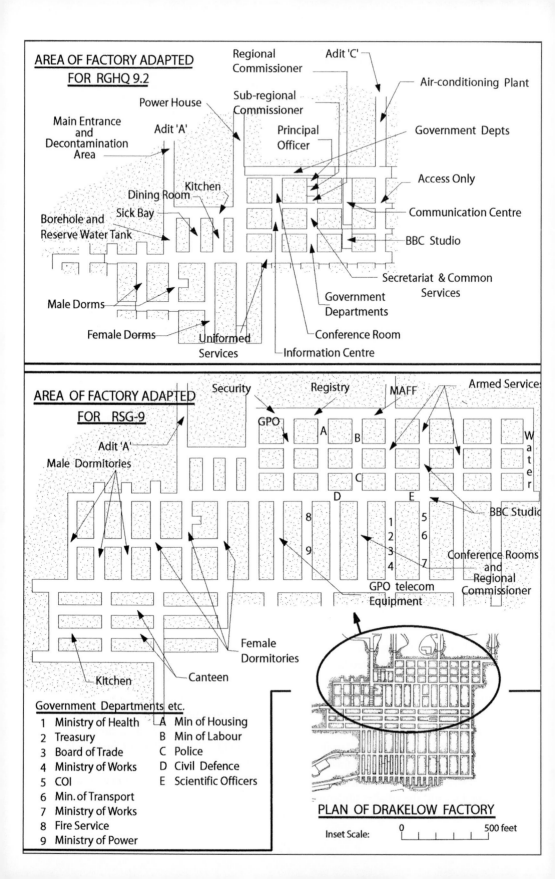

AREA OF FACTORY ADAPTED FOR RGHQ 9.2

Main Entrance and Decontamination Area

Adit 'A'

Power House

Regional Commissioner

Sub-regional Commissioner

Principal Officer

Adit 'C'

Air-conditioning Plant

Government Depts

Access Only

Communication Centre

BBC Studio

Kitchen

Dining Room

Sick Bay

Borehole and Reserve Water Tank

Male Dorms

Female Dorms

Uniformed Services

Information Centre

Conference Room

Government Departments

Secretariat & Common Services

AREA OF FACTORY ADAPTED FOR RSG-9

Security

Registry

MAFF

Armed Services

GPO

Adit 'A'

Male Dormitories

A

B

C

D

E

Water

BBC Studio

8

9

1
2
3
4

5
6

7

Conference Rooms and Regional Commissioner

GPO telecom Equipment

Female Dormitories

Kitchen

Canteen

Government Departments etc.

1 Ministry of Health
2 Treasury
3 Board of Trade
4 Ministry of Works
5 COI
6 Min. of Transport
7 Ministry of Works
8 Fire Service
9 Ministry of Power

A Min of Housing
B Min of Labour
C Police
D Civil Defence
E Scientific Officers

PLAN OF DRAKELOW FACTORY

Inset Scale: 0 ———— 500 feet

existing, long-abandoned quarry workings, the Drakelow site consisted of some 250,000 square feet of purpose-built tunnels laid out in a regular grid pattern. Buried fifty feet below the Blakeshall estate near Kidderminster, the Drakelow factory, which was operated by the Rover Car Company, limped along until 1955 with a dribble of peacetime production contracts, but by the end of the decade was in use only as rough storage for the Ministry of Supply.

By 1962, however, Drakelow, like its sister factories at Warren Row and Spring Quarry, had found new roles to justify the vast sums of public money poured into them for two decades, as Regional and National Seats of Government. Most of the old underground office complex at Drakelow, including the works canteen and recreation area, was sealed off from the main factory tunnels and fitted out as RSG-9.

The existing Rover kitchens and dining rooms were retained and upgraded, new, steel-partitioned offices laid out, telecoms equipment installed and a BBC radio studio constructed. Fitting out was completed by May 1961, just in time for the new bunker to take part in the Civil Defence exercise MERCIAN TRUMP II. Drakelow required a staff of 325 (including seventy-five women), led by a Regional Commissioner who was a government minister of Cabinet rank, assisted by a Principal Officer who was a civil servant, and two Deputy Commissioners.

In 1982 Drakelow underwent a £2,000,000 refurbishment to bring it to the necessary standard to operate as a Regional Government Headquarters. With a reduced staff of only 134 personnel, a limited remit in the field of civil emergency government, and more modern communications systems, a much more compact area was required. Many of the offices at the east end of the old RSG were sealed off, including the original BBC studio, which was replaced by a smaller and more modern one. New air-conditioning was provided and two new 147kVA generators installed in a power-house formed out of one of the entrance adits. The old kitchens, which predated the RSG era, were abandoned and replaced by new facilities built to a standard design common throughout all the RGHQs built or refurbished in the 1980s.

The ROTOR operations rooms lent themselves well to conversion into hardened headquarters during the various phases of Regional Government war planning. The Hope Cove GCI station, which served as a headquarters in several guises for the south-west of England, is typical of those, like Kelvedon Hatch, that underwent only minimal physical alteration to make them suitable for their new task. The major change in both cases was the insertion of a floor across the main operations well, which was no longer required. At Kelvedon Hatch, Hope Cove and Barnton Quarry the original, highly specified air-conditioning equipment was retained.

Whilst the three-storey Sector Operations Centres at Barnton Quarry and Kelvedon Hatch provided sufficient floor space for the staff of 350-400 required by the RSG, the two-storey GCI stations did not. At Hope Cove the extra accommodation was provided by a Second World War 'Happidrome' operations room that still remained intact just a few yards from the modern bunker. This was extended to provide a new kitchen and dining room, while the old structure was refurbished, with only minimal internal alterations, to provide sleeping, recreational and medical facilities. With the lower staffing levels required under the later RGHQ programme, the 'Happidrome' fell into disuse and was demolished in 1985.

THE SUB-REGIONAL HEADQUARTERS

By the beginning of 1962 it was realized by the Home Office that the re-orientation of the RSG structure towards a more Central Government biased role had effectively destroyed the link, previously maintained by the Regional War Rooms, between Whitehall and the next lower level of Civil Defence control, ie. the Local Authority. To re-forge the link an intermediate level of control, the Sub-Regional Headquarters or SRHQ, was developed. The original conception envisaged each Region divided into three sub-regions each with a purpose-built, fallout-proof bunker providing for a staff of 280. This three-element plan was to have been replicated in the county control structure also, with each county having a northern, central, and southern sub-control bunker reporting to the county main. Financial stringency prevented either system from being fully implemented however, before a further reorganization was proposed in 1965. A few SRHQs were completed in the early 1960s, due to the availability of several redundant, hardened MoD buildings which were suitable for cost effective conversion.

SUB-REGIONAL HEADQUARTERS COMPLETED PRIOR TO 1966	
REGION	SRHQ BUNKER
4 – East	Under control of Cambridge RSG: (a) BAWBURGH 'Rotor' bunker. (b) KELVEDON HATCH 'Rotor' Sector Control bunker. (c) HERTFORD: basement of new government office block.
7 – West	Under control of Bolt Head RSG: (a) ULLENWOOD (Gloucester), Anti-Aircraft Operations Room. (b) BRISTOL Regional War Room. (Later passed to Bristol City Council and subsequently to Avon County Council.)
9 - Midland	Under control of Drakelow RSG: (a) SWYNNERTON (Staffordshire). Conversion of two redundant, semi-underground HE magazines at a former ROF filling factory.
12 – South	TUNBRIDGE WELLS Regional War Room.

Like the later development of S-RC 8.2 at Brackla, the Swynnerton Regional Government Headquarters is a conversion of two adjacent explosives magazines on the site of a former Royal Ordnance filling factory. Because the nature of the ground at Swynnerton precluded tunnelled magazines, a cut and cover technique was used instead, which allowed the building of rectangular concrete, box-section storage chambers, larger and more suitable for later adaptation than the tunnels at Brackla. Similar arrangements to those made at the Welsh bunker, incorporating two-storey entrance buildings housing standby generators and air-conditioning equipment at each sub-bunker are employed at Swynnerton, together with a buried, reinforced concrete corridor linking the two sections.

The bunker was abandoned in 1990 following the end of Home Defence war planning in the UK and was sealed up by the Army, who now occupy the site as a training area, due to Health and Safety risks posed by asbestos contamination.

SUB-REGIONAL CONTROLS (S-RCs)

A radical rethink of both the national and regional emergency government plans, undertaken in 1966, resulted in a scheme that was more flexible than the previous, static structure, and more responsive to the pattern of nuclear war that dominated strategic thinking in the mid-1960s. A target assessment made by the Joint Intelligence Committee in the following year indicated that the prime targets of a Soviet attack would now be British and (more importantly) US radar stations and military bases in the UK, together with military and civil command and control centres. Included within the latter category were all the former RSGs, the existence of which would have been well known to Soviet intelligence. The broad sweep of the anticipated attack legitimized government propaganda regarding the 'stay-put' home defence policy and the presumption that no part of the United Kingdom was safer than another.

SOVIET TARGET ASSESSMENT – 1967

MILITARY COMMAND & CONTROL CENTRES	
Bentley Priory - RAF Fighter Command HQ High Wycombe - HQ Bomber Command Ruislip - HQ US 3rd Air Force Bawtry - HQ No.1 Group Bomber Command Northwood - Channel Command HQ Plymouth Pitreavie Fort Southwick - HQ, C-in-C Home Station	2 x 1-3 MT air-burst bombs over each location.
FIGHTER BASES	
Coltishall Leuchars Wattisham Binbrook	2 x 500 KT airburst bombs over each location.
MISSILE BASES	
Woodhall Spa North Coates West Raynham	2 x 500 KT airburst bombs over each location.

RAF BOMBER BASES

Scampton Wittering Waddington Honington Marham Coningsby St Mawgan Lossiemouth Machrihanish Leeming Gaydon Piningly Valley Bedford Brawdy Yeovilton Lyneham Wyton Pershore Boscombe Down Kinloss Manston Ballykelly Filton Leconfield	2 x 500 KT missile launched airburst, and 2 x 1MT aircraft dropped groundburst bombs on each location.

USAAF BOMBER BASES

Alconbury Bentwaters Woodbridge Wethersfield Lakenheath Upper Heyford	2 x 500 KT missile launched airburst, and 2 x 1MT aircraft dropped groundburst bombs on each site.

SEABORNE NUCLEAR DETERRENT BASES

Gareloch Holy Loch Rosyth Portsmouth Devonport Rugby (communications)	2 x 500 KT missile launched airburst, 2 x 1 MT aircraft dropped groundburst bombs on each site. 1 x 500 KT missile launched airburst and

Criggion (communications) Anthorn (NATO communications) Inskip (communications) North Waltham (US communications) Londonderry (US Navy communications) Thurso (US Navy communications)	1 x 500 KT aircraft dropped airburst bomb on each location.

BMEWS EARLY WARNING RADAR

Fylingdales	2 x 500KT airburst.

RADAR STATIONS

Boulmer Patrington Bawdsey Neatishead Buchan Saxa Vord Staxton Wold Feltwell	2 x 500KT airburst bombs over each location.

CENTRAL GOVERNMENT

London Cheltenham GCHQ	8 x 1 MT and 2 x 500 KT airburst. 2 x 1 MT and 2 x 500 KT airburst.
(Note: the Emergency Government War HQ at Corsham was omitted from this list for security purposes)	

REGIONAL GOVERNMENT HEADQUARTERS

Catterick York Preston Cambridge Dover Reading (Warren Row) Salcombe (Hope Cove) Brecon Kidderminster (Drakelow) Armagh Edinburgh (Barnton Quarry) Nottingham	2 x 0.5-3MT missile launched, and 2 x 1MT aircraft dropped groundburst bombs on each location. These sites are to be regarded as *possible* rather than *probable* targets.

MAJOR CITIES	
Glasgow Birmingham Liverpool Cardiff	4 x 1MT and 2 x 500 KT airburst bombs over each city.
Manchester Southampton Newcastle Bristol Sheffield Swansea Hull Middlesbrough Coventry Wolverhampton Leicester Stoke on Trent Belfast Edinburgh Nottingham	2 x 1MT and 2 x 500 KT airburst bombs over each city.

A further significant result of the 1966 reassessment was the decision that henceforth the sub-regional control should be the highest level of regional government during the pre-strike, wartime and immediate post-war periods. Its primary function was to be in many ways similar to that of the old Regional War Rooms but with a wider remit, ie. to oversee the reorganization of resources and the creation of social stability within its region. The previous conception of regional government as a large-scale devolved central government, carrying much of the traditional Whitehall baggage in microcosm, ceased to exist as it became increasingly clear that many months or even years might elapse before such a wide-ranging body could achieve legitimacy or assume authority. The 'Regional Seat of Government' in its new guise would rise from the post-war ashes long after the battles were over and fallout dissipated: there would be no need for hardened or radiation-proof bunkers; instead a suitable existing office complex within the region would be used (if such a site survived), maybe a University campus or local authority headquarters, within which surviving members of the ruling elite from the SRHQs and other government bunkers would regroup to mould the new democracy.

The abandonment of the earlier RSG concept and rationalization of the SRHQ network in 1966 left a number of ex-RSG sites vacant that were absorbed into the new structure of sub-regional bunkers, now renamed Sub-Regional Controls (S-RCs) to reflect their modified role. Many other classes of building also became available at this time, including several Royal Ordnance Factory explosives magazines and a number of Second World War cold stores, which were immensely strong surface structures built in the 1940s to house strategic supplies of frozen foods. The following table outlines the system of S-RCs as it existed in 1970, by which time it was virtually moribund following the run down of Civil Defence in 1968:

Region No. 1 – NORTH
Shipton: ROTOR bunker
Hexham: Second World War Cold Store

Region No. 2 – NORTH EAST
Ilkley: Craiglands Hotel
Conisbrough: AAOR
Bempton: ROTOR bunker

Region No. 3 – NORTH MIDLANDS
Loughborough: Cold Store
Skendleby: ROTOR bunker

Region No.4 – EASTERN
Bawburgh: ROTOR bunker
Hertford: Basement of new government office block
Kelvedon Hatch: ROTOR bunker

Region No. 5 – LONDON
London ceased to be a Home Defence region; its territory being divided amongst the surrounding regions.

Region No. 6 – SOUTHERN
Warren Row: Second World War underground aircraft component factory.
Basingstoke: Unallocated

Region No. 7 – SOUTH WEST
Hope Cove: ROTOR radar bunker.
Ullenwood: AAOR

31. **Hope Cove Regional Seat of Government.** The central operations room, created by inserting a new floor spanning the operations well of the former ROTOR R4 bunker. *Author's collection*

32. **Hope Cove Regional Seat of Government.** Interior view of the bunker showing the top floor access corridor and the east stair well to the lower level. *Author's collection*

REGION NO. 8 – WALES

Bangor: Hardened basement at the University of Bangor.
Bridgend: Converted explosives magazine at former Brackla ROF.

REGION NO. 9 – MIDLANDS

Drakelow: Second World War underground aircraft engine factory
Swynnerton: Converted explosive magazines at former ROF.

REGION NO. 10 – NORTH WEST

Southport: Basement of new government office block
One other, undefined *ad-hoc* location.
Plans to develop the underground bomb store at Harpur Hill, and possibly also two explosives magazines at Newton Aycliffe ROF, were abandoned at an early stage.

REGION NO.12 – SOUTH EAST

'Dumpy' – Tunnels below Dover Castle.
Guildford: Stoughton Barracks

33. **RGHQ 8.2, Brackla, Bridgend.** An external view of one of the two identical bunkers, linked by an underground walkway, that would have governed South Wales in the aftermath of nuclear attack. *Author's collection*

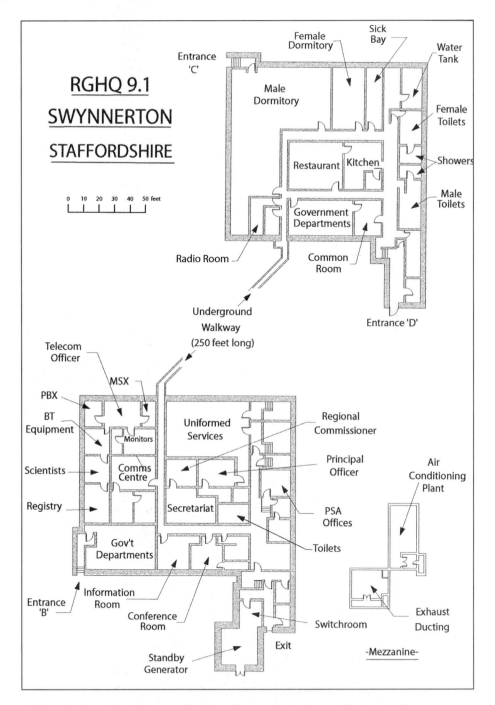

RGHQ 9.1

SWYNNERTON

STAFFORDSHIRE

0 10 20 30 40 50 feet

Entrance 'C'

Female Dormitory

Sick Bay

Water Tank

Male Dormitory

Female Toilets

Restaurant   Kitchen

Showers

Government Departments

Male Toilets

Radio Room

Common Room

Underground Walkway (250 feet long)

Entrance 'D'

Telecom Officer

MSX

PBX

BT Equipment

Monitors

Scientists

Comms Centre

Registry

Gov't Departments

Entrance 'B'

Information Room

Conference Room

Standby Generator

Uniformed Services

Secretariat

Exit

Switchroom

Regional Commissioner

Principal Officer

PSA Offices

Toilets

Air Conditioning Plant

Exhaust Ducting

-Mezzanine-

S-RC 8.2, at Brackla near Bridgend was one of two Regional Government bunkers created by the conversion of underground explosives magazines at redundant Royal Ordnance filling factories. The Brackla ROF was bounded to the south by the Brackla hills, an area of sharply rising high ground composed principally of shale. When the factory was built in 1941 it was decided to bury seven explosives magazines in the hill; five to contain filled shells awaiting

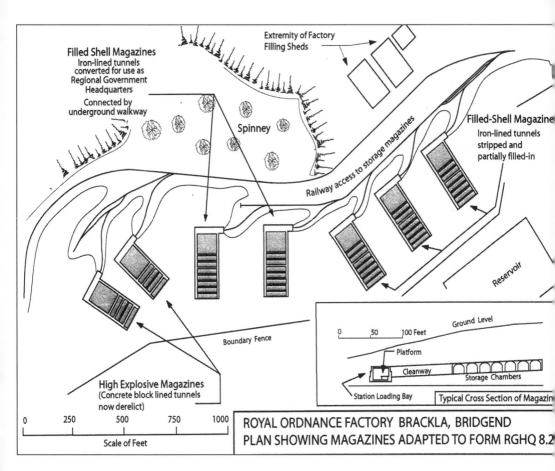

Filled Shell Magazines
Iron-lined tunnels
converted for use as
Regional Government
Headquarters
Connected by
underground walkway

Extremity of Factory
Filling Sheds

Spinney

Railway access to storage magazines

Filled-Shell Magazine
Iron-lined tunnels
stripped and
partially filled-in

Reservoir

Boundary Fence

Ground Level

0   50   100 Feet

Platform

Cleanway

Storage Chambers

Station Loading Bay

Typical Cross Section of Magazin

High Explosive Magazines
(Concrete block lined tunnels
now derelict)

0   250   500   750   1000

Scale of Feet

ROYAL ORDNANCE FACTORY BRACKLA, BRIDGEND
PLAN SHOWING MAGAZINES ADAPTED TO FORM RGHQ 8.2

despatch and two to hold raw explosives.

Construction of each magazine involved boring two parallel tunnels 300′ long and 100′ apart through the unstable shale strata and then excavating a series of lateral tunnels, (eight in the filled shell magazines, three in the HE magazines) joining the main access tunnels or 'cleanways'. 'Cut and cover' railway loading bays enclosed the ends of each cleanway.

The loose nature of the shale required that the tunnels should be round in section and fully lined to ensure stability. False, reinforced concrete floors were built into the tubes and rectangular passageways and storage areas built upon them, with voids at the sides and top. Concrete skew headwalls of a complicated design were required at the junction of the clearways and magazine compartments. The Ministry of Works specified that heavy, bolted cast-iron ring girders, similar to those used on the London Underground, should be used for tunnel lining. Construction was delayed by shortages in the iron allocation for the ring girders, so the contractors, McAlpine, resorted to the use of pre-cast, curved concrete blocks of various dimensions in substitution. The first two magazines, for High Explosives, were completed with this material but difficulties in the manufacture of the blocks to adequate tolerances and other problems led to its abandonment in the remaining five magazines, which were eventually complete with conventional iron girders.

The Home Office acquired the site in October 1961 and selected an adjacent pair of iron-lined tunnels for the Regional Government Headquarters. Scrap contracts were later let for the demolition of the disused tunnels as the value of the cast-iron content was considerable. The iron lining was removed from the three remaining shell magazines which have now suffered severe collapses of the loose shale strata, but the smaller HE magazines remain undamaged because the concrete lining blocks are valueless.

The nature of the tunnel construction left the Home Office with little scope for alteration in the magazine areas which have been turned into offices and all the typical paraphernalia of an RGHQ. Alterations to the entrances, however, have been considerable. New dual-level, reinforced concrete structures have been built, where once the railway tracks entered the loading bay, to form air-lock entrances and decontamination chambers, together with standby generator rooms on the lower floors and air-conditioning and filter plants on the upper floors. A newly excavated covered walkway joins the two sets of tunnels.

Of the twenty-two R-SCs fourteen were more or less useable at the end of the decade. Despite the final curtain having been brought down upon the old and anachronistic Civil Defence organization and the improving east-west tolerance, the early 1970s saw further significant structural change in the emergency control programme. London, once again, became an independent Home Defence Region, taking over the Kelvedon Hatch control bunker which became SRC 5.1. At that time the five London Groups were reinstated with the following group control bunkers reporting to Kelvedon Hatch:

1. Northern Group: MILL HILL War Room.
2. North-East Group: WANSTEAD War Room.
3. South-East Group: KEMNAL MANOR War Room / PEAR TREE HOUSE
4. South-West Group: CHEAM War Room.
5. North-West Group: SOUTHALL re-used Second World War Civil Defence Centre.

Economies in the Emergency Government budget meant, however, that, with few exceptions, new works and improvements to existing structures were minimal. Expenditure on communications equipment was particularly inadequate throughout the decade.

The whirlwind arrival of the conservative Thatcher government in 1979 heralded the greatest and most radical resurgence of Home Defence emergency planning since the 1930s. Although much of the building was done in great secrecy, the guiding policy was overt and proactive; Civil Defence had become just another weapon in the nuclear arsenal. The 1980 Home Defence Review called for seventeen modern, effective and highly specified protected regional headquarters, to be known as Regional Government Headquarters (RGHQs), provided with the most up-to-date communications equipment, housed in either refurbished former Sub-Regional control premises or in completely new, purpose-built underground buildings.

SCOTLAND SOUTH AND SCOTTISH CENTRAL CONTROL

Kirknewton (upgraded 1950s Regional War Room)
Replaced by - Purpose-built Headquarters at **Cultybraggan.** Commissioned in 1990.

SCOTLAND NORTH

Anstruther (upgraded SRHQ constructed within shell of underground ROTOR two-level R3 bunker)

REGION 2 - NORTH EAST

(New group created by the integration of the former Eastern and North Eastern)
2.2 - **Hexham** former Second World War cold store
2.1 - **Shipton** underground ROTOR station

REGION 3 - NORTH MIDLAND

3.1 - **Skendelby** underground ROTOR station
3.2 - **Loughborough** former Second World War cold store

REGION 4 - EASTERN

4.1 – **Bawburgh** underground ROTOR station
4.2 – **Hertford** basement of government offices

(In 1991 Hertford was replaced by the former ROC Group Control at Bedford)

REGION 5 - LONDON

5.1 – **Kelvedon Hatch** former ROTOR sector operations centre.

REGION 6 - SOUTH

Plans put forward in 1982 to reconstruct and enlarge the former **'Dumpy'** RSG site below Dover Castle were abandoned in the early 1980s due to the exorbitant cost of the project.

The earlier **Warren Row** site having been abandoned; due in part to its sensational disclosure by 'Spies for Peace', and partly by its inherent unsuitability, the only remaining Regional HQ was the office suite below Alencon Link in **Basingstoke**, which became RGHQ 6.2.

Plans were prepared in 1988 to develop the former Home Office radio station at **Crowborough** into a modern Regional Government Headquarters to the standards of those built at Chilmark and Cultybraggan. The Crowborough bunker was commissioned in 1992 at a cost of £80 million and disbanded shortly afterwards.

REGION 7 - SOUTH WEST

Initially the former S-RCs at **Bolt Head** and **Ullenwood** were upgraded to become, respectively, RGHQ 7.1 and 7.2. The old ROTOR bunker at **Bolt Head** was refitted for its revised function, and the nearby Second World War

'Happidrome' operations centre was redeveloped to provide additional domestic accommodation. It was linked to the modern bunker by a covered walkway.

In 1985 the **Bolt Head** site was downgraded and the 'Happidrome' domestic site demolished. Shortly afterwards, the ex AAOR site at **Ullenwood** was closed and work began on a spectacular, new underground bunker on land adjoining the RAF bomb store at **Chilmark** near Salisbury.

REGION 8 - WALES

Although Wales was supposed to have two RGHQs, during most of the cold war only the **Brackla** ex S-RC bunker existed.

Work started but was soon abandoned in 1986 upon the conversion of the former Second World War cold store at **Llandudno Junction** to provide a RGHQ for North Wales. The project was stopped due to excessive cost, and until 1992 North Wales remained without suitable accommodation.

North Wales finally got its bunker, RGHQ 8.1, following the disbanding of the ROC in 1992, when the group control centre at **Wrexham** became available. Little development had been completed, however, by the time regional government in Wales was finally abandoned in 1994.

REGION 9 - WEST MIDLANDS

Both S-RC period bunkers at **Drakelow** and **Swynnerton** were revamped in the mid 1980s to meet the new RGHQ specification. At Drakelow much of the existing S-RC infrastructure was abandoned and a further, much smaller, area of the Second World War underground factory was developed into RGHQ 9.2. Plans were made to close Drakelow and transfer the Regional Headquarters to the recently vacated UKWMO Headquarters at **Lawford Heath**, but the end of the cold war put paid to this before it could be fully implemented.

REGION 10 - NORTH WEST

Initially The North West was served by only the old S-RC at **Preston**, which was poorly constructed and quite unsuitable. In 1985 the former ROTOR GCI bunker at **Hack Green**, which had latterly operated in a civil ATC mode, became available, and was developed at great expense to be the principal North West bunker; RGHQ 10.2. The earlier facility at Preston was closed down and for a while Hack Green effectively functioned as a dual establishment; i.e RGHQs 10.1 and 10.2.

Early in 1992 the **Longley Lane** ROC HQ bunker at Preston became available. Conversion of this site, to become RGHQ 10.1, was not fully completed before the abandonment of Regional Government.

REGION 11 - ULSTER

A detailed discussion of emergency planning in Northern Ireland is beyond the scope of this volume. Three bunkers were envisaged for the province, built to a design similar to that at Chilmark, but construction at all but one site was dilatory and none were fully commissioned.

34. **Crowborough Regional Government Headquarters.** The original underground bunker was the wartime, Foreign Office radio transmitter station code-named 'Aspidistra', but it was completely gutted and rebuilt as an RGHQ to replace 'Dumpy', the existing sub-standard accommodation below Dover Castle. The squat concrete ventilation towers are part of the new works completed in the 1980s. *Nick Catford*

The three new bunkers (or rather two new bunkers and one radical reconstruction of an existing bunker) built in the late 1980s represent the final phase of Regional Emergency Planning and mark the ultimate apotheosis of bunker building in the United Kingdom. Built irrespective of cost, (the final bill for the Chilmark RGHQ is reputed to have been £80,000,000), these bunkers were overt symbols of the Thatcher government's contempt for the old Soviet Union.

RGHQ 6.1 at Crowborough near King's Standing in Sussex was commissioned in 1990 to replace the highly unsuitable, damp and crumbling tunnels below Dover Castle. The RGHQ was constructed within the shell of an earlier bunker built by Canadian Army personnel over a nine-month period in 1941 and used by the Political Warfare Executive during the Second World War to house wireless transmitters that broadcast subversive radio messages into Europe. After the war the Foreign Office made use of the station, code-named Aspidistra, for its Diplomatic Wireless Service, and later the BBC leased the equipment to broadcast World Service programmes.

Built in a natural hollow and only just underground, with the upper floor slightly mounded over with earth, the original Aspidistra bunker was built on two floors with the entrance on the lower level approached by a slight incline. The site was acquired by the Home Office in 1984 and was completely gutted and rebuilt internally. Due to the availability of several feet of extra headroom achieved by the removal of under-floor cable ducts, it was possible to incorporate a third, mezzanine, floor within the shell of the bunker. Further additional floor space was made available by extending the upper level with the construction of a new wing to contain a modern standby power plant and air-conditioning equipment. The distinctive ventilation towers from this plant room, similar to the vent towers at Chilmark, are now a conspicuous landmark. Three new entrances were constructed on the upper floor near the plant room extension together with an emergency exit stairway serving all three floors at the far end of the bunker. The original bottom-level entrance was retained as a supplementary emergency exit.

The upper floor houses a power-house with two diesel generators, air-conditioning equipment and dormitory accommodation for the bunker's 150 staff. The middle floor contained departmental offices and conference rooms while the lower floor was occupied by scientific officers' accommodation, a private suite for the Regional Commissioner, a BBC studio and telecommunications equipment.

Crowborough was in service less than two years before the RGHQ network was stood down, but the site was retained by the Home Office and now thrives as a police training centre.

The Chilmark and Cultybraggan bunkers are similar though not identical in design and both are built on Ministry of Defence land within secure boundaries. The Cultybraggan bunker is situated on the Cultybraggan Army training ground fifteen miles north of Stirling, and was opened in 1990. The Chilmark bunker stands in a triangle of land between the main railway line and the Ham Cross interchange yard which serves the underground RAF bomb store at Chilmark.

Construction of the Chilmark bunker began in 1985 and was completed within three years. The two-storey building is a magnificent structure built almost completely underground with just part of the upper floor mounded with earth. The local geology was ideal for this type of construction. Having chosen a

35. **Cultybraggan, The Scottish Central Government Bunker.** Built in the 1980s to replace Barnton Quarry, this, along with the south-west regional bunker at Chilmark in Wiltshire, was one of the few completely new, purpose-built bunkers built since the early 1960s. *Nick Catford*

36. **Cultybraggan.** The fully fitted BBC studio from which government warning and advice messages would be broadcast to Scotland's civil population in time of nuclear war. *Nick Catford*

37. **Chilmark RGHQ.** External view of the bunker showing ramp to the main entrance on the upper floor and the emergency exit from the plant room on the lower floor. *Author's collection*

very gently sloping hillside consisting of some fifteen feet of soft earth overlying the limestone bed below, it was possible for the builders to scoop out an excavation in the earth and then level a shelf in the underlying rock upon which to build the bunker's foundation. After construction of the two-foot-thick concrete shell, which consists of an elongated rectangular box with central mid-feather walls running along the long axis, the excavated earth was backfilled and mounded over the roof level to a depth of ten feet. Service plant is contained within separate sections of the bunker spread over both floors at the southern end. Here the bunker is wider in plan to accommodate ventilation shafts which are built into a cavity some ten feet wide which separates a pair of inner and outer blast-proof walls that rise through both levels of the structure to protrude above ground forming external ventilation towers. This array of towers is arranged as three sides of a square and gives the impression of something rather intimidating down below.

The bunker is fitted out to the highest standards; carpeted throughout and illuminated by concealed fluorescent fittings, it has the air of a rather luxurious corporate headquarters rather than the last bleak refuge from nuclear Armageddon. The lower floor is devoted almost entirely to military and civilian offices, a BBC radio studio, BT telecoms equipment room, secretariat office,

38. **Chilmark RGHQ.** Upper floor central access corridor. *Author's collection*

39. **Chilmark RGHQ.** Like all the bunkers built or refurbished in the 1980s, the kitchen and dining room at Chilmark was fitted to a remarkably high standard.
Author's collection

military communications centre, strong-room, etc. The upper floor is devoted to domestic services and contains male and female dormitories, common rooms, a large dining room with tiled floor and a very well equipped kitchen with matching stainless steel appliances. An odd feature of the bunker is its sewage system, and

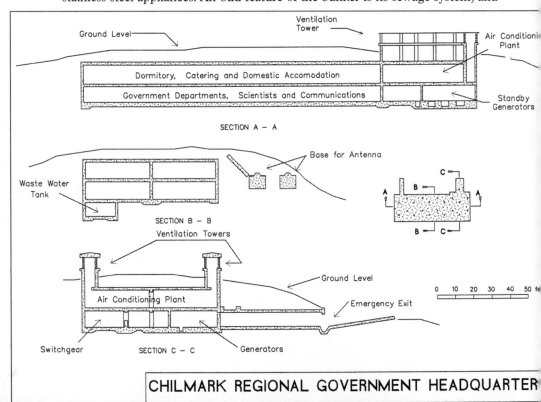

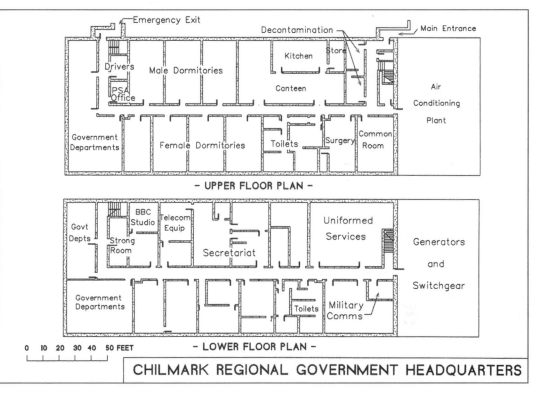

- UPPER FLOOR PLAN -

Emergency Exit

Decontamination

Main Entrance

Drivers

Male Dormitories

Kitchen

Store

PSA Office

Canteen

Air Conditioning Plant

Government Departments

Female Dormitories

Toilets

Surgery

Common Room

- LOWER FLOOR PLAN -

Govt Depts

BBC Studio

Telecom Equip

Strong Room

Secretariat

Uniformed Services

Generators and Switchgear

Government Departments

Toilets

Military Comms

0 10 20 30 40 50 FEET

CHILMARK REGIONAL GOVERNMENT HEADQUARTERS

40. **Chilmark RGHQ.** Standby generators in the plant room. *Author's collection*

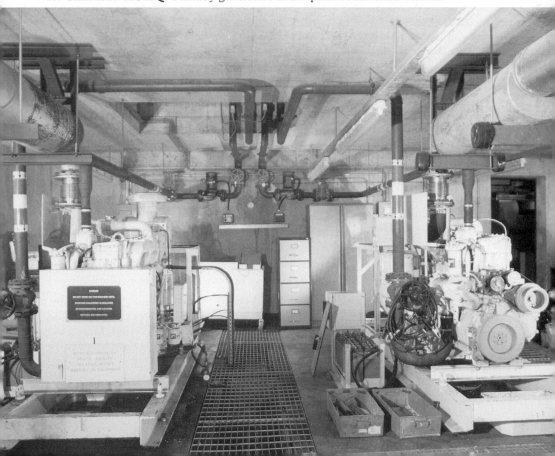

41. **Chilmark RGHQ.** Main switch room. *Author's collection*

in particular an enigmatic illuminated sign above a manhole in the gentlemen's
toilet which reads 'DO NOT REMOVE THIS COVER IF GAS WARNING
LAMP IS ILLUMINATED'. This has nothing to do with the risk of toxicological
attack, as might be imagined. Connection to the main drains would run the risk
of contamination being forced into the bunker through the sewers by external
overpressure resulting from a nuclear detonation, so instead a very large sump or
cesspit was constructed below the bunker's lavatory annexe. The sign refers to the
very real risks from a build-up of sewer gas in this sump after prolonged use.

THE BUNKER'S DEMISE

The sudden, internal collapse of the Soviet Union in 1992 which exposed the
fragility of the Russian military threat and brought about the end of the cold war
virtually overnight was fortuitous for the British Government. Facing ruin from
financial mismanagement during the dying years of Conservative rule, Whitehall
leaped with unseemly haste to embrace the benefits of the 'peace dividend'.
Perhaps the most obvious, though debatable, consequence of the 'peace
dividend' was the increasingly swingeing series of Defence Reviews, which saw
the wholesale closure of Naval dockyards, Ordnance Factories and other
military bases. Another significant consequence was the immediate dismantling
of all except the very core of the 'continuity of government' bunker network.

10

LOCAL AUTHORITY BUNKERS

Whilst plans for emergency regional government in the UK were reasonably well developed by 1961, the system at county level and below still reflected the fragmented, quasi-amateur, volunteer characteristics of the Second World War Civil Defence organization. Although abandoned along with much of the other civilian paraphernalia of war in 1945, the Civil Defence Corps was reconstituted just three years later in response to the worsening international situation and the largely American-fuelled east-west animosity which, as a consequence of the somewhat cynical US 'forward defence' policy, would put the UK on the front line of the Third World War.

The post-war Civil Defence structure remained virtually identical to its wartime forebear throughout its twenty-year life until its demise in 1968; although subject to broad guidance and partial financing from the Home Office, day-to-day management and the organization of the almost wholly volunteer workforce was solely a local authority responsibility. Throughout the Second World War the County, District, and City councils had utilized whatever facilities existed as Civil Defence control centres on an ad-hoc basis. Often the inherently secure basements of the massively constructed Victorian city halls had sufficed, or odd rooms in council owned properties remote from the city centres; perhaps country houses which in pre-war years had been taken over by local authorities as hospitals or mental institutions. In some areas, particularly in the industrial conurbations which were prime Luftwaffe targets, purpose-built bomb-proof control bunkers and a number of substantial training and operational complexes were built and survived into the nuclear era. For the most part the strongest surviving wartime Civil Defence buildings were the very conspicuous gas-cleansing centres.

The *Civil Defence Act* of 1948 contained wide-ranging powers 'including any measure not amounting to actual combat for affording defence against any form of hostile attack by a foreign power'. The provisions of the Act embraced the functions of most of the Home Ministries, including those of the Cabinet Home Defence Committee, but was principally administered by the Home Office, which delegated day-to-day operations to the County and Borough authorities. Regulations issued in the following year further detailed the responsibilities of these 'Corps Authorities' which included: the collation, in co-operation with the Royal Observer Corps and other bodies, of attack intelligence; post-attack co-ordination of local resources; rescue of the trapped and injured; protection against radioactive fallout, and the dissemination of advice to the public. Following the establishment of the Regional War Rooms, Regional Directors of Civil Defence were appointed in 1955 to oversee the local authority administration on behalf of central government.

A lack of clear guidance from Central Government, a dire paucity of funding at both central and local level and a curiously dichotomous view of the nature of future warfare, meant that the provision of protected accommodation – the Civil Defence Corps Bunkers – or a viable Civil Defence infrastructure of any type was at best patchy throughout the country during the early years. The following brief overview of the first phase of cold war Civil Defence in Wiltshire is typical of developments nationally.

Throughout the Second World War Wiltshire's Civil Defence headquarters had been located in the basement of Roundway House, a council-owned property on the outskirts of Devizes. Following the revival of Civil Defence in 1948 the Roundway HQ was refurbished and maintained its function until at least 1957, and probably survived until the new, semi-hardened County Control was constructed in the basement of County Hall, Trowbridge, in the early 1960s. Civil Defence controls were also provided for the larger towns and boroughs, including Chippenham, Salisbury and Swindon, but the low-risk status of these towns, at least during the early years, ensured that funding was minimal and accommodation consisted of little more than a couple of rooms in a council-owned building. The Salisbury sub-control was initially in Friary Lane, but by 1957 the centre was relocated to the Council House in Bourne Hill, from where all the emergency sirens in the City were remotely controlled.

Reiterating the ambitious proposals outlined in an early circular of 1951, a Home Office memorandum issued in March 1952 instructed all the County and Borough Councils in the United Kingdom to prepare bomb-proof main and subordinate Civil Defence control centres. It was expected that substantial progress should be made with these preparations by the end of 1952, although actual construction was to proceed only in the most vulnerable areas. Little guidance was issued, however, as to what constituted a 'most vulnerable area', and no council was particularly eager to be so assessed, for, although the construction of emergency centres would attract substantial Central Government grants, such a venture would still represent a considerable drain on ratepayers' resources at a time when much more pressing and publicly acceptable demands existed.

Early in 1952 officers from the Home Office and from the South West Region debated whether Swindon should be included in the 1952 capital investment budget. This was an important matter to the local authority at that time as it was considering the construction of a major extension to the Swindon Civic Centre and the incorporation of a new Civil Defence control within this extension would be financially advantageous. A representative from the Home Office pointed out that

> the present policy is that the degree of protection provided should normally be the same as that planned for public shelters in its immediate vicinity.

This requirement caused some consternation, as Swindon, along with virtually every other Borough, City and County Council in Britain, had made no public shelter provision at all.

Swindon's wartime Civil Defence HQ control room had been in the basement of the Civic Offices, with training and depot facilities in huts at the rear of these offices in Savernake Street. An emergency standby centre was established in a small private school in Westlecote Road. The existing centre was quite inadequate to meet the needs of the Third World War, and in compliance with one element of the early post-war plan, it was proposed in 1951 to move the Civil Defence control away from the supposedly more vulnerable town centre area to Lydiard Park, with the alternative centre at Foxhall stud farm. This scheme, however, ran contrary to another Home Office recommendation that the emergency centres should be as close as practicable to the peacetime Council administrative headquarters and was abandoned.

Instead, it was proposed to strengthen the existing Savernake Street gas cleansing centre by the addition of a new, six inch thick concrete roof, to produce a building similar to the then current, more-or-less standard Home Office bunker design. Council engineers pointed out, however, that the existing walls would be unable to support the weight of the new roof and that the cost (£5,500) of all the additional work required, including reinforcement of the existing walls and foundations, would result in an inherently unstable structure which was more costly and less satisfactory than a purpose-built bunker. A subsequent, more modest proposal envisaged modification of the existing gas cleansing station by covering the entire building with a redundant 'Robin' aircraft hangar which in turn would be covered with a thick layer of earth. This concept, too, was seen as impracticable, and the situation remained unresolved until 1962, when work finally started on the Civic Centre extension.

By the time work finally started on the Civic Centre bunker Civil Defence planning had entered a new phase and the requirement was now for a facility orientated more towards an emergency administrative, rather than life-saving, role. Plans were prepared for a comprehensive control centre in the basement of the new extension, but these were greatly reduced in scope when it was discovered that the high water table precluded any major underground works.

After 1962 Wiltshire was divided into three geographical areas for Civil Defence purposes:

North Wiltshire:	74C	Operations centre in Chippenham
Mid Wiltshire:	74A	Operations centre in Devizes
South Wiltshire:	74B	Operations centre in Salisbury

Inevitably, a shortfall in funding prevented much concrete progress, although, for reasons that are difficult to understand, Salisbury was categorized as a high-risk City and Home Office cash made available. Early in 1959 Salisbury City Council laid plans to build a new, heavily protected control bunker on the south-west outskirt of the city at a site beside the old Blandford Road. When completed in 1962 it consisted of a large, single-floored concrete structure built into rising ground designed so that, while the entrance was just below ground level, the main building was protected by some twenty feet of earth and rock. Access was by means of a single, blast-resistant pedestrian door leading through an air-lock. A twenty-foot vertical emergency escape shaft containing an iron ladder was provided at the western extremity of the building. Hidden in a small roadside copse in an affluent, peripheral residential district of the city, the bunker is

42. **Salisbury Civil Defence Bunker.** An overhead view of the bunker's inconspicuous entrance, hidden in a roadside copse to the south of the city. *Author's collection*

43. **Salisbury Civil Defence Bunker.** Arrangement of air locks and blast doors sealing the bunker from the access tunnel. *Author's collection*

44. Salisbury Civil Defence Bunker.
A view of the control room shortly after decommissioning. The structure is now used for the storage of ballot boxes and voting booths.
Author's collection

45. Salisbury Civil Defence Bunker.
Nuclear, chemical and biological filters installed when the bunker was upgraded during the 1980s. This equipment, which is electrically powered but can be operated manually in emergency, was standard throughout the smaller bunkers built or refurbished since 1979.
Author's collection

almost invisible to the casual observer, the most conspicuous features being two tall, slender concrete ventilation towers that provide fresh air for the ventilation system and an exhaust for the standby Lister generator.

What facilities to include in the new bunker generated considerable debate among members of the Salisbury Civil Defence Committee. The committee minutes referring to a discussion as to whether or not underground dormitories should be provided offer an interesting insight into the thinking of pre-Cuba local authority emergency planners. It was decided, for example, that dormitories were not required, as:

> It would only be if fallout was serious that people would have to stop a long time underground – unless the enemy introduced bacteriological or chemical warfare, which would be just too bad!

Elsewhere, in those areas deemed more vulnerable to nuclear bombardment, similar semi-buried or massively hardened surface bunkers had already been built. In Bristol, for example, four massive surface blockhouses were built during 1954 at Banwell Close in Bedminster; Henleaze Road; Clayton Road in Avonmouth, and at the junction of Brook Road and Crofts End in the Speedwell district. Only the Bedminster bunker now survives although long disused. The Avonmouth control was swept aside to make room for the new Customs House in the 1970s, while of the other two, the only remaining evidence is a couple of overgrown concrete patches in the corners of municipal playing fields. These, like similar bunkers at Basset Green Road and Bitterne Road East in

46. **Bedminster Civil Defence Control.** Built in a quiet residential district on the outskirts of Bristol in 1954, this anonymous concrete blockhouse is typical of dozens of similar Civil Defence controls erected in and around conurbations thought most vulnerable to attack from atomic bombs. *Author's collection*

47. **Bedminster Civil Defence Control.** Locked up and forgotten in 1968, this is a view of the control centre, mouldering away nearly forty years later. *Author's collection*

Southampton and others in numerous other industrial towns and cities, were built on the outskirts of the built-up areas they were to serve in order to minimize the risk of destruction should the centres of those towns be targeted.

The years after 1962 were marked by a new rationalism in Civil Defence planning, following the shock of Cuba. Before that time it appears that the antagonistic regimes of East and West were genuinely prepared to go to war in order to ensure the ascendancy of their respective ideologies. This period was perhaps the last in history to carry the stigma of the 'curious dichotomy' remarked upon earlier in this chapter, which reflected in part the comments of Lloyd George, made in 1914, that governments and military strategists

> ... prepare, not for the next war, but for the last one or the last but one. Unfortunately, they only remember the lessons which were best forgotten because they were inapplicable, and forget all the experiences by which they ought to have profited because they were a foretaste of modern warfare.

Until Cuba it seems that the strategists thought that, despite the acknowledged, awesome destructive power of the nuclear missile, the next war, in which their use would be inevitable, would somehow be just like the last war. And therein lies the dichotomy: most cities would be destroyed yet most, as in the Second World War, would survive untroubled by conflict; entire populations would die in the holocaust, but most would survive unscathed and the unfortunate few would be plucked unharmed from the debris. Survival could be planned for, and the plans would be those for the last war, or the war before last. In 1962 the scales fell from their eyes, and those who brought the world to the brink of annihilation realized, at the eleventh hour, the full awfulness and futility of their philosophies. Two consequences of Cuba directly influenced UK Civil Defence assumptions for the rest of the decade: first, it to some extent brought western and eastern leaders to their senses, largely deflating the post-war tensions that brought the world to the precipice of annihilation; secondly it highlighted the futility of the pre-nuclear culture that still invested Civil Defence thinking into the 1960s. It was the realization of the totality of nuclear obliteration – that there would be no trapped and wounded for the heavy rescue squads to save, nor bewildered but hearty homeless to drink tea brewed in WRVS mobile canteens, nor burning but reclaimable factories and homes for the AFS to extinguish – that led, at an accelerating pace, to the final and inglorious end of the traditional Civil Defence Corps structure in 1968. With no real remaining role, and with a new optimism abroad, the end was inevitable. There was no longer a need for the numerous and patently useless, hardened Civil Defence controls in the cities and most were quietly abandoned.

Emergency planning continued, because, although war was now less likely than it had been in any year since 1947, in the words of the 1965 *Home Defence Review*, 'misunderstandings and miscalculations need to be prepared for'. But the emphasis was now firmly upon the concept of 'continuity of government'. Survival of the nation-state was more important – or at least probably more feasible – than survival of the population. Local authorities in conjunction with Home Office agencies including UKWMO could advise and warn the public, but beyond that the people must fend for themselves. Local councils were empowered to organize what remained of the post-war industrial, commercial and social structure within their areas, and when conditions had stabilized to transfer most of their previously delegated power upwards to the Sub-Regional Controls, the Regional Seats of Government, and ultimately to the National Seat of Government, wherever that might reside.

In practical terms, the local authority Civil Defence bunker-building programme remained in limbo throughout the mid-1960s and, with few exceptions, those that were already built reverted to care and maintenance from 1968 until the start of the next decade. The policy that had seen the end of the RSG system and the institution, in its place, of the Sub-Regional Control structure, also modified the role of the local authority. New regulations issued in 1963 and 1964 required County Councils to provide protected emergency headquarters and defined more clearly their wartime responsibilities. The principal tasks would henceforth be *restoration* of services rather than rescue. The prime County responsibility was to forge a link in the chain of command (and thus help maintain the continuity of government), but the more visible roles were: to maintain law and order, the provision of foodstuffs, fuel and power, maintenance of a minimal level of public health and clearance of essential transport routes.

During this period about half of the County councils had either started or completed construction of their County War Headquarters, generally underneath their Shire Halls or civic centres. In Wiltshire, the basement of County Hall, a 1930s structure in Bythesea Road in the county town of Trowbridge, was converted into a reasonably secure nuclear bunker for the County Council and for elements of the County military headquarters staff. Most of the sub-basement windows were bricked-up, and where this was not practicable heavy steel sliding shutters were fabricated to seal the openings.

Access to the centre was via two external stairways, fitted with sliding steel blast doors, and internally via a lift from the peacetime administrative area above. A steel blast door protected the lower lift landing, but, like one of the external stairway blast doors, was erected the wrong way around, so that a nearby explosion would blow the door open rather than seal it against its frame. The steel window-shutters suffered similar shortcomings. In addition to the fixed blast-proofing, a stockpile of 1288 nine-inch high-density concrete blocks was provided with which to build extra radiation protection for the most important and vulnerable rooms. Service installations included a 25 Kva alternator, hand-operated ventilation filters and an extensive kitchen that in peacetime operates as the staff canteen for the entire County Hall complex.

County bunkers were generally designed for a staff of up to eighty; in Wiltshire the full establishment was fifty-three:

Chief Executive
Officer in Charge of control centre
Deputy controller
Military Headquarters staff (eleven)
West Wilts District Council staff *(from 1974 until 1982)* (two)
Operations and Information staff (seven)
Communications staff (seven)
Scientific advisors (three)
Civil Liaison officers (eight)
Police liaison officer
Administrative personnel (four)
Clerical staff (seven)

Elsewhere, a wide range of structures of variable effectiveness had been adopted or built to house the County control bunkers, as the following few examples will indicate. (A comprehensive though incomplete gazetteer of local authority bunkers can be found at the end of this chapter.) Somerset's emergency control was a well designed and equipped purpose-built bunker deep below an underground car park adjacent to the old County Hall in Taunton. In Dorset a less well protected bunker was built in the basement of Dorchester library. Because of its vulnerable south-coast location, Hastings Borough Council sought and received Home Office funding for a purpose-built control bunker in 1965, to replace its earlier, rather inadequate Civil Defence controls at Jackson Hall and Marine Court. The new, block-house pattern bunker was built in the grounds of Ashdown House, a Ministry of Works property at Harrow Lane in the north-west suburb of the town. The building was intended for a staff of fifty, with additional accommodation available in the cellars of Ashdown House. It was suggested in 1966 that a tunnel be constructed to link the two buildings but this was considered superfluous by the cost-conscious local authority.

Birmingham utilized a fascinating array of bunkers between 1954 and 1999, as responsibility for Emergency Planning shifted, with the changes in local authority organization, from Birmingham City Council to the old West Midlands County Council, and finally to West Midlands Fire Service. The earliest protected accommodation was the Council House War Room which consisted of three small rooms in the basement of the Victorian City Hall. The ceilings are reinforced with heavy RSJs overlain by corrugated sheeting. Whilst not heavily blast-protected, the innermost room is sealed by a substantial steel door. The 'war-room' has seen continuous service in many guises and today, after a recent refurbishment, provides a dedicated District Emergency Co-ordinating Centre. At some time during the 1970s the outside of the Council House, including the bunker rooms, was reinforced with steel mesh as a precaution against terrorist bombs.

Following the winding-up of the Civil Defence Corps in 1968, Birmingham Corporation took control of the heavily protected Civil Defence bunker built in 1954 in the grounds of No. 8 Meadow Road, Harborne, Birmingham. This is a typical early 1950s single-storey concrete structure, similar to the Salisbury bunker with a single pedestrian entrance and emergency exit tunnel, buried under a grass bank at the rear of the house. This building continued in use through the change of responsibility for emergency planning in 1974 (when it became the responsibility of the West Midlands County Council), and through the subsequent change in 1986 when responsibility was transferred to West Midlands Fire & Civil Defence Authority. Its function ceased in 1989 when the house in Meadow Road and its bunker were sold to a private engineering company for offices.

The third, and most impressive, of the Birmingham bunkers is the ex ROTOR period Anti-Aircraft Operations Room located at St Bernard's Road, Wylde Green, Sutton Coldfield. This standard, two-storey, semi-buried AAOR was built in 1954 to control the guns of the Birmingham gun-defended area (GDA). Following the demise of Anti-Aircraft Command just a few years after the building was completed, the Wylde Green bunker was transferred to the Territorial Army, but by 1962 it had been purchased by Warwickshire County Council for use as the county Civil Defence headquarters. As a consequence of the 1974 local authority reorganization, Sutton Coldfield was absorbed by the new West Midlands County Council, and the Wylde Green bunker was refitted to serve as the West Midlands county main Civil Defence and emergency planning centre, with a designated staff of forty. When the council was devolved in 1986, responsibility was transferred to the West Midlands Fire and Civil Defence Authority, which maintained it until its disposal in 2000. A few years earlier, following the apparent end of the cold war, the peacetime rump of emergency planning was transferred to a suite of unprotected offices in the Fire Service headquarters.

Six other redundant AAORs were acquired during the early 1960s by local authorities for similar conversion, including the Barrow AAOR in Cumbria and the Frodsham bunker in Cheshire which formerly controlled the guns of the Liverpool and Manchester GDA. The latter building, which was constructed in 1951, was purchased by Cheshire County Council in October 1961 and re-fitted over the following twelve months. The internal layout was considerably altered to meet the council's requirements, but the original balcony around the two-storey plotting room was retained. The upper floor of the bunker contains the dormitories and domestic services, while the lower floor is put over to offices, communications and service plant.

In Scotland the old Second World War RAF Group Control Centre at Craigmore, near Inverness, found new uses in the nuclear era. The wartime centre consisted of three earth-mounded bomb-proof buildings built of brick and concrete, comprising an operations room building, a separate filter room and a communications centre. Following its abandonment by the RAF in 1946, the operations room was taken over by the recently re-formed Royal Observer Corps as its Group Headquarters, and over twenty years later the adjacent two-storey Filter Room complex was acquired by the Highland Council for conversion into its blast- and fallout-protected emergency centre. The bunker underwent a major refit, at a reputed cost of £5 million in 1990, and continues to function into the twenty-first century. Highland Council also acquired the long-disused AAOR at Gaerloch which was refitted as the county standby emergency headquarters in 1988 but has never been used.

Following the 1968 stand-down, all central government funding for Civil Defence was withdrawn except for minuscule Home Office grants for the demolition of wartime air-raid shelters and for the minimal care and maintenance of the Regional Government bunkers. The majority of the county emergency structures ceased to exist, although a few of the Shire counties, and, exceptionally, a couple of London boroughs, maintained full Civil Defence organisations through local financing and voluntary management by council staff. Somerset, for example, continued to maintain regular exercises throughout the nadir of Civil Defence, despite the cutbacks. The incoming 1971 Conservative government put renewed emphasis upon nuclear emergency planning – now renamed 'Home Defence', and during the first three years of its tenure a series of Home Office circulars redefined the nature of regional government and the role of the local authorities. County councils were obliged to establish two protected county control bunkers: the County Main, which should ideally be contiguous with the peacetime administrative headquarters, and a remote County Standby that could take over if the Main, which was likely to be in a city centre and thus vulnerable to attack, should be disabled. At this time, too, London was reconstituted as a discreet wartime region, responsibility having previously been distributed amongst the surrounding regions on the assumption that in the event of nuclear war the Capital would be obliterated during the first nuclear exchange.

April 1974 saw a major reorganization of local government, with the formation of District Councils as a tier of government below County level, replacing the archaic assortment of Rural District Councils, City Boroughs, Urban Districts, etc. The newly defined role of the local authority reflected the move away from 'rescue and succour' that began in 1963, and further emphasized the pre-attack 'warning period' and immediate post-attack responsibilities for collating attack information, co-ordinating surviving resources and advising the public. The few local authority Civil Defence exercises conducted during the early 1970s were predominantly co-operative exercises with the UKWMO; the other responsibilities, for billeting survivors, disposing of bodies, maintaining public health and controlling food supplies were of secondary importance. Throughout this period of relative international calm the emphasis was upon *planning* rather than construction, and until the cold war became noticeably warmer in 1979/80 few practical advances were made.

Another *Home Defence Review* published in 1980 (as a response to increased Soviet aggression and American posturing) saw the evolution of Civil Defence into its final and most mature form; the birth of a strong, visible and overtly challenging weapon in the national armoury of deterrence. District Councils, along with all the Utility Companies and nationalised industries, were pressured into building emergency bunkers to complement the existing County structure. Over the following four years central government policy, issued as a series of Home Office circulars, was rationalised into a comprehensive and demanding instruction manual – the *Emergency Planning Guidelines for Local Authorities* – published in 1984. The last and greatest spurt in bunker building reached its peak in 1987 when the Home Office announced that it would offer one hundred per cent funding for approved bunker schemes and for other emergency-planning projects, including the construction of standby switching centres for the National Grid, underground emergency control centres and hardened pumping installations for the various water boards, as well as blast protection for existing electricity sub-stations and distribution centres. Decades earlier, strategic stockpiles of materials for the repair and restoration of the national grid had been established in huge, moderately protected hangar-like depots in countryside locations, and the BBC had already provided remote transmitters, complete with independent power supplies in isolated rural areas. A central BBC emergency control centre complete with broadcast studios, was established

48. National Grid Strategic Reserve Depot, Cirencester, Gloucestershire. Hangar-like structures similar to this were constructed in each of the home defence regions to store emergency stocks of material required to re-establish essential power lines. *Author's collection*

under its training college at Wood Norton Hall, near Evesham.

The promise of Central Government funding led to a rash of new building, even by local authorities that had previously been antagonistic to the whole ethos of nuclear war planning. Compelled to build bunkers, many authorities designed structures that were suspiciously similar to the day nurseries and social centres that their local councillors demanded but their hard-pressed budgets could previously ill afford. Often the 1980s District Council bunkers materialized as the basements of old people's homes and care centres, and it is a matter of speculation as to how large a proportion of the total building costs were attributed to these basements. Propelled by Conservative support for the free enterprise culture, several private companies benefited from this bunker-building boom, the most prominent being probably Tom Butler and Company, which produced a range of standard design bunkers adopted by numerous local authorities and utilities. The design of these latter period bunkers draws heavily on Swiss research, and many of the components adhere closely to standards issued in Switzerland many years earlier, where the construction of household or public bunkers was mandatory under all new buildings.

Perhaps unfortunately for private enterprise, the cold war ended abruptly before many of the new bunkers were complete. Through inertia, some local authorities continued construction through into the early 1990s, but the majority of those still incomplete by 1992 were left unfinished and adapted for less sinister purposes. Most of the water board bunkers, too, were never completed and exist today as mere shells; strange, semi-underground protuberances near rural reservoirs, often, indeed, mis-identified as reservoirs themselves. Most counties retain their County Main bunkers as peacetime emergency planning centres for use during civil contingencies or natural disasters, but the standby sites have generally been abandoned. Similarly, most District Councils have been keen to divest themselves of their cold, forbidding bunkers, those that still maintain an emergency planning function preferring to use conventional office accommodation.

THE EMERGENCY GOVERNMENT OF GREATER LONDON

During the first bunker-building frenzy of the early 1950s London was divided into four sectors for administrative purposes: North-East, North-West, South-East and South-West. Each sector was provided with a smaller, single-storey version of the Regional War Room, designated 'Sub Regional Commissioners Offices'. The four war rooms were located at:

- Mill Hill (Partingdale Lane)
- Wanstead (Northumberland Avenue)
- Chislehurst (Kemnal Manor)
- Cheam (Church Road)

These sub-regional war rooms reported directly to the Central Government Civil Defence War Room, and each controlled, and received reports from, six or seven subordinate Borough control bunkers. This system was retained, with decreasing effectiveness, until the end of the Civil Defence and the reorganization of regional government that saw the emergence of the Sub-Regional Control as the most significant layer of emergency government. At that time London, for reasons discussed elsewhere in this volume, ceased to be an independent administrative unit and responsibility for its various Boroughs was transferred to the surrounding regions. The Borough control at Hackney, for example, reported to S-RC 4.2 at Kelvedon Hatch.

By 1972 London once again was reconstituted as an independent entity for Home Defence purposes and became responsible for its own post-nuclear destiny. The region was divided into five geographical sectors similar to those that existed during the Second World War, at the head of which was a 'Group Control'. These controls were essentially the Regional War Rooms revamped and reorganized, reporting now to the Kelvedon Hatch S-RC which was redesignated 5.1 and was responsible only for the London region. Initially the four 1950s blockhouses continued much as before, serving the Northern, North Eastern, South Eastern and South Western groups of London Boroughs. A new bunker, created in 1972 by the adaptation of an existing Second World War Civil Defence Centre at Southall, controlled North West London. The bunker is buried below the playground of Hanborough Infants School in South Road, Southall, and is an impressive structure even in its current state of dereliction. Three of the four original entrances were bricked up, a new generator and air-conditioning plant were installed and three rooms underground were fitted with vault doors to form secure registries for important papers.

At around this time the Kemnal Manor bunker in Chislehurst was abandoned in favour of a newly constructed control centre established above ground in the lower floors of Pear Tree House, a recently constructed block of flats in Lunham Road, SE19. The following table shows the Greater London organization immediately prior to the final phase of Home Defence development that occurred in the early 1980s:

GROUP	NORTH EAST	SOUTH EAST	SOUTH WEST	NORTH WEST	NORTHERN
Control Centre	Wanstead War Room	Kemnal Manor War Room Function taken over by Pear Tree House	Cheam War Room	Southall Civil Defence Centre	Mill Hill War Room
Dependant Boroughs	• Havering • Barking and Dagenham • Newham, • Tower Hamlets • Hackney • Waltham Forest • Redbridge	• Greenwich • Bexley • Bromley • Croydon • Southwark • Lewisham	• Wandsworth • Lambeth • Merton • Sutton • Kingston • Richmond	• Harrow • Brent • Kensington and Chelsea • Hammersmith and Fulham • Hounslow • Ealing • Hillingdon	• Enfield • Haringey • Islington • City of London • Westminster • Camden • Barnet

During the 1980s plans for London became confused. By the middle of the decade the Mill Hill and Southall bunkers had ceased to operate and the remaining three were transferred to the control of the London Fire and Civil Defence Authority, a sure indication of the changed emphasis of emergency planning. Tentative plans were made earlier to refit the Mill Hill War Room as an emergency centre for the London Borough of Barnet but this came to nothing. Similarly, a scheme to adapt Brompton Road underground station as a replacement for Southall and as a comprehensive Emergency Control for the whole of London was soon abandoned.

None of the London Group controls remain in service: Cheam was demolished and its site redeveloped, Southall is abandoned and partially flooded, and Mill Hill has long been empty and is destined to be demolished in the year 2001. The rather bizarre 'bunker' in Pear Tree House has recently been abandoned, and the Chislehurst war room at Kemnal Manor is to be redeveloped as a rather unusual private residence.

TABLE OF LOCAL AUTHORITY BUNKERS

This list is not exhaustive and its accuracy cannot be guaranteed, due to varied reliability of the sources from which it is compiled. The Civil Defence records in dozens of County Archives have been searched with varying results: some yield treasures immediately, others are frustratingly sparse, while in those counties where Civil Defence Committee minutes are filed with the Chief Executive's papers, they are often closed for thirty years. Much of the information was provided by current local authority Emergency Planning Officers, but one must remember that many of the events recorded are three generations old, far beyond immediate personal memory. The final source is personal investigation on the ground, which often yields exciting results, but is necessarily open to misinterpretation.

Avon County Council
For some years the short-lived Avon County Council used the former Regional War Room at Flowers Hill, Brislington, as an emergency control centre. In 1981 the Home Office increased the annual rent for the premises from £400 to over £4,000. Avon County Council seized this opportunity to announce its 'nuclear-free' status, refused to pay the increased rent, abandoned the bunker and ceased to cooperate with all future Home Office war plans.

Berkshire
The County main bunker is underneath Shire Hall in Reading. Built in 1990, it is now used as document repository. County Standby is beneath Newbury District Council offices.

Buckinghamshire
County Main is in the basement of Aylesbury Town Hall, and the Standby beneath Bletchley fire station. Both were built in the early 1970s, and are predated by an earlier Civil Defence HQ the location of which has not been identified.

Significant improvements were made in 1981 with the aid of a Home Office grant, with further improvements in the late 1980s.

Upgrading of the Bletchley Standby was planned but not implemented before the grant was withdrawn.

Radiation protection was not absolute at either site: some rooms of the Aylesbury HQ, for example, had exposed windows above ground level that would be sandbagged in emergency.

Cheshire

County Main bunker was established in the ex-AAOR at Frodsham in 1961. An earlier war room was maintained in the basement of Chester County Hall.

Specially designed octagonal bunkers were built in the basements of Ellesmere Port Council HQ, and Vale Royal Borough Council HQ in the mid 1980s.

Clwyd

County main emergency centre is below Mold fire station.

Conwy

(Conwy is a 1996 amalgamation of Aberconwy and Colwyn councils)

There are reinforced basement bunkers, each provided with blast doors and standby generators, underneath the Council HQ in Bodlondeb and the Civic Offices at Colwyn Bay.

Cornwall

County main bunker is a lightly protected suite of rooms in the basement of County Hall, Treyew Road, Truro, built in 1982.

Corporation of London

The hardened Civil Defence control underneath the Guildhall is now used for document storage.

Devon

County main emergency centre is in the basement of County Hall, Exeter. The County Standby was to be a very inadequate affair built at Fort Austin by walling up the main entrance of the fort and adapting the chamber thus formed.

Durham

The emergency planning centre is within the Fire Brigade Headquarters at Framwellgate Moor. Previously, there was a Civil Defence control in the basement of Durham County Hall, with a Standby under Darlington Town Hall.

Essex

The first Essex county main bunker was built underneath an extension to the County Hall in 1963. This survived until the late 1970s, when a nearby building development created a change in the water table which threatened to flood the bunker.

County Standby bunker is a converted AAOR at Mistley. This was never properly fitted out, and in the words of the current County EPO, was 'very much for the County second eleven'.

The present centre is incorporated in a further extension to the County Hall, complete in 1985, and is a lightly protected office suite finished to minimum Home Office specifications, suitable also as a peacetime conference centre or offices. It is provided with filtered ventilation but has ordinary fire doors rather than blast doors.

Glamorgan County Council
During the early 1960s an unusual joint venture between the County Council and British Steel, (which was a major employer in the region) resulted in the construction of a large, semi-underground bunker at Brombil. After the construction of the M4 motorway the local water table changed dramatically and rendered the bunker untenable. After decades of disuse it was sold in 1996 and its roof now forms the foundation slab for two modern bungalows.

Gwent
County Standby consisted of two semi-basement rooms below a residential college on high ground overlooking Abergavenny. Protection was minimal. Steel joists were inserted to support the wooden floor of the room above, and arrangements made with a local builders merchant to tip several tons of sand through the ground floor windows as a measure of radiation protection. A flight of steps from the rear of the 'bunker' leads to a lean-to annexe that housed a small standby generator and racking for the storage of food supplies and stretchers.
Gwent's emergency centre was established in 1985 in the basement of the 1972 Council HQ in Cwmbran. The bunker has a low protective rating, and has high-level windows that would be sealed in emergency with sandbags. The bunker ceased to function in 1998.

Gwynedd
The County emergency control centre was first established as a Civil Defence Corps control in the basement of the County Court building in Caernarfon in the early 1950s. After a period of decline this was refitted to a high standard in 1986. The County Standby is in Dolgellau.

In 1968 Meirionnydd adapted a disused school building about a mile from their headquarters office as a Civil Defence centre. Following the Three Mile Island incident, this centre was rebuilt, with a new, one-foot thick concrete roof, as an emergency centre for the nearby Trawsfynydd nuclear power station.

Hampshire
County main bunker is a specially constructed underground structure below part of the medieval castle complex in Winchester.

County Standby is in an ex-Civil Defence centre built in one of the old ammunition magazines at Fort Widley. This site is now only used by the local Raynet group.

Hereford (Old County)

Between 1950 and 1974 the County main bunker was in a series of adapted cells in the basement of the Magistrate's Court, which is a solidly constructed Victorian building detached from the Civic Centre. This was taken over as the Standby centre for the newly formed Hereford & Worcester County in 1974.

Hereford and Worcester

The Emergency Planning unit of the new combined County authority was allocated a suite of rooms in the basement of the 1970s County Hall. This had a very low protection factor, and whilst a few rooms are still used as a peacetime Emergency Control Centre, most of the area is now used for storage.

Hertfordshire

Hertfordshire appears to have been sparsely provided with nuclear protection after 1968. A proper County main bunker was never provided but the Council offices in Hemel Hempstead housed the standby, which was an inadequate and ill-equipped site.

Prior to that the county was divided into three Civil Defence regions, North, West and South-West. The North control was to have been built at Hitchin but was never completed, the Western control was at Carpenter's Park, Hemel Hempstead, and the SW control was built at Reed's School, Watford, between 1953 and 1956.

Highland

Regional main bunker is in the ex-RAF Sector Operations block at Craigiebarns.

The AAOR at Gaerloch was acquired by Highland Council as a standby bunker and was partially fitted out in 1988.

Humberside

The post-war AAOR at Wawne was converted into a county control for the East Riding of York in the early 1960s and subsequently became the Humberside county control. Demolition of the building is currently under discussion in 2001.

Kent

County main was built in the basement of the Council's Springfield office complex on the outskirts of Maidstone in 1964; this location was selected in order to avoid congestion in the centre of Maidstone. The bunker was refurbished and extended in 1984 when modern concrete and steel blast doors were fitted. A structural survey taken some time later indicated that the ceiling reinforcement was inadequate. Like the Dorset HQ at Dorchester and elsewhere, the bunker was not provided with an internal emergency power supply, but relied upon external connections to mobile generators which would be set up in an adjacent car park. Plans were drawn up for strengthening work but the centre was closed down in 1999 before the work was put in hand.

A County Standby bunker proposed for Canterbury was never completed.

Earlier Civil Defence Corps plans for Kent had been much more comprehensive, but were never fully implemented due to funding shortages. The scheme envisaged protected controls at: Gravesend, to oversee the Dartford and Northfleet RDCs; at Canterbury (in the basement of the old Municipal Building) to control the area from Sheppey to Herne Bay; and Orpington (where a standard 1954-style bunker was built), to control metropolitan Kent. No suitable site could be found in the Thanet district, which included the strategically important port of Dover, and the Civil Defence authorities there were told to use any suitable Second World War shelter that was not waterlogged, or if that was not possible to simply requisition a suitable building at the start of an emergency.

The Maidstone district was controlled from a Civil Defence headquarters in the basement of Mote House, the Cheshire Home in Mote Park. There is no surviving evidence of this centre at the house.

No protected accommodation was provided in the Folkestone area, where, between 1952 and 1968 the Civil Defence control consisted of a series of prefabricated huts.

Leicestershire
A radiation-proof bunker with a protection factor of 100 was provided under the new County Hall in Glenfield, Leicester, in 1968.

Norfolk
The County Main emergency centre is below the nine-storey County Hall building and the adjacent Police training centre in Martineau Rd, Norwich. Built in 1961 and subsequently upgraded on several occasions, the centre has one-metre-thick concrete walls and ceilings, its own 32KvA generator and 3,500 gallon reserve water supply. A high-specification air-conditioning and filtration plant is capable of one complete air change every twenty minutes.

The county standby, beneath a Social Services day centre in Grimston Road, Kings Lynn, was deemed unsuitable and abandoned in the 1980s.

Nottinghamshire
Nottinghamshire was relatively ill-prepared for nuclear war, but had a small emergency centre under a 1960s extension to the County Hall in West Bridgeford. The County standby was, unusually, co-located with the main Severn-Trent Water emergency control bunker under their headquarters in Mansfield.

Oxfordshire
County main bunker is an underground structure built partially below Wood Eaton Manor, a council-owned special-needs school north of Oxford. The original structure closely conformed to the standard Civil Defence control pattern. Access was via a pair of light steel doors, which in time of war would have been rendered radiation and blast resistant by several tons of sand piled against them. Egress would then have been by means of a vertical shaft

211

emergency exit which was also filled with sand that would require digging out. This was a common feature of most European bunker designs of the 1960s. During a 1980s refurbishment the bunker was substantially rebuilt with an additional emergency exit fitted with conventional, heavy-duty blast doors.

Powys
The 'bunker' is an ordinary basement room in the District Council Headquarters at Llandrindod Wells, which was previously a Victorian spa hotel. The pf factor is estimated to be in excess of 2000 on account of the density of the bricks employed in its construction. Very little provision was made to strengthen the bunker other than arrange to tip several tons of sand from a nearby quarry around the ground floor of the building.

Somerset
County main bunker was a purpose-built centre deep below an underground car park adjacent to County Hall in Taunton. The Taunton centre was closed in 2000 and is now used as a repository for the county archive. County Standby was below the ambulance station in Yeovil but is now just used for general storage.

49. **Somerset County Emergency Centre.** Entrance vestibule with switchgear for the air-conditioning and standby generator plant. Steps from the main entrance descend to the right of the picture, while the passageway in the background lead to an alternative entrance. Toilets are to the left of this passage with dormitories and a kitchen to the right. *Author's collection*

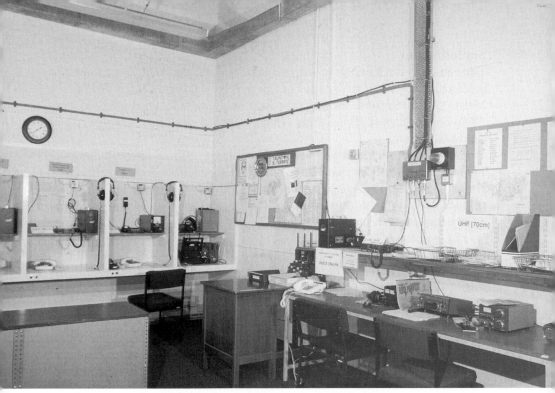

50. **Somerset County Emergency Centre.** The communications centre showing a variety of radio communication equipment including RAYNET sets providing emergency links with local amateur radio operators. *Author's collection*

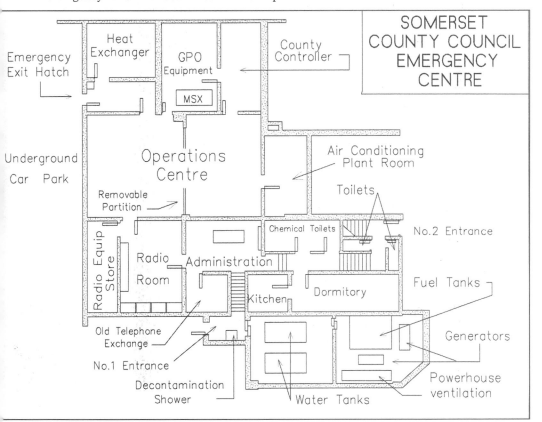

Staffordshire

The county council first provided emergency accommodation in the form of a protected ARP HQ in the basement of its massive Victorian County Building in Martin Street, Stafford, in 1939. This was continually updated until the early 1990s and contained all the usual features: blast doors, generators, filtered air conditioning, etc.

The basement of Hanley library was nominated as the county standby from 1974 until 1997 but was never fitted out to a high standard. Work started on the Hanley centre in 1971 when it was the responsibility of Stoke on Trent City Council, but it was transferred to County in 1974 following the local government reorganization.

Suffolk

The first post-war county bunker was a heavily protected structure built in the early 1950s below the new Ipswich Divisional police HQ. It originally served both East Suffolk and Ipswich Borough Councils, and, following the amalgamation of East and West Suffolk in 1972 it functioned for the joint Council and Ipswich Borough.

Before 1972 West Suffolk maintained an emergency bunker in the basement of the Shire Hall, Bury St Edmunds.

Surrey

The earliest Civil Defence County Main bunker for Surrey was built in 1960 partially below Guildford Technical College and partly into an adjacent hillside. It has been recently decommissioned and adapted for use as a gymnasium for the college and for archive storage. The blast doors have been retained, but all other features such as the generators and air-conditioning plant have been removed.

Surrey's current emergency planning centre is based in County Hall, Kingston-upon-Thames and meets the needs of both the County and the Borough of Kingston. The County Standby centre was returned to Reigate & Banstead Borough Council in the early 1980s, while all the other Surrey District bunkers have been relegated to storage use.

Tayside

The Tayside bunker was at Craigiebarns House to the east of Dundee within a site occupied by the Caledonian Sector Control of UKWMO. In recent years the house has been converted into private flats.

None of the Tayside Regional Councils (Angus, Dundee, Perth, Kinross) had emergency planning centres.

Warwickshire

Until it was absorbed into the new West Midlands local authority in 1974, Warwickshire's County Main had been, since its acquisition in 1962, the ex AAOR in Sutton Coldfield.

The new County Main is beneath a council owned property called 'The

Retreat' in Rugby, with a standby in the basement of Stratford District Council's offices.

West Glamorgan County Council
For many years this council utilized the former AAOR at West Cross, but following the Welsh local government reorganization in 1986 it was transferred to the City & County of Swansea Authority. Due partly to the local geology, the two-storey bunker is completely above ground with main and emergency exits on the lower floor. Internally the building retains many of its original features, including the curved perspex screens on two of the three sides of the balcony overlooking the operations well.

West Sussex
Because of its prime coastal target location, West Sussex was one of the earliest counties to be granted Home Office funding for the construction of bomb-proof Civil Defence shelters. County Main was constructed in the basement of County Hall, Chichester, in the early 1950s, and the standby, in Horsham, was a standard design surface blockhouse, recently demolished to make way for a housing development.

Wiltshire
County Main is in the basement of County Hall, Trowbridge (see main text). Standby was built underneath Devizes library, but is now used only for archive storage.

Yorkshire
County Main bunker built below County Hall in Northallerton.

DISTRICT, BOROUGH, AND CITY COUNCIL BUNKERS

Ashford Borough Council
Semi-basement below car-park under council offices.

Aylesbury Vale District
Two rooms in basement of Aylesbury Civic Centre were earmarked for conversion but never completed.

Barrow District Council
This authority utilized the Barrow AAOR which was substantially upgraded in 1984. Previous to that it had lain disused for some years following its abandonment as a Civil Defence Corps control in 1968, having been first adopted for this function in the late 1950s.

Basildon District Council
Although a traditionally Tory constituency, Basildon council was avowedly anti-

nuclear, and their emergency plans verged upon farce. Their 'nuclear bunker' consisted of two portacabins pitched in the middle of a field far from anywhere, at the council's Barleyland depot. In event of nuclear war they would be surrounded by rubbish skips filled with earth and piled two-high, with RSJs covered with earth propped between them.

Basingstoke
The County standby bunker is below Basingstoke Old Town Hall.

Beaconsfield
There is a purpose-built Civil Defence centre under the old Police Station and Courts. Constructed in 1954 and continuously upgraded, it was subject to a major revamp in the 1980s.

Bermondsey
Work started on a hardened Civil Defence bunker under Spa Gardens in Spa Road in 1953, but the project was halted two years later before building work was finished. Temporary accommodation was found in the Spa Road municipal offices until 1961 when a new bunker was opened under the Neckinger Garage adjoining the civic offices.

Bexley
An underground Civil Defence control was built in Bexley Broadway in 1953, to the standard design replicated, for example, at Gravesend. It consists of a central corridor protected by a heavy steel door at the bottom of a flight of access steps; service and domestic accommodation including a switchroom with Lister generator and a small kitchen to one side and operations rooms on the other. The modern Bexley Civic offices have been built over the bunker, the access steps emerging in an enclosed patio in the middle of the office complex.

Birmingham Corporation
A small wartime Civil Defence centre under the Victorian City Hall has remained in constant use, but in 1968 the City Council took possession of a redundant, purpose-built Civil Defence Corps bunker (built in 1954) in the garden of No.8 Meadow Road, Harborne. This was transferred to West Midlands council in 1974. (See main text for details).

Brecklands District
A purpose-built bunker was built in the 1980s close to the District Council offices in Dereham and offices there are still in use as an emergency planning centre.

Brentford and Chiswick
During the 1950s the local authority approached the Lucozade Company with a view to converting the cellar of their factory into a Borough Civil Defence control, but were told that the company had already earmarked it as a fallout shelter for factory staff.

Bristol City Council
Main bunker under the Council House, College Green. Four Civil Defence controls were built in 1954 in Bedminster, Avonmouth, Henleaze and Speedwell. (See main text for details.)

Broadlands District Council
Purpose-built 1980s bunker close to the District Council offices in Norwich; still occasionally used for exercises.

Bromsgrove District
No hardened facilities provided.

Camden
During the 1950s an underground Borough Civil Defence control was built beneath a green area at 163 Highgate Road.

Camberwell
Civil Defence Control opened under the Town Hall in Peckham Road in 1954, with Civil Defence training centres at Kirkwood Road and Brayards Road.

Canterbury
This authority chose not to develop a hardened control centre and opted instead for conventional, unprotected offices which acted as both an emergency centre and peacetime conference room.

Castle Morpeth Borough Council
Immediately after the local council reorganization in 1974 proposals were made to build a bunker in the cellars of the Town Hall in Morpeth, but these were never implemented.

Castle Point Borough Council
A Thatcher-period bunker built below an extension to the council offices at Thundersleigh near Southend in 1992. The design is very similar to that of the Severn-Trent Water bunker in Gloucester with multiple blast doors protecting the main entrance and duplicate emergency exits accessed via two dormitories at the rear.

Charnwood
Modern bunker to standard post-1982 design as part of an extension to new council offices in Loughborough, built circa 1990. Now used only for general storage.

Chelmsford
Bunker in the basement of an extension to the Civic Centre built in the mid-1980s.

Cherwell
The emergency control centre below Banbury Town Hall was decommissioned in the mid-1980s and is now used as a council leisure resource.

Chiltern
The council's bunker, built in 1985 below a new council office block, was transferred to county control in 1990 and is now used for storage.

Chislehurst
No. 7 Group Civil Defence control bunker was built in 1954 in the garden of "Sunnymeads" in Perry Street, only half a mile from the large London Group Control bunker at Kemnal Manor. The building fell into disuse around 1962 and was demolished in the 1980s.

Crawley Borough Council
The basement of Crawley Town Hall accommodates a bunker built in 1979. The bunker is secured by three sets of blast doors and contains a small power station, ventilation equipment and decontamination showers. An emergency exit, in the form of a low, horizontal passageway leading to a vertical shaft fitted with a ladder, has been sealed in recent years.

Dacorum Borough Council
Small basement bunker below the council headquarters in Hemel Hempstead, built in 1966. Very few improvements have been made to this site over the decades other than the removal of the blast doors and their replacement by conventional wooden doors in recent years.

Dagenham Borough Council
Purpose-built underground single-storey Civil Defence bunker built in 1953 in the grounds of the Civic Centre at the junction of Wood Lane and Rainham Road. The bunker has been disused since 1968.

Dartford
Emergency centre consists of a reinforced refuge within the Civic Centre.

Dover
Converted basement below municipal offices, completed 1989.

Ealing
Ealing was a steadfastly 'nuclear-free' authority and was unwilling to provide any sort of Civil Defence accommodation. Eventually the authority was compelled to take up space in the North West Group Control at Southall.

Eastbourne
Rooms in the basement of the council offices were designated as the County Standby bunker, detailed architects plans were prepared but never implemented.

Eastleigh Borough Council
The authority utilized a hardened Civil Defence bunker, possibly of Second World War vintage, beneath the old Town Hall (currently the Point Art & Dance Centre). Now used for storage, although the original blast doors and ventilation plant are still in situ.

Eden District Council
A comprehensive emergency centre was constructed below the Mansion House, Penrith, during the 1980s. Communications and service plant were housed in a fully protected basement area, while the control room, kitchens and domestic services were on the ground floor. Under emergency conditions the ground floor area could be segregated from the rest of the building by temporary works involving steel framing and sandbags.

Edinburgh
Lothian Regional Council and Edinburgh District Council both had financial interests in the Eastern Zone HQ at Corstorphine Hill in Edinburgh (Barnton Quarry), but neither authority occupied any part of it as an emergency centre.

Epping Forest District Council
The Epping Forest bunker is one of the most interesting in the Home Counties, in that it is a conversion of a Second World War RAF Sector Operations Centre and still retains most of its original external features. The large L-shaped building, which is just south of the North Weald airfield control tower, is

51. **Epping Forest District Council Bunker.** Main entrance. *Nick Catford*

52. Epping Forest District Council Bunker. The control room of this former RAF Sector Operations Centre has been much altered since the Second World War.
Nick Catford

partially mounded over with a short entrance tunnel in the mound protected by blast walls. Much of the original interior layout is still discernible, with the operations well retained as the council operations room, still overlooked by the control balcony. Elsewhere the wartime layout has been lost where rooms have been subdivided to form modern offices. The bunker was adapted as a local authority control only in 1986, at which time new external blast doors and air-tight internal doors were fitted.

Epsom and Ewell
The original 1950s Civil Defence bunker was a semi-underground structure at the far end of the council HQ car park, but was relocated to the new HQ building in 1992 when this was erected on the site of the car park.

Fareham
Protected accommodation was provided reluctantly in the late 1980s in response to Home Office pressure. The authority chose to adapt an existing 1950s AAOR at Fort Fareham which was about two miles from its headquarters. The Fareham AAOR, unlike the majority of the Anti-Aircraft Operations Rooms of the period which were built in concrete to a standard design, was an adaptation of one of the fort's existing casemates. Many of the original 1950s features remain, including the massive blast doors and the ventilation system.

Greater Manchester
The County Main bunker was located in Cheadle, a suburb of Stockport, and

was maintained in recent years by Greater Manchester Fire & Civil Defence Authority. The authority took control of the ex-Regional War Room for their own purposes some time after 1972. It stands in the grounds of the Nuffield Hospital and has recently been converted into a pharmaceutical store for the hospital.

County Standby is in the basement of Bolton Town Hall.

Gravesham
Converted basement in council HQ, now abandoned in favour of conventional offices.

Hackney
A substantial semi-underground concrete bunker was built in 1953 behind Stoke Newington town hall. Typical of many of the local authority Civil Defence bunkers built as part of the Civil Defence organisation based upon the Regional War Room concept, it consists of a series of underground rooms on each side of a central corridor, accessed via a dog leg stairway from a hardened concrete surface blockhouse. It was provided with its own generator and air filtration and circulation plant and an extensive land-line communication system.

Hammersmith
Emergency centre in the basement of the Guildhall, Kingston.

Harrow
The Second World War Civil Defence Group control situated at the corner of Uxbridge Road and Uxbridge Lane was scheduled for demolition in 1954 and replacement by a new blockhouse in a nearby car park. This plan never came to fruition and the original structure survived as the Harrow Borough Council control until 1966.

Hastings Borough Council
A substantial, reinforced concrete Civil Defence control bunker was built on ground adjacent to Ashdown House in the Round Wood area of the town. Ashdown House was previously a Ministry of Works office. The bunker was constructed between 1965 and 1968 and was designed to house a staff of fifty, with cooking and dormitory facilities provided. An overflow staff of thirty would be housed in Ashdown House, and there were plans to link the two buildings by means of a tunnel, but a council minute recorded in 1966 reveals that this proposal was voted down because 'no movement was anticipated during fallout'.

Before 1965 two buildings in the town centre, Jackson Hall and Marine Court, had fulfilled the Borough's Civil Defence needs. The council records indicate that in 1965 the Home Office was making Hastings a special case for building, as they were the weak link in the South East defences.

Hereford City
Basement of Old Town Hall.

Horsham District Council
Horsham District Council's bunker, which also acts as the West Sussex County Standby, is in the basement of a council office block built opposite Horsham Town Hall in 1984.

Huntingdon
A modern bunker was built in 1983 in the basement of Castle Hill House, the former HQ of RAF Pathfinder Force. Used only for storage since 1995.

Ipswich
This authority did not provide any blast or fallout protected premises, but a basement room in the council HQ was fitted with emergency communications equipment in 1988/9.

Leominster District Council
New, purpose-built bunker incorporated in the basement of Arkwright Court, an old people's home in Leominster now owned by the Leominster Marches Housing Association and used for storage. In an arcaded, semi-basement frontage, two apparently innocent louvered wood doors disguise a pair of massive steel blast doors a few feet behind them.

Luton
No special provision other than to fit out a basement room in the council HQ with a few additional telephone sockets.

Malden District Council
A small basement bunker was built under a purpose-built brick building on an estates department nursery in Providence Park in 1982. The site was vacated by the Emergency Planning department in 1985 when a new centre was opened in the town centre council offices.

Malvern Hills District
The authority was allocated a suite of rooms under a new building erected for the County Treasurer's Department in Malvern in the late 1980s, but it was never fitted out. The rooms are now used for storage.

Mansfield District Council
Emergency control centre built below new Civic Centre constructed in 1990.

Matlock
Emergency centre beneath council headquarters building.

Medway
Medway Unitary authority inherited two Civil Defence bunkers, at Gillingham and Rochester, when it was created in 1998.

The 1950s purpose-built, single-storey underground concrete bunker in the car park of the Council offices in Gillingham was given over to storage in the early 1980s when the second Medway centre, a surface bunker in the car park of the Rochester Civic Centre, was upgraded to a high standard.

Melton Borough Council
Thatcher-period bunker built under new headquarters building in late 1980s.

Merseyside
With a nuclear-free legacy, it is to be expected that the region was ill-provided with emergency bunkers, and such is the case. Merseyside utilized as its main bunker a very small installation built for Liverpool Corporation underneath the Walker Art Gallery. The County Standby is beneath an extension to Southport Technical College built in the late 1960s.

Birkenhead Corporation bunker is beneath the Glenda Jackson Theatre.

Mid-Devon
The Mid-Devon bunker is one of several that was started in the late 1980s but never completed following the end of the cold war. Nevertheless, the bunker, in the basement of the Town Hall, Fore Street, Tiverton, is equipped with a fully functional air-conditioning and filtration system, a TSX50 telephone exchange and a standby generator.

Milton Keynes
Milton Keynes attempted to adopt 'nuclear-free' status, and refused to build its own bunker, but was allocated space in the County Main.

New Forest District
Emergency centre below the Council offices in Ringwood.

Northallerton
Small bunker beneath Northallerton Civic Centre.

North Devon
Bunker constructed underneath the Civic Centre and Police Station in Barnstaple during the early 1980s.

North East Lincolnshire
Emergency centre in basement of council offices in Brigg.

North Somerset
No special provisions was made other than to allocate two small rooms in the basement of council offices in Bridgwater.

North Weald
Emergency centre established in a converted RAF Sector Operations block, refurbished to a high standards in the 1980s.

North Wiltshire

Semi-underground bunker built in the basement of 1960s annexe to council offices in Monks Park, Chippenham. The annexe, which is built on a steeply sloping riverside site, housed the council's planning department until it was demolished in 2000. The emergency centre was in a suite of basement rooms which was buried into the hillside at the rear but was quite exposed on the front, riverside, elevation. To have built it deeper would have taken it below river level.

Rather oddly, the main entrance was via a heavy steel and concrete blast door from an internal stairway, but within the centre only lightweight doors separated the various rooms, three of which had glazed frontages overlooking the river. This arrangement rendered useless the row of pressure release valves built into the concrete wall above the main door.

The main operations room was an austere concrete chamber containing the usual maps, etc. together with a small hand-operated air filter. Behind this room was an even smaller one containing the telecoms equipment. A lightweight door separated the ops room from a series of three rooms on the river frontage that comprised the dormitory, kitchen and conference room.

North Yorkshire

Hardened premises below Grove Road School, Harrogate.

Oxford City

The early 1950s concrete Civil Defence blockhouse built by the Borough Council is now a commercial broadcasting station.

Poole

A small emergency centre was established in the basement of the Civic Centre but no trace of this now survives.

Portsmouth

Emergency centre established at Fort Widley in 1965.

Redditch Borough Council

A purpose-built facility was erected in the basement of the new town hall, erected in the 1980s. The rooms were later revamped to provide a children's creche for employees.

Restormel Borough Council

A hardened emergency centre was included as an integral part of the council offices when the new HQ was built in Penwinnick Road, St Austell in 1982. Although it forms the South East corner of the basement area, access is only possible from an external stairway. The design of the bunker is very similar to most of those constructed after 1982: heavy steel and concrete blast doors protect an entrance lobby which gives access, via more blast doors, to a generator room to the right, or, via a series of decontamination showers, to the main operations area to the left. The emergency exit consists of a thirty-foot long concrete-pipe walkway leading to a vertical shaft that emerges via a hatch into the HQ car park. The length of the emergency exit tunnel is calculated to ensure that the exit hatch is far enough from the building not to be covered by debris should the building collapse.

Richmond Upon Thames
During 1985-6 a bunker was built beneath Thameslink House, a new office block not occupied by the council, some way from Richmond town centre. It was designed to sustain a staff of forty for two weeks and has a protection factor in excess of one hundred.

Rotherham
Concrete bunker, probably constructed as a Civil Defence control in the 1950s and periodically upgraded, located in the compound of a council depot on the outskirts of the town.

Rutland
This authority has no protected accommodation of its own, other than an emergency communications room in the basement of its headquarters, but shares its Emergency Planning function with Leicestershire.

Salisbury and South Wiltshire
Hardened, single-storey underground control built between 1959 and 1962 beside Old Blandford Road on S.W outskirts of the city. Now used for storage. (See main text.)

Sevenoaks
Protected basement in modern council headquarters.

Shepway (Kent)
Converted basement of council offices now abandoned in favour of unprotected surface accommodation.

Southampton
In compliance with Home Office requirements, Southampton City Council, which was another of the so-called 'nuclear-free zones', made just minimal war plans. Between 1983 and 1993 the City authority leased from Hampshire County Council one of the two hardened 1954-era bunkers which the county had retained since the days of the Civil Defence Corps. The City bunker, which still exists though now in commercial ownership, is in Basset Green Road, near the M27. The other, which seems to have fallen into disuse in 1968, is in Bitterne Road East. Until 1968 both bunkers were subordinate to a main Civil Defence centre below the council HQ in the city centre.

South Cambridgeshire
Emergency control centre built by Tony Leadley, the EPO, in 1985 in basement

of the council offices, Cambridgeshire House, Hills Road, Cambridge. The District authority had considerable difficulty gaining planning permission to build the bunker because the City authority in whose area it resides had declared itself a nuclear-free zone. Construction involved the insertion of a reinforced roof spanning the whole of the basement area and the erection of very substantial blast doors.

South Gloucestershire District Council
A hardened control centre, complete with standby generators and air-lock blast doors was included in the basement of the new council headquarters in Thornbury, originally constructed for Northavon District Council. A basement area in Kingswood Civic Centre was also allocated as an emergency centre but never fitted out.

South Herefordshire District Council
The District applied for a Home Office grant for a shelter below the new, 1980s headquarters, but it was never built. A female Conservative councillor raised objections and managed to block the planning permission. Her grounds for opposition were that it would require the removal of an oak tree which, being a prime example of its species, she succeeded in having a preservation order issued on. It came out later that she did not realize that she was preventing the construction of a nuclear bunker intended for her own survival, and when this was pointed out, wanted the tree down immediately: too late, for planning permission was already granted for the new HQ, sans bunker.

South Oxfordshire
Control bunker built in 1988 as an above-ground extension to an existing office block in Wallingford. (The high water table in the area precluded an underground structure.) Since the end of the cold war the bunker has been decommissioned and is now used for storage. The Council Chamber is currently designated as an emergency planning centre.

South Scurlough District Council
Emergency centre built in the basement of council offices in Hornsea.

Southwark
Southwark Borough Control was an underground, post-war Civil Defence bunker (circa 1952) at the junction of Peckham Road and Vestry Road, opposite the Town Hall. Later a temporary health centre was constructed on top of this, but in 1984 all the surface features were swept away and the bunker sealed when the land was redeveloped to build the Heygate Estate. The bunker contained forced air ventilation, a diesel generator, a 'four-minute-warning' indicator and two teleprinters connected to the GLC area bunker at Gypsy Hill. Ten years prior to closure the bunker was refitted to act as Southwark's emergency flood control centre.

St Albans
Emergency centre with all the usual features: blast doors, comms centre, standby generator, etc, built under St Albans council offices in 1989.

Strathclyde
Single-storey bunker similar (although not identical) to a London Group Control. Now under commercial occupation.

Stroud
Purpose-built centre in Ebley Mill, the new council HQ built in 1989. The bunker consists of an above-ground extension to the existing mill building and doubles as a stationery store and party meeting room. A typical Butler design with solid concrete walls, concrete slab roof and triple air-lock doors at the main entrance.

Swale Borough Council
Converted basement abandoned in favour of conventional office space.

Tendring District Council
This authority never built its own bunker but was allocated two rooms in the Essex County Standby at Mistley, an ex-AAOR.

Test Valley
This is a dual-located authority with its HQ split between Romsey and Andover, both of which had protected accommodation. A converted basement below the Romsey HQ sufficed, while at Andover a hardened bunker, now abandoned, was built at an outlying Council depot.

Thanet
Plans for a protected emergency centre were prepared in 1986 but construction never got under way.

Thurrock
Emergency centre in basement of council offices.

Tonbridge and Malling
Specially constructed concrete bunker built between two wings of former RAF buildings which were taken over for conversion to new council offices.

Torbay
Building works on the Borough bunker under the council headquarters were completed in 1988.

Uttlesford District Council
A fully featured emergency bunker with radiological, biological and chemical protection was built under the council offices in 1989.

Wallasey Borough Council
Emergency centre beneath Wallasey Town Hall.

Wealden District Council
Lightly protected semi-underground structure adjacent to council offices.

Wellingborough
When the new combined Fire and Ambulance Station was planned for
Wellingborough in 1962 it was decided to incorporate a Civil Defence control
centre in the basement, accessed from a flight of steps within the Fire Station.
Much of the original equipment has been stripped out in recent years and the
premises are now used as storage for the Fire Brigade.

West Devon
Following its move to new premises in Kilworth Park, West Devon Council
contemplated plans for a new bunker on several occasions but these were never
brought to fruition due to a lack of funding, despite a possible fifty per cent
Home Office grant. The existing plans, as described by Nick Payne, the current
EPO for West Devon, are thus:

> The story goes that the survival of WDBC was ensured under a plan in
> which one of the chief officers and a small team would leg it to the bowels
> of one of the forts above Plymouth in the event of a threat, and the
> remainder would be protected by a scheme in which a number of ad-hoc
> lean-to shelter affairs using sheets of corrugated iron would be erected
> against the walls of the cliff up to Kilworth House. These were to be
> reinforced with sandbags, and staff would scuttle into them when the sirens
> sounded.

West Oxfordshire
Bunker in the basement of council offices at George Green.

West Wiltshire District Council
A well equipped bunker was built in 1984 underneath a detached medical centre
in the car park of council offices in Bradley Road, Trowbridge. A substantially
constructed surface blockhouse contains the bunker's standby generator and air-
conditioning plant.

Wigan
The cold war emergency control centre was situated in a Second World War Civil
Defence station in the basement of the council's town centre administrative
building.

Worcester City Council
This was a 'nuclear-free' authority and took little interest in bunker building, but
in minimal compliance with Home Office regulations it nominated part of the

Guildhall basement as an emergency centre. No work was done to provide even limited nuclear protection.

Woking
Modern bunker built under the civic offices in 1982 and upgraded in line with Home Office guidelines until 1990. Now used for storage, but the original bunk beds in the dormitory are utilized as stationery racks. While in use, the EPO was concerned that there were no emergency exits provided, and the main entrance door opened outwards, which meant that it could be jammed shut by debris should the building above collapse.

Wychavon
Emergency centre in basement of Civic Centre in Pershore, with ventilation and exhaust outlets visible adjacent to the centre's car park. Now used for storage.

Wycombe
Established in the basement of Court Gardens Leisure Centre, about four miles from the town centre. The EPO had little confidence in the suitability of this site and it was never completely fitted out for service.

11

THE GPO SECRET UNDERGROUND EXCHANGES AND THE ESSENTIAL SERVICE BUNKERS

Throughout the Second World War most of the development in telecommunications technology in the United Kingdom had been undertaken by the GPO, principally as a result of the long-established Post Office monopoly of telephone services. Even during the pre-war years, GPO standard equipment had been the only types acceptable for most government contracts. It is not surprising, therefore, that when the government called for a major revamp of the communications systems to support the post-1948 Civil Defence programme the GPO should be deeply involved. In fact, the organization was so deeply immersed in secret construction projects connected with military and Civil Defence communications systems and with the ROTOR radar project that its normal commercial and domestic activities suffered as a consequence. During 1948 and 1949, plans were developed for the construction of a hardened, 'survivable' trunk cable network linking the major administrative and industrial cities and strategic defence sites such as naval dockyards and RAF communications centres. The new works would have collateral peacetime benefits, but in the straitened times of the 1950s when most of the work was implemented, Parliament could not have authorized, nor the Exchequer sustained, such a project as a purely commercial venture.

Important components of this new-works programme were two trunk cable routes, the first from Glasgow to London via Manchester and Birmingham, and the second from London to Bristol that later incorporated the transatlantic telephone links from land-stations in Cornwall. Spurs to the south and east would serve other strategic locations. It was planned that these cables would be intercepted by very heavily protected, bomb-proof underground emergency telephone exchanges in the centres of Glasgow, Manchester, Birmingham, Bristol and London. Additional cables would be routed around the perimeters of these cities to avoid the more vulnerable central target areas. By 1950 certain aspects of the programme had been downgraded, including the abandonment of the underground city centre exchanges at Glasgow and Bristol, but the final scheme still retained three of the planned underground telephone trunk exchanges:

- London 'KINGSWAY'
- Birmingham 'ANCHOR'
- Manchester 'GUARDIAN'

These were supplemented by eight semi-underground 'PR1' and 'PR2' Intermediate Carrier Repeater Stations, the two designations signifying only that they differed slightly in the lengths of their main equipment rooms. The 'PR' repeaters were located at:

• WARMLEY	on the eastern outskirts of Bristol
• PORTSDOWN	overlooking Portsmouth Harbour
• QUESLETT	north-west of Birmingham
• LYNDON GREEN	south-east of Birmingham
• SWINTON	north-west of Manchester
• STOCKPORT	south-east of Manchester
• ROTHWELL HAIGH	south-east of Leeds and UDDINGSTON

Implementation of this scheme met with continued delays and it was not completed until late in 1958, by which time much of its function had been overtaken by the Post Office microwave network (the erroneously named 'BACKBONE' system, which has been described at length in Duncan Campbell's *War Plan UK*, and is only touched upon briefly below). As the project neared completion, the underground trunk exchange in the government's emergency war headquarters at Corsham was integrated into the London-to-Bristol cable.

The KINGSWAY exchange in London was the only one to be built in an existing underground structure, the wartime deep-level shelter underneath Chancery Lane tube station, and was the first to be completed, in October 1954. By the mid-1950s most of the wartime tube shelters had descended into obscurity, although future research may prove that obscurity was not synonymous with lassitude. Files in the Public Records Office indicate that a prolonged works programme was undertaken in the tunnels by the civil engineers Mott, Hay and Anderson, who were also responsible for construction of the ROTOR radar stations. What this work entailed is still secret, for the files are closed to public scrutiny until the year 2006. Chancery Lane, though, was acquired by the Post Office under Emergency Powers in 1949, and in 1951 work began there on the construction of the 'KINGSWAY' trunk exchange.

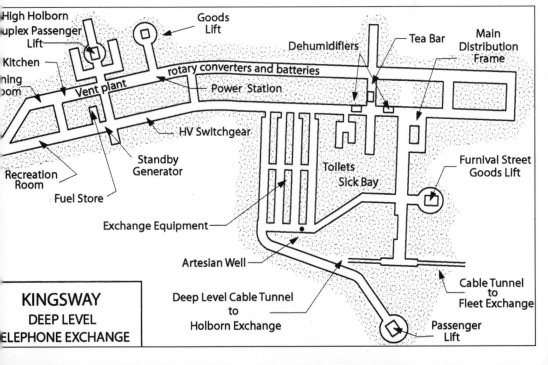

53. **Kingsway Telephone Exchange.** The passageway carrying communication cables from the exchange into the government deep-level cable tunnel system below Whitehall. *Nick Catford*

54. **Kingsway Telephone Exchange.** Switchgear in one of the main tunnels that was once part of the wartime deep-level shelter built adjacent to the Holborn tube station. *Nick Catford*

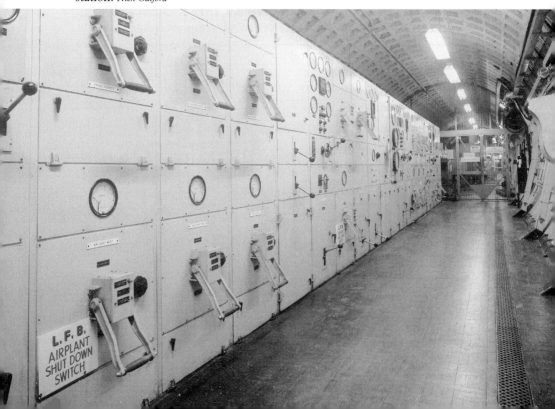

L.F.B. AIRPLANT SHUT DOWN SWITCH

55. **Kingsway Telephone Exchange.** A section of the Main Distribution Frame that occupies most of the north-east section of the original wartime deep shelter tunnel. *Nick Catford*

The civil engineering task involved the excavation and lining of four additional tubes running south from the existing pair of shelter tunnels, with interconnecting cross-passages and subsidiary service tunnels. Several new lifts were installed and a connecting tunnel dug to the existing GPO deep-level cable tunnel. The western ends of the original tubes were given over to staff catering facilities and service plant, which included a 1.5 megawatt power station with a 22,000-gallon fuel reserve, together with high-voltage transformers and associated switchgear. Power supplies for the telecom equipment, including motor generators and the station DC batteries, were housed in the north tunnel. The main distribution board and exchange apparatus were located at the east end of the wartime tubes and in the four new extension tunnels. KINGSWAY was a non-director exchange handling principally through traffic to other exchanges, including the continental exchange in the Faraday building, and the Wood Street international exchange. Emergency dormitory accommodation was provided for the 150 operators and other staff, and the bunker, like so many London buildings, had an artesian well providing an independent supply of fresh water. Access to the underground complex was via discreet passenger lifts in High Holborn and Took's Court, and there was a goods lift in Furnival Street.

By the mid-1980s the importance of KINGSWAY to the defence communication network and as a domestic exchange was in decline. In 1986 British Telecom redeveloped parts of the redundant tunnel system as the KINGSWAY Computer Centre, (KYCC) to house secure back-up systems for ICARUS, the computerized International Circuit Allocation Record Update System. Shortly after, two of the new tunnels in the southern sector of the complex were refurbished to a very high standard to provide a briefing room and other accommodation for what is presumed to have been a government bunker of unknown provenance. It has been suggested that it served as a temporary, central government briefing room while PINDAR (the new government war headquarters built in the 1990s to replace Corsham) was under construction as a result of the delays in completing the latter bunker, but this is only speculation.

Construction of the exchanges beneath Manchester and Birmingham city centres started in 1954 and involved the boring of new, one thousand-foot long, large-diameter tunnels at each location, over one hundred feet below the city streets. Disposing of the vast amounts of excavated rock and earth without compromising the secrecy of the project in such highly visible, city centre locations added enormously to the difficulty of the task.

Like KINGSWAY, both Manchester GUARDIAN and Birmingham ANCHOR are non-director exchanges, designed to handle predominantly through-traffic, although at all three sites twenty percent of the boards were reserved for terminal circuits. Both exchanges required sophisticated air-conditioning equipment to maintain stable atmospheric conditions within the tunnels, and the installation and commissioning of this apparatus contributed to the delay in completing the project. The ventilation equipment and its associated circulating fans occupies the lower floor of a large, two-storey plant room at one end of the main tunnel. The upper floor houses a standard GPO power station with two diesel generators, one supplying AC current for station services such as the lifts, air-conditioning equipment, lighting and cooking, etc, while the other provides DC current for the telecoms equipment.

Birmingham ANCHOR was finally commissioned on 9 November 1957. The exchange was built beneath the conventional GPO exchange in Colmore Row and was accessed via a lift within the building.

Manchester GUARDIAN was completed, at a cost of £4,000,000, just over a year later, on 7 December 1958. One hundred and twelve feet below the Rutherford exchange in George Street, it runs the length of Back George Street and houses six large manual plug-board panels. During the 1960s a piano was infiltrated into the operators rest room and the walls were decorated with 'picture window' murals in an attempt to relieve the underground oppression, should staff be confined there for the duration. Emergency dormitories were built for staff forced to remain underground for any length of time during fallout conditions and the underground canteen had sufficient provisions to maintain an adequate diet for several weeks. Like KINGSWAY and ANCHOR, Manchester's underground telephone exchange was manned continuously on a twenty-four-hour basis throughout the cold war years until it was decommissioned in the 1970s.

Pedestrian entry was gained to GUARDIAN via lifts in the Rutherford exchange. A separate shaft-head building off George Street contained the winding gear for a large goods lift, used for transferring heavy machinery underground. The shaft was accessed by means of four short flights of stairs that terminatied at an upper landing from which the lift descended a further eighty feet to the tunnels. The top of the shaft was sealed by a five-ton concrete slab that could be slid horizontally over the opening and could sustain the weight of the building should it collapse. Hydraulic rams were provided to force open the slab, but should this prove impossible then two alternative emergency exit routes were available. These exit routes utilized the deep-level cable tunnels that ran for approximately one mile east and west of the exchange, terminating at vertical shafts in Ardwick and Salford. Unassuming, small red-brick buildings mark the position of these shafts. Identifiable by their ventilation louvres and padlocked steel blast doors, they can be found in Lockton Close, Ardwick, and Islington Street in Salford.

THE 'PR' REPEATERS

It is generally accepted that during the first half of the 1950s the technical and financial resources of the GPO were entirely committed to new works associated with operation ROTOR and its ancillaries to the exclusion of all else. It has been argued that the Post Office microwave system was developed as an integral part of the ROTOR radar network, but this is not supported by the technology nor chronology. ROTOR generated large volumes of data and depended entirely upon the GPO land-line cable network for its transmission. Because ROTOR data consisted of simple narrow-band signals, the requirement was for lots of conventional copper wire rather than the high-tech broad-band capabilities that microwave technology promised. Even had microwave transmission been necessary, its development would have come too late for ROTOR. Although the GPO had established a series of pilot microwave installations between 1949 and 1952, its large-scale implementation only became feasible from 1957, by which time ROTOR was obsolete. Microwave communication would have had more relevance to the broad-band video broadcasting of processed radar data required by LINESMAN/MEDIATOR, but even then its usefulness was limited due to the inadequacies of the contemporary technology.

There has been continued debate as to whether the microwave network was established as a necessary, peacetime communication system or primarily for defence purposes. The unequivocal answer is that it was indeed a *defence* asset, but was authorized by Parliament on the understanding that it had joint civil and military capabilities, just as LINESMAN, the air-defence radar, was authorized only because of its integration with MEDIATOR, the civil aviation surveillance radar system. The moral soundness of this arrangement does not matter, it is simply a fiction that allows Parliament to authorize expenditure that would have otherwise have been difficult to justify. Retrospectively, the government has argued that the microwave system was developed to pave the way for 625-line UHF colour television transmission. 625-line television was not, however, even a twinkle in the eye of electronics engineers in 1957, when the microwave links were at an advanced planning stage, and, anyway, more than adequate co-axial land-line distribution cables were already in existence.

The true nature of the microwave system was revealed at a planning inquiry into the siting of a tower near Stokenchurch in Buckinghamshire in 1957, at which a Ministry of Housing & Local Government officer commented that the tower was 'primarily for the purpose of national defence but it will also have civilian uses.'

The Stokenchurch enquiry rumbled on for three years, much to the government's embarrassment, and in January 1961 it was forced to admit that

the tower was part of

a national network of communications which would be vital in time of attack when normal landline communications might be destroyed.

The following year Mr J Merriman, who was later to become the Post Office Director of Technology, told a similar enquiry at Wotton-under-Edge in Gloucestershire, that:

The Post Office is responsible for ensuring that in the event of attack on this country adequate communications for the administration of the country are available up to the time of the attack and as far as possible to assist in the work of restoration afterwards.

The microwave system was primarily a defence asset, but was *not* primarily a feature of ROTOR or any other radar system. These systems, and the government communications systems upon which the survival of the nation was to depend in time of crisis, had, in the early 1950s, to rely upon existing copper-cable technology.

The cable system that existed in 1950 was insufficient for the tasks required of it and furthermore, much of the network, although underground, passed through the centres of cities that were vulnerable to enemy attack. Over the next five years hundreds of miles of new trunk cables were laid, special deeply-buried telephone exchanges were constructed below the most vulnerable cities and new, alternative cable routes laid by-passing the city centres. Eight enormous, semi-underground reinforced concrete bunkers were built at nodal points on these cable routes to house vitally important repeater equipment. The two largest installations, at Rothwell Haigh, near Leeds, and Warmley, near Bristol, were slightly larger than the rest and were designated type 'PR2'. The other six stations were type 'PR1' and were identical to the PR2s except that the equipment rooms were some twenty feet shorter. Along with other circuits, Warmley handled traffic from the Corsham government complex, while Rothwell Haigh served another important RAF sector communications centre.

Superficially similar to the two-level R4 ROTOR operation centres, the PR2

56. **Warmley PR2 GPO Repeater Station.** An external view of the bunker just prior to demolition in 2001. The power station fuel tanks have been removed from the excavation in the foreground. *Author's collection*

bunkers were designed and built by the Ministry of Works for the Post Office. The bunkers were double-level, windowless structures, two hundred feet long and eighty feet wide, with the lower floor completely underground. The exposed upper storey had a roof, walls and floor-slab of eighteen-inch-thick reinforced concrete. A single-storey annexe attached to the right-hand front elevation comprised office and domestic accommodation and was not blast-proofed. Inside the main entrance lobby a heavy steel blast door secured the main bunker from the office block. An integral, rectangular concrete ventilation tower the full width of the bunker rises from the right-hand end of the building to a height of some ten feet above roof level. Within the main structure, this tower descends through both floors as a separate entity, sealed from the main chambers by thick concrete walls which are pierced for the connection of filters and ducts associated with the station's ventilation and power plant.

The upper floor is divided into three chambers of roughly equal size. Viewed from the front elevation, the room to the right, adjoining the ventilation stack, contains the main air-conditioning units, including the circulating fans, dehumidifiers and filter packs. Installation of the trunking between the filters and the main external ducts proved something of a headache for the ventilation contractors, Messrs Troughton & Young. They were advised that the plant might need to provide

air purification additional to normal dust filtration for an emergency period of up to four weeks, and that during the emergency four week shutdown period the plant should run using a recirculated water supply of no more than 100 gallons.

They were to install standard Vokes filters for normal peacetime conditions, but for the emergency period 'special filters will be provided by the Post Office.'

A special jig was to be provided to change the filters when necessary, but the Post Office was unwilling to give details of the 'special filters' which rendered it impossible for Troughton & Young to arrange connections for them in the ductwork. Unable to elicit the necessary information, their engineer wrote:

In the absence of more detailed information regarding this equipment it is assumed that single-duct connections will be required to the inlet and outlet of the fan and similar single connections to the inlet and outlet of the filter unit.

The contract specified that:

The air-conditioning plant should provide reasonably comfortable air conditions for staff in a semi-underground protected building. The number of occupants would not exceed twenty. The plant should maintain a positive pressure throughout all parts of the building to prevent infiltration of contaminated air.

Troughton & Young responded that:

With regards to the stipulation that the plant should maintain a positive pressure throughout all parts of the building, we would suggest that the pressure created by the plant is not relied upon to prevent the infiltration of outside contaminated air, as the pressure created by a high wind could be greater than the pressure created inside the building by the supply fans. We would suggest that all external openings are provided with gas-tight doors. In addition, all air openings which are open to atmosphere should be provided with gas-tight dampers so that in the event of a power failure these could be closed until the failure was overcome.

The middle room contained two motor generators on plinths to supply DC power for the telecoms plant and to charge the station batteries which were in a quarry-tiled chamber to the rear of this section. This room also contained a range of voltage regulators and other control equipment, and the main station DC distribution boards and switchgear mounted on heavy slate panels. The motor-generator sets were double-ended units with a 415 volt 50 amp AC drive motor and two 100 amp DC generators running at 960 rpm.

The third main chamber, to the left-hand end of the building, contained racks of PRE 51 repeaters, supplementing those in the main equipment room downstairs.

A steel stairway led to the lower floor, which was divided into two main chambers and an annexe which contained switchgear for the 11,000 volt incoming mains supply and two 11Kv/415v transformers in fire-proof cubicles. The right-hand chamber was the main plant room and contained two standby diesel generators and the refrigeration compressors, which were three-cylinder

57. **Warmley PR2 GPO Repeater Station.** 11Kv transformer and switchgear cubicles in the lower floor of the bunker. *Author's collection*

58. **Warmley PR2 GPO Repeater Station.** A general view of the bunker's underground power-house. *Author's collection*

59. **Warmley PR2 GPO Repeater Station.** Low tension switchgear in the station's underground power-house. *Author's collection*

machines built by L Sterne & Co and were identical in every respect to those installed in the R4 ROTOR bunkers. Duplicate compressors were provided, although only one was run at any time.

Two diesel-driven AC generators were installed; one was nominally a standby to power the telecoms plant via the motor generators and the other to drive the station plant (air-conditioning compressors, fans, sundry pumps and motors, lighting, heating, etc), but switchgear was installed to enable either engine to assume either role in emergency. The telecoms generator set was arranged to start automatically on mains failure, whereas the station generator was started manually.

TELECOMMS STANDBY GENERATOR

Engine: Davey Paxman V12, type 12RPH2, 400 horsepower at 1000 rpm.
Alternator: 269 Kva 346/440 volts

STATION STANDBY GENERATOR

Engine: National Gas 8 cylinder type R4A8, 400 horsepower at 600 rpm.
Alternator: 313 Kva 415 volts.

Tender documents for the power station specified that:

the engines shall be capable of running continuously without attention for periods of up to fourteen days. During this period no maintenance attention will be given to the plant.

Fuel was stored in two external buried storage tanks, each with a capacity of 6,000 gallons. The tanks were in chambers only a foot or so below ground level,

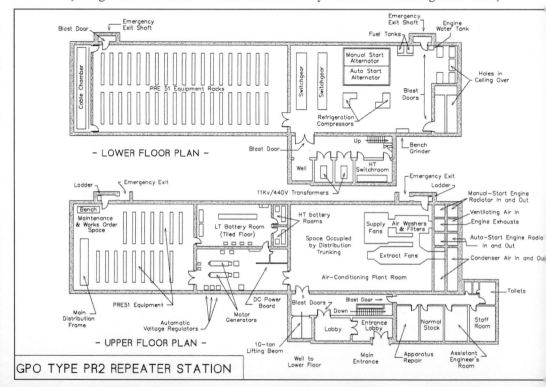

GPO TYPE PR2 REPEATER STATION

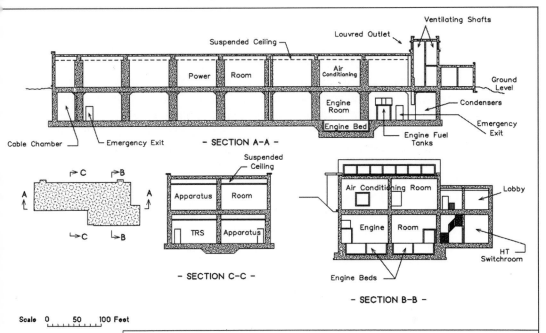

GPO TYPE PR2 REPEATER STATION

- SECTION A-A -

Suspended Ceiling — Power Room — Air Conditioning — Engine Room — Engine Bed — Louvred Outlet — Ventilating Shafts — Ground Level — Condensers — Emergency Exit — Engine Fuel Tanks — Cable Chamber — Emergency Exit

- SECTION C-C -

Suspended Ceiling — Apparatus Room — TRS — Apparatus

- SECTION B-B -

Air Conditioning Room — Engine Room — Engine Beds — Lobby — HT Switchroom

Scale 0 50 100 Feet

which, in light of the deteriorating winter weather conditions experienced in the early 1960s, was not considered deep enough to guarantee against the fuel thickening under adverse conditions. Early in December 1963 it was ordered that as a precautionary measure sufficient fuel for fourteen days' continuous running should be stored in drums inside the bunker.

The left-hand chamber on the lower floor, which occupied slightly more than half of the nett floor space, was the main equipment room and was packed with racks of PRE 51 repeaters. A small chamber at the far end of this room contained the termination pots of the incoming cables, all of which were fitted with gas-tight valves. Two emergency escape ladders, enclosed by heavy steel blast doors, rose in a narrow shaft between floors to emergency exits that protruded from the otherwise blank rear wall of the bunker.

Had the 'PR' repeater stations been built solely to service traffic from the ROTOR radar stations then they, like ROTOR itself, would have been redundant before they were built. Although initial plans were prepared early in 1950 and detailed drawings for the elevations were approved in April 1951 construction did not begin for another year, and even by the summer of 1954 very little plant had been installed. Later that year the two diesel generators passed their acceptance tests, but agreement had only just been given for the layout of power bus-bars in the equipment rooms, so it seems likely that the telecoms equipment could not have been installed any earlier than 1955. This would have been a year after the ROTOR Sector Control bunkers were supposed to be completed, although it is interesting to note that delays on the part of the GPO were given as the reason for the slippages in their commissioning dates.

Surviving records indicate that the air-conditioning and filtration plants were not finally handed over by Troughton & Young until 10 April 1958, although it is possible that, given the changing nature of the nuclear threat during the mid-1950s, the plant was subject to continuous revision.

During the five years after the first transatlantic telephone cable was laid from Clarenville in Newfoundland to Oban in 1956, several further cables were laid, terminating at different locations in the United Kingdom. There have been persistent rumours circulated by old employees of Cable & Wireless, who were responsible for constructing the ground station and laying the inland section of a transatlantic cable that came ashore at Widemouth Bay near Bude in Cornwall, that the cable in question carried the hot-line connection between Whitehall and the White House. This has been dismissed in many quarters as just another cold war myth, but a series of memos discovered in the PR2 station at Warmley lend a small degree of credence to the suggestion. Covering the period from just after the Cuban Missile Crisis until December 1963, the memos exhort the site engineers to ensure that every endeavour is made

> to minimise the potential risk of shutting down for maintenance purposes the Ocean Telephone Cable System, London to Widemouth Bay, Inland Section.

By the end of the 1970s the defence role of the PR repeaters and the land-line network had been pretty well usurped by the GPO microwave system and they gradually fell into disuse.

ESSENTIAL SERVICES

Earlier studies have looked at what was essentially the 'Civil Defence' approach to the preservation of essential services, such as the Auxiliary Fire Service, Civil Defence mobile columns, strategic food reserves, Home Office vehicle stockpiles, dusty garages filled with 'Green Goddess' fire engines and emergency welfare centres catering for everything and anything from children to animals. Although active throughout the 1950s, these things were already anachronistic throwbacks, with their roots firmly in the Second World War, and it is not intended to pursue this subject further in this volume. Instead, in this final chapter, we will look briefly at the measures taken to ensure the continuity of the major public utilities - the railways, the national grid and the water authorities. This is a subject that has received scant attention to date but appears to offer fertile ground for further research.

Among the first of these industries to seek protection against the atom bomb was the National Grid. This organization had prior experience in this field, having temporarily transferred its national control centre during the Second World War from Bankside power station (now the Tate Modern) to an underground emergency suite in a disused lift shaft in St Paul's tube station.

Post-war, each of the eight Regional Boards had peacetime regional control centres, and plans were prepared between 1950 and 1955 to build alternative, emergency controls at remote locations within each region. Construction proceeded slowly, but most were completed by the early 1960s. The earlier buildings, like that at Rothwell Haigh near Leeds (close to the GPO PR2 repeater station), were substantial concrete bunkers, but the later ones had the superficial appearance of an ordinary office building, though to a very distinctive design.

The National Grid national emergency control centre is housed in a bunker-like building at Becca Hall, near Leeds. Although the building is not fully hardened, the control room is within a reinforced semi-basement and windows in the ground floor are fitted with steel, sliding blast-shutters. Becca Hall also housed the north-eastern region peacetime control centre. Its emergency standby control is at Rothwell Haigh and consists of a long, squat concrete bunker built in the early 1950s and very much like a pair of typical Civil Defence control bunkers of the period joined end to end.

The south-west region emergency control is housed in a rather sinister building, partially hidden among trees atop a small hillock in the grounds of Durley Park in Keynsham, near Bristol, beside the A4 Keynsham by-pass. Early in 2000 the building was declared redundant and is now occupied by sections of the Meteorological Office. Elsewhere, the south-east emergency control is in East Grinstead, that for the north-west is in the Bramley area of Greater Manchester, and the midland region bunker is in Redhill Avenue, a residential area of Kings Norton on the southern fringe of Birmingham.

The National Grid also established several strategic reserve stores in remote locations around the country. These depots contained stockpiles of equipment, transformers, and distribution line components necessary to aid the restoration of electricity supply in the post-war recovery period. Somewhat incongruous in their remote rural locations, and almost invariably surrounded by woodland, the warehouses bear a striking resemblance to aircraft hangars, with high, broad roofs and multiple-leaf sliding doors at each end. An excellent example, decommissioned in 1999, can be found near the village of Barnsley, west of Cirencester in Gloucestershire.

Measures proposed by the Conservative government to protect the water supply industry and, more specifically, to ensure a minimum emergency supply of two litres per day to every survivor of their next war, were not implemented until the late 1980s, by which time it was patently obvious that the cold war was rapidly drawing to a close. Consequently, despite the availability of one hundred per cent Home Office grants to cover the cost, the various Water Boards faced the task of building emergency control bunkers with mixed enthusiasm.

With cost only a minor consideration, several Water Boards built numerous magnificent bunkers in compliance with specifications set by the Swiss Civil Defence Organization, which were generally accepted as international standards and aspirational targets. Yorkshire Water and Severn-Trent Water were prime examples in this category. Yorkshire Water built ten emergency controls in its region, at Bradford, Doncaster, Harrogate, Huddersfield, Hull, Leeds, Northallerton, Sheffield, Skipton and York. Severn-Trent is reputed to have built at least eight emergency bunkers, including two at their regional offices in Gloucester and Mansfield, the latter being shared with Nottingham County Council which used it as the county standby.

The Severn-Trent bunker in Gloucester is a purpose-built underground structure deep below a new office block, designed in 1987, at their Staverton depot in Gloucester. It is a perfect example of late cold war underground architecture incorporating all the best design features developed over the

60. **Severn Trent Water Control Bunker.** Blast doors and air locks protecting the headquarters bunker in Gloucester. *Author's collection*

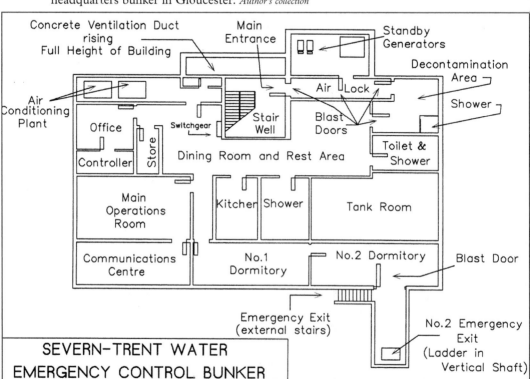

Concrete Ventilation Duct rising Full Height of Building

Main Entrance

Standby Generators

Decontamination Area

Air Lock

Shower

Air Conditioning Plant

Office

Switchgear

Stair Well

Blast Doors

Controller

Store

Dining Room and Rest Area

Toilet & Shower

Main Operations Room

Kitchen

Shower

Tank Room

Communications Centre

No.1 Dormitory

No.2 Dormitory

Blast Door

Emergency Exit (external stairs)

No.2 Emergency Exit (Ladder in Vertical Shaft)

SEVERN-TRENT WATER EMERGENCY CONTROL BUNKER

previous forty years. The bunker, which was completed in 1992, is approached via a dog-legged concrete stairway from the main foyer of the surface building and is sealed at the base of the stairs by a large, concrete-filled steel-framed blast door that leads into a spacious air lock. To the left of the air lock a similar door gives access to the bunker's power station, while straight ahead yet another blast door leads into the decontamination area. This chamber is secured from the main area of the bunker by yet another massive blast door. Once through the chain of air locks, the visitor is in a central corridor off which are several large rooms. Two of these are dormitories for the staff of twenty personnel, and two are designated as communications and operations rooms, although in peacetime they are quite empty. In an emergency, equipment would be transferred from the peacetime operations centre in the office block above. There is a small kitchen and a range of toilets, waste water from which is collected in a 600-gallon interceptor tank and pumped to the surface by hand.

Air and exhaust ducts for the bunker's two 275 Kva generators and for the comprehensive ventilation, air filtration and dehumidification system are all contained in a reinforced concrete duct that rises to the very top of the surface building. This duct, which is disguised by a cladding of mellow red brick that matches the main façade of the building, is a central element of the building's design. It is an immensely strong structure and its height ensures that should the office block be destroyed by blast there would be no risk of the vital ventilation shafts being blocked by rubble. The same consideration influenced the design of the emergency exits. A short passageway, secured by a nine-inch-thick blast door similar to others in the bunker, leads off one of the underground dormitories and branches into two routes. A dog-leg passage, designed to dissipate blast, gives access to a flight of steps up to a conventional door at the rear of the main building, but the other route takes the form of a narrow pipe about thirty feet in length which leads to a vertical shaft and ladder that emerges via a manhole into the office car park. The position of this manhole was carefully calculated to ensure that it was beyond the perimeter of the rubble heap that would be formed should the building completely collapse.

A raised mound adjacent to a series of covered reservoirs at Blunsdon waterworks, beside the A419 north of Swindon, conceals a large emergency control bunker built by Thames Water in 1987. At first glance the mound appears to be just another reservoir, but closer inspection reveals that a lightweight steel door let into one end of the mound conceals a much heavier blast door a few feet behind it. At the west end of the bunker a deep vertical shaft with iron rungs in its wall gives access to another steel and concrete blast door sealing the emergency exit. Louvred concrete ventilation towers rising from the top of the mound serve an underground power-house. A similarly massive bunker, partially disguised as a reservoir, was built by Southern Water at its Brede waterworks north of Hastings.

Other water authorities, perhaps more aware of the pointlessness of what they were being asked to do, took a more considered, cautious approach. Wessex Water, for example, chose to build its emergency centre in a disused semi-underground reservoir on the site of the former Royal Navy Cordite Factory at

61. **Brede Waterworks Control Bunker.** *Nick Catford*

Holton Heath, near Poole in Dorset. A large hole was knocked in one end of the reservoir and protective outer doors fitted, but little more was done before work at the site was permanently suspended. Similarly, Bristol Water chose to adapt a pair of disused underground reservoirs at a very remote waterworks at Holcombe Bottom, near Radstock in Somerset. Connecting doorways were cut in the walls separating the two reservoirs and a blast-protected entrance formed in one side, complete with the usual paraphernalia of blast doors, air locks, pressure relief valves and decontamination showers. Within the bunker, a small plant room contained a Lister generator and a simple air filtration and ventilation system. Internal partitions were erected to form a range of offices and a small dormitory complete with wooden bunks, but final fitting out of the bunker was still unfinished at the end of 1999 when the project was abandoned and the site offered for sale by public tender.

British Gas, too, had nuclear contingency plans, though little detailed information has yet been released. A national emergency control centre was built at Washwood Heath in Birmingham and several protected strategic pumping stations have been identified, including examples at Eye and Aylesbury.

During the Second World War a number of protected control bunkers were built at strategic locations around the railway network in order to safeguard the movement of trains should the existing peacetime communications system become disrupted. Several of these wartime buildings still survive, including a fine example at Bawtry in South Yorkshire which consists of a long, low utilitarian red brick structure with a bomb-proof concrete roof and steel shutters over the window openings. A similar scheme to maintain railway operations was proposed in the early 1950s in response to the threat of Soviet aggression. Plans were prepared for the construction of twenty-five atom-bomb-proof control bunkers at key junctions and traffic centres throughout the United Kingdom, but only two were completed, at Bricket Wood near Watford and at Knebworth in Hertfordshire, and one at Burntisland, near Edinburgh partially completed, before the idea was abandoned in favour of mobile control trains using converted railway carriages.

THE ART TREASURE REPOSITORIES

During the Second World War many of the Treasures of the British Museum and the V & A were secretly transported to a specially prepared, 25,000-square-foot underground repository at Westwood Quarry, near Bradford-on-Avon in Wiltshire. Similarly, pictures from the National Gallery and a number of private collections were stored in air-conditioned chambers constructed deep inside a disused slate mine at Manod, near Blaenau Ffestiniog in North Wales. By 1948 most of the exhibits had returned to their respective museums and galleries except for an insignificant quantity of V&A material that remained at Westwood until the early 1960s.

Both repositories were retained by the government throughout most of the cold war. Leases on Manod were regularly renewed until 1980, and the repository at Westwood was retained until 1983 when the site was returned to the Bath & Portland Stone Company, from whom it had been requisitioned in 1940. At both sites, new standby generators had been installed in the early 1950s. Records held in the archives of the National Gallery indicate that small-scale exercises were conducted at irregular periods between 1956 and 1975 to test procedures for the evacuation of pictures from the gallery and from the Royal Collection to the safety of Manod should an international crisis arise. The Westwood repository seems not to have been involved in these exercises, but this may be because more sinister things were happening there in the early 1950s. At that time the site was maintained by the Ministry of Works & Buildings, but was still under the control of the British Museum. In 1952 the museum directors were approached by officers from the government's top-secret Microbiological Research Department at Porton Down who requested that they might use the 'Carpet Room' in the Westwood repository for high-dosage experiments with the pathogen *Serratia Marcesens*. Special equipment was installed to disseminate the organism, but things went wrong and quantities of the bacterium were released into other areas of the quarry and, via a ventilation shaft, into the open air. At the time *Serratia Marcesens* was considered relatively harmless, but its use subsequently aroused more controversy in scientific circles than any other agent. Questions about its safety became a central issue during a US Federal Court trial in 1981, in which the US government was charged with responsibility for the death of a civilian as a consequence of a germ warfare test over San Francisco thirty years earlier.

Since the early 1980s the European Union has taken steps to formulate a unified approach to the protection of the cultural treasures of member countries in global war. These measures are limited to not just museum and library artefacts and works of art, but also buildings and public works of cultural significance, although it is difficult to imagine what actions could be taken to safeguard the latter categories.

It has been suggested that as a result of the abandonment of both Manod and Westwood in the early 1980s space was either prepared, or at least allocated, for Britain's art treasures in sections of the Spring Quarry Central Government War Headquarters at Corsham released following the 1979/82 refurbishment programme.

12

THE CENTRAL GOVERNMENT
EMERGENCY WAR HEADQUARTERS

During the 1930s, as war in Europe became ever more inevitable, the reaction of the British government to the approaching conflict was, predictably, first to panic and contemplate flight (for 'the bomber would always get through') and then to close ranks and concentrate its power base within Whitehall even more completely than in times of peace. Early in 1937, with war on the horizon, a sub-committee of the Committee of Imperial Defence, convened the previous year under the Chairmanship of Sir Warren Fisher, issued its first report on alternative working locations for the various government departments should central London become untenable. Later that year a further committee, chaired by Sir James Rae, re-examined a number of the Warren Fisher proposals, and expanded them to include special provision for the War Cabinet and Service Chiefs. Their key proposals, which included the evacuation of central government either to locations in the west country or to protected accommodation in north London, were noted but were not acted upon for over a year.

Meanwhile, a special Sub-Committee of the Committee of Imperial Defence proposed the construction of three hardened, underground citadels to house the political and military heads of the three Service Departments: Admiralty, War Office and Air Ministry, together with their key planning staffs, at locations near Harrow to the north-west of the capital.

The proposed War Office Citadel, later appropriated by the War Cabinet, was built below a new office block at the Post Office Research Establishment in Dollis Hill. 'Station-Z', the Air Ministry's underground redoubt is below an HMSO factory in Headstone Drive, Wealdstone, in Harrow, and the Admiralty bunker, appropriately enough, was buried below the Admiralty Charts Depot (now a Health & Safety laboratory and disused), in Cricklewood. Following the appropriation of the Dollis Hill site by the War Cabinet, the Army was offered much less satisfactory accommodation at Kneller Hall, Twickenham.

Construction of a fourth bunker for the War Cabinet, Winston Churchill and his immediate staff, was completed by the autumn of 1938. This, the Cabinet War Room, was built just ten feet below ground in the basement of what is now the Cabinet Office but what was at that time the headquarters of the Office of Works. A suite of basement rooms, previously used for rough storage, was strengthened by the addition of stout timber struts internally and reinforcement of the roof-slab with three feet of reinforced concrete to provide private quarters for Churchill, the War Cabinet, a central map-room, and service accommodation. A small broom cupboard was adapted to provide what was euphemistically described as the 'transatlantic telephone exchange', but which in fact contained no more than an ordinary telephone and enciphering machine connected to a nearby external telegraph via which the messages traversed the

248

Atlantic Ocean.

The establishment of the Cabinet War Rooms in Whitehall was coincident with the Munich crisis and marked the first backward step in the faltering dispersal plan which had envisaged the removal of key government establishments to safe, rural retreats when war threatened. Faced with a *real* rather than a hypothetical crisis, government reacted by drawing in the centre of power. As the first bombs fell this policy was reversed: the bomber, they said, would always get through and central London would be quickly and comprehensively reduced to rubble. Dispersal, after all, might be a wise move.

Earlier, in October 1938, Eric de Normann, an officer of the Ministry of Works and a key player in the construction of the Cabinet War Rooms in Storey's Gate, put forward a plan for a deep underground alternative War Room at Dollis Hill in North London at the location already under consideration as a War Office emergency citadel. Construction of the bunker, code-named PADDOCK, began in January 1939 and was completed by June 1940. The finished building retained most of the features incorporated in de Normann's original plans: over forty feet below ground, the lower and smaller of the two floors was protected by six feet of reinforced concrete while the upper floor had a roof slab three feet thick. The lower floor consisted of eighteen rooms including the main Cabinet Offices, a large map room and an emergency generating plant. The slightly larger upper floor contained a further nineteen departmental offices. A central stairway

62. **PADDOCK - Churchill's Second World War National Government Headquarters at Dollis Hill.** Built fifty feet underground below the Post Office research laboratory, this bunker was abandoned and forgotten over sixty years ago. This view shows the main operations room, now partially flooded. The window at the far end gives onto Winston Churchill's private office. *Nick Catford*

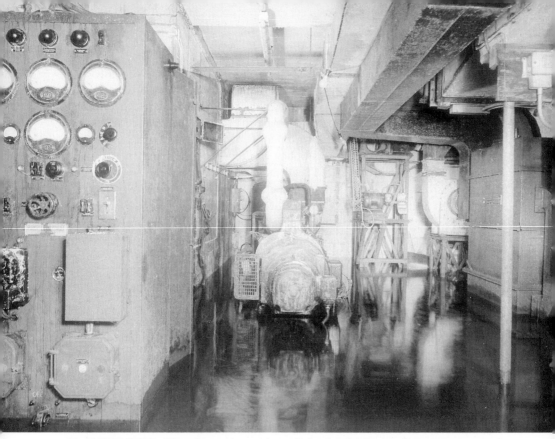

63. **PADDOCK.** The decayed remains of the bunker's standby generator and ventilation plant. *Nick Catford*

gave access to both floors from the main Post Office building on the surface, while spiral staircases at each end formed emergency exit routes.

As early as 1940 Winston Churchill formulated the concept of 'continuity of government' which was later to be the central thesis of cold war strategic planning. Writing speculatively of the German plans for the invasion of Britain, he commented that:

> The German method is to make the disruption of the Central Government a vital prelude to any major assault on the country. They have done it everywhere. They will do it here.

To counter this threat, Churchill, with personal reservations, agreed to the evacuation of key elements of government to the protected underground citadels, instructing his subordinates that:

> We must make sure that the centre of Government functions harmoniously and vigorously. This would not be possible under conditions of almost continuous air raids. A movement to PADDOCK by echelons of the War Cabinet, War Cabinet Secretariat, Chiefs of Staff Committee and Home Forces GHQ must now be planned... . Pray concert all the necessary measures for moving out not more than two or three hundred principal persons and their immediate assistants.

The continuing debate as to the strategic value of the Harrow citadels delayed construction such that by the time they were ready in mid-1940 the policy of dispersal was being seriously questioned once again. Indeed, as early as February, 1939 Cabinet had already done a partial about-turn, having decided that:

> to enable essential services work to be carried on during a bombardment, deep bomb-proof quarters should be provided **in the Central Area** for the five War Rooms of the Cabinet, Service Departments [Admiralty, Air Ministry and War Office] and the Home Security Organization.

The Dollis Hill bunker was used only briefly by the Cabinet Office as a Central Government War Headquarters, and with only limited success. The first and only Cabinet meeting was held there, simply to test its facilities, on 3 October 1940, but Winston Churchill didn't like it, noting that:

> The accommodation at 'PADDOCK' is quite unsuited to the conditions which have arisen. The War Cabinet cannot live and work there for weeks on end while leaving the great part of their staffs less well provided for than they now are in Whitehall... 'PADDOCK' should be treated as a last resort.

The location was used on one other occasion by the War Cabinet, in March, 1941, as an exercise in propaganda to impress the visiting Australian Prime Minister, Robert Menzies. From that date the Cabinet assembled in the Storey's Gate War Room below the old Ministry of Works building until the autumn of 1943, when it was decided that the North Rotunda – a purpose-built bunker in Horseferry Road (*see below*), – refitted and now code-named ANSON, should be used as the Cabinet War Room. Most of the equipment from PADDOCK was transferred to ANSON, leaving just sufficient for a small Army contingent that continued in occupation there until the end of 1944, after which the site was abandoned.

The problems with the North London citadels were threefold and the least of these was the potential effect upon public morale should it leak out that the nation's leaders had abandoned the Capital for a distant and safer haven, whilst leaving six million inhabitants to an undefined but probably awful fate. Secondly, the suite of only thirty-seven rooms was far too small to accommodate an effective staff, which would have to work with widely dispersed support departments elsewhere. The greater problem was communication. The vulnerability and unreliability of contemporary radio technology rendered it useless for the dense and mainly secret communications needs of a government at war, and the pre-war and early wartime telephone system, too, suffered from a fragility that to some extent still exists today. The network was inflexible; manual exchanges, which represented the bulk of the exchanges at that time, were slow, unreliable and subject to the fallibilities of the human operators; while the few electro-mechanical exchanges, with their delicate relays and selectors, were difficult to maintain under adverse conditions and highly vulnerable to air-raid damage. To compound this vulnerability, most of the lines were carried overhead and were inevitably the first casualties of bombardment.

The proposed solutions to these problems were twofold: new underground bunkers up to one hundred feet below ground would be built within the precincts of Whitehall and the GPO would construct a system of tunnels that would allow the routeing of telephone cables between these bunkers safe from the heaviest aerial bombing. Just before the war the London Passenger Transport Board were making plans for significant additions and improvements to the underground system and their engineering and planning staffs were very much orientated towards that task. It was not surprising, therefore, that the War Cabinet should turn to the LPTB Chief Engineer, Sir Horace Dalrymple-Hay, for technical assistance in planning the proposed Whitehall bunkers. Dalrymple-Hay's scheme envisaged a network of four parallel steel-lined tunnels running the length of Whitehall at a depth of one hundred feet providing sufficient space to accommodate a staff of three thousand. The cost of this proposal (little short of £2,000,000), was, however, more than the exchequer was prepared to bear, and the two-and-a-half-year construction estimate quite unrealistic for a war emergency measure.

By the end of 1939, when work finally began, the Whitehall tunnel scheme had been whittled down to no more than a single tube to carry Post Office telephone cables linking government exchanges and emergency war rooms in the basements of various ministries. In conjunction with these developments, in the spring of 1940, the GPO began construction of a heavily fortified extension to the Faraday House exchange in Carter Street, its existing trunk exchange which was built in 1902. The extension, Faraday House North, or 'The Citadel', is a massively built, windowless concrete monolith with walls six feet thick and a seven-foot-thick reinforced concrete roof. To support its continued operation under emergency conditions, 'Citadel' was equipped with standby generators, gas filtration and air-conditioning systems, dormitories for the staff and an artesian well to provide an independent water supply. Faraday House North was completed in just seven months and opened in December 1940.

Meanwhile, a series of somewhat *ad-hoc* sites within Whitehall had been located for bunkers for the service departments and the Ministry of Home Security. Prior to the war the Westminster Gas Company owned a large plot of land near Horseferry Road on which stood two enormous gas-holders; these were demolished in 1937 and were not replaced, although the gas company intended to do so at some future date. After demolition two huge, brick-lined cylindrical pits over forty feet deep that previously contained the bases of the steel gasometers remained, forbiddingly large and empty. The two vacant holes were requisitioned by the government, roofed over with twelve feet of reinforced concrete and became the North and South Horseferry Rotundas; each spread over three floors and homes, respectively, for the Ministry of Home Security War Room (and later the War Cabinet) and for the Air Ministry war room. A third bunker, incorporated in a new, heavily constructed steel-framed office block on an adjacent plot to the south of the rotundas accommodated the Army GHQ Home Command. An alarmingly ugly concrete edifice on the corner of Horseguards Parade was built as a bunker to house the Admiralty staff, which functioned in parallel with the citadel at the Harrow charts depot until 1944.

Although not large individually, these structures, together with a pair of basement bunkers built for the War Office underneath Montague House in Whitehall, (now the MoD Main Building) between them gave shelter to the required core government staff of three thousand. As the war progressed the network of Post Office cable and communication tunnels was extended to interconnect these various underground war rooms and to link them to a number of hardened or semi-hardened Post Office and private telephone exchanges on the surface.

While the Central Government bunkers were being planned and built under conditions of great secrecy, the development of another series of bomb-proof underground shelters within the capital was subject to much broader review and, in the later war years, was to become the subject of open contention in the press and among the London population at large. These tunnels - the Deep Tube Shelters - were, like most of the similarly ill-fated underground factories built at much the same time, conceived at the height of the German Blitz in 1940 and were more or less redundant by the time they were completed in 1942. The British government had always been ideologically opposed to the concept of deep-level shelters for the mass of the urban industrial population, ostensibly on the grounds that such shelters would sap morale in the long term by engendering a shelter mentality, and that industrial output would be adversely effected as a result. Privately, ministers were fearful of the prohibitive cost of building and operating shelters on such a scale.

Eventually the Home Office was persuaded, in October, 1940, to go ahead with the construction of ten shelters which would be built by London Transport at government expense. The decision to go ahead with the tube shelter project was considerably influenced by a vague undertaking on the part of London Transport to purchase the tunnels at the end of hostilities and incorporate them in a projected underground express-way. The deep shelters were to be built some forty feet below existing stations on the Northern Line; five would be south of the Thames at Clapham South, Clapham Common, Clapham North, Stockwell, and the Oval; three in the Central area at Goodge Street, Chancery Lane and St. Paul's, and two further north at Camden Town and Belsize Park. The St Paul's tunnel was quickly abandoned when fears were raised that the excavations might damage the foundations of the cathedral, and tunnelling at the Oval was abandoned soon after, when an underground watercourse was breached and threatened to flood the workings. Construction of the remaining eight shelters was completed by the summer of 1942 in the face of vehement parliamentary opposition and at a cost greatly in excess of the original estimate. It was initially calculated that shelter space could be provided at £15 per head, but the final per capita cost was found to be in excess of £40.

Each shelter consisted of a parallel pair of iron-lined tunnels, 16′ 6″ in diameter and 1,200 feet long, linked at intervals by cross passages. Each tube was divided into two floors, and access was by means of electric lifts in vertical shafts, supplemented by dual, spiral stairways that encircled the lift shaft and served each of the underground levels independently. Each shelter was provided with bunks for 9,600 people and had adequate catering and sanitary provision. Later, the capacity was reduced to 8,000 and conditions became rather more humane. The shaft-top entrance buildings, all of which are still extant, are easily identifiable, circular, pill-box-like brick structures without windows or other external features.

By the time they were finished in 1942 there was no longer a pressing need for the deep shelters following the relaxation in the German aerial assault. This situation allowed the government, in pursuance of its anti-shelter policy, to defer their opening to the public despite opposition from the LPTB which had looked to the deep shelters to relieve the nightly burden on its stations. The War Cabinet successfully suppressed the use of the deep-level shelters by the general public until the arrival of the flying bombs, and later the V2 rockets, forced a change of attitude. In the meantime all had been pressed into service for various military purposes, mainly as transit hostels for British and American troops, but in July 1944 Clapham North, Clapham South, Camden, Belsize Park and Stockwell were finally opened to the public. Of the remaining three, Goodge Street had already been allocated to Eisenhower as a secure Command Centre for the invasion of Europe; Chancery Lane was used by the Public Record Office for storage and, like Clapham Common, was earmarked as a possible government citadel should the rocket bombardment make the existing bunkers untenable.

This system of tunnels and citadels below Whitehall, together with the deep tube shelters, comprised the wartime legacy upon which the earliest plans for the protection of government within the capital during the first phase of the cold war would be based.

Following a brief period of post-war euphoria, the government was again, in 1948, bracing itself for war; this time with the Soviet Union. War plans at that time envisioned a conventional conflict very similar to the last, and even the detonation of the first Soviet atomic bomb did little to change this view. Although it was accepted that London would be the prime target for attack and would, most likely, be utterly destroyed, the government was confident that suitably upgraded existing bunkers like those in Horseferry Road would survive and thus maintain the fiction of London as the heart of the British Empire.

The North Rotunda, by then known as ANSON, had been used as a Central Government War Room since the middle of 1943, and for a short time the west tunnel at Chancery Lane was also considered as a possible government citadel, although nothing came of this plan. The east tunnel was already occupied by the Public Record Office as an emergency repository, along with parts of the Camden shelter. By 1952/3, with the onset of the cold war, the North Rotunda and the Admiralty Citadel were firmly established as emergency war rooms to house 5,800 key government workers and major new works were under way to link these and other key locations by means of extensions to the Post Office cable tunnels. Should war break out, the remaining lower orders of the Whitehall establishment would progressively evacuate to far-flung country retreats in a manner reminiscent of the 'Yellow Move' of the Second World War.

Thus far the British government had drifted somewhat rudderlessly as regards its plans for the next war, but the emergence of the Hydrogen bomb, with its spectre of a land aglow with radiation and the sun obscured by dense and deadly clouds of fallout, kick-started the Cabinet into belated action. During 1953 and

1954 four influential committees investigated the vulnerability of Britain's economy, military forces, and social institutions to the effects of nuclear war. Both the Hall Committee, whose primary focus was upon the effectiveness of the current Civil Defence and Regional Government organization, and the Maclean Committee, which studied the likely disruption to the armed forces under nuclear attack, concluded that the dislocation of communication would be the most serious immediate consequence. Weaknesses in the nation's communication systems, particularly in its trunk telephone network, had been highlighted during the war years and the GPO, in consultations with the defence departments, had been preparing large-scale improvements since 1948.

Meanwhile a Treasury committee under the chairmanship of Thomas Padmore was studying the financial implications of current and future plans for the Machinery of Government in War and the location of the wartime Seat of Government. Padmore's first report, whilst acknowledging the city-busting destructive power of the Hydrogen bomb, still considered London as a viable seat of central government. It was accepted that a widespread dispersal of day-to-day departmental operations to the rural areas would be appropriate, but the committee recommended that the existing Whitehall bunkers should be retained and extended to house an expanded central staff of 7,700.

Padmore recognized that London might eventually become untenable and suggested that a reserve headquarters, later code-named SUBTERFUGE, should be established somewhere outside the main target areas in a west country location. Even at this early stage Padmore probably already had in mind the huge Spring Quarry underground complex at Corsham, in north Wiltshire, for this site had been a grave embarrassment to the Treasury since 1941. Within months of the first Padmore report, the Strath enquiry began a detailed analysis of the implications of nuclear radiation and radioactive fallout upon the UK 'Continuity of Government' plans. The conclusions of the Strath Report, circulated in March 1955, was critical of the existing system of emergency regional government via the Regional War Rooms, arguing that the highly interactive form of tactical control from Whitehall that it envisaged would be impossible under the changed circumstances. Until that time it was presumed that the reporting chain between the Regional War Rooms and the Central Government War Room in the North Rotunda would survive the nuclear onslaught, allowing central government to maintain control throughout the periods of survival and recovery.

Strath heralded the end of the Regional War Rooms and the introduction of the larger, more sophisticated, and virtually self-sufficient RSGs. Following Strath, it was no longer assumed that the Seat of Government would remain in London. Indeed, by the beginning of 1956 it was firmly established that the government would abandon London and that the Spring Quarry site at Corsham should be developed as 'SUBTERFUGE', the Emergency Government War Headquarters. It was further decided that a reserve site should also be developed and, although concrete evidence is not yet forthcoming, it is generally supposed that the recently decommissioned storage tunnels at the

Rhydymwyn mustard gas factory near Mold in North Wales were earmarked for this function. No development, however, was ever undertaken at Rhydymwyn, and for the last forty years the tunnels there, bereft of the sinister storage tanks that once contained thousands of tons of toxic war-gases, have remained dark, dank and empty.

Despite these developments, a central Home Defence War Room remained at Horseferry Road until at least 1962 when, as 'CHAPLIN', it controlled the Regional Headquarters in exercise FALLEX 62. Evidence suggests that the new government emergency headquarters at Corsham was either complete or nearing completion in 1962, but the London 'CHAPLIN' bunker was used as a substitute in exercises to maintain its secrecy.

In later years the North Rotunda maintained a minor role in the nuclear war plan, as the home of the central telephone exchange for the Government Telephone Network. This exchange, known as the 'Horseferry Tandem', was finally decommissioned in the late 1990s. Meanwhile, the South Rotunda, with its original power-house with triplicate diesel generators and air-conditioning plant still intact but disused, became the Civil Service Sports Club.

THE WARTIME ORIGIN OF THE SPRING QUARRY COMPLEX

The underground complex that was to become Britain's alternative seat of government in the event of nuclear war was subject to a slow gestation that started in the mid 1930s in response to the growing threat of conventional war in Europe. During the century prior to 1934 the quarrymen of north Wiltshire had extracted building stone of the finest quality from mineral reserves one hundred feet below the villages of Box and Corsham. As they progressed they left behind a ramified network of worked-out chambers and galleries that extended, under Corsham Down alone, to some three thousand acres. It was said that one could walk in a straight line underground from the edge of Box Hill to Pockeredge Farm near the eastern portal of Box railway tunnel – a distance of over two miles – without seeing daylight. The construction of Box tunnel by the Great Western Railway in 1938 had exposed the vast reserves of oolitic limestone under Corsham Down, and the largest of the quarries was subsequently developed close by. Directly to the north, Tunnel and Huddswell quarries sprawled over two million square feet and came to within twenty feet of the tunnel lining. Immediately to the south lay Spring Quarry, even larger at 3,500,000 square feet. By 1934 the stone industry was in terminal decline; Tunnel Quarry had been abandoned six years earlier while Spring Quarry was nearing the end of its reserves and was only marginally profitable.

Early in 1934 Tunnel Quarry was purchased by the War Office and over the next six years was converted into a huge underground ammunition depot designed to store the entire war reserves of ammunition for the British land forces. At an early stage in the Tunnel Quarry project, the Army Council minuted to the Treasury that:

It is a programme which may cost £100,000 or £250,000, or £500,000 according to the amount of work which must be done. Whatever is the case it is not open to us to be content with anything less.

As the project progressed it became apparent that even the largest of these estimates was hopelessly optimistic and would represent just a tiny fraction of the true final cost which was in excess of £4.4 million.

It was, then, with considerable alarm that the Treasury learned in December, 1940, that under pressure from Lord Beaverbrook, the Minister of Aircraft Production, Churchill had been persuaded to sanction the conversion of Spring Quarry into the largest underground factory in the world, producing Centaurus radial engines for the Bristol Aeroplane Company. This plan was an ill-conceived panic response to the intensive German attacks upon the British aircraft industry. Mindful of the forty-fold increase in cost of the War Office underground depot in Corsham, a Treasury official noted to his Minister in December 1940, when the estimated cost of the project had already reached £2,341,000, that:

> I think there is no alternative to sanction the scheme in principal, but to ask that a close watch be kept on development.

A year later very little work had been completed on site other than the removal of stone debris from underground, but the estimate had passed £6,000,000. Waste removal alone had already absorbed over £2,000,000, prompting the same Treasury official to ask the Minister for Works & Buildings:

> Quarry development at £2,227,000 looks **Pretty Sinister**. Is this a repetition of the War Office experience at Corsham? Why have we not been told of this enormous increase of cost at an earlier stage?

This, however, was only the start of the troubles. The factory was still not ready for occupation by the end of 1942, by which time the German bombing had reduced to insignificance and the whole underground factory scheme had become an irrelevance. No one, other than Beaverbrook, was enthusiastic. Neither the Bristol Aeroplane Company management nor the employees wanted to go underground. The Treasury had been vehemently opposed to the project from the start and the War Office was convinced that development of the factory would prejudice the security of its own underground establishments in the Corsham area. Badly managed, poorly executed, and overshadowed by accusations of profiteering on the part of some of the contractors involved, the Spring Quarry project had acquired an evil reputation and an unstoppable internal momentum. Construction continued despite its patent irrelevance in a manner that defied logical analysis.

The completed factory extended over 2,200,000 square feet of underground space and was divided into three major sections divided by geological faults. The main offices, workshops, and canteens were concentrated in the larger eastern section which encompassed over half the available area. The west end of the quarry was divided by a second, lateral, fault to provide two smaller areas, each of approximately 500,000 square feet. The southernmost of these was also converted into engineering shops but the northern area was never fully developed. To facilitate the easy movement of some 20,000 employees in and out of the factory each day two inclined shafts were fitted with 'Otis' electric escalators requisitioned from St Paul's and Holborn tube stations in London. These were supplemented by four high-capacity electric passenger lifts in vertical shafts, while a further five heavy-duty lifts were installed to move goods and materials in and out of the quarry. Process steam was provided by two underground boilerhouses each with six large coal-fired boilers, and for the benefit of the employees there were five underground restaurants that could jointly cater for over six thousand diners at a sitting.

By April 1945, when the factory finally closed, the bill for its construction had passed £20,000,000, with half as much again spent on machine tools. Yet it had produced virtually nothing of note except a small number of Centaurus engines, many of which failed at the test stage due to the poor conditions under which they were assembled. The overspend at Spring Quarry was so notorious that it prompted an unprecedented House of Commons Public Accounts Committee enquiry, the only time that such an inquiry had investigated a defence project in wartime.

More problems arose immediately after the war when questions as to the disposal of the shadow factories and other wartime emergency construction projects were examined. It was revealed that while the Treasury was authorising increasingly uncontrolled expenditure at Spring Quarry, it was unaware that these huge sums were being spent upon a property which had been requisitioned, and about which matters of long-term tenure or ownership had not been properly addressed. A subsequent internal memorandum, quoted below, gives the first hint of what the future held for the quarry:

> As to the requisitioning position, one thing that was abundantly clear was that having spent such an enormous sum here [ie. Corsham] we would want to buy-out some of the quarries and keep some kind of citadel for future emergencies.

A year earlier, as the German rocket bombardment gained momentum, parts of Spring Quarry had been allocated to the 'Crossbow' committee, which was tasked, *inter alia*, with relocating the seat of government should the situation become critical. There is, however, no record of any concrete action having been undertaken to implement the plan at that time.

By 1946 the property was in the hands of the Ministry of Supply which had been progressively letting parts of the underground area to the Admiralty for temporary storage. When questioned about the long-term future and eventual disposal of the quarry, Mr A.K. Davis, the officer in charge, noted to his superior that 'I gather that the policy is to hold on firmly to our best refuge from the Atom Bomb.'

A year later a request from the Courtaulds company to view the underground factory in order to obtain data that might be relevant to the design of a 'windowless factory' they planned to build elsewhere was met with a polite refusal, on the grounds that 'the future use of the site may be somewhat sensitive'.

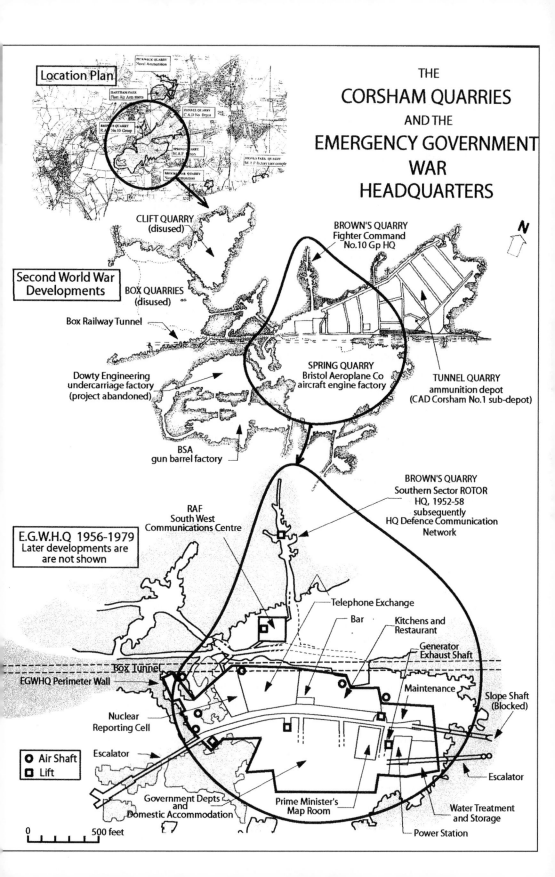

THE CORSHAM QUARRIES AND THE EMERGENCY GOVERNMENT WAR HEADQUARTERS

Location Plan

PICKWICK QUARRY
Naval Ammunition

HARTHAM PARK
Fleet Air Arm stores

TUNNEL QUARRY
C.A.D No. Depot

BROWN'S QUARRY
R.A.F No. 10 Group

SPRING QUARRY
M.A.P stores

BROCKHAM QUARRY
Naval Ammunition

MONKS PARK QUARRY
M.A.P factory tool compts

CLIFT QUARRY
(disused)

BROWN'S QUARRY
Fighter Command
No.10 Gp HQ

N

Second World War Developments

BOX QUARRIES
(disused)

Box Railway Tunnel

Dowty Engineering
undercarriage factory
(project abandoned)

SPRING QUARRY
Bristol Aeroplane Co
aircraft engine factory

TUNNEL QUARRY
ammunition depot
(CAD Corsham No.1 sub-depot)

BSA
gun barrel factory

BROWN'S QUARRY
Southern Sector ROTOR
HQ, 1952-58
subsequently
HQ Defence Communication
Network

RAF
South West
Communications Centre

**E.G.W.H.Q 1956-1979
Later developments are
are not shown**

Telephone Exchange

Bar

Kitchens and
Restaurant

Generator
Exhaust Shaft

Box Tunnel

EGWHQ Perimeter Wall

Maintenance

Slope Shaft
(Blocked)

Nuclear
Reporting Cell

○ Air Shaft
□ Lift

Escalator

Escalator

Government Depts
and
Domestic Accommodation

Prime Minister's
Map Room

Water Treatment
and Storage

Power Station

0   500 feet

THE EMERGENCY GOVERNMENT WAR HEADQUARTERS

Although it is probable that Spring Quarry was earmarked as the site of the alternative emergency war headquarters before 1950, it was not until 1954 that the first steps were taken to bring the tentative plans to fruition. In April the government finally bought the quarry freehold from the Bath & Portland Stone Company along with one hundred acres of surface land. A group of surface hostels that had housed employees of the Bristol Aeroplane Company during the war years, and latterly provided temporary accommodation to several hundred East European refugees, were peremptorily cleared and an embargo put on commercial and residential development in the immediate vicinity.

During the following eighteen months the Padmore working party, in co-operation with the various civil ministries and service departments, calculated the manning requirements of the emergency headquarters. Based upon Padmore's findings, architects and engineers from the MOWB drew up plans for the conversion of the factory into a secure citadel for the central government nucleus. Meanwhile the GPO, with advice from the British Joint Communications Electronics Board and the Emergency Government Headquarters Communications Planning Panel, were designing the necessary communications systems.

By the beginning of 1957 the final layout of the Corsham bunker was firmly established. A gross area, including support pillars, of approximately 2,000,000 square feet in the northern half of the east side of the quarry was selected, which would provide in excess of 1,000,000 square feet of useable office space. This area would be sufficient to house the proposed military and government staff of 7,700 personnel. The Box railway tunnel and the perimeter wall of the Army's Tunnel Quarry ammunition depot formed its northern boundary, while to the south a broad new reinforced concrete wall divided it from the rest of the quarry, which continued to function as an Admiralty store. Beyond the main perimeter wall a lighter barrier built of concrete blocks created a vacant 'buffer-zone' between the Central Government and Admiralty areas.

Within the government zone a wide roadway ran east to west with lifts and passenger escalators at each extremity. To the north of this roadway most of the chambers were put over to service installations: the telephone exchange, workshops, air-conditioning, catering and domestic facilities, etc. The southern section housed most of the departmental offices and living quarters, while the Cabinet and main executive functions were concentrated in the central, eastern area.

With the layout agreed, construction initially proceeded quickly. By March 1957 the redundant slope shaft 'B' had been securely blocked by a massive concrete plug and contractors were awaiting the final engineer's drawings to enable them to get on with modifications to the ventilation shafts B1 and E2, scheduled for completion by the end of June. It had been planned to cap the chimney shaft and coaling shaft for underground boilerhouse No. 1 at the same time, but it was later decided to remodel these when it was decided that the existing underground plant was to be partially included in the new

64. BURLINGTON Under Construction. A view of the main access road during an early stage of conversion of the former Bristol Aeroplane Company underground engine factory in 1959. The headquarters' underground telephone exchange and the legendary 'Rose & Crown' bar were later established in chambers to the right of this passageway. *Author's collection*

arrangements. By November the shaft-head buildings for lifts PL1, PL2 and GL1 had been made blast-proof by sealing the original openings with five-foot-thick concrete walls on massive foundations and building new, concrete access passageways at right-angles to the existing openings. The head of Machinery Lift No. 1, which had previously consisted of an open gantry and travelling crane, was completely rebuilt as an enclosed, reinforced concrete structure with a blast-proof entrance. A spiral staircase was fitted in this shaft for use as an emergency exit.

Late autumn saw work start on the most difficult of the surface features, the inclined escalator shafts. When it was first decided, in 1942, to fit escalators in shafts 'A' and 'C' the Ministry of Aircraft Production was forced to requisition second-hand units from the LPTB because new ones were unobtainable due to

Escalator Shaft 'C'

Ventilation Shaft 'E2'

Goods Lift 'GL1'

Passenger Lift 'PL1'

Ventilation Shaft 'E1A'

ML1 Shaft Converted to Power Station Exhaust Shaft

Passenger Lift 'PL2'

Ventilation Shaft 'E1'

65. **The Central Government War Headquarters at Corsham.** This aerial view shows most of the surface features, including the escalator shaft and lift-head buildings, and the specially adapted ventilation shaft caps.

66. **BURLINGTON Under Construction.** This photograph, taken in 1959, shows work under way on the reconstruction of the entrance blockhouse enclosing the escalators in slope shaft 'C'. The original building, dating from 1942, was partially demolished and enclosed within a massive concrete edifice. The tall building to the right is goods lift GL1, which was also reconstructed later in 1959. At that time the corrugated shedding that partially encloses it was removed and the structure covered in earth. A further passenger lift, PL1, is just visible in the background. *Author's collection*

material shortages. Problems arose when it was discovered that none of the units available were quite long enough for the incline shafts at Corsham. At the east end of the quarry, slope shaft 'A', which was fitted with the No. 4 escalator from Holborn tube station, was modified by sinking two vertical shafts from the surface to meet the incline at the highest point of the escalator. Spiral stairs in these shafts connected the incline to a small surface building. Construction of a new, bunker-like concrete shaft-head began in November 1957. The old escalator was rewired and partially refurbished, but it is unlikely that it was ever used. Very significant alterations were made to the escalator in slope shaft 'C' and its associated surface building. Here, too, the original unit terminated some distance below ground level and was connected to the surface via a broad flight of steps in the upper section of the incline. Through the winter of 1957/8 most

67. **The Central Government War Headquarters at Corsham.** The inconspicuous pedestrian entrance to passenger lift PL1 beside Westwells Road in Corsham. Most of the large concrete shaft head building is concealed beneath a grassy mound. *Author's collection*

of the original surface building was demolished and a huge new concrete edifice constructed, enclosing what remained of the original structure. Below this building the ground had been opened out to the top of the existing escalator where a large chamber was constructed to form a circulating area, and from there a second, new escalator rose to the surface building. The whole structure was then mounded over and grassed, leaving only two small, gated pedestrian entrances visible at each side.

By April 1959 most of the major building works were completed; the surface works were finished, the underground perimeter walls were built and most of the internal partitioning was complete. Three sets of massive blast doors had been erected to seal emergency exits into the adjoining Admiralty depot, emergency generators were installed, though not yet operative, and some of the domestic equipment such as bakery ovens and much of the air-conditioning plant was in place. Special measures had been taken to protect the tops of the ventilation and boilerhouse shafts, which had originally taken the form of light brickwork cowlings surmounted by wire-mesh guards. These were replaced by lightweight brick support walls, pierced at intervals to allow a flow of air, and surmounted by immensely heavy, three-foot-thick octagonal reinforced concrete caps. The shaft-tops terminated in shallow pits or bunds slightly larger than the diameter of the octagonal capstones and the whole was designed so that the effect of a nearby nuclear blast would demolish the light support walls allowing the concrete cap to fall into the bund, thus effectively sealing the shaft. Thereafter the inhabitants of the nether world would rely on recirculated air for ventilation. Alternatively, in an emergency, small, fixed explosive charges could be used to demolish the supporting structures in a controlled manner.

By the summer of 1959 progress at Corsham had slowed markedly; work on the ventilation and air filtration systems was yet to start, fuel tanks for the generators and air-conditioning boilers were on site but not yet installed, and much of the internal plumbing was incomplete. There were as yet no proper sewage facilities (although it was planned to install nearly a thousand toilets), the proposed waste-water recycling plant did not exist and construction of the huge underground fresh water lagoon had not begun. The shell of the GPO telephone exchange was finished, but no equipment was yet installed. When eventually completed, the telephone exchange, which was a major trunk installation, was a showpiece of the site and a 'must-see' element of the tour for the very few outsiders who were ever privileged to visit. An enormous, double-sided manual plug-board exchange, large enough to service a small city, sat in an immaculate hall with a polished black and white tiled floor, its equipment contained in typical 1950s mahogany cabinets with clocks suspended on ornate brackets at intervals along its considerable length. Nearby was a supplementary electro-mechanical equipment room with rack upon rack of Strowger selectors, while in an adjacent chamber, also with black and white tiled floor, stood a pair of motor generators to supply the necessary DC power. Another room contained hundreds of glass-cased batteries, like fish tanks, stacked on wooden racks. Further away, in the GPO power station, there were dedicated standby diesel generator sets to ensure a continuity of supply to all the telecommunications plant.

With completion of the telephone exchange and other communication systems still two years away in June 1959, progress at Corsham was suddenly reduced to a crawl when Civil Defence spending was allocated a drastically reduced priority in the defence budget. The Defence Departments called for the rapid completion of 'SUBTERFUGE', but it was argued that the central government bunker, without a parallel network of suitable regional government bunkers (which currently did not exist), would be impotent. This situation did not last long however, and by the end of 1960 the job was well in hand. Impatient of the slow progress with the installation of the communications systems, the RAF, which had over a decade's experience of such work in the Corsham quarries, took over much of the task. Thereafter, operation of the Corsham communications equipment was shared jointly between the RAF and the central government organization.

Other major tasks undertaken at Spring Quarry included the construction of several large operations rooms with glazed mezzanine balconies, which involved a great deal of new excavation in order to obtain the necessary headroom. At least two capacious vaults fitted with huge safe doors were built at the east end of the depot, one of which functioned as a central registry. The use of the other is unclear, but it has been suggested that this may have been intended for the Bank of England gold reserves. Certainly, in both the United States and Canada (where a special vault had been built for the Bank of Canada gold reserves in the 'Diefenbunker') the preservation of the monetary system had been an important element of the war-plan.

A minor, but controversial, item that taxed the architects of the EGWHQ was whether or not to provide a licensed bar for the inmates. At first, the idea was rejected by the Treasury 'Machinery of Government in War Planning Team' because of:

> the austerity conditions which would prevail at SUBTERFUGE, the number of additional staff who would be required to run the wet canteen, and the difficulties of arranging supplies of beer.

By 1962, however, these problems were obviously overcome, because a bar was built serving not only beer but spirits too. And it was not an austere affair, but a replica of a typical stylish club bar of the 1960s, complete with mirrors, optics, and tasteful fittings in polished chrome.

In 1960 it was stated that, although 'SUBTERFUGE' was far from complete, it *could* be used by a limited staff of about 1,500 should a crisis suddenly develop. At that time it was envisaged that the Corsham bunker would be manned late in the 'precautionary' period, that there would be a short nuclear exchange, and that thereafter it would deal in detail with issues such as international relations, strategic supplies and the management of defence strategy, while giving just broad, tactical direction to the lower levels of Regional Government, with whom a limited two-way dialogue would be established. It was this mix of strategic and tactical control, of short war and prolonged recovery, very much under central government control, that necessitated the hugely complex communications system with its staff of over 1,000 operators.

As the new decade opened, western assessments of the nature of future warfare changed, as did the perceived function of the Corsham nucleus. It was realized that total war might develop with great speed, maybe within two or three days, and that thereafter it could drag on for months or even years. An embunkered central government would be stretched to prosecute an extended war and could no longer hope to exercise control over a ruined, decimated country for any length of time. Under these conditions, which were the conditions that gave rise to the RSG organization, control of the country at large was devolved almost completely to the Regional Seats of Government, while the function of the Corsham nucleus became increasingly orientated towards military command and to the prosecution of the war. Only core departmental staffs would remain to deal with international affairs and act as the skeleton upon which the regional structures would coalesce as reconstruction got under way. Accepting the principle of a rapid spiral into war, it was expected that the Seat of Government would remain in London during the short precautionary period and flee to Corsham at the last moment.

With the new decade and new function came another new code-name. In 1961 the underground complex at Corsham became the fabled city of 'BURLINGTON'.

In the early autumn of that year a top secret Chiefs of Staff committee, the 'Emergency Government War Headquarters Inter-Service Committee (EGWHISC), under the chairmanship of G.R.D. Fitzpatrick, examined the staffing and operational requirements of BURLINGTON. Introducing its findings, the committee's report, issued on 8 September, noted that:

> We have undertaken this examination in the light of the revised concept which envisages control being exercised from London during the Precautionary period, with BURLINGTON as the Seat of Government in the Survival and Reconstruction period, *and as an alternative centre for authorizing nuclear retaliation.*

The report, which was essentially an analysis of Service staffing requirements, excluded references to the Service Directors of Intelligence and their staffs who would form part of the War Cabinet Organization. An annexe detailed the functions of the various departments and their manning requirements:

Cabinet Organization -
To act as the ultimate source of authority during the period of survival and reconstruction and to be an alternative centre to London for authorizing Nuclear Retaliation. It is assumed that the Prime Minister would take on the responsibility for defence and that the War Cabinet would consist of a small number of Senior Ministers, with other Ministers and Chiefs of Staff attending meetings as required.

The Chief of the Defence Staff would be housed in the War Cabinet Organization area, but other Chiefs of Staff would be elsewhere in the Headquarters.

The War Cabinet Organization would include a number of supporting staffs, e.g Secretariats (civil and military), Intelligence and Map Room staffs, Ministry of Defence representatives and common services such as Registry and Typing.

A senior staff of sixty-three military personnel were included in the Cabinet Organisation:

> ... including the Chief of the Defence Staff and his staff, the Chiefs of Staff Secretariat, the Joint Planning Staff, and staff for the Prime Ministers Map Room. Additional personnel will be provided by the Ministry of Defence.

The task of the Admiralty contingent was:

To provide the government with professional Naval advice that will enable it to intervene effectively to influence the conduct of the war at sea where the National Interest requires.

A breakdown of the total staff of 123 naval personnel was included in an appendix to the report, which is detailed below.

The Home Office function was to oversee:

- Overall policy of maintenance / restoration of Law & Order.
- Advice to the Army Council and Chiefs of Staff.
- Implementation of Army Council and Chiefs of Staff directives.
- Provision of members of Joint Service Committees.
- Re-deployment of manpower and logistic resources between commands.
- Preparation for survival and recovery.

Aware that the resources of the Police might be quickly over-extended, it was noted that: 'The implementation of certain of the functions will be delegated to the United Kingdom Land Forces.'

The function of the Air Ministry, which still held the keys to the UK nuclear deterrent, was stated thus:

- *To operate nuclear retaliation, or those aspects of nuclear retaliation that remain to be completed.*
- To provide liason in connection with, and logistic support of, those elements of the RAF which are or will be assigned to SACEUR and SACLANT.
- To control global RAF activity, in particular operation of the air transport forces.
- To contribute support, both in manpower and logistically to joint action during the survival phase.
- *To liaise with any surviving USAF in the United Kingdom.*

The role of the UK Commander in Chief's Committee was still under review as the EGWHISC committee sat, but the following provisional function was agreed:

C-in-C UKLF
- Operational command of the Armed Services in support of the Civil Authorities.
- Administrative command of the Army in the United Kingdom.
- Land defence of the United Kingdom.

A.C.H.D.F
- To provide backing for Air Force units engaged in active air operations.
- Subsequently, to afford the most effective possible assistance that air support, principally in transport and communications, can render to national survival and recovery.

The following table of military manpower requirements for BURLINGTON is collated from the appendices to the EGWHISC report:

Chief of the Defence Staff and his Staff	
Chief of the Defence Staff	1
DCDS or ACDS	1
Support staff	7

Chiefs of Staff Secretariat	
Secretary	1
Deputy Secretary	1
Support staff	11

Joint Planning Staff	
Deputy or Assistant Secretary	1
Support staff	8

Prime Minister's Map Room	
Captain, R.N, Colonel, or Group Captain	1
Admiralty Component	10
War Office Component	11
Air Ministry Component	10

The Ministry of Defence will provide forty-seven staff from the Permanent Secretary's department, the Chief Scientific Advisor's department, the Joint Communications Electronic Staff, and contributions to the registry and typing services.

The Deputy Chief of Staff MoD Collation Centre will fill the senior Staff appointment in the Prime Minister's Map Room. One senior watchkeeper and one watchkeeper will be found from the Collation Centre and each will be of a different Service from the officer filling the senior appointment in the Map Room.

Admiralty Contingent	
First Sea Lord	1
Secretary to the First Sea Lord	1
Naval Assistant to First Sea Lord	1
Naval Staff	113

The above figures include Officers for the Joint Movement Staff and the Joint Administrative Planning Staff – one of the appropriate rank for each staff.

In addition, the Admiralty has a commitment to provide twenty-four messengers for the common user staff.

WAR OFFICE CONTINGENT

Chief of the Imperial General Staff	1
Advisors to CIGS	2
Department of VCIGS	38
Department of DCIGS	32
Department of A.G	35
Department of Q.M.G	51
S os S and PUS Departments	24

The above list includes Officers of the Joint Movement Staff and the Joint Administrative Planning Staff, but takes no account of the requirement for Message Control Staff.

In addition to the staff shown above who will be required for Staff functions, the War Office has a commitment to provide the following common user staff:
Camp Commandant and staff, Medical and Dental staff, Security staff, Catering staff, and laundry services. The total for this commitment amounts to 409 Officers and other ranks.
A further commitment is the provision of guards.
The Camp Commandant's staff of 30 messengers will be provided by the Cabinet Office (6), and the Admiralty (24).

AIR MINISTRY CONTINGENT

Air Marshal	1
Air Vice Marshal	1
Air Commodore	3
Group Captains	12
Wing Commander and other Officers	39
Civilian staff	66

COMMANDER IN CHIEF - HOME STATION

C-in-C Home Station, representative and staff	11
C-in-C, Chief of Staff and staff	10
General Staff	29
Attached General Staff	5
M.G.A and staff	9
A.G Branch	14
Attached A.G staff	27
Q. Staff	13
Attached Q. staff	10
Administration	10
A.C.H.D.F	20

When the time came for London to be evacuated, a small party of VIPs would leave Horseguards Parade aboard a helicopter bound for Corsham. Amongst the helicopter party would be:

- The Prime Minister and his immediate advisors
- Chief of the Defence Staff
- Secretary to the Chiefs of Staff Committee
- The First Sea Lord, his Secretary and Naval Assistant
- Chief of the Imperial General Staff and two advisors
- Chief of the Air Staff and two immediate advisors

The rest of the military component, five Senior Ministers, and those government civil servants who were allocated desks at BURLINGTON, would travel to the west country in a fleet of 200 buses that were requisitioned earlier. These buses would not go directly to Corsham but would assemble at a secret location some twenty miles distant, probably RAF Lyneham, or possibly the Staff College at Shrivenham, from where they would proceed to their final destination by a discrete fleet of twenty locally hired coaches.

Except for completion of the telecoms system, very little work remained undone at BURLINGTON by September, 1962, but, with the Cuban problem becoming critical the Chiefs of Staff voiced their anxiety, asking in a secret minute: 'Will the facilities at BURLINGTON be ready in time to launch a retaliatory attack?'

One question, the solution to which has eluded researchers since the 1960s, is that of the fate of the Royal Family in event of a global nuclear war. Suggestions that they might fly off to a safe refuge in Canada, as was proposed should the Germans have mounted a successful invasion in 1940/41, have been dismissed because the geographical location of Canada, bordering the USA and thick with American radar bases, made it even more vulnerable than the United Kingdom.

The common perception is that space would be provided at BURLINGTON, and people working at and responsible for the Corsham bunker speak openly of it being 'The Queen's bunker'. No documents have been released to substantiate this theory and the Cabinet Office remains tight-lipped about the Royal connection, as they have about all aspects of Corsham.

Throughout the Second World War completely groundless and erroneous rumours circulated that Tunnel Quarry, the Army's ammunition depots at Corsham, was prepared as an emergency home for the Royal Family; there were similar rumours regarding the underground store at Westwood, near Bradford-on-Avon, that was in fact built to house many of the treasures from the V&A and British Museum. Had London become utterly untenable through constant German bombardment then the Royal Family would, in fact, have been moved to Madresfield Court, near Malvern, a location considered beyond the range of German bombers.

It would be easy to dismiss the concept of royal quarters at BURLINGTON as equally groundless, just another element in the emotive Corsham mythology. But there are serious constitutional reasons why such protection should be afforded the reigning monarch. Just as in the United States the President is the embodiment of the nation state, (the whole US 'Continuity of Government' programme revolves around the preservation of the person of the President and the demonstration of his continued survival to the nation and the world at large), so the survival of the Queen symbolizes the survival of her Nation and Empire. Despite the apparent impression that the Royal Prerogative is no more than an anachronistic formality, the authority of the Monarch, as Head of State, is required to declare war and peace and to legitimize international treaties, even with the nation *in extemis*. Throughout the vicissitudes of nuclear war planning this element of constitutional legitimacy has been maintained, as the following extract from a Home Office letter to the Local Authorities Association, circulated in 1977, illustrates:

> Full powers of constitutional government would be vested constitutionally in the Regional Commissioner on behalf of the Crown.

Beyond the strictly constitutional level, there are other reasons to maintain the Monarch at the centre of government and at the heart of what might remain of the national communication network. It can be assumed that the country at large would blame their political leaders for forcing the nation along the road to war once again. Given the level of public respect for the Royal Family that existed in the 1950s and 1960s, public perception that the Queen was still at the helm would have been of incalculable value. Public appearances by royalty in times of crisis or hardship have always been major boosts to the morale of the British people. Great efforts were made throughout the Second World War to keep King George VI and Queen Elizabeth in the public eye, and there is no doubt that broadcasts from the BBC studio in the Corsham bunker very early in the recovery phase of nuclear conflict would have been of immense value.

'BURLINGTON' becomes 'TURNSTILE'

When the first detailed plans for the Corsham Emergency Government War Headquarters were prepared in the mid-1950s, it was expected to be a comprehensive joint establishment that was both an alternative Seat of Government from which the civil concerns of the nation would be addressed, a National Civil Defence War Room from where the immediate welfare of a broken nation would be co-ordinated and, as the Cabinet War Room, the site from which the retaliatory strike would be authorized and the war directed. By 1962, as BURLINGTON, it had become principally an expanded headquarters for the War Cabinet and the Chiefs of Staff organization, with a limited central government role maintaining just the absolute core government functions.

By the mid-1960s the name and emphasis changed again. This time the name was TURNSTILE and its notional Civil Defence role, with its outdated concepts of rescue and recuperation, slipped away and was gone by 1968. It is argued that after the 'safety-valve' of Cuba, emergency planning at all levels slipped into virtual oblivion and that much of the bunker infrastructure was left to rot for the rest of the decade. Whilst there may have been an easing of tension that enabled western governments to cut back on the most visible elements of

Civil Defence expenditure, central planning continued. In reaction to the rapid escalation of the Cuban crisis, the Machinery of Government Home Defence Committee published a paper in 1965 introducing a new approach to nuclear crisis-management. Recognizing that the manning and working-up of the Corsham juggernaut during a short precautionary period might not be practicable, the committee outlined its 'Python' concept. This envisaged a core complement of 600 or so Ministers and military chiefs assembling into eight smaller, more manageable and widely dispersed groups, the survivors of which would coalesce in later phases of the war. Whilst this concept may have influenced strategic thinking in the 1980s and 1990s, when advances in communication technology made its implementation more feasible, there is little evidence of its earlier implementation.

Certainly, during the late 1960s few changes occurred at Corsham, but a PSA maintenance staff of seventy were permanently employed. Major developments were undertaken around 1975 at the EGWHQ in connection with the improved United Kingdom Warning and Monitoring Organization, when civil defence spending elsewhere was stagnant. A large section of the north-west corner of the quarry was physically separated from the rest of the bunker and developed as a UKWMO Nuclear Reporting cell, manned by some 600 RAF personnel, and supplying fallout information to the Emergency Government War Headquarters and the adjoining RAF communication units. Information from around the country was collated at a central control room, filtered and distributed as required. A disused section of the quarry which had previously been part of the Bristol Aircraft Company's senior staff canteen was converted into a series of airmen's dormitories, while elsewhere within the new unit – later known as the Quarry Operations Centre – offices were converted into smaller dormitories for the centre's WRAF contingent. The manpower of this unit was in marked contrast to other Nuclear Reporting cells at the various armed forces headquarters. At RAF Upavon, for example, the Transport Command cell had a staff of just four, who between them undertook a task roughly equivalent to that of an ROC Group Control.

Among other improvements scheduled at that time, but not completed, was the construction of a new emergency exit from the north-west corner of the bunker, that would have taken a route through the old Box stone quarry to a new concrete-lined vertical shaft in Box fields. A heavy blast door was positioned at the end of a long passage in the old workings, known to local cavers as the 'wind tunnel', and a route laid out leading to the new shaft. A spiral stairway destined for the vertical shaft was never installed and further work on the project was inexplicably abandoned in 1977.

Within two years, though, a major upgrade of the EGWHQ was put in hand under the Thatcher regime as part of the government's new, aggressive approach to civil defence. Between 1979 and 1982 the headquarters was dramatically reduced in scale to reflect its diminishing importance as a centre for civil government, but the facilities there were substantially upgraded for its more focused role as a central government Command Nucleus. New kitchens were installed and a new generating station with four diesel alternator sets was established near the bottom of the ML1 machinery-lift shaft, which was adapted as an exhaust duct. As this work progressed, increasing doubts were raised as to the long-term suitability of the quarry as a nuclear shelter. Its name, 'Spring Quarry', reflected one of its major drawbacks. Several underground springs drained into the quarry necessitating almost continual pumping, with pipelines passing through adjacent areas controlled by the Admiralty and the British Railways Board. Common-user and inspection rights to these ducts, one of which runs below the rails in Box Tunnel, required inconvenient contractual agreements. Of greater concern, however, was the damaging effect of water percolating through the rough stone ceiling of the bunker from the strata above. This was a problem that had dogged not just Spring Quarry, but all the Government-controlled quarries in the Corsham area since they were first developed in the Second World War, and for which no adequate cure had ever been found.

OTHER COLD WAR FACILITIES AT CORSHAM

During the inter-war years, quarries to the north of Box Tunnel were converted for ammunition storage, and by 1942 the fifty-acre Tunnel Quarry complex was probably the most sophisticated underground storage facility in the world. A branch from the standard gauge London to Bristol main line entered a side-tunnel at the east portal of Box Tunnel to feed a half-mile-long underground station, whose facilities included a four-bay underground engine shed and a refuge siding that could hold a fifty-wagon train. Within the quarry, ammunition was moved using eleven miles of conveyor belt and a complex system of narrow gauge railways. There was a one megawatt power station with two huge Ruston & Hornsby diesel generators, underground barracks that could sleep 300, an underground telephone exchange and offices that included every function of a surface army camp from Commandant to Chaplain.

An area to the west end of the complex in close proximity to Spring Quarry remained undeveloped until 1942 when it was acquired by the Air Ministry who wished to establish a secure teleprinter switching centre there. Built at a cost of £50,000, the South West Switching Centre was opened in August 1943, under command of No. 10 Group, Fighter Command, whose underground Sector Headquarters was in nearby Brown's Quarry.

The centre continued in operation through the post-war years using wartime equipment that was now rapidly becoming obsolete. In 1960 a radical refit was undertaken to bring it to the standards required for its cold war role. New communications equipment was commissioned and, impatient of the slow progress made to date, responsibility for the adjacent EGWHQ communications centre was thereafter operated as a shared facility, with day-to-day maintenance undertaken by GPO engineers.

Following the reorganization, South West Signals Centre was renamed 'South West Commcen', and then, in May 1961, when the station became an autonomous unit, 'RAF Hawthorn'. Four years later, in June 1965, Hawthorn came under the umbrella of RAF Rudloe Manor, and in this role saw steady growth in its communications facilities for over a decade.

In 1977 a further change of name, which saw the unit designated 'RAF No.6 Signals Unit', coincided with a general overview of RAF communications requirements until the end of the century. Previously the service had relied primarily on equipment that was based upon technology introduced during the Second World War, and upon analogue land-line telecoms equipment leased from the GPO. This situation was both inflexible and expensive. An assessment conducted by the Ministry of Defence concluded that the current configuration of the communication system was inadequate to face the assessed military threat and that future ground systems needed to be based on the twin pillars of security and survivability. It was also recommended that all types of communication traffic should be integrated into a single network.

The new system, which took over ten years to develop, was the 'RAF Fixed Telecommunications System' (RAFFTS), and at its core were projects UNITER, which provided the system framework, terminal equipment and digital switches, and BOXER, which provided MoD-owned communications bearers, the physical links between the switching centres. A weakness of RAFFTS is that it still relies to some extent upon bearers rented from third-party providers like British Telecom, both for elements of UNITER and for the legacy telegraph network and the defence voice networks (GPTN and AOTN). Control of the entire RAFFTS network is exercised from the old South West Signals Centre site, which has, in recent years been re-designated yet again, as RAF No.1 Signals Unit Rudloe Manor.

During 1988/9 No.2 Signal Brigade, the Home Forces principal strategic communications unit, vacated the ex-ROTOR bunker at Sopley which had served as its emergency headquarters for many years and transferred to Basil Hill Barracks at Corsham. It had been proposed that the Brigade should take over the underground Quarry Operations Centre when the nuclear reporting cell there was wound up in 1992, but this plan was later abandoned.

The most recent development in defence communications to affect the previously disparate units at Corsham was the creation, in April, 1998, of the Defence Communication Service Agency (DCSA). The result of a study initiated in 1993 and announced to Parliament in 1996, the DCSA is a tri-service organization bringing together units from the RAF, Royal Navy, Army and MoD Centre into one agency with functional responsibility for satellite, radio and land-line communication, including voice, data, fax and E-mail. The Defence Fixed Telecommunications Service (DFTS), which was already based at Corsham, is a key element of the DCSA providing conventional telecom services within Great Britain. The Headquarters of the DCSA is at Basil Hill Barracks.

By 1989 the deficiencies of the Corsham Emergency Government War Headquarters were becoming increasingly obvious; it was a fifty-year-old facility first constructed under emergency wartime conditions for a completely different purpose, with inadequate preparation carried out by inexperienced contractors and labourers under distinctly adverse environmental conditions, with persistent high humidity and the ever-present risk of roof-falls. The only motivating factor that ensured its continued survival was the half-century's investment of public funds that no one in government was willing to either write off or explain. As the cold war drew to a close its role was being gradually usurped by smaller, more modern nodal command and control centres utilizing modern communications technology. In 1986 a statement in the *Bath Evening Chronicle*, attributed to the Ministry of Defence, announced that the emergency headquarters at Corsham was to be abandoned because 'at a depth of eighty feet it is no longer safe against modern nuclear weapons.'

The statement went on the explain that

> although the site was no longer to be the Central Government War Headquarters, considerable work was currently in hand to prepare it for another vital function, in connection with a new satellite based military communication system.

The report was a little misleading as the new development referred to was in fact in a separate part of the quarries and involved the construction of a new military Command Control and Communications centre, which consolidated the existing military (as opposed to the civil government) control capability at Corsham. Details of these systems are beyond the scope of this volume. It has been suggested that the new satellite communications centre at Corsham has a secondary role beyond that of strategic communications, having absorbed the functions of the Atlantic Submarine Monitoring station at Brawdy in Pembrokeshire. The Brawdy station was one of three similar two-storey bunkers built in 1957 to monitor the movements of Soviet submarines, and presumably those of every other maritime nation, friend or foe. The others were in the western Atlantic at Harrison Point, Barbados, and on the island of Antigua, near the international airport. All were rendered redundant by satellite technology in 1986.

Both the Cabinet Office and the MoD still refuses to comment in detail about the current status of the Corsham EGWHQ, but the available evidence suggests that it ceased to function between 1989 and 1992, although maintenance work continues at the site at a much reduced level. What emergency provision now exists for central government in the post cold war era is a matter of speculation. Since 1968 Whitehall has progressively shed its responsibility for the protection of the civil population, firstly by the abolition of the Civil Defence Corps, which in many ways was a tacit recognition of the fact that there *was* no viable protection, and later by an increasingly comprehensive transfer of civil emergency powers to the regional government organization and the local authorities.

Henceforth, Central Government in war would consist of a War Cabinet and Chiefs of Staff Committee, and its remit be limited exclusively to the conduct of war. The wartime homes for these elite few appear be HMS *Warrior*, the Fleet Headquarters at Northwood, and the PINDAR bunker under the Ministry of Defence Headquarters in Whitehall. It is probable that PINDAR will remain active throughout the precautionary period with executive staff there only evacuating to Northwood at the last moment.

During the early 1960s an underground Navy command centre was established at Northwood in Middlesex. This has grown over the intervening forty years to become the most important Command and Control centre in the United Kingdom and is assumed to be the location from which the War Cabinet and Chiefs of Staff will function in nuclear war. HMS *Warrior* at Northwood controls the UK nuclear deterrent and is home to, among other organizations, an important NATO headquarters, the Royal Navy Commander in Chief Fleet, the Flag Officer Submarines, Headquarters 11/18 Group RAF, and, since 1996, the United Kingdom Permanent Joint Headquarters. Functions established at Northwood include the Tomahawk Land Attack Cruise Missile Support Centre and Royal Navy UHF SATCOM shore station.

Born of the Conservative government's 'Front Line First' defence review, the Permanent Joint Headquarters was inaugurated on 3 April 1996 and has a core staff of some 330 who were previously spread amongst the three Armed Services headquarters and the Ministry of Defence in Whitehall. With a staff of tri-service military personnel, together with civilian planners and specialist medical and scientific advisors, the PJHQ is well positioned to respond quickly to emerging crises and develop appropriate contingency plans. Although primarily a military command centre, a Select Committee on Defence report published in 1999 is careful to describes it as 'an integrated civilian-military organization'.

THE PINDAR BUNKER

Plans for the PINDAR bunker beneath the Ministry of Defence Main Building in Whitehall were first laid by the Conservative government in the latter half of the 1980s. Just as previous administrations had in times of crisis drawn in the centre of power to the bastions of Whitehall, the Thatcher government, having by its US inspired policy of brinkmanship brought the world close to nuclear annihilation, built, in a broad Churchillian gesture, its own bunker beneath the streets of the capital.

PINDAR was commissioned on 7 December 1992 just as the last of the civil government facilities at Corsham were wound down. Construction of the bunker, on a site that had previously been developed as a bunker for the War Office during the Second World War, was fraught with difficulties and was completed several years behind schedule. Details of PINDAR were made public during a House of Commons Debate in April 1994 when Jeremy Hanley, Secretary of State for the Armed Services, told the House that:

> The purpose of the PINDAR joint operations centre is to provide the Government with a protected crisis management facility. It became operational on 7 December 1992. A number of plans exist for the use of PINDAR and the centre is manned by a permanent staff, which is augmented in times of crisis. There are a number of categories of personnel allocated space in PINDAR, including Ministers, senior military and civilian personnel, plus service and civilian operational and support staff. It would be inappropriate to give any more detailed information than this as it would relate to operational capability.

Refusing to be drawn on details of the size of the bunker, where its access points were or how many floors it spread across, Mr Hanley confirmed that it was not connected to the deep-level tube system, and stated that:

> The PINDAR facility is located beneath the Ministry of Defence main building in Whitehall. Details of its size and layout are of an operational nature and it is not our practice to reveal such information.

Asked to disclosed the cost of construction, the Secretary of State replied:

> The total cost of the PINDAR facility has been £126,300,000, of which £66,300,000 was spent on the civil works programme.

The commission date of PINDAR was delayed for over a year due to a serious fire that destroyed one floor of the bunker while construction was in progress. Much of the bunker is contained within the shell of an underground Second World War communication centre that had continued in use by the MoD throughout the post-war years. One level, seven floors below ground and consisting of a single large chamber 350′ by 150′, had served as a Lamson Tube exchange for the whole of Whitehall. Because the machinery that drove the Lamson pneumatic-tube system was so noisy, the interior of the room had been clad in a one-foot-thick layer of cork for acoustic insulation. Cutting equipment used by contractors to remove the cork caused it to overheat and smoulder, but this went unnoticed while workmen were on site. Overnight, however, the fire took hold and by morning the whole chamber was well alight. With access limited to one small door at each end of the room the fire proved difficult to extinguish and the burnt cork, by now reduced to a three-foot-deep pile of glowing embers that filled the entire room, took weeks to damp down and remove. For several days a thick pall of black smoke hung over Whitehall, but the Ministry of Defence resolutely refused to comment upon its origin.

PINDAR and elements of the PJHQ at Northwood jointly compose the government's Defence Crisis Management Organization (DCMO). Both centres are linked together by live video conferencing facilities and to a number of other Command and Control centres including Land Command HQ at Wilton, RAF Strike Command, the Defence Transport and Movement Agency at Andover and to various NATO headquarters.

A post-operational analysis of the DCMO management of the crisis in Kosovo notes that the organization

> works well, but there was a tendency for Whitehall staff to stray into operational business – the domain of PJHQ – often at the expense of providing more strategic guidance.

Ministerial control of the UK crisis management machinery, which includes bringing together key government departments to co-ordinate the United Kingdom's political, military and economic responses to home or overseas crises, is exercised by the Cabinet Office Defence Secretariat.

CONCLUSION

We have now examined in some detail the early warning radar systems that were the first lines of defence in the war that never was and at the wide range of control bunkers and fallout shelters that offered sanctuary to those lucky few who were in a position to respond to the radar warnings.

Throughout this book we have, almost by default, considered all these structures to be secret and, therefore, by extension malign and sinister. Indeed, in common usage the word 'bunker' is unable to stand on its own two feet and must always be propped up by the adjective 'secret', or better still (and with yet more sinister undertones) both 'secret' *and* 'nuclear'. The rural roads of Essex, where several of these once mysterious underground bolt-holes are now no more than tourist attractions, are littered with road signs bearing the curiously contradictory and often multi-lingual message: 'This way to the secret nuclear bunker'.

But how secret were they in reality? Tens of thousands of local authority employees were well aware of the multitude of county and district council bunkers. For twenty years the Civil Defence Corps openly touted for new members to replenish its ever-dwindling ranks. All these men and women, and their families and friends, knew all there was to know about the hardened Civil Defence bunkers in which they played their weekly war games. The same is true of the Royal Observer Corps and UKWMO. The situation is more blurred in relation to the Regional Seats of Government and their successors. It was not a hanging offence for the uninitiated to know of their existence. Their perimeter fences were not, like every airfield, army base and Territorial Army centre in the UK, decked with signs warning that 'This is a prohibited place under the *Official Secrets Act*'. (Probably the most absurd official notice ever devised: 'this place is very secret, so we thought we had better tell you in case you were unaware'). Instead, they hid behind a veil of embarrassed anonymity. Embarrassed because the Home Office Ministers who ruled over them were acutely aware of public opinion regarding their function – bolt holes for the privileged few.

What of the radar stations? Were they secret? Their locations were obviously not, for it is impossible to hide a hillside full of gigantic iron dishes and rotating scanners; the Fylingdales golfballs, for example, were visible from halfway across the North Sea. Even the underground control bunkers for these stations were not 'secret' for they all had terrestrial footprints easily identifiable by those who cared to look. The secrets lay in the technology hidden inside the control bunker rather than in the structure itself. But even the pressing need to obscure the science from prying eyes was not adequate reason for burying it, cocooned in steel and concrete, fifty or 100 feet below ground. They are buried simply to protect against blast and radiation and the secrecy is an incidental bonus.

Secrecy is, however, a potent weapon in its own right; its manipulation is fundamental to international diplomacy and has always been a key element in nuclear strategy. To claim you have a new, secret weapon of hitherto unimaginable power that will comprehensively defeat the most advanced weapons of ones enemies, be it real or chimerical, can change the balance of world power overnight. Hitler accomplished this when he spoke at Danzig in September 1939 of 'a secret weapon against which no defence would avail', and Reagan's 'Star Wars' project, although well and truly in the chimerical category, nevertheless hastened the fall of Soviet Communism.

During the cold war there were ample reasons not to make secrets of the passive defence measures. To demonstrate that the West had bunkers and shelters strong enough to protect its administration, weapons and command structure against any missiles the Soviet Union cared to hurl at it, and could use those bunkers to launch a retaliatory attack or a second strike, was a powerful deterrent. If your enemy perceives that you are defenceless is he not more likely to attack you than if you can exhibit a credible defence?

Nevertheless, there is often political value to be had from enveloping certain government establishments with the aura of often undeserved secrecy – especially if this fulfils the dual purpose of confounding external enemies and, on the domestic front, avoiding questions that might prove ethically embarrassing to answer. While trying, with no little success, to dissuade me from a particular line of research in the preparation of this book, a Ministry of Defence spokesman explained that

> governments, if they wish to act upon the world stage, **must have secrets.** Even if they do not have secrets they must give the impression that they do for then it appears that they control a force more formidable than they actually possess.

The paramount fear is not that a long-guarded secret – like the ingredients of Coca Cola or, as in the early 1950s, the secrets of Los Alamos – will be revealed to a wicked and corrupt competitor, but that a long-vaunted chimera will be exposed for what it has been all along – nothing at all.

Despite contrary evidence it is still a common assumption that what governments most avidly want kept secret *will* be kept secret, so when one of these great secrets is let slip via a government-sponsored leak, it is a tacit admission that an even bigger secret is waiting in the wings. Alternatively, governments often find it advantageous to maintain the aura of mystery surrounding a hitherto secret site long after its significance has faded in order to distract attention from the bigger secret that is its successor.

There are far fewer secrets now, and there is relatively little left to learn about the Anglo-American archaeological legacy of the cold war. Most of the bunkers, shelters and buried headquarters have been abandoned, sold to private enterprise for use as secure storage facilities or turned into visitor centres. As much of their history as has not been lost through departmental negligence has been collated and recorded. Even those few sites about which their respective political masters still doggedly refuse to disclose invaluable historical data – Mount Weather in the USA, for example, and the BURLINGTON bunker at Corsham in the United Kingdom – have revealed their chronologies and structural details. We know when and how they were built, we know what they look like inside and, for the most part, how they are equipped.

What we do not know for sure are details of the policies that governed their operation. British Cabinet Office and Ministry of Defence papers relating to the Machinery of Government In War, which, *inter alia*, deal with the functioning of the Corsham Emergency Government War Headquarters, are, almost without exception, closed for at least a hundred years. A considerable amount of information regarding the manning and operation of BURLINGTON during the very early years is available in various Chiefs of Staff papers that are now open and more can be extrapolated from a series of Home Office documents that have been less closely censored. Policy documents created by the Thatcher government, particularly those created since 1979 when, coincidentally, Burlington was rebuilt, may never see the light of day. Many suspect that this over-zealous secrecy conceals a callous, miscalculated policy of social abandonment perpetrated by a belligerent, bankrupt government that was prepared to renege all responsibilities to its people in pursuit of the capitalist ideal. But until the Cabinet Office is prepared to admit that the maintenance of a coherent historical record is of greater importance than the reputations of one or two flawed, transitory administrators, we shall never know.

INDEX

ABM programmes, 52
Admiralty Citadel, 254
Afghanistan, Soviet invasion of, 53, 69, 254
Agency Logistics Division, 15
'Air Defence of Great Britain during the ten years following the defeat of Germany' UK Chiefs of Staff paper, 71
Air Defense Information System (ADIS), 86
'Air Force One', 9
Air Ministry War Room, 252
Air Staff Requirement, 888, 94
Alaska, 25, 36, 40
Alaska Radar, 25, 40
Aleutian Islands, 36, 37, 40
Alternate Joint Communications Centre, 6
Alternate National Military Command Centre, 9
AN/FPS-115, 62
AN/FPS-117, 37, 40
AN/FPS-124, 37, 40
AN/FPS-14, 26
AN/FPS-19, 36
AN/FPS-23, 36
AN/FPS-26, 30
AN/FPS-27, 30
AN/FPS-3, 30, 83, 84
AN/FPS-49, 61
AN/FPS-50, 59
AN/FPS-6, 30
AN/FSQ-7, computer, 28
AN/SS-17A, 37
AN/TPS-502, 30
ANCHOR, 230, 234
Anchorage, 40
  Operations Centre, 40
Andrews AFB, 9, 27
'Anik' communications satellite, 36
ANSON, 251, 254
Anstruther ROTOR station, 75, 91, 95
  Conversion of ROTOR station to RSG, 91
Anti-Aircraft Command, demise of, 89
Anti-aircraft Operations Rooms, 74
  history, 114
  details of construction, 115
  non-standard designs, 116
AOTN, 275
Armed Forces HQ for Scotland, Inverbervie, 104

ARP, 152
Art Treasures Repositories, 19, 247
Ashdown House, Hastings, 221
Ashford Borough Council Local Authority bunker, 215
'Aspidistra', 184, 186
AT&T, 46
Atom Bomb, Soviet, 6, 7, 254
Attack Warning System (Canada), 68-69
AUTOVON, 10
Avon County, Local Authority bunker, 207
Avon Fire Brigade Control Centre, 140, 142
Aylesbury Vale District Local Authority bunker, 215

BACKBONE, 231
'Backfire' bomber, 37
Backscatter radar, 40
Baffin Island, 36
Bankside power station, 242
Barnton Quarry ROTOR station, 76, 95, 173
  conversion to RSG, 163
Barrow District Council Local Authority bunker, 215
Barrow in Furness, AAOR, 116
Barter Island, 36, 38, 42
Basildon District Council Local Authority bunker, 215
Basingstoke Local Authority bunker, 216
Bath & Portland Stone Company, 260
Battle Management Centre (NORAD), 55
Bawburgh ROTOR station, 75, 76, 91, 93, 94, 97, 184
  Sub-Regional Headquarters, 174
  use as S-RC, 179
Bawdsey ROTOR station, 97-98
BBC emergency transmitters, 204
Beachy Head ROTOR station, 75, 91, 98
Beaconsfield, Local Authority bunker, 216
Beale AFB, 28
Beaverbrook, Lord, 171, 257
Becca Hall, National Grid emergency control centre, 243
Bedminster, Civil Defence centre, 198
Belsize Park Deep Level Tube Shelter, 253-254

Bempton ROTOR station, 75, 91, 98
  use as S-RC, 91
Benbecula, 95
Bendix Corporation, 26
Beneath the City Streets, viii
Bentley Priory, 151
Berkshire Local Authority bunker, 207
Berlin crisis, 1, 6, 25, 40, 73, 147, 152
Bermondsey Local Authority bunker, 216
Bernard Harbour, 38
Bexley Local Authority bunker, 216
'Bhangmeter', 130
Big Bay, 39
Bikini atom bomb tests, 22, 126
Bird, Manitoba, 34
Birkenshaw AAOR, 116
Birmingham, Civil Defence Control, 201
Birmingham Corporation Local Authority bunker, 216
Bishops Court, 94
'Blackjack' bomber, 37
Bloodhound missile, 91-92, 97-98
  and Type 80 Radar, 91
Blue Streak missile, 127
Blunsdon, Water Board bunker, 245
BMEWS, 42, 52, 54, 58, 61, 93, 136, 148-149
  threat from Soviet jamming, 93
BOMARC, 29, 51
Bomb Alarm System, 14
Bomb Power Indicator, 130
Bothwell, Seattle, 24
Boulmer ROTOR station, 75, 87, 91, 94, 98
  Type 80 Radar, 87
  UKASACS role, 98
Box ROTOR station, 98
  RAF No.10 Group HQ, 98
  Sector Operations Centre, 76
Box Tunnel (GWR), 99, 256
BOXER, 275
Brackla, 181-185
  conversion of ROF into S-RC, 181
  layout plan of RGHQ 8.2, 182
  Sub-Regional Headquarters, 174
Bradford, Yorkshire, Water Board bunker, 243
Bradford on Avon, ROC post, 137-138

Bramscote RTS, 92
Bray Island, 39
Brecklands District, Local
  Authority bunker, 216
Brede, Water Board bunker, 245
Brentford and Chiswick, Local
  Authority bunker, 216
Brevoort Island, 39
Bricket Wood, British Rail
  emergency control bunker, 246
BRIDGE (Canadian government
  bunker programme), 65
Brislington, 157
Bristol, Civil Defence, 157
Bristol Aeroplane Company, 257
Bristol Centaurus aero engine,
  257
Bristol City Council, Local
  Authority bunker, 217
Bristol War Room, 174
Bristol Water, Emergency bunker
  at Holcombe, 246
British Gas Emergency pumping
  stations, 246
British Joint Communications
  Electronics Board, 260
British Museum, 19
British Rail Control bunkers, 246
British Rail Control trains, 246
Broadlands District, Local
  Authority bunker, 217
Brompton Road tube station, 206
  use as AAOR, 116
Bromsgrove District Local
  Authority bunker, 217
Broughton Island, 39
Brownlow Point, 38
Buchan ROTOR station, 42, 75,
  87, 91, 92, 94, 95, 98, 99,
  Type 80 Radar, 87
  RTS, 92
  Control and Reporting Centre, 95
  Communications facilities, 42
Buckinghamshire Local Authority
  bunker, 207
BUICC, 30
BUICC III, 30
Bull Report (1947), 21
Bullen Point, 38
BURLINGTON, 266-269, 271-
  272
  Admiralty contingent, 267
  Air Ministry responsibilities, 268
  and Cuba missile crisis, 271
  becomes 'TURNSTILE', 272
  Cabinet Organization, 267
  licensed bar, 266
  military manpower requirements,
    269
  role of ACHDF, 268
  role of C-in-C UKLF, 268

transfer of staff in emergency,
  271
Burns & Roe, 28
Business Continuity
  Programmes, 18
Byron Bay, 38

Cabinet War Room, 248-249, 251
Calvo ROTOR station, 75, 89,
  100
  abandonment, 89
Camberwell, Local Authority
  bunker, 217
Cambridge Bay, 39
Cambridge War Room/RSG, 164
  layout plan, 164
  new works associated with RSG
    status, 164
Camden Local Authority bunker,
  217
Camden Town Deep Level Tube
  Shelter, 253
Campbell, Duncan, vii
Camp Borden, 65
Camp David, 8
Camp Gagetown, 65
Canada Survival Plan (1967), 69
Canadian bunkers, 63 et seq
Canadian/American Military
  Study Group, 34
Canterbury Local Authority
  bunker, 217
Cape Dyer, 36, 39
Cape Hooper, 39
Cape Kiglapait, 37, 39
Cape Lisburne, 38
Cape McLoughlin, 39
Cape Mercy, 39
Cape Parry, 38
Cape Peel West, 39
Cape Perry, 36
Cape Sabine, 38
Cape Sarichef, 38
Cape Simpson, 38
Cape Young, 38
Carcinitron valve, 89
Cardiff (Wenalt) AAOR, 116-117
  BT Emergency Control Centre
    for Wales, 117
Carmarthen Civil Protection
  Unit, 143
Carp, Ottawa, 64
Carrier Warning System, 136-137
Carter AFB, 22
Cartwright AFB, 37, 39
Castle Morpeth Local Authority
  bunker, 217
Castle Point Borough Council
  Local Authority bunker, 217
Central Ammunition Depot
  Corsham, 99

Central Government Emergency
  War Headquarters, 248-265
  alterations to escalators, 263
  development at Corsham, 260
  installation of communications
    equipment, 265
  layout plan, 259
  pre-war plans for, 248
Chancery Lane Deep Level Tube
  Shelter, 253
Chancery Lane tube station, 231
CHAPLIN, 256
Charlottetown, 65
Charmy Down ROTOR station,
  75, 89, 100
  abandonment, 89, 100
Charnwood District Local
  Authority bunker, 217
Cheam (London Group Control),
  153, 183, 205
Chelmsford, Local Authority
  bunker, 217
Chenies ROTOR station, 75, 100
Cherry Report, 73
Cherwell Local Authority bunker,
  218
Cheshire Local Authority bunker,
  118, 208
Cheshire County Emergency HQ,
  118
Cheyenne Mountain, 1, 6, 13, 49,
  53, 54
  upgrade Programme, 54
  systems failures, 53
Chilmark RGHQ, 184-188
  development of new RGHQ, 187
  plans and sections, 187, 188
Chiltern Local Authority bunker,
  218
Chislehurst Local Authority
  bunker, 218
Churchill, Winston, 248, 249
Cincinnati, 24
Cirencester, National Grid
  strategic supply store, 243
Civil Defence (UK), 147, 149, 150,
  157, 198, 201, 242, 276
  abolition of, 276
  Bedminster, 198
  Birmingham, 201
  Bristol, 198
  Bristol Group Controls, 157
  Devizes, 194
  funding for 1981 expansion, 150
  Hastings, 201
  in the United Kingdom 1945-68,
    147
  Swindon, 194
  Trowbridge, 194
  wartime, 242
  Wiltshire, 194

Civil Defence Act, 153
Civil Defence Corps, Local
  Authority responsibilities, 193
Civil Defense Policy (US), 20
Civil Service Sports Club, 256
Clapham Common Deep Level
  Tube Shelter, 253
Clapham North Deep Level Tube
  Shelter, 253-254
Clapham South Deep Level Tube
  Shelter, 253-254
Clear, Alaska, 42, 59
  (BMEWS), 59
Clinton Point, 38
Clubhouse Quarry, 18
Clwyd, Local Authority bunker,
  208
CND, 148, 149, 163
Code Translation Data Service, 46
Cold Hesledon ROTOR station,
  75, 100
Cold Stores, WWII, adaptation
  as S-RCs, 185
Colorado Springs, 52
Comberton ROTOR station, 75,
  100
Comprehensive Radar Stations,
  89, 91
CONAD, 49
Conisbrough AAOR, 117
Contingency Impact Analysis
  System, 15
'Continuity of Government', 13,
  59, 255, 271
Control and Reporting Centres,
  95
'Control Chain', viii
Controller, Defence
  Communications Network
  (CDCN), 99
Conwy Local Authority bunker,
  208
Cornwall Local Authority
  bunker, 208
Corporation of London Local
  Authority bunker, 208
Corsham (Wiltshire) 99, 136, 151,
  255, 256, 271, 273, 274,
  Brown's Quarry, 274
  cold war facilities at, 274
  Emergency Government War
  Headquarters, 136
Corsham Emergency Government
  War Headquarters, 151
Corsham quarries, 99, 273
  new government works, 1979-82,
  273
Counterfeit banknotes, 17
County War Headquarters, 200-201
  legislation, 200
  Dorchester, 201

Taunton, 201,
Trowbridge, 201
Craigiebarns House, 146
Craigiehall AAOR, 117
Craigmore, Inverness, 202
Cranberry Portage, 34
Crawley Borough Council, Local
  Authority bunker, 218
Cricklewood, Admiralty Charts
  Depot, 248
Crisis Relocation Planning (CRP),
  23
Croker River, 38
Crosslaw ROTOR station, 76, 100
Crowborough RGHQ, 184-186
Cruise missiles in Britain, 149
Cruise missiles, Soviet, 53
Cuba, 11, 14, 22, 68, 147, 163,
  199, 271, 272, 273,
Cultybraggan, 187

Dacorum Borough Council Local
  Authority bunker, 218
Dagenham Borough Council
  Local Authority bunker, 218
Dalrymple-Hay, Sir Horace, 252
Danby Beacon, 75
'Danger Official Secret RSG-6':
  Full text of 'Spies for Peace'
  pamphlet, 165
Dartford Local Authority bunker,
  218
Dartmoor Prison, 18
Dawson Creek, 34
DCMO, 278
DCSA, 275
De Normann, Eric, 249
Deep Level Tube Shelters, 253-254
  Belsize Park, 253-254
  Camden Town, 253
  Chancery Lane, 253
  Clapham Common, 253
  Clapham North, 253-254
  Clapham South, 253-254
  Goodge Street, 253
  Oval, 253
  St Paul's, 253
  Stockwell, 253-254
Defence Communication Services
  Agency (DCSA), 275
Defence Crisis Management
  Organization (DCMO), 278
Defence Fixed Telecommunications
  Service (DFTS), 275
Defence Support Programme
  communications satellites, 60
Defence Transport and
  Movement Agency, video link
  to DCMO, 278
Defence White Paper 1946, 123
Defence White Paper 1947, 123

Defence White Paper 1957, 148
Delbert, 65
Demarcation Bay, 38
Denton, Texas, 24
Denver, Colorado, 24
Department of Defence
  Directorate 5100.30, 9
'Deterrence' policy, 90
Devizes Civil Defence control, 194
Devon Local Authority bunker,
  208
Dewar Lakes, 39
DFTS, 275
Diefenbaker, John, 64
Diefenbunker, 14, 64-66, 266
Disaster Finance Office, 15
Disaster Personnel Operations
  Division, 15
Distant Early Warning Line, 25-53
  upgrading of, 37, 53
  closure dates, 38
District Councils, Formation of,
  203
Dollis Hill, 248-251
Doncaster, Water Board bunker
Doppler principle, 34, 36, 37
Dorchester, Dorset County War
  HQ, 201
Douglas Wood, 75
Dover AAOR, 117
Dover, Local Authority bunker,
  218
Drakelow, 141, 163, 171-173, 185
  development as RSG, 171
  layout plans, 172
  conversion to RSG, 163
Drakelow Unearthed, viii
Driftwood Bay, 38
Drone Hill, 75
Drytree, 75
Dudley Zoo, Tunnels beneath, 171
Duluth, Minnesota, 26
'Dumpy', 184
Dunkirk, 75
Durham Local Authority bunker,
  208

Ealing Local Authority bunker,
  208
East Kilbride (Torrance House),
  AAOR, 117
East Kilbride (Torrance House)
  Scottish Zone HQ, 117
Eastleigh Borough Council Local
  Authority bunker, 219
Eden District, Local Authority
  bunker, 219
Edinburgh Local Authority
  bunker, 219
Edinburgh Island, 38
Eisenhower, General D, 34, 254

Electronic Counter Counter measures, 61
Elvaston AAOR, 117
Emergency Broadcasting Facility (Canada), 68
Emergency Government Headquarters Communications Planning Panel, 260
Emergency Government War Headquarters, 265-277
closure of Corsham site announced, 276
upgrading, 1979-82, 273
Emergency Government War Headquarters Inter-Service Committee (EGWHISC), 267 et seq
Emergency Measures Organization (EMO), 64
Emergency Planning Canada (EPC), formation of, 69
Emergency Planning Guidelines for Local Authorities 1984, 204
Emergency Regional Government in the United Kingdom, 152
EMO, 68
Ent AFB, 26, 52
Epping Forest Local Authority bunker, 219
Epsom and Ewell Local Authority bunker, 220
Essential Services bunkers, 242
Essex Local Authority bunker, 208
Essex County Standby War Headquarters, 120

Faeroes, 36, 94
Fairbanks, 40
Fairford, 1
Fairlight ROTOR station, 76, 101
Fallout protection, 12, 22
Faraday House, 252
Fareham, Local Authority bunker, 220
Farrid Head, 91
Federal Government Emergency War Headquarters (Canada, 64-65
Federal Reserve (USA), 20
FEMA, 14, 15, 22-24
regional bunkers, 23-24
Fitzpatrick, G.R.D, Chairman of EGWHISC, 267
Flag Officer Submarines, at Northwood, 277
'Flexible Response' policy, 94
Folly, 75
Foreness ROTOR station, 76, 101
Fort Bridgewood AAOR, 117
Fort Custer, 27
Fort Fareham AAOR, 117

use as Fareham Borough council bunker, 117
Fort Knox, Kentucky, 27
Fort Lee, 27
Fort Pepperell, 31
Forward Defense, 3
Four Minute Warning, 58, 136
Fox, Steve, viii
Foxe Channel, 36
FRC-56 tropospheric scatter , 45
Frodsham AAOR, 118
Frodsham, Cheshire County Emergency HQ, 118
Fylingdales, 25, 42, 58, 60-62, 93, 136-137
BMEWS, cost of construction, 60
choice as BMEWS site, 60
upgrade programme, 62

Gaerloch AAOR, 202
Gailes ROTOR station, 75, 101
General Strike, 1926, 152
George, Southern California, 26
Germany, plans for invasion of Britain, 250
Gjoa Haven, 39
Gladman Point, 39
Glamorgan Local Authority bunker, 209
Gloucester, Water Board bunker, 243
Gold Reserves , storage of
Goldsborough ROTOR station, 76, 101
underground fire, 101
Goodge Street, Deep Level Tube Shelter, 253
Goose Bay, 31, 34
GPO, 230, 252, 275
GPO deep level cable tunnel, 233
GPO Repeater Stations, 231, 234-242
Portsdown, 231
Queslett, 231
Rothwell Haigh, 231
Stockport, 231
Swinton, 231
Warmley, 231
GPO Telecommunication System, post-war weakness of, 255
GPO, involvement in ROTOR, 74
GPTN, 275
Grand Forks AFB, 30, 52
Gravesham Local Authority bunker, 221
Great Falls, Montana, 34
Great Whale River, 34
Greater London, emergency government of, 205
Greater Manchester Local

Authority bunker, 220
'Greek Island', 15
'Green Garlic', installed at Bawdsey, 97
Greenbrier, 14-17
Greenland, 36
Griffiss, New York, 26
GUARDIAN, 230, 234
'Guardian' Class vessels, 37
Gulf War, 55
Gwent Local Authority bunker, 209
Gwynedd Local Authority bunker, 209

Hack Green ROTOR station, 75-76, 101-102, 185
civilian ATC role, 102
conversion to RGHQ, 102
Hackney Local Authority bunker, 221
Hall Beach, 36, 39, 41
Hall Committee, 255
Hamilton, San Francisco, 26
Hammersmith, Local Authority bunker, 221
Hampshire Local Authority bunker, 209
HANDEL, 137
Hanley, Jeremy, 277
Hanscomb Field, 52
Happidrome, 82, 100, 105, 173
Hope Cove, 173
Murlough Bay, 105
Comberton, 100
Harding River, 38
Harrogate, Water Board bunker, 243
Harrow Local Authority bunker, 221
Harrow, Wartime bunkers, 248
Harrow Citadels, Communications problems, 251
Hartland Point ROTOR station, 75, 102
Hastings Borough Civil Defence Control, 201, 221
Hat Island, 39
Hawaii, 37
Hayscastle Cross, 75
Herefordshire Local Authority bunker, 210
Hereford City Council Local Authority bunker, 221
Hertford, Sub-Regional Headquarters, 174
Hertfordshire Local Authority bunker, 210
Hexham Cold Store, 179, 184
'High Point Special Facility'
High Street, 75
High Wycombe, 95

Highland Council Local
  Authority bunker, 146, 203, 210
Hill Head, 75
Hofn, 42
Holabird, Root and Burgee, 26
Holborn, LPTB escalators, 258
Holcombe (Shepton Mallet),
  Bristol Water emergency
  bunker, 246
Holmpton ROTOR station, 75,
  102
Home Defence Planning
  Assumptions 1957, 149
Home Defence Review 1980, 182,
  204
Home Defence War Room, 256
Home Office Working Party on
  War Rooms, 1949, 153
Hope Cove ROTOR station, 75,
  91, 102-103, 157, 163, 173, 179,
  184-185
  abandoned, 91
  RAF Fighter Control School, 102
  conversion to RSG-7, 103, 163
  conversion to RGHQ, 103
  conversion of adjacent
Hopedale, 34
Hopton ROTOR station, 76, 103
Horseferry Road, 254-256
Horseferry Rotundas, 252
Horseferry Tandem, 256
Horseguard's Parade, Admiralty
  Rotunda, 252
Horsham District Local
  Authority bunker, 222
Horton River, 38
House of Representatives,
  accommodation for, 15
Huddersfield, Water Board
  bunker, 253
Hull, Water Board bunker, 243
Humberside Local Authority
  bunker, 210
Humberside County War HQ, 122
Huntingdon Local Authority
  bunker, 222
Huntington, Samuel, 23
Hydrogen Bomb, 6, 147, 90, 254
  effect of fallout, 147
  Soviet, 6, 254
  Soviet, effect upon ROTOR
  project, 90

IBM, 28
ICARUS, 233
Iceland, 36
Icy Cape, 38
IFF, 30
Ilkley, use of Craiglands Hotel as
  S-RC, 179
Inter-Departmental Working

Group on War Measures
  (Canada), 63
Inverbervie ROTOR station, 75,
  104
Ipswich Local Authority bunker,
  222
Ipswich, AUTOVON station, 10
IUKADGE, 94

Japan, 152
Jenny Lind Island, 39
Joint Strategic Target Planning
  Staff

K I Sawyer AFB, 28
Kangok Fjord, 39
Keats Point, 38
Keflavik, 42
Kelvedon Hatch, 76, 104, 173-174,
  179, 183-184, 206
  RGHQ, Sub-Regional
  Headquarters, 174
  use as S-RC, 179
Kelvin Hughes projector, 86, 105,
  113
  at Portland, 105
  at Wartling, 113
Kemnal Manor, 156, 183, 205
Kent Local Authority bunker, 210
Kenton Bar, 155
Keynsham, National Grid
  emergency control centre, 243
Kilchiaran ROTOR station, 88,
  105
Killard Point ROTOR station,
  function as RTS, 92
Kilworth Park, Devon, 228
Kings Standing, Sussex, 186
KINGSWAY, 230-234
  plan of underground exchange,
  231
Kirknewton War Room,
  Conversion to RSG, 164
Kirtland, New Mexico, 26
Knebworth, British Rail control
  bunker, 246
Kneller Hall, 248
Knob Lake, 34
Kogru, 38
Kulusuk, 39
KYCC (Kingsway Computer
  Centre), 233

L4 communication network, 51
Lac St. Denis, 31
Lady Franklin Point, 38
Lailor River, 39
Langtoft ROTOR station, 75, 105
Lansdown AAOR, 118-120, 137
  occupation by Royal Observer
  Corps, 118, 137

layout plan, 119
  occupation by Avon Fire
  Brigade, 120
Larson AFB, 27-28
LASHUP, 25-27
'Launch on Warning' policy, 59
Lawford Heath RGHQ, 141, 185
Leeds, Water Board bunker, 243
Leicestershire Local Authority
  bunker, 211
Leominster District Local
  Authority bunker, 222
Library of Congress, 20
LINESMAN, 93-94
LINESMAN/MEDIATOR, 93,
  235
  land-line communications for,
  235
Lippit's Hill AAOR, 120
Lippit's Hill
  Metropolitan Police North
  London War Headquarters, 120
Lisburn AAOR, 120
Liverpool Bay, 38
Llandudno Junction Cold Store,
  185
Lloyd George, 11
Local Authority bunkers, 193-229
  Ashford Borough Council, 11
  Avon County, 207
  Aylesbury Vale District, 215
  Barrow District Council, 215
  Basildon District Council, 215
  Basingstoke, 216
  Beaconsfield, 216
  Berkshire, 207
  Bermondsey, 216
  Bexley, 216
  Birmingham Corporation, 216
  Brecklands District, 216
  Brentford and Chiswick, 216
  Bristol City Council, 217
  Broadlands District, 217
  Bromsgrove District, 217
  Buckinghamshire, 207
  Camberwell, 217
  Camden, 217
  Canterbury, 217
  Castle Morpeth, 217
  Castle Point Borough Council,
  217
  Charnwood District, 217
  Chelmsford, 217
  Cherwell, 218
  Cheshire, 208
  Chiltern, 218
  Chislehurst, 218
  Clwyd, 208
  Conwy, 208
  Cornwall, 208
  Corporation of London, 208

Crawley Borough Council, 218
Dacorum Borough Council, 218
Dagenham Borough Council, 218
Dartford, 218
Devon, 208
Dover, 218
Durham, 208
Ealing, 218
Eastbourne, 218
Eastleigh Borough Council, 219
Eden District, 219
Edinburgh, 219
Epping Forest , 219
Epsom and Ewell, 220
Essex, 208
Fareham, 220
Gazetteer, 206
Glamorgan, 209
Gravesham, 221
Greater Manchester, 220
Gwent, 209
Gwynedd, 209
Hackney, 221
Hammersmith, 221
Hampshire, 209
Harrow, 221
Hastings Borough Council, 221
Hereford, 210
Hereford City Council, 221
Hertfordshire, 210
Highland Council, 210
Horsham District, 222
Humberside, 210
Huntingdon, 222
Ipswich, 222
Kent, 210
Leicestershire, 211
Leominster District, 222
Luton, 222
Malden, 222
Malvern Hills, 222
Mansfield, 222
Matlock, 222
Medway, 222
Melton Borough Council, 223
Merseyside, 223
Mid-Devon, 223
Milton Keynes, 223
New Forest District, 223
Norfolk, 211
North Devon, 223
North East Lincolnshire, 223
North Somerset, 223
North Weald, 223
North Wiltshire, 224
North Yorkshire, 224
Northallerton, 223
Nottinghamshire, 211
Oxford City Council, 224

Oxfordshire, 211
Poole, 224
Portsmouth, 224
Powys, 212
Redditch Borough Council, 224
Restormel Borough Council, 224
Richmond upon Thames, 225
Rotherham, 225
Rutland, 225
Salisbury and South Wiltshire, 225
Sevenoaks, 225
Shepway (Kent), 225
Somerset, 212
South Cambridgeshire, 225
South Gloucestershire, 225
South Herefordshire, 226
South Oxfordshire, 226
South Scurlough, 226
Southampton, 225
Southwark, 226
St Albans, 227
Staffordshire, 214
Strathclyde, 227
Stroud, 227
Suffolk, 214
Surrey, 214
Swale Borough Council, 227
Tayside, 214
Tendring, 227
Test Valley, 227
Thanet, 227
Thurrock, 227
Tonbridge and Malling, 227
Torbay, 227
Uttlesford District, 227
Wallasey Borough Council, 228
Warwickshire, 214
Wealden District, 228
Wellingborough, 228
West Devon, 228
West Glamorgan, 215
West Oxfordshire, 228
West Sussex, 215
West Wiltshire, 228
Wigan, 228
Wiltshire, 215
Woking, 229
Worcester City Council, 228
Wychavon, 229
Wycombe, 229
Yorkshire, 215
Loks Island, 39
London Group Controls, 156, 161, 183
and S-RC organization, 183
plans and section, 161
Lonely, 38
Longley Lane ROTOR station, 76, 105
occupation by Royal Observer Corps, 105

Longstaff Bluff, 39
'Looking Glass', 6
Loughborough Cold Store, 179, 184
use as S-RC, 179
LPTB (London Passenger Transport Board), 252, 258
escalators, Holborn, 258
escalators, St Paul's, 258
involvement in government tunnel construction, 252
Luke AFB, 28
Luton Local Authority bunker

Machinery of Government Home Defence Committee, 273
Machinery of Government in War Planning Team, 266
Mackar Inlet, 39
Mackenzie King, 25
Mackenzie River, 36
MacLean Committee, 255
Macmillan, Harold, 93
Malden Local Authority bunker, 222
Malmstrom AFB, 28
Malvern Hills, Local Authority bunker, 222
Manchester AAOR, 120
Manod Quarries, storage of art treasures, 247
Mansfield Local Authority bunker, 222
Mansfield, Water Board bunker, 243
Marconi 246 A/H Radar, 102, 111
Marconi company, 74, 84, 99, 102, 108
Marconi S259 Radar, at Buchan, 99
Marconi T264A Radar, 108
'Martello', 112
Martlesham Heath, 42
Master Control Centres, 92
Master Radar Stations, 92
Matlock Local Authority bunker, 222
McChord, Washington, 26
McGill University, 34
McGuire AFB, 27
McGuire AFB, 28
McIntyre AFB, 38
MEDIATOR, 93
Medway Local Authority bunker, 222
Melton Borough Council Local Authority bunker, 223
Mercian Trump III' Civil Defence exercise, 173
Merriman, J, 235
Merseyside Local Authority bunker, 223

Merstham AAOR, 120
Metropolitan Police North
London Emergency War
Headquarters, 120
Metropolitan Police South
London Emergency War
Headquarters, 120
Mid-Canada Line, 25-35
Mid-Identification Zone, 34
Mid-Devon, Local Authority
bunker, 223
Mill Hill, London Group
Control, 157, 183, 205, 206
Milton Keynes, Local Authority
bunker, 223
Minimal Essential Emergency
Communications Network, 10
Ministry of Home Security, 252
Minot AFB, 28, 30
Mistley AAOR, 120
Essex County Standby War
Headquarters, 120
MIT, 27, 28, 43
MITRE Corporation, 46
Monkton Farleigh, 19
Montague House, Whitehall, 253
Mormond Hill, 42
Mott, Hay and Anderson, 231
Moulton, AVM, AOC RAF No.
90 Group, 93
Mount Pony, 14-20
Mount Weather, 13-15
Murlough Bay ROTOR station,
88, 105
Mutual Vulnerability concept, 53
Mutually Assured Destruction
(MAD), 59

Nanaimo, 65
National Attack Warning System
(Canada), 67
National Command Centre
Afloat, 6
National Emergency Airborne
Command Post, 9, 11
National Grid, 204, 242, 243
emergency control centre Becca
Hall, 243
emergency control centre East
Grinstead, 243
emergency control centre
Keynsham, 243
emergency control centre Kings
Norton, 243
emergency control centre
Manchester, 243
emergency control centre
Rothwell Haigh, 242
St Paul's tube station, 242
Wartime emergency measures,
242

Grid strategic supply stores,
243
National Military Command
Centre, 9
National Processing Service
Centre, 15
NATO, 63, 277
Neatishead ROTOR station, 63,
75, 91-92, 98, 105,
Comprehensive Radar Station,
105
Control and Reporting Centre,
95
fire in underground control
room, 105
LINESMAN/MEDIATOR, 105
PLAN AHEAD, 105
RTS, 92
underground fire, 105
Netherbutton, 75
New Forest District Local
Authority bunker, 223
Nicholson Peninsula, 38
'Night Watch', 6, 9
NIKE, 29, 51
NIKE-X, 29
Nikolski, 38
Nixon, Richard, 13
No.2 Signals Brigade, 275
at Basil Hill Barracks, 275
at Sopley, 275
NORAD, 1, 6, 13, 29-30, 34, 36,
40, 42, 49, 52, 427-M project, 52
Direction Centres, 29
Sectors, 29
Norfolk Local Authority bunker,
211
North Warning System, 54
North American air defence
communication systems, 41
North American Air Defence
Modernization Agreement, 37
North American Radar, 25 et seq
North Atlantic Radio System, 42
North Coates, 92
North Devon Local Authority
bunker, 223
North East Lincolnshire Local
Authority bunker, 223
North Rotunda, 251, 254, 255,
256,
North Somerset Local Authority
bunker, 223
North Warning System, 37, 58
North Weald Local Authority
bunker, 223
North Wiltshire Local Authority
bunker, 224
North Yorkshire Local Authority
bunker, 224
Northallerton Local Authority

bunker, 223
Northallerton Water Board
bunker, 243
Northwood, 151, 276-277
Norton, 28
Nottingham War Room, 162, 164
conversion to RSG, 162
new works associated with
RSG status, 164
Nottinghamshire Local Authority
bunker, 211
Nuclear Detonation & Fallout
Reporting System (Canada), 64
Nuclear Reporting Cell, 99, 136,
273
Nudluardjuk Lake, 39

Offut AFB, 9-10
Oliktok, 38
Olney, Maryland, 24
Operation CLOVERLEAF, 127
'Orange Yeoman', 118
'Orlit' posts, 125
Oval, Deep Level Tube Shelter,
253
Oxford City Council Local
Authority bunker, 224
Oxfordshire Local Authority
bunker, 211

Packard Foundation, 20
PADDOCK, 20, 249-250
Padmore Working Party, 255, 260
Padmore, Thomas, 255
Patrington ROTOR station, 91,
92, 94, 97
'Patriot' missile system, 12, 55
PAVE PAWS, 60
Pear Tree House, 156, 183
Peard Bay, 38
Pearl Harbor, 1, 6, 58
Pembroke AAOR, 120
Penhold, 65
Pentagon, 6-7
Permanent Joint Board on
Defence, 25
Pershing missile, 69
Pevensey, 75
Phased Array Radar, 40, 53
Phoenix Report (Canada), 69
PINDAR, 276-278
commissioned 1992, 277
cost of construction, 278
details revealed to Parliament,
277
serious fire during construction,
278
Pinegap radars, 37
Pinetree Line, 25-40
PJBD, 24-25
PLAN AHEAD, 92

Proposed R12 bunkers, 92
Plan position indicators
    (installation in ROTOR
    stations), 76
Plymouth AAOR, 121
Point Barrow, Alaska, 36, 38
Point Lay, 38
POLEVAULT, 34, 41-42
Police National Computer, 160
Poling, 75
Poltimore Park, 142
Poole Local Authority bunker, 224
Port Heiden, 38
Port Moller, 38
Portland ROTOR station, 75,
    84-85, 87, 105
    FPS-3 equipment, 84-85
Porton Down, trials at Westwood,
    247
Portreath, 95
Portsdown, GPO Repeater
    Station, 231
Portsmouth Local Authority
    bunker, 224
Powys Local Authority bunker, 212
PR1 & PR2 Repeaters, 230, 235,
    237, 240-241,
    air conditioning, 237
    construction details, 237
    cross section drawing, 241
    layout plans, 240
    special air filters, 237
Presidential Directive 41, 22
Presidential Succession Act,
    1947, 13
Prestatyn ROTOR station, 88, 108
Prestwick, proposed BMEWS
    site, 59
Protect & Survive, 150
Provincial Government
    Headquarters (Canada), 65
PSA, 273
Public Record Office, 254
Public shelter (Canada), 68
Python concept, 273

Quarry Operations Centre, 273, 275

RAF Barton Hall, 139
RAF Caledonian Sector
    Operations Room, 134
RAF Fixed Telecommunications
    System, 275
RAF Hawthorn, 274
RAF No.1 Signals Unit Rudloe
    Manor, 275
RAF No.10 Group HQ, 99, 274
RAF No.6 Signals Unit, 275
RAF South West Switching
    Centre, 274
RAF Strike Command HQ, video

link to DCMO, 278
RAF Strike Command Interim
    Alternate War Headquarters, 98
RAF Upavon, 273
RAF Waddington, 141
RAFFTS, 275
Raigmore, 146
Raven Rock Mountain, 6, 10-14
Raytheon, 36
RCAF, 25, 31
Reading War Room,
    Communication centre for
    Warren Row RSG, 165
Reagan, Ronald, 23, 37
Redditch Borough Council Local
    Authority bunker, 224
Regional Government
    Headquarters (RGHQ), 184-187
    'Dumpy', 184
    Anstruther, 184
    Bawburgh, 184
    Brackla, 185
    Chilmark, 184-187
    Crowborough, 184-186
    Cultybraggan, 187
    Drakelow, 185
    Hack Green, 185
    Hertford, 184
    Hexham, 184
    Hope Cove, 184
    Kelvedon Hatch, 184
    Lawford Heath
    Llandudno Junction, 185
    Loughborough, 184
    Preston, 185
    Shipton, 184
    Skendleby, 184
    Swynnerton, 185
    Ullenwood, 184
    Warren Row, 184
    Wrexham (Boras) ROC HQ,
    185
Regional Seats of Government,
    160-164, 178, 266
    Anstruther ROTOR station, 163
    Barnton Quarry, 163
    Brecon Barracks, 162-163
    Cambridge War Room, 162-164
    Catterick Barracks, 162-163
    Demise of RSG scheme, 178
    Devolution of power to, 266
    Drakelow, 163
    Easingwold CD College, 162
    Fullwood Barracks, Preston,
    162, 163
    Hope Cove, 162-163
    Kirknewton, 164
    Nottingham War Room, 162-164
    Reading War Room, 162
    Shipton ROTOR station, 163
    Shrewsbury Barracks, 162

Specifications for, 162
Torrance House, 163
Tunbridge Wells War Room, 163
Warren Row, Henley on Thames,
    163
Regional War Rooms, 152-162
    Birmingham, 153, 159
    Bristol, 153
    Cambridge, 153, 155-156
    Cambridge, Conversion to
    RSG, 156
    Cardiff, 153, 159
    Construction, 154
    Kirknewton, 153, 159
    Leeds, 153, 155
    London sub-regions, 153
    Manchester, 153, 159
    Newcastle, 153, 155
    Nottingham, 153, 155
    Plans and section, 154
    Plans for provision of, 153
    Reading, 153, 157
    Tunbridge Wells, 153, 160
Reserve Bank of Richmond, 20
Reserve UK Air Defence
    Operations Centre, 144
Resource Interruption
    Management System, 15
Restormel Borough Council Local
    Authority bunker, 224
RGHQ (Regional Government
    Headquarters), 103, 121, 141
    Hope Cove, 103
    Lawford Heath, 141
    Ullenwood, 121
Rhydymwyn, 256
Richards-Gebaur AFB, 27
Richmond upon Thames Local
    Authority bunker, 225
Ringstead, 75
Robin's, Georgia, 26
Roosevelt, 2, 25
Rotherham Local Authority
    bunker, 225
Rothwell Haigh GPO Repeater
    Station, 231, 236
Rothwell Haigh National Grid
    regional control, 242
ROTOR, 26, 27, 71-122, 123,
    235-236
    1958 Plan, 90
    Comprehensive Radar Stations,
    89
    construction of SOCs, 83
    entrance guardhouse, plan, 79
    GPO involvement, 74
    'Happidrome' conversion, 82
    impact of hydrogen bomb, 90
    installation of fixed coil
    displays, 87
    Kelvin Hughes projectors, 86

Land-line communications, 235, 236
map of stations, 77
Marconi company, 74, 84
Operations room designations, 78
origins of, 71
Plan position indicators, 76
R1 bunker plan, 79
R3 bunker plan, 80
R4 bunker plan, 80, 82
ROC involvement, 123
SOCs abandoned, 91
table of radar stations, 96
Type 80 Radar, 85-90
typical site description, 81
US AN/FPS-3 radar, 83
US AN/FPS-3 radar, 85
ROTOR 1, 73-75
locations of stations, 75
ROTOR II, 86
ROTOR III, 87-88
principal components, 87
Rowley Island, 39
Royal Family, emergency accommodation, 271
Royal Family, role in recovery phase of nuclear war, 272
Royal Navy Commander in Chief Fleet, at Northwood, 277
Royal Navy UHF SATCOM shore station at Northwood, 277
Royal Observer Corps, 74, 123-146,
Caledonian Sector, 145
function within ROTOR, 74
Group and Sector Headquarters, 130
history, 123
increased funding for, in face of nuclear threat, 127
re-formation, 1947, 123
re-organization in mid 1950s, 124
Sector organization, 1950, 124
Sector re-organization, 1954, 124
Sector re-organization, 1968, 138
standown of wartime organization, 123
underground observation posts, 127-129
upgrade of communications equipment, 139
Royal Observer Corps Group Headquarters, 141-146,
Aberdeen, 146
Ayr, 145
Bedford, 141
Boras (Wrexham), 143
Bristol, 142
Bromley, 134, 141
Carlisle, 145
Carmarthen, 143

Colchester, 140
Dundee, 146
Durham, 145
Edinburgh, 134, 145
Exeter, 142
Fiskerton, 134, 139, 141
Glasgow, 145
Horsham, 139, 140
Inverness, 146
Lansdown, 139-140
Lawford Heath, 141
Leeds, 134, 139, 141
Lisburn, 132, 145
Maidstone, 134, 139
Norwich, 141
Oban, 139, 145
Oxford, 134, 140
Preston, 132, 139, 144
Shrewsbury, 143
Truro, 139, 142
Watford, 139, 140
Winchester, 140
Yeovil, 142
York, 142
RSG-7, Hope Cove, 103
Russia, 2
Rutland Local Authority bunker, 225
Rye, 75

'Safeguard' ABM system, 52-53
SAGE, 26-40
integration of Texas Towers, 45-46
Saglek, 37
Salisbury Civil Defence bunker, 194-195, 225
SALT, 52
SALT II, 53
Sandwich ROTOR station, 75, 91, 108
LINESMAN/MEDIATOR, 108
Civil ATC function, 108
Sango ROTOR station, 75
Satellite Teleregistration Centre, 15
Satellite warning, 14
Saxa Vord ROTOR station, 88, 91-92, 94, 109
wind damage, 109
Scarnish ROTOR station, 75, 91
School Hill, 75
Scottish Zone Control, 159
Sea of Okhotsk, 40
Seaton Snook ROTOR station, 75, 91, 109
Secret Underground Cities, vii
Sector Operations Centres, abandonment, 91
SEEK IGLOO, 40
Selfridge, Michigan, 26
Senate, accommodation for (USA), 15

Sennen, 75
Serratia Marcesans, 247
Sevenoaks Local Authority bunker, 225
Severn Trent Water, Gloucester emergency bunker, 244-245
Shadowgraph Ground Zero Indicator, 130
Sheffield Water Board bunker, 243
Shepherd Bay, 39
Shepway (Kent) Local Authority bunker, 225
Shetland, 36
Shilo, 65
Shingle Point, 38
Shipton ROTOR station, 76, 109, 163, 184
conversion to RSG, 163
SRHQ, 109
'Short sharp war', 23
Short Term Plan (ADGB), 73, 123
Simpson Lake, 39
Sisimut, 39
Skendleby ROTOR station, 75, 91, 110, 184
RGHQ, 110
Skipton, Water Board bunker, 243
SLEWC, 94
'Smart' weapons, 12
Snaefell ROTOR station, 88, 110
Somerset Local Authority bunker, 212-213
Sopley ROTOR station, 75,91, 110-111
civil ATC function, 111
UK Land Forces National Military Command Centre, 111
South Cambridgeshire Local Authority bunker, 225
South Gloucestershire Local Authority bunker, 226
South Herefordshire Local Authority bunker, 226
South Oxfordshire Local Authority bunker, 226
South Scurlough Local Authority bunker, 226
South West Switching Centre (RAF South West Control), 274
Southall London Group Control, 157, 183, 206
Soviet Target Assessment, 1967, 175-178
Space Control Centre (NORAD), 55
Space Defence Operations Centre, 52
Space Surveillance Centre, 52
'Spies for Peace', 148, 163, 165, 184
Spokane, 34

Spring Quarry, 18, 171- 173, 247, 255-258
aircraft engine factory, 171
closure of aero engine factory, 258
conversion to aero engine factory, 257
storage of art treasures, 247
S-RC (Sub-Regional Controls), 157, 179-181
Bawburgh, 179
Bempton ROTOR bunker, 179
Brackla, 181
Craiglands Hotel, Ilkley, 179
Hertford, 179
Hexham Cold Store, 179
Hope Cove, 179
Kelvedon Hatch, 179
Loughborough Cold Store, 179
Shipton ROTOR bunker, 179
Ullenwood, 179
Warren Row, 179
SSPAR (BMEWS), 62
St Albans Local Authority bunker, 227
St Anne's ROTOR station, 75, 91, 111
Civil ATC function, 111
St Margaret's ROTOR station, 75, 91, 111
St Margaret's, New Brunswick, 31
St Paul's Tube Station, 242, 253, 258
Deep Level Tube Shelter, 253
LPTB escalators, 258
National Grid wartime control centre, 242
St Twynell's ROTOR station, 75, 91, 111
Staffordshire Local Authority bunker, 214
Stage 1 radar (ROTOR), 73
Standard Oil Company, 19
'Station Z', 248
Staxton Wold, 75, 92, 94
'Stay Put' Home Defence policy, 175
Stead, 28
Stenigot, 75
Stewart AFB, 27
Stewart, New York, 26
Stockport, GPO Repeater Station, 231
Stockwell, Deep Level Tube Shelter, 253-254
Stoke Holy Cross, 75
Stokenchurch, microwave tower, 235
Stoney Mountain, 34
Storey's Gate, 249

Storm Hills, 38
Strategic Air Command, 10, 56
Strath Report, 255
Strathclyde Local Authority bunker, 227
Stroud Local Authority bunker, 227
Sturt Point, 39
Sub Regional Controls (S-RCs)
Sub-Regional Headquarters, 174
Bawburgh, 174
Brackla, 174
Bristol War Room, 174
Hertford, 174
Kelvedon Hatch, 174
Ullenwood, 174
SUBTERFUGE, 255, 256
Delays in construction, 256
Suffolk Local Authority bunker, 214
Surrey Local Authority bunker, 214
Swale Borough Council Local Authority bunker, 227
Swansea AAOR, 121
West Glamorgan County War Headquarters, 121
Swindon, construction of Civil Defence bunkers, 194
Swingate, 75
Swinton GPO Repeater Station, 231
Swynnerton ROF, 174, 181, 185
layout plan of RHHQ 9.1, 181
Sub-Regional Headquarters, 174
Sub-Regional Headquarters, 174

Taunton, Somerset County War HQ, 201
Tayside Local Authority bunker, 214
Tayside Regional Council, 146
Teeside AAOR, 121
Telephone Exchanges, underground, 230
Tendring Local Authority bunker, 227
Test Valley Local Authority bunker, 227
Texas Towers, 43-48
building contracts, 43
collapse of TT4, 45
integration into SAGE, 45
locations, 44
shut down and dismantling, 48
Thames Water, Blunsdon emergency bunker, 244
Thanet Local Authority bunker, 227
Thomasville, Georgia, 24
Thompson, E.P, 150

Thor missile, shortcomings, 60
Thule - Cape Dyer troposcatter system, 41
Thule, Greenland (BMEWS), 59
Thurrock Local Authority bunker, 227
Tin City, 40
Tinker, Oklahoma, 26
TOCSIN, 64
Tom Butler & Co. Ltd, 205
Tomahawk Missile Land Attack Cruise Missile Support Centre, at Northwood, 277
Tonbridge and Malling Local Authority bunker, 227
Topsham, Maine, 27
Torbay Local Authority bunker, 227
Torrance House AAOR, 159
conversion to RSG, 163
TPS-43 Radar, Spoils of Falkland War, 99
Transatlantic Cable, via Warmley, 242
Trelanvean, 75
Treleaver ROTOR station, 75, 91, 111
Trewan Sands ROTOR station, 75, 112
Trimingham ROTOR station, 75, 91, 112
Type 91 Radar, 112
'Tripwire' policy, 12, 59, 90
Tropospheric scatter, 36
Trowbridge, Wiltshire, 194, 201
Civil Defence, 194
Wiltshire County War HQ, 201
Truax AFB, 27
Truleigh Hill ROTOR station, 76, 84, 112
FPS-3 equipment, 84
Truman, Harry, 7, 22
Tukialik, 39
Tuktoyaktuk, 38
Tunbridge Wells War Room, conversion to RSG, 162
Tunnel Quarry, 99, 256-257, 274
cost of construction, 257
TURNSTILE, 272
Type 80 Radar, 85-92, 90, 92, 118
weakness of, 89
retained at PLAN AHEAD stations, 92
Type 84 Radar, 92, 94,, 97, 105
installed at Bawdsey, 97
Type 85 Radar, 92, 94
Type 91 Radar, 112

Uig ROTOR station, 88, 91, 112
UK Civil Defence, 147 et seq
UK Land Command HQ,

Wilton, video link to DCMO, 278
UKCAOC, 95
UKWMO, 133-136, 138, 145-151, 273,
  abandonment, 151
  at Corsham, 273
  Home Office funding for, 136
  National HQ, Longley Lane, Preston, 133-135
Ullenwood AAOR, 121, 157, 174, 179, 184-185
  Gloucester County War Headquarters, 121
  Regional Government Headquarters, 121
  Sub-Regional Headquarters, 174
  use as S-RC, 179
Underground factories, adapted as cold-war citadels, 17
United Kingdom, Emergency Government plans, 152
United Kingdom Permanent Joint Headquarters, at Northwood, 277-278
UNITER, 275
Upavon, 273
US Army Information Systems Command, 11
US Departments of State, emergency accommodation for, 14
US Emergency Broadcasting System, 24
US Federal Reserve, 17
US Navy Bureau of Yards, 43
USAF Air Defence Master Plan, 53
Uttlesford District Local Authority bunker, 227
V2 Rocket, 254
Valcartier, 65
Vancouver, 31
Vange AAOR, 121
V-bomber force, reaction time
Ventnor ROTOR station, 75, 113
  Civil ATC function, 113
Wainwright, 38
Wallasey Borough Council Local Authority bunker, 228
Wansdyke Security, 19
Wanstead, London Group Control, 156, 183, 205

War Plan UK, vii
Warmley GPO Repeater Station, 231, 236
Warren Fisher Committee, 248
Warren Row, 163-165, 171, 173, 179, 184,
  conversion to RSG, 163
  description of RSG, 165
  layout plan, 165
  new works associated with RSG status, 164
  use as S-RC, 179
Wartling ROTOR station, 75, 91, 113
  Kelvin Hughes projector, 113
Warwick County Council Civil Defence HQ, 122
Warwickshire Local Authority bunker, 214
Washington, 7, 13, 14
Washington Post, 15
Water Board bunker, 150, 243
  Blunsdon, 245
  Bradford, 243,
  Brede, 245
  Doncaster, 243
  Gloucester, 243
  Harrogate, 243
  Huddersfield, 243
  Hull, 243
  Leeds, 243
  Mansfield, 243
  Northallerton, 243
  Sheffield, 243
  Skipton, 243
  York, 243
Wawne AAOR, 122, 210
  Humberside County War HQ, 122
Wealden District Local Authority bunker, 228
Wellingborough Local Authority bunker, 228
Wessex Water, Holton Heath emergency bunker, 245
West Beckham, 75
West Devon Local Authority bunker, 228
West Drayton, proposed Tactical Control Centre, 93

West Glamorgan Local Authority bunker, 121, 215
West Midlands Council War HQ, 122
West Myne ROTOR station, 88, 114
West Oxfordshire Local Authority bunker, 228
West Prawle, 75
West Sussex Local Authority bunker, 215
West Wiltshire Local Authority bunker, 228
Westwood Quarry, 19, 247
  storage of art treasures, 247
  toxic weapons trials, 247
Weymouth AAOR, 122
WHITE ALICE, 42
White House Situation Room, 10
White Sulphur Springs, 15
Whitehall tunnel scheme, 252
Whitehall, Montague House, 253
Whitelaw, Willie, comment on provision of public shelters, 150
Widmouth Bay (Cornwall), transatlantic cable ground station, 242
Wigan Local Authority bunker, 228
Wiltshire, Civil Defence, 194
Wiltshire Local Authority bunker, 215
Winisk, 34
Woking Local Authority bunker, 229
Worcester City Council Local Authority bunker, 228
Wotton-under-Edge, microwave tower, 236
Wrexham ROC Group HQ, proposed RGHQ for Wales, 143
Wychavon Local Authority bunker, 229
Wycombe Local Authority bunker, 229
Wylde Green AAOR, 122

'Yellow Move', 254
York Water Board bunker, 243
Yorkshire Local Authority bunker, 215